# The material body

Manchester University Press

# Social Archaeology and Material Worlds

Founding editors
Joshua Pollard and Duncan Sayer

Series editors
Chantal Conneller, Laura McAtackney and Joshua Pollard

*Social Archaeology and Material Worlds* aims to forefront dynamic and cutting-edge social approaches to archaeology. It brings together volumes about past people, social and material relations and landscape as explored through an archaeological lens. Topics covered may include memory, performance, identity, gender, life course, communities, materiality, landscape and archaeological politics and ethnography. The temporal scope runs from prehistory to the recent past, while the series' geographical scope is global. Books in this series bring innovative, interpretive approaches to important social questions within archaeology. Interdisciplinary methods which use up-to-date science, history or both, in combination with good theoretical insight, are encouraged. The series aims to publish research monographs and well-focused edited volumes that explore dynamic and complex questions, the why, how and who of archaeological research.

## Previously published

*Neolithic cave burials: Agency, structure and environment*
Rick Peterson

*The Irish tower house: Society, economy and environment, c. 1300–1650*
Victoria L. McAlister

*An archaeology of lunacy: Managing madness in early nineteenth-century asylums*
Katherine Fennelly

*Communities and knowledge production in archaeology*
Julia Roberts, Kathleen Sheppard, Jonathan Trigg and Ulf Hansson (eds)

*Images in the making: Art, process, archaeology*
Ing-Marie Back Danielsson and Andrew Meirion Jones (eds)

*Early Anglo-Saxon cemeteries: Kinship, community and mortuary space*
Duncan Sayer

*An archaeology of innovation: Approaching social and technological change in human society*
Catherine J. Frieman

# The material body

## Embodiment, history and archaeology in industrialising England, 1700–1850

Elizabeth Craig-Atkins and Karen Harvey
(eds)

MANCHESTER UNIVERSITY PRESS

Copyright © Manchester University Press 2024

While copyright in the volume as a whole is vested in Manchester University Press, copyright in individual chapters belongs to their respective authors, and no chapter may be reproduced wholly or in part without the express permission in writing of both author and publisher.

An electronic version is also available under a Creative Commons (CC BY) licence, thanks to the support of University of Sheffield Library, which permits distribution and reproduction provided the author(s) and Manchester University Press are fully cited and it is indicated if any modifications or adaptations are made. Details of the licence can be viewed at https://creativecommons.org/licenses/by/4.0/

Published by Manchester University Press
Oxford Road, Manchester M13 9PL

www.manchesteruniversitypress.co.uk

British Library Cataloguing-in-Publication Data
A catalogue record for this book is available from the British Library

ISBN   978 1 5261 5278 7   hardback

First published 2024

The publisher has no responsibility for the persistence or accuracy of URLs for any external or third-party internet websites referred to in this book, and does not guarantee that any content on such websites is, or will remain, accurate or appropriate.

Typeset
by New Best-set Typesetters Ltd

# Contents

*List of figures* vii
*List of tables* xi
*List of contributors* xii
*Acknowledgements* xv

Introduction: the material body in archaeology and history
 – Elizabeth Craig-Atkins and Karen Harvey 1
1 Archives of embodiment: body and experience in the
 archaeological and historical record – Karen Harvey 22
2 Marking maternity: integrating historical and archaeological
 evidence for reproduction in the late eighteenth and early
 nineteenth centuries – Elizabeth Craig-Atkins and
 Mary E. Fissell 47
3 Embodying the history of shoes: footwear and gender in
 Britain, 1700–1850 – Matthew McCormack 81
4 'The Corporation of Corpse-stealers': archaeological and
 historical evidence of bodysnatching in early eighteenth-century
 London – Robert Hartle 100
5 Who smokes anymore? Documentary, archaeological and
 osteological evidence for tobacco consumption and its
 relationship to social identity in industrial England,
 1700–1850 – Anna M. Davies-Barrett and Sarah A. Inskip 133
6 Uncovering the lives of late-eighteenth- and nineteenth-century
 inhabitants of Bristol through osteoarchaeological and
 documentary analysis – Heidi Dawson-Hobbis and
 Jocelyn Davis 170

7 Disability, gender and old age in the Industrial Revolution: cultural historical and osteoarchaeological perspectives – Sophie L. Newman and David M. Turner   205

*Index*   236

# Figures

Note: Unless otherwise stated, all rights are reserved. For permission to reproduce any of these images please contact the rightsholder.

1.1 The Simpson gravestone at Carver Street Chapel. Photograph courtesy of Brian Irwin. 31
1.2 Skeletal remains of Ann Purvis. Photograph courtesy of Sophie Newman, University of Sheffield. 38
2.1 Location of St Hilda's church and the surrounding town of South Shields as represented on Richardson's map of 1768 and Fryer's map of 1773. The area of excavation which revealed the fetal and perinate group discussed in this chapter is overlain. Redrawn from historic mapping and Raynor *et al.*, 2011 by I. Atkins. 49
2.2 Plan of the lower level of the western section of the excavated area, indicating the locations of human skeletal and coffin remains. Redrawn from Raynor *et al.*, 2011 by I. Atkins. 51
2.3 Age at death distribution of the fetal and perinatal individuals from St Hilda's based on dental development (Al Qahtani *et al.*, 2010), basi occiput dimensions (Scheuer and McLaughlin Black, 1994) and femoral length (Kiserud *et al.*, 2017; Scheuer *et al.*, 1980). Four fetal/perinatal individuals are omitted from this chart as none of the required skeletal elements could be assessed (Sks 703, 796, 842, 1007). 58
3.1 Wellington boots, 1800–25. Courtesy of Northampton Museum and Art Gallery (2000.27.33.1). 85
3.2 Slip-on men's shoe, 1700. Courtesy of Northampton Museum and Art Gallery (P.22/1974.1). 87

| | | |
|---|---|---|
| 3.3 | Men's shoe, 1828. Courtesy of Northampton Museum and Art Gallery (P25/1970.14). | 91 |
| 3.4 | Children's pumps, *c*.1830. Courtesy of the Museum of Leathercraft (274.53). | 93 |
| 4.1 | Burial [3999]/[4000], 0.5 m scale. Photograph courtesy of Crossrail/Museum of London Archaeology (MOLA) and reproduced with permission of MOLA. | 103 |
| 4.2 | Key locations mentioned in this chapter, plotted on Rocque's map of London, 1746. | 105 |
| 4.3 | William Cheselden giving an anatomical demonstration to six spectators in the anatomy-theatre of the Barber-Surgeons' Company, London. Oil painting, *c*.1730/1740. Wellcome Collection 47339i CC BY. | 110 |
| 4.4 | A nightwatchman disturbs a body-snatcher who has dropped the stolen corpse he had been carrying in a hamper, while the anatomist runs away. Etching with engraving by W. Austin, 1773. Wellcome Collection 25668i CC BY 4.0. | 121 |
| 5.1 | Two prostitutes bargaining with a naval man. Thomas Rowlandson's *Sea Stores*, 1812. The Metropolitan Museum of Art, New York; The Elisha Whittelsey Collection, The Elisha Whittelsey Fund, 1959. CC0. | 140 |
| 5.2 | Circular pipe-notch in the left dentition of a middle adult male caused by abrasion of the enamel surfaces by the habitual smoking of a clay pipe (PSN208, Sk134130, St James' Gardens). | 145 |
| 5.3 | Staining caused by tobacco smoking on the lingual (inner-facing) surfaces of the upper left canine, premolars, and first molar of a young adult possible male (PSN157, Sk1963, Barton-upon-Humber). | 146 |
| 5.4 | Magnified image of lingual staining on the upper right first molar of an older adult female (PSN25, Sk417, Holy Trinity Church). | 147 |
| 5.5 | The anterior dentition is divided into nine 'sites' (circles), made up of the intersection between two teeth. At least one of either the corresponding upper or lower sites, consisting of both teeth, for all nine sites must be present for the accurate observation of a pipe-notch. Molars (black) were not recorded for pipe notches since the pipe stem is very unlikely to be in contact with these teeth due to their position at the back of the mouth. | 148 |
| 5.6 | Heavy lingual staining on the upper right dentition of Sarah Green (PSN25, Sk417), an older adult female buried | |

| | | |
|---|---|---|
| | within the post-medieval burial ground for Holy Trinity Church, Coventry. | 154 |
| 5.7 | Complete degeneration of Sarah Green's left temporomandibular joint (arrow), causing flattening and atrophy of the joint surface. | 157 |
| 6.1 | Burials on excavation a) SK293, b) SK7, c) SK48, and d) SK273 (upper) and SK272 (lower). Reproduced with permission of Avon Archaeology Ltd. | 176 |
| 6.2 | Death certificates of Maria Taylor and Thomas Rokeby Price, Crown Copyright. | 177 |
| 6.3 | Destructive lesions on the sacrum and fifth lumbar vertebrae of SK293, Maria Taylor. Photograph by Heidi Dawson-Hobbis. | 178 |
| 6.4 | Endocranial lesions on the frontal bone of SK293, Maria Taylor. Photograph by Heidi Dawson-Hobbis. | 179 |
| 6.5 | Healed fracture of the left tibia and fibula of SK48, Mark Kelson. Photograph by Heidi Dawson-Hobbis. | 185 |
| 6.6 | Death certificates of Mark Kelson and George Cumberland, Crown Copyright. | 187 |
| 7.1 | Skeletal elements present and pathological changes seen in Skeleton 15, Hazel Grove, Stockport. a) Antemortem tooth loss of the left and right lower molars of the mandible (arrows); b) thoracic and lumbar vertebrae of the spine, demonstrating kyphoscoliosis and fusion of the 9th–11th ribs on the right side; c) remaining right ribs (1st–8th) showing straightening of the shafts and degenerative changes to the heads (point of articulation with the vertebrae); d) bowing of the right femur, tibia and fibula. | 210 |
| 7.2 | Skeletal elements present and pathological changes seen in Skeleton 235, St Hilda's Churchyard, South Shields. a) Anterior view of the left and right scapulae, highlighting evidence of dislocation of the right glenohumeral (shoulder) joint; b) posterior view of the left and right humeri, demonstrating extensive changes seen on the joint surface of the right proximal humerus; c) well-healed fracture seen on the midshaft of the right 3rd rib; d) evidence of possible trauma (arrow) on the right lunate; e) possibly associated osteoarthritic changes seen on the distal joint surfaces of the right radius and ulna, leading to eburnation (arrows); f) medial view (left image) of the right 1st metacarpal (associated with the thumb) showing a well-healed fracture of the proximal joint surface (arrow), and proximal view | |

|     | (right image) of the fractured joint surface of the right 1st metacarpal. | 214 |
| --- | --- | --- |
| 7.3 | Skeletal elements present and pathological changes seen in Skeleton 502, St Hilda's Churchyard, South Shields. a) Antemortem tooth loss of the right 2nd premolar and molars; b) evidence of osteoarthritis in the right superior articular facet of the second thoracic vertebra, showing porosity and eburnation of the joint surface (arrow); c) posterior view of the left proximal femur, with mushroom-like deformity of the femoral head, and osteoarthritic changes to the joint surface; d) posterior view of the left acetabulum (hip joint) showing extensive secondary osteoarthritic changes; e) posterior view of the right patella, showing patches of eburnation (arrows) indicative of osteoarthritis; f) anterior view of the right distal femur with patches of eburnation (arrows) matching that seen on the posterior surface of the patella. | 217 |

# Tables

5.1 Prevalence rates of evidence for smoking in populations from Coventry, Barton and London. Prevalence rates are presented in three groups: rate of pipe-notches; rate of lingual staining; rate of pipe-notches and/or lingual staining combined. 150–151

5.2 Prevalence rates of evidence for smoking in different status groups, ranging from high to low, from St James's Gardens, London. 153

7.1 Spinners employed in Nineteen Fine Spinning Mills in Manchester, 1832 (Shuttleworth, 1842: 270–1). 226

# Contributors

**Elizabeth Craig-Atkins** (e.craig-atkins@sheffield.ac.uk) is Senior Lecturer in Human Osteology at the University of Sheffield where her research investigates human skeletal remains from Christian burial grounds in England to consider questions concerning health, lifestyle and identity. Recent projects have focused on the archaeology of children and childhood and on the funerary manipulation and management of human remains during the medieval period. She has published papers in the Society for the Study of Childhood in the Past's monograph series and the *American Journal of Biological Anthropology* on the motivations behind differential funerary treatment of perinates and infants in early medieval cemeteries, integrating funerary and skeletal data with isotopic analysis of diet and physiological status.

**Anna M. Davies-Barrett** (a.daviesbarrett@leicester.ac.uk) is an osteoarchaeologist with a specialism in respiratory disease and its relationship to environmental, social and economic changes in the past. She is currently the research associate in palaeopathology on the *Tobacco, Health and History* project, investigating changes in the prevalence of disease in relation to the introduction of tobacco to Europe. Previously, she worked as a lecturer in human osteoarchaeology and later prehistory at Cardiff University and as a bioarchaeologist at the British Museum. Publications of her research into past prevalence rates of respiratory disease and the impact of aridification and increasing urbanism can be found in the *American Journal of Physical Anthropology* and the *International Journal of Paleopathology*.

**Jocelyn Davis** is an archaeologist working for Avon Archaeology Ltd and has an MA in Osteoarchaeology from the University of Southampton and an MA in History from the University of Bristol.

**Heidi Dawson-Hobbis** (heidi.dawson-hobbis@winchester.ac.uk) is a Senior Lecturer in Biological Anthropology at the University of Winchester and an honorary research associate at the University of Bristol. Her PhD research focused on the associations between health and burial status of medieval children which formed the basis for her book entitled *Unearthing Medieval Children: Health Status and Burial Practice in Southern England* (BAR Publishing British Series 593, 2014).

**Mary E. Fissell** (mfissell@jhu.edu) is Professor in the Department of the History of Medicine at the Johns Hopkins University, where she also co-edits the *Bulletin of the History of Medicine*. Her scholarly work explores how ordinary people in early modern England understood health, healing and the natural world. *Vernacular Bodies* (Oxford University Press, 2004) explored how everyday ideas about making babies mediated large-scale social, political and religious change. Her current work continues to examine vernacular knowledge – ideas about the natural world that ordinary people used, made, shaped and practised. She connects the histories of gender, the body and sexuality with those of popular culture and cheap print in the Atlantic world in a project about an extraordinary medical book called *Aristotle's Masterpiece*. First published in 1684, it was still for sale in sleazy London sex shops in the 1930s, having somehow retained its currency for over two centuries.

**Robert Hartle** has twenty years' experience in commercial archaeology, including sixteen years with Museum of London Archaeology, where he worked till 2023. He is a historical archaeologist, whose research interests include early modern burial practices, co-author of numerous articles and author of the book *The New Churchyard: From Moorfields Marsh to Bethlem Burial Ground, Brokers Row and Liverpool Street* (Museum of London Archaeology, 2017).

**Karen Harvey** (k.l.harvey@bham.ac.uk) is Professor of Cultural History at the University of Birmingham. She has published extensively on the history of gender, masculinity, sexuality, the home and material culture. Her books include *Reading Sex in the Eighteenth Century: Bodies and Gender in English Erotic Culture* (Cambridge University Press, 2004), *The Little Republic: Masculinity and Domestic Authority in Eighteenth-Century Britain* (Oxford University Press, 2012) and the edited collection *History and Material Culture*, 2nd edition (Routledge, 2018). *The Imposteress Rabbit-Breeder: Mary Toft and Eighteenth-Century England* was published by Oxford University Press in 2020.

**Sarah A. Inskip** (s.inskip@leicester.ac.uk) is a bioarchaeologist with a specialism in the interdisciplinary analysis of human skeletal remains. At present she is a UKRI/AHRC funded Future Leaders Fellow and is PI of the *Tobacco, Health and History* Project at the University of Leicester. The aim of this project is to assess how the arrival and commodification of Tobacco in Western Europe had an impact on health and disease patterns from the sixteenth to nineteenth century, and how this relates to modern-day health trends. Previously, she was a Research Associate at the University of Cambridge on the *After the Plague* Project, and was a lecturer in Bioarchaeology at Leiden University, the Netherlands.

**Matthew McCormack** (matthew.mccormack@northampton.ac.uk) is Professor of History at the University of Northampton. He works on masculinity, politics and war in eighteenth-century Britain. His publications include *The Independent Man: Citizenship and Gender Politics in Georgian England* (Manchester University Press, 2005), *Embodying the Militia in Georgian England* (Oxford University Press, 2015) and *Citizenship and Gender in Britain, 1688–1928* (Routledge, 2019). His current research is on men's footwear, on which he published 'Boots, material culture and Georgian masculinities' (*Social History* 42(4) (2017)).

**Sophie L. Newman** (sophie.newman@ed.ac.uk) is a Teaching Fellow in Human Osteoarchaeology in the School of History, Classics and Archaeology, University of Edinburgh. She completed an AHRC-funded PhD at Durham University in 2016, and has previously worked for York Osteoarchaeology Ltd, the University of Sheffield and the University of the Highlands and Islands. Her research interests include the bioarchaeology of children, eighteenth/nineteenth-century health, vitamin D deficiency and the impact of social inequality on health. Her more recent research has focused on the biological and social impact of the ageing process in the eighteenth and nineteenth centuries. She has co-authored peer-reviewed journal articles in the *International Journal of Osteoarchaeology*, the *American Journal of Biological Anthropology* and *Bioarchaeology International*, and has contributed to edited volumes Beauchesne and Agarwal *Children and Childhood in Bioarchaeology* (University Press of Florida, 2018) and Kendall and Kendall *The Family in Past Perspective* (Taylor and Francis, 2021).

**David M. Turner** (d.m.turner@swansea.ac.uk) is Professor of History at Swansea University. He has published widely in the field of disability history, including the books *Social Histories of Disability and Deformity* (edited with Kevin Stagg; Routledge, 2006) and *Disability in Eighteenth-Century England* (Routledge, 2012), which won the Disability History Association Outstanding Publication prize. His recent work, supported by Wellcome Trust funding, has focused on disability in the British coal industry. His latest book, *Disability in the Industrial Revolution: Physical Impairment and British Coalmining*, written with Daniel Blackie, was published by Manchester University Press in 2018.

# Acknowledgements

This book has its genesis in the collaborative research project 'The Material Body: An Interdisciplinary Study in History and Archaeology' (British Academy Small Grant SG151375; 2015–2018), led by Elizabeth Craig-Atkins and Karen Harvey. This project brought a team of interdisciplinary researchers to the University of Sheffield to explore the potential of osteoarchaeologists and historians of the body working together. Several who took part in that pilot research project have contributed to this volume: Elizabeth Craig-Atkins, Mary Fissell, Karen Harvey and David Turner. Other contributors spoke at the project conference held at the University of Birmingham in 2018: Robert Hartle, Sophie Newman and Matthew McCormack. The editors wish to thank the British Academy for research funding, and all those who participated in the project workshops. We are especially grateful to Vanessa Campanacho, Nigel Cavanagh, Diana Swales and Hannah Wallace who undertook research in support of that project. The editors also thank the University of Birmingham for supporting the conference, 'The Material Body, 1500–1900: A Conference of Archaeologists and Historians' (4–5 July 2018), Hannah Wallace for her support at the event and all the speakers and participants at the conference.

# Introduction: the material body in archaeology and history

*Elizabeth Craig-Atkins and Karen Harvey*

*The Material Body* exploits the possibilities of studying embodied lives in the past through the sources and approaches of the disciplines of archaeology and history, and the interdisciplinary field of material culture studies. These academic disciplines share the objectives of exploring the lived experience of people in the past through material remains and archival records, whether these be human skeletons, material objects or written or visual documents. Archaeologists and historians alike seek to examine the body, to reconstruct embodied experiences and understand changing forms of 'embodiment'. This book explores a range of approaches to the material body. It advances the ambitions of both historians and archaeologists to explore the material and experiencing body in an account of embodied subjects. In its integration of the sources, concepts and methods of history and archaeology, this book explores precisely how the biological, physical, environmental, social, cultural and psychological interacted to produce embodied experiences. In its focus on categories of identity – including age, gender, class and disability – the book highlights the structures of matter, thought, culture and power through which these experiences were formed. This interdisciplinary and embodied approach, created by bringing historical and archaeological disciplines into explicit dialogue, allows us to better account for the experiences of men, women and children in the past.

The collection comprises seven chapters that study the body using documentary evidence alongside collections of human remains and material culture from Britain during the period 1700–1850. This is a period that witnessed considerable fast-paced transformation in the material world, the working and living conditions of men, women and children, and the organisation and relationships of a changing social structure. It is also a period for which there is a rich documentary and material record around which historians, archaeologists and material culture scholars can collaborate. This project began with the explicit recognition among ourselves that archaeological and historical research agendas align in the study of the body and with particular potency in the study of the material body. The volume grew from a desire to explore the nature and extent of our shared understanding and to encourage synergy between the two disciplines in scholarship, by undertaking collaborative research. To complement this focus on collaborative working, the authors adopt a reflective and critical perspective on their own practices throughout the volume, and this introduction will consider the process of interdisciplinarity, specifically of interweaving archaeological and historical methods and practices. We will discuss the context for these, focusing particularly on the material turn, new materialism and phenomenological approaches and the opportunities and challenges they offer for a study of 'embodiment'. The introduction will also highlight the particular dividends of uniting archaeological and historical perspectives for an understanding of the embodied past, and specifically for the study of industrialising England during the period 1700–1850.

## The material turn

The place of material things in our understandings of the past has played a crucial role in the development of academic thought during the twenty-first century, particularly for those social science, humanities and arts disciplines which examine human experience. The shift has been referred to as the 'material turn', a 'turn towards materiality' and 'a Material-Cultural Turn' (Gerritson and Riello, 2015: 3; Hamling and Richardson, 2010: 1; Hicks, 2010). In history, this took the form of integrating material culture and the physical within accounts of the past. The material turn has seen historians recognising objects to be as rich a source for historical research as documents and images (e.g. Bennett and Joyce, 2010; Davidson, 2019; Gerritsen and Riello, 2015; Grassby, 2005; Harvey, 2017; Hicks and Beaudry, 2010; Tilley *et al.*, 2006). This was an understanding long established in archaeology, design history and museology, of course. But while objects have long been a primary source material in archaeological studies, the frameworks within which they were interpreted have also changed. From the focus on collecting among nineteenth-century antiquarians, researchers grew to prioritise typology, technology and function, then human behaviour and ideology in their understandings of the material world. In moving away from explicitly functionalist approaches – following archaeology's so-called cultural turn – archaeological thought undertook conceptual shifts that aligned with other humanities disciplines. The material turn thus created fertile shared ground for archaeologists and historians to explore materiality in the past through key points of understanding and prompted new, shared agendas. Of particular relevance to this volume is the argument presented by both British anthropological archaeologist Dan Hicks (2010: 28) and social historian Patrick Joyce (2010), that we need to cast off the distinction between the material and the cultural in studying the human past.

## New Materialism

Within the 'material turn', a useful distinction can be made between studies of 'materials' or distinct objects and an epistemic turning towards viewing the past through the lens of 'materiality' (Harvey, 2017: 9). The small-scale focus of the first contrasts with the large-scale approach of the second, an approach which envisions all aspects of the past as rooted in material conditions. Materiality has been defined as 'a fundamentally relational process, not a substance, and what really matters is the relations between entities' (Lucas, 2012: 167–8). This has been at the centre of the work of Tim Ingold, the British anthropologist. His vision of the arena of materiality is one in which humans and things are enmeshed in ways that deny both the anthropocentric emphasis on the agency of humans and the division between the social and the material world (Hicks, 2010: 77–9; Hodder, 2012). For Ingold, humans are merely one part of a larger environment in which all manner of physical things have an agentive role.

The broader intellectual shift within which Ingold's writing can be situated has been termed 'new materialism' or the 'new materialisms' (Fowler and Harris, 2015; Hamilakis and Jones, 2017; Marshall and Alberti, 2014; Witmore, 2014). This is an eclectic and inclusive group of perspectives that embrace post-humanist and non-representationalist visions of an entangled world of people, things and relational properties (Fowler and Harris, 2015). New materialism frames materiality using ideas of matter and assemblage. Matter, in this sense, is a form of materiality that can be articulated in post-humanist terms – inclusive of all objects, beings and entities without centring humanity or human agency (Govier and Steele 2021; Hamilakis and Meirion Jones, 2017; Schouwenburg, 2015). Matter is itself agentive and productive, and entangled in heterogeneous, relational, unbounded and ever-mutable 'assemblages'. Much of this work has not engaged directly with the material body as we will describe it here; however, Attala and Steele (2019) (who term the approach described above 'New Materiality') offer a sustained exploration of its relevance to both the 'materials of the body' and the association of bodily and material words. Their insistence that 'people and the material world are inextricably co-constitutive' (2019: 234) reflects, to us, a form of new materialism that integrates the body itself.

The extent to which a focus on 'materiality' is new, for both historians and archaeologists, is debatable. For the English social historian Patrick Joyce, the turn to materiality was in fact a return to the 'social' in social and cultural history. He argued that a too-common adherence to the primacy of the cultural in our understanding of human experience implicitly relegates the material and the economic to a separate sphere (Joyce, 2010: 221). As Joyce (2010: 226) puts it, a turn to materiality means reconsidering the distinction between representation and things, erasing 'the familiar conceptual distinctions between the natural and the social'. In envisaging materiality as comprising relational processes shaped by society, culture and matter, such work reshapes what 'material' means.

## Experience and embodiment

The burden of much of this scholarship is to integrate materiality into studies of the past and often to envisage humans as just one aspect of past materiality among others. In this way, human actors can be situated within a material world in which a range of forces and relationships are at work. For bioarchaeologists (or osteoarchaeologists) in particular, the study of the body as material is not at all new. Human bodies have been a longstanding focus of archaeological research, both directly as a result of the survival of human remains as tangible traces of the past and indirectly through their role in creating and interacting with material culture, buildings or landscapes. However, for much of the twentieth century, research with the potential to illuminate embodied experience was separated into distinct sub-fields, operated by different practitioners. Bioarchaeologists studied human remains, most commonly in their skeletonised form, and tended to focus on questions of a biological nature – past demography, diets, disease. In line with the scientific fields to which these studies are closely aligned (e.g. palaeodemography to contemporary demography, palaeopathology to medicine) the focus of research rested on population-level patterns indicative of broad-scale environmental and biological processes. The individual appears usually only as a case study representing the population or a population-level process; for example, of a particular disease state or when the individual themself is deemed historically significant. The adoption of a biological model of the body that primarily operated at the population scale meant that variation between individuals, or within individuals over their lives, and the small-scale, personalised insights they offer were subjugated to large-scale, long-term processes. Individual variation tended to be hidden by generalisation and complexity dismissed as statistical noise (Hosek and Robb, 2019; Stodder and Palkovich, 2012). An essentialist understanding of the body meant naturalised bodily states went unquestioned, including transhistorical and Western-centric understandings: the masculine body as default, the particularity of human experience and the individual existing in a static, bounded body. Socially and theoretically informed bioarchaeology is a relatively recent development (Gowland and Kacki, 2020).

In contrast, artefacts (both from the grave and other contexts) were examined by archaeological material culture specialists whose focus rested on technology and the role of objects in bodily display (e.g. dress) and its representation of social roles and ideologies (Crossland, 2010). Here, the concept of agency focused attention on making, albeit initially at the expense of the maker (Hodder, 2012). Indeed, the body is referenced in multiple ways through material culture: in representations of bodies and their parts in illustration and sculpture, through impressions of the living body inscribed on objects during their making or use – such as fingerprints in pottery clay or wear on a tool that describes the body part used in its operation, and in metaphorical references to bodies through shape and form (Pluciennick, 2002). With hindsight it seems strange that a connecting factor between these enquiries – the body itself – was marginalised in discourses for so long.

Over the past three decades, these distinctive approaches within archaeology have been brought together in a variety of ways. Initial synergies emerged through the pioneering work of gender archaeology, which Crossland (2010: 388) states 'acted as a common node of interest for archaeologists from very different backgrounds and traditions and brought bioarchaeologists and those engaged with more artefact-focused archaeologies into conversation'. The archaeologist Sarah Tarlow (2011: 8) has commented that her work examines the 'material body', not the 'experiencing body'. Yet explorations of the body have gone on to explore the links between the biological and social, realising the potential of different scholarly viewpoints and modes of analysis to form pieces of the larger puzzle of experiences of the body (e.g. Baker and Agarwal, 2017; Blakey and Rankin Hill, 2016; Sofaer, 2006; Tilley and Oxenham, 2011). However, the opportunities offered by these approaches must be tempered with an appreciation of selectivity and inadequate representation in the sources of data for such studies, which render the lived experiences of some people in the past more visible than others (e.g. Gowland, 2018; Mant and Holland 2019). The shared understandings of the material body as a route to reconstructing lived experiences that emerged from these new conversations are foundational to the chapters in this volume.

In one regard, the bodies that bioarchaeologists discuss are physical things: material entities composed of biological material that create a human form. These bodies are tangible and sufficiently durable to survive millennia, in the majority of the UK at least, as buried skeletal remains in a grave. Bodies are at once a form through which we interact with the world, but also a plastic object which is created by its engagement with the world (Buikstra et al., 2011; Ingold, 2011; Schrader and Torres-Rouff, 2021; Sofaer, 2006). The biological structure of the human body is a marriage of genetic and environmental influences formed over the life course. Developmental environment influences the expression of genetic traits resulting in patterns of both discrete and continuous variation in bodily characteristics. The body is a biologically dynamic structure that adapts and heals over time, even after growth has ceased. Exposure to environmental stress in childhood can retard growth and development, creating bodies of different sizes and proportions. Intense and habitual physical activity during developmental and post-developmental life will lead to robust muscle insertions and alter the cross-section shape of bones in ways that better withstand force; or, when the body is pushed beyond its physical limits, the residual evidence of trauma can be detected in fracture calluses and misaligned bones. Lifetime experiences can be written into (and therefore read from) its structure and form, and the epigenetic nature of these processes dictates that some of these experiences also influence bodies of subsequent generations, writing the experiences of parents and grandparents into the bodies of their children (Gowland, 2015). Bodies are thus material in their physicality, and material in their creation. This emphasis on experience is important to bioarchaeology, which has developed its own theoretical frameworks rooted in the biocultural approach, in which the combined contribution of dynamic interactions between people and their physical, social and cultural worlds to human variation is explicitly recognised (Zuckerman and Armelagos, 2011: 20).

The material turn's impact on the study of the body is also fully evident in scholarship on the history of the body. Cultural history and its attendant focus on language was the dominant approach in the early history of the body (Porter, 2001). Yet, subsequent approaches have been driven by materialist approaches (Csordas, 1990; Ruberg, 2020). As Harvey has noted, 'The human body is a material archive of experience that—unlike the written, visual, and material object sources that typically inform our studies of the past—cannot be read with literary approaches to discourse alone' (Harvey, 2020: 138). Some historians have drawn attention to the biological aspects of the body. A key intervention was by Daniel Lord Smail, who offered a neuro-historical account of the past, drawing attention to the explosion in addictive substances in the eighteenth century and the combined impact of the resultant chemical and social changes on Enlightenment culture (2007). Drawing on Smail's work and discussing the eighteenth century, Dror Wahrman called for 'a corporealist critique' of cultural histories of representations, for example. Though Wahrman acknowledges the dangers of essentialism when studying the body, gender and sexuality, he seeks a way for historians to integrate 'the extra-cultural domain' into their analyses. His '"corporealist" (or "neo-essentialist") critique' he characterises as occupying 'the unpredetermined boundary' between 'unreflective essentialism' and 'unreflective constructivism' (Wahrman, 2008: 599). Such approaches bring to the fore the material body, though firmly in the context of human culture.

Other historians of the period have drawn on new materialist approaches as a way to correct the occlusion of 'the materiality of the body' in their discipline. Clever and Ruberg deploy the method of praxiography, or a material history of practice, to get 'beyond interpretations *of* the body to the actions of physical bodies in practice' (Clever and Ruberg, 2014: 562, 553). A different approach explores how individuals were positioned in relation to other material things. The historian of early modern Europe, Ulinka Rublack (2013: 84), has argued that the increasing range, circulation and availability of material items during the Renaissance meant that, 'Subjectivity was increasingly experienced in relation to this transient or durable object world'. In this account, the material world interacted with emergent internalised personal identities. Who a person was – to themselves and to others – was constituted by the material world of which they were a part. Materiality is important to historians who are not concerned only with the evidently physical aspects of past lives, but with the full range of human experience. We might agree that consciousness, identity and selfhood, for example, are not in themselves material. Yet even those aspects of experience which may not be considered as simply material – if material at all – are nevertheless shaped by and situated within a material context. Materiality shapes human experience. Indeed, materiality *is* human experience, both in the sense that the person exists in a physical context and that the person is, to some extent, themselves physical.

In some of these respects, then, the body may be investigated as an 'object' like many others – it is material, occupies space, can be touched, marked, owned; it is changed by its interaction with the environment and is organic – like landscapes, for example. Archaeologists Dušan Borić and John Robb (2008) advocated for 'body-centred' research while Joanna Sofaer (2006) framed 'the body as material culture' and as a particular kind of material culture that is both biologically and socially constructed. Accounts of the body as 'always in the process of being created and recreated through a lifetime of activities and interactions with other people and objects in the world' bear the mark of the impact of new materialism (Wesp, 2015: 141). Attala and Steele's *Body Matters* (2019: 9) responds to what they envisage as 'the stubborn tendency to see materials as inert as well as the representations that disassociate the living body from the material world' in archaeology. They aim a 'new materialities' approach at 'the matter of the body, demonstrating how it enables us to situate people within the material, physical world and thus to better understand how people forge relationships, and come into being, both with each other and with other things' (10).

Yet, for many scholars, this is not sufficient. The body is arguably a particular kind of 'object' or form of material culture for many scholars, particularly those working in humanistic disciplines. Indeed, new materialist approaches are considered by both bioarchaeologists and historians as limited in their capacity to account for all aspects of human experience, even as those aspects are shaped by the material world in which the body interacts with other matter. Fredengren's application of the idea of 'figurations' to refer to 'conceptual personae' and enable archaeologists to discuss 'identity, personhood and subjectivity' (2013: 56, 66) actually excludes a large component of what a historian understands as 'subjectivity': cognition, self-identity and the emotions. For Rublack, the material world interacted with people's 'social and emotional experiences' (2013: 84–5). As Roper puts it, with a psychoanalytic inflection: 'By subjectivity I mean the way an individual mentally and emotionally organises experience' (2010: 312). This sentiment is shared by archaeologists, for whom materiality is a principal key to understanding the past lives of people as thinking, feeling, moving, dynamic individuals in time and place (Dornan-Fish, 2012). As Alexandra Ion remarks of Attala and Steele, 'I am left wondering if a new materialist agenda manages to capture the full and complex nature of relationships when it comes to bodies and humans' (2021: 1028). Bodies interact with other material objects and processes of human thought build on this material interaction, but the lived experience of being a feeling and thinking person cannot be accounted for in new materialism. The body is – or is often experienced as – continuous with the person as a thinking self.

A focus on the lived experience which combines the physical body and immaterial consciousness has been fostered by the impact of phenomenological approaches in both archaeology and history. Merleau-Ponty, a principal phenomenological theorist, envisaged '[t]he experience of one's own body' as defying the distinction between subject (person) and object (thing): 'I am my body', he wrote, 'and reciprocally my body is something like a natural subject, or a provisional sketch of my total being' (1945; 2002: 205). Phenomenological approaches, including those of Merleau-Ponty, have been adopted in archaeology and applied to things, bodies and landscapes (Hodder, 2012: 27–30). Historians draw on phenomenology, too, specifically 'to lay bare the lived experience of the body in the past' (Ruberg, 2020: 91). Such approaches encourage small-scale studies that delve into the necessarily intimate, personal, individual and interiorised components of lived experience. Historians of the eighteenth century turn to first-person 'ego-documents' or detailed third-person records such as doctors' notes to reconstruct the lived experience of the body through the metaphors in written language (Duden, 1991; Pilloud and Louis-Courvoisier, 2003). The scale of archaeological enquiry has also shifted to recognise the individual or the person more explicitly, and in doing so align more neatly with scales of historical enquiry, which often focus on the microhistorical (Brewer, 2010; Fowler, 2004; Hosek, 2019; Magnússon and Szijártó, 2013; White, 2014), directing the two disciplines along parallel paths in their explorations of lived experiences of the body. A biographical approach to artefacts has also been adopted, both to illuminate people through their material worlds (Gilchrist, 2012; Hoskins, 1998; Mytum, 2010) and examine the lives of the objects themselves (Beaudry, 2011; Meskell, 2004). Hosek and Robb (2019: 4) draw attention to the development of what they call 'text-aided' osteobiographies to explore social differences in past societies and Hosek, Warner-Smith and Novak (2021) examine the process of 'doing bioarchaeology with archives' – approaches which several of the authors in this volume seek to extend and deepen. The process of osteobiography begins with assembling a comprehensive set of skeletal data from a single individual to create a life narrative (Hosek and Robb, 2019; Saul, 1972). Advances in biomolecular techniques that extract increasingly detailed information about individuals – DNA sequences, isotopic evidence for diet, migration and health, pathogenic DNA from infected individuals and oral microbiome data, among others – facilitate richer, multifaceted, personal datasets on which to build more nuanced understandings of lived experience. Certainly, disciplinary specialisation remains a barrier to integrating the biocultural, historical, political-economic and sociocultural approaches in the study of embodiment (Leatherman and Goodman, 2020). Yet, recent development of the theoretical underpinning of osteobiographies have reinforced their power as a research tool for socially contextualised bioarchaeology – something that is intrinsically complementary to an embodied approach to the past (Hosek and Robb, 2019: 2; Hosek et al., 2021).

'Embodiment' is a keyword for historians, too, and is used to describe lived experience as created out of the intersection between the physical body and the internal world of the mind. As Roper (2010) suggested, historians should study people in the past as 'embodied subjects' whose subjectivity is grounded in the physical body. The term expresses a shared concern among archaeologists and historians working on the body to adopt a critical engagement with a biological/social distinction. For historians, experience of the body is the product of an interaction between different phenomena which include the material, social, cultural and emotional. As Canning writes of the history of the body, subjects 'are not simply the imposed results of alien, coercive forces; the body is internally lived, experienced and acted upon by the subject and the social collectivity' (1999: 506). In their study of an eighteenth-century Swiss doctor, Pilloud and Louis-Courvoisier demonstrate that bodily experience is layered from an external aspect (one that is constructed or observed by another) and an internal aspect ('purely interior and intimate'); these are combined in what they term 'biological-cultural corporeal maps' (2003: 452). Together, the chapters in this book consider the multiple dimensions of bodily experience, including its material, cultural and subjective components. The shared interests of historians and bioarchaeologists in the material body, embodiment and individual experience have driven the chapters in this volume. The experience of bodies – or the experiencing body – is a key focus of much of the scholarship in this field and several of the chapters in this book. It is this multifaceted bodily experience that we refer to here as 'embodiment', and one that is recorded in a range of types of evidence that include written documents and the material body itself.

## About this book

This book recognises that we – as researchers trained and encultured in the disciplines of history, archaeology and material culture studies – cannot realise the potential of the material turn and embodied approach unless we work together. Archaeologists studying both skeletons and objects acknowledge that the material culture approach to the body cannot provide 'a comprehensive view of embodied experiences' (Wesp, 2015: 145) and that 'cultural information is required to interpret the biological data' (Schrader and Torres-Rouff, 2021: 21). Historians search for approaches – particularly practice-theory and praxiography – that allow them to deconstruct 'the binary opposition between biological essentialism and social constructionism' and focus on 'the material, experiencing body', yet they generally do so without turning to the physical bodies themselves (Clever and Ruberg, 2014). Despite each discipline having eloquently defined the gaps in their own scholarship, very few studies attempt to combine these approaches, especially for the post-medieval period, which is the focus of the chapters presented here (e.g. Gowland, 2018; Mant, 2016). This is the challenge taken up by the contributors to this book. We argue that, by bringing together historians' and archaeologists' approaches to the changing social and cultural contexts of bodies and the extant record of the physical body, we can engage with the challenges posed by theoretical advances that have characterised the first quarter of the twenty-first century, adequately mobilise the rich range of evidence at our disposal for historical periods and, in integrating social and material, transform our understanding of people's lived experiences of the body.

But what does an effective interdisciplinary study of the material body entail? First, we need to engage in a sustained dialogue across disciplines that realises the potential of our varied research materials. Understandings of the socio-materiality of the body have been developed by scholars in both archaeology and history over the last 30 years, resulting in a refined epistemological framework for embodied research. As historians increasingly study people in the past as 'embodied subjects', archaeologists have begun to view the body through a material lens, at once the physical locus of embodied experience and a product of accumulated embodied actions. Uniting these impulses requires negotiation between these ways of thinking and the diverse forms of research materials at our disposal – the creation and interrogation of an 'archive of embodiment' (Harvey, 2020).

Second, we need to establish new ways of working that prioritise the creation and interrogation of this archive. Some contributors use past interactions with the materiality of dead bodies as a way to uncover new social practices amongst the living. Other contributors study the material body as an experiencing body, exploring the lives of men and women, young and old, able and disabled. Further contributions are concerned with the reciprocal interactions between objects associated with or worn upon the body and bodies themselves. The authors utilise different source materials and take different approaches, but together and in dialogue they each commit to examine how the social and material are combined in the making of embodied experience. All exploit the possibilities of studying the material body in the past in interdisciplinary ways, drawing specifically upon the disciplines of history, archaeology and material culture studies. This interdisciplinarity arises in these chapters not only by combining the evidence and approaches that are typically associated with either historians or archaeologists, but also through a sustained collaborative process. The book itself is the outcome of a collaborative project. In the first stage, a group of archaeologists and historians (including Craig-Atkins, Fissell, Harvey, Newman and Turner) took part in a series of research workshops, experimenting with shared research materials and interpretive approaches. In the second stage, this group came together with others (including Hartle, McCormack) to present research on the material body. This book reflects this interdisciplinary collaborative process: three chapters and the introduction are each co-written by an archaeologist and historian, two are written by a historian and two by archaeologists.

## Why 1700–1850?

The period explored in these chapters is one that both historians of the body and bioarchaeologists have identified as witnessing significant change in people's living and working conditions in Europe, particularly but not exclusively in urban areas. Significant transformations occurred which had a huge impact on the body. Bioarchaeological scholarship has examined the negative impacts of the process of industrialisation; the accompanying large migration from rural to urban environments transformed human demographics with wide-ranging impacts upon human health. Higher rates of infectious disease – including tuberculosis and metabolic disease – such as rickets, trauma and neoplastic disease have been discussed (Bekvalac and Western, 2016; Brickley et al., 2007; Lewis, 2002). Historians, too, have explored the impact of industrialisation on the body, specifically how new urban contexts damaged life expectancy while also changing attitudes to bodies that defined new social identities and social relationships, notably a new class of poor labouring bodies, newly sexed bodies and hardening concepts of the able and disabled body (Cody, 2005; Laqueur, 1990; Siena, 2019; Szreter and Mooney, 1998).

Industrial England is a major growth area in archaeological studies, but past research has lacked the explicit contribution of historians who have considerable expertise in this period. Yet, this is a period for which the rich evidence from many large skeletal collections can be linked directly to extensive surviving documentary evidence in the form of biographical material over the life course. A growing skeletal record for this period, combined with an extraordinarily rich documentary, historical and material culture record, presents an opportunity to take a significant new direction in the study of eighteenth- and nineteenth-century bodies. Work that draws on the methods and data from both disciplines to understand the historical body is undertaken for earlier periods, but this is rarely done for the study of the post-medieval body. Within archaeology, the work of post-medieval bioarchaeologists of industrialising England most often produces population-level studies of larger groups, rather than of small communities and individuals. Cases where a fuller historical record is integrated with an analysis of skeletal remains are very rare but have been shown to lead to valuable new knowledge about healthcare, attitudes towards individuals and the role of women (Owsley et al., 2018). The combination of materials which create our archive of embodiment enables us to undertake a holistic treatment not just of elite bodies but those that might be considered 'ordinary' and 'marginalised' bodies – men, women and children of the middling sort and labouring poor, reproducing female bodies, disabled bodies, the old and young, and bodies that were stolen, traded and handled. The larger extent of historical documentation pertaining to a broad social range of individuals in particular, combined with the excavation of large cemeteries in major urban centres, offers an exciting possibility for a new history of embodied experiences of industrialising England. It gives us the opportunity, for example, to combine first-person reports of experience with the evidence of the physical body, allowing us to put these in dialogue with one another in ways that are not possible for pre-modern archaeologists or those who work on objects alone. This is the ideal context within which to test ideas associated with the material turn, new materialism and phenomenology.

### Evidence and themes

One of the hallmarks of the chapters that follow is the combination of written historical documents – parish registers, newspapers, medical books – with data on skeletal remains, coffin plates and cemetery layouts. This patterns the particular approach or approaches that the chapters take to the material body. Yet, while the emphases that each author gives to the different types of evidence vary, they all align the various data and place them, as Newman and Turner put it, 'in dialogue with' each other (p. 206). These chapters show unequivocally that one set of evidence (be it historical or archaeological) can provide context for the other, illuminating what might be most distinctive or extraordinary in either the archaeological or historical record. These sets of evidence can also complement and, arguably, complete each other. The illicit practice of bodysnatching was not often recorded in historical documents, but the newly discovered example of a protected grave discussed in Hartle's chapter 'is a rare physical manifestation of contemporary antipathy toward bodysnatching but also the undocumented anxiety of bereavement' (p. 121). Yet all chapters avoid what Craig-Atkins and Fissell refer to as the '*handmaiden problem*' in which one discipline is placed in the helper role to another (p. 52). No chapter deploys the evidence, methods or scholarship of the other discipline as 'background' but instead strikes a balance between the distinct scholarly approaches and the range of available evidence.

At times one set of evidence aligns with another in ways that enrich, consolidate and deepen the overall reconstruction of the embodied experience of the past. The dialogue between different forms of evidence does not always lead the conversation in one unified direction, however. There are misalignments, gaps and inconsistencies between datasets that prompt queries, often turning on the tensions between the body as represented, recorded, described or experienced. Combining skeletal data with written sources can also expose tensions between them. Several of the chapters in this book expose these tensions. For example, though the historical record strongly suggests that women were generally not smokers in this period, Davies-Barrett and Inskip present clear bioarchaeological evidence to the contrary: 43% of female skeletons in their sample show evidence of regular tobacco use. Here, the historical record – in this case, often socio-cultural representations

– is a poor record of practice. In contrast, the material evidence of the body itself presents clear evidence of experience. In other cases, the written sources record the embodied past in ways that the bioarchaeological simply cannot. In their discussion of unwanted pregnancies, Craig-Atkins and Fissell position the archaeological and historical material in 'productive tension' (p. 55). The significant numbers of abortions suggested by textual evidence is in tension with a stark archaeological absence in graveyard excavations: aborted foetuses would not receive a sacred burial. The tension in the record generates a discussion about attitudes towards pregnancy and reproduction: '[i]nfants were paradoxically both highly valued and often unwanted' (p. 68). In the case study of George and Elizabeth Cumberland, Dawson-Hobbis and Davis expose similarly productive tensions between the archaeological and historical record. George's skeletal remains provide some physical evidence of gout, while Elizabeth's skeleton yields no evidence of gout, perhaps because relevant parts of the foot were missing. In the written accounts of their health given in George's letters, gout was a condition from which they both suffered and for George it clearly shaped his lived experience. Surprisingly, though, his letters do not mention pain. The discrepancies cause Dawson-Hobbis and Davis to speculate that Elizabeth's complaints were misdiagnosed, and to reflect on the difficulties of surmising the lived experience of pain from the skeletal evidence alone. In this case, the evidence of the material body is a poor record of embodied experience.

Nevertheless, combining evidence in these ways can significantly enhance our accounts of individuals' embodied lives in the past. In her study of the 18-year-old James Simpson, Harvey uses historical evidence of the context of early nineteenth-century masculinity to interpret the apparent silence of his skeletal record. Bringing together the historical and bioarchaeological develops a textured picture of both the risks attendant on young men and the dual privileges of rank and gender. Harvey's second case study prompts a reconsideration of the experiences of middle-aged women in this period. Here, the physical processes of ageing and poverty visible on Ann Purvis' skeleton seem inconsistent with the status she was accorded and that is traceable through other evidence. In this case, bringing together different bodies of evidence demonstrates that the physical body did 'not correlate consistently with social status or social identity in the past' (Harvey, p. 40). A similar approach to ageing can be found in the chapter by Newman and Turner. They set out, 'not just to *compare* skeletal and documentary evidence, but to explore how archaeological and social historical methodologies can be more fully integrated to understand ageing and disability in this period' (p. 206). The result is to reposition what might be considered 'exceptional pathological case studies' and instead to interpret these as 'the remains of people whose experiences were shaped both by their physical characteristics and by the wider culture that gave them meaning' (p. 228). A humanistic impulse to bring into focus the embodied experiences of the integrated person is strong throughout these chapters.

The individual, embodied and experiencing person is a principal unit of analysis throughout this book. Several authors employ the method that we term 'from skeletal biography to social biography'. This involves 'record linkage of osteoarchaeological information and historical documents (parochial records and other sources) for any named individuals in archaeological collections', and allows the researcher 'to connect the population-level studies of skeletal collections to both general historical and specific biographical research' (Harvey, p. 28). Case studies of named individuals are central to three chapters: Dawson-Hobbis and Davis examine George and Elizabeth Cumberland of Bristol, Harvey discusses James Simpson of Sheffield and Ann Purvis of South Shields, Davies-Barrett and Inskip focus on Sarah Green of Coventry. Other individuals, whose names are not known, allow for detailed case studies in other chapters: the three skeletons from Hazel Grove and St Hilda's in Newman and Turner, the single skeleton from the 'New Churchyard' in Hartle, and the thirty-four burials of fetuses and perinates at St Hilda's in Craig-Atkins and Fissell. The scale of these analyses is significant. It is this scale that creates a precise meeting point for bioarchaeological and historical evidence and accompanying approaches, avoiding either discipline becoming mere background to the other. As Harvey outlines, the personal embodied biography or 'life reconstruction' is one important focus shared by scholars in both history and archaeology (p. 26). Even in studies where personal names are missing, it is at the level of what Craig-Atkins and Fissell refer to as 'small stories' where the interpretation of skeletal remains for an understanding of the living is most fruitful (p. 48).

The human scale is evident in the insistent focus on identities throughout the book. Women and gender feature prominently in chapters by Craig-Atkins and Fissell, Dawson-Hobbis and Davis, Harvey and McCormack; though a range of social ranks feature in chapters by Davies-Barrett and Inskip and McCormack, the labouring poor are the main subjects of Craig-Atkins and Fissell, Dawson-Hobbis and Davis, Harvey and Newman and Turner. Ageing is discussed by Dawson-Hobbis and Davis, Harvey and Newman and Turner; debility/disability is a principal focus for Newman and Turner in particular, though it is also discussed by McCormack. In their treatment of these identities, the authors underscore that the social identities of gender, rank, age and dis/ability were embedded in the physical body and shaped by this material experience.

The socio-physical nature of the human body is palpable in those chapters which focus on the interaction between the body and object. These chapters show the influence of the various strands of the material turn in their account of the body as one material object in assemblages with other material objects. The notches worn into men's (and just one woman's) teeth by the 'cutty' tobacco pipes in Davies-Barrett and Inskip's chapter bespeak gendered forms of practice. The impression left in shoes by the shape, excretions, warmth and movement of the body in McCormack's 'embodied history of shoes' provides clear examples of how the body moulds things and is itself moulded by things (p. 84). The physical changes made to the body by its interaction with the environment are evident throughout many other chapters, whether in the account of the extensive permanent change to the right shoulder of *Skeleton 235* following a dislocation most likely caused by an accident in Newman and Turner, or the skeletal lesions in the vertebrae of Maria Taylor who died aged 23 from tuberculosis in 1845, and whose life as a member of the working poor is reconstructed in Dawson-Hobbis and Davis. Though Dawson-Hobbis and Davis note that the reporting of such details might appear clinical to non-archaeologists, they also provide 'an embodied physicality to the study of past lives, which offers its own form of intimacy' (p. 194). When such physical changes are accompanied by historical sources, especially self-reports describing the attendant agony, the degree of intimate reconstruction is arguably much greater. These accounts trace the impact of phenomenological approaches which foreground individual and interior experiences. Eighteenth-century reports of corns, calluses, blisters and bunions generate a vivid picture of shoe-wearing in the past, for example. Such studies offer compelling and substantive data on experience to embodied histories.

The power of this intimate small-scale arises from its situation within the large-scale, though. In the dialogue between these different levels of analysis emerges the deeper and wider understanding of past embodied experience. Population-level analysis of particular burial sites is an important component of many of these chapters (especially Dawson-Hobbis and Davis, Harvey, Davies-Barrett and Inskip, and Newman and Turner), though all of these chapters situate their examples and case studies in a broader context. The use of a range of types of evidence collated from deep and thorough research into the historical record in the chapters by McCormack and Hartle enable the authors to situate their material objects within a richly reconstructed wider vision. McCormack's shoes are read in the context of 'the subjective, the emotional and the economic' approaches to the object, set against medical and literary attitudes towards footwear and examined in the light of men's and women's feelings about wearing shoes (p. 82). Hartle's account of a protected grave is set against a range of wider attitudes towards the dead and their treatment and the professional networks of the men who sustained the theft of corpses. The commodified object of the body was at the very heart of these networks.

## Conclusions

The chapters presented in *The Material Body* demonstrate how interdisciplinary collaborative working among historians, archaeologists and scholars of material culture can realise the potential of the material turn and embodied approach, harness the rich range of evidence at our disposal for historical periods and, in integrating social and material, transform our understanding of people's lived experiences of the body. In this introduction, we have situated our embodied approach within each discipline's material turn, focusing on how the sources, concepts and methods of each discipline can engage us with the challenges posed by theoretical advances of the first quarter of the twenty-first century. Interweaving scholarship from both history and archaeology, we have demonstrated that embodied experience is centred within but not solely determined by the physical body. We have also traced at the convergence of archaeological and historical understandings of embodiment a rich material basis for researching embodied subjects – an 'archive of embodiment' – and demonstrated the need for new ways of working that prioritise the creation and interrogation of this archive.

Together, the chapters collected here develop and test new methods for interrogating the archive of embodiment. In doing so, they advance understanding of how the social and material are combined in the making of embodied experience in ways that bring particular dividends for our understanding of the early modern period. They have facilitated a sharper focus on bodies that might be considered 'ordinary' and 'marginalised' and, in revealing productive tensions between the many different types of evidence and scales of enquiry that are available for historical periods, have pushed against the boundaries of not only our interpretations but of the disciplines of history, archaeology and material culture studies themselves. Our original aim for the Material Bodies project was to promote the dividends of archaeologists and historians working together. This book offers a new and fruitful way forward in this endeavour.

## References

Attala, L. and Steele, L. (2019). 'Introduction', in L. Attala and L. Steele (eds), *Body Matters: Exploring the Materiality of the Human Body* (Cardiff: University of Wales Press), pp. 1–18.

Baker, B. J. and Agarwal, S. C. (2017). 'Stronger together: Advancing a global bioarchaeology', *Bioarchaeology International*, 1(1–2): 1–18.

Beaudry, M. C. (2011). 'Stitching women's lives: Interpreting the artefacts of sewing and needlework', in M. C. Beaudry and J. Symonds (eds), *Interpreting the Early Modern World: Transatlantic Perspectives* (New York: Springer), pp. 143–58.

Bekvalac, J. and Western, G. (2016). 'The impact of industrialization on London health', *Radiology Open Journal*, 2(1): 1–3.
Bennett, T. and Joyce, P. (2010). *Material Powers. Cultural Studies, History and the Material Turn* (London and New York: Routledge).
Blakey, M. L. and Rankin-Hill, L. M. (2016). 'Political economy of African forced migration and enslavement in Colonial New York: An historical biology perspective', in M. K. Zuckerman and D. L. Martin (eds), *New Directions in Biocultural Anthropology* (Hoboken: John Wiley & Sons), pp. 107–32.
Borić, D. and Robb, J. (2008). *Past Bodies: Body-Centered Research in Archaeology* (Oxford: Oxbow Books).
Brewer, J. (2010). 'Microhistory and the histories of everyday life', *Cultural and Social History*, 7(1): 87–109.
Brickley, M., Mays, S. and Ives, R. (2007). 'An investigation of skeletal indicators of vitamin D deficiency in adults: Effective markers for interpreting past living conditions and pollution levels in 18th and 19th century Birmingham, England', *American Journal of Physical Anthropology*, 132(1): 67–79.
Buikstra, J. E., Baadsgaard, A. and Boutin, A. T. (2011). 'Introduction', in A. Baadsgaard, A. T. Boutin and J. E. Buikstra (eds), *Breathing New Life into Evidence of Death: Contemporary Approaches to Bioarchaeology* (Santa Fe: School for Advanced Research Press), pp. 3–28.
Canning, K. (1999). 'The body as method? Reflections on the place of the body in gender history', *Gender & History*, 11(3): 499–513.
Clever, I. and Ruberg. W. (2014). 'Beyond cultural history? The material turn, praxiography, and body history', *Humanities*, 3(4): 546–66.
Cody, L. F. (2005). *Birthing the Nation: Sex, Science and the Concept of Eighteenth-Century Britain* (Oxford: Oxford University Press).
Crossland, Z. (2010). 'Materiality and embodiment', in D. Hicks and M. C. Beaudry (eds), *The Oxford Handbook of Material Culture Studies* (Oxford: Oxford University Press), pp. 386–405.
Csordas, T. J. (1990). 'Embodiment as a paradigm for anthropology', *Ethos*, 18(1): 5–47.
Davidson, H. (2019). 'The embodied turn: Making and remaking dress as an academic practice', *Fashion Theory*, 23(3): 329–62.
Dornan-Fish, J. (2012). 'Motive matters: Intentionality, embodiment, and the individual in archaeology', *Time and Mind*, 5(3): 279–98.
Duden, B. (1987; 1991). *The Woman Beneath the Skin: A Doctor's Patients in eighteenth-century Germany* (Cambridge, Mass.; London: Harvard University Press).
Fowler, C. (2004). *The Archaeology of Personhood: An Anthropological Approach* (London: Routledge).
Fowler, C. and Harris, O. J. T. (2015). 'Enduring relations: Exploring a paradox of new materialism', *Journal of Material Culture*, 20(2): 1–22.
Gerritsen, A. and Riello, G. (2015). *Writing Material Culture History* (London: Bloomsbury).
Gilchrist, R. (2012). *Medieval Life: Archaeology and the Life Course* (Woodbridge, Suffolk: The Boydell Press).

Govier, E. and Steele, L. (2021). 'Beyond the "thingification" of worlds: Archaeology and the New Materialisms', *Journal of Material Culture*, 26(3): 298–317.

Gowland, R. (2015). 'Entangled lives: Implications of the developmental origins of health and disease hypothesis for bioarchaeology and the life course', *American Journal of Physical Anthropology*, 158(4): 530–40.

Gowland, R. (2018). '"A Mass of Crooked Alphabets": The construction and othering of working class bodies in industrial England', in P. K. Stone (ed.), *Bioarchaeological Analyses and Bodies: New Ways of Knowing Anatomical and Archaeological Skeletal* Collections (Cham: Springer), pp. 147–63.

Gowland, R. and Kacki, S. (2020). 'Theoretical approaches to bioarchaeology. The view from across the pond', in C. M. Cheverko, J. R. Prince-Buitenhuys and M. Hubbe (eds), *Theoretical Approaches in Bioarchaeology* (Abingdon: Routledge), pp. 170–83.

Grassby, R. (2005). 'Material culture and cultural history', *The Journal of Interdisciplinary History*, 35(4): 591–603.

Hamilakis, Y. and Jones, A. M. (2017). 'Archaeology and assemblage', *Cambridge Archaeological Journal*, 27(1): 77–84.

Hamling, T. and Richardson, C. (2010). 'Introduction', in T. Hamling and C. Richardson (eds), *Everyday Objects: Medieval and Early Modern Material Culture and its Meanings* (Farnham: Ashgate), pp. 1–26.

Harvey, K. (2017). 'Introduction: Historians, material culture and materiality', in K. Harvey (ed.), *History and Material Culture: A Student's Guide to Approaching Alternative Sources*, 2nd edn (Abingdon: Routledge), pp. 1–26.

Harvey, K. (2020). 'One British thing: A history of embodiment: Ann Purvis, ca.1793–1849', *Journal of British Studies*, 59(1): 136–9.

Hicks, D. (2010). 'The material-cultural turn. Event and effect', in D. Hicks and M. C. Beaudry (eds), *Oxford Handbook of Material Culture Studies* (Oxford: Oxford University Press), pp. 25–98.

Hicks, D. and Beaudry, M. (eds) (2010). *Oxford Handbook of Material Culture Studies* (Oxford: Oxford University Press).

Hodder, I. (2012). *Entangled: An Archaeology of the Relationships Between Humans and Things* (Chichester: Wiley-Blackwell).

Hosek, L. (2019). 'Osteobiography as microhistory: Writing from the bones up', *Bioarchaeology International*, 3(1): 44–57.

Hosek, L. and Robb, J. (2019). 'Osteobiography: A platform for bioarchaeology research', *Bioarchaeology International*, 3(1): 1–15.

Hosek, L., Warner-Smith, A. L. and Novak, S. A. (2021). 'The Body as (in, and with) text: Doing bioarchaeology with archives', *Archaeological Review from Cambridge*, 36(2): 45–68.

Hoskins, J. (1998). *Biographical Objects: How Things Tell the Stories of Peoples' Lives* (London: Routledge).

Ingold, T. (2011). *Being Alive: Essays on Movement, Knowledge and Description* (London: Routledge).

Ion, A. (2021). 'Review of Attala, Luci & Steel Louise (eds), *Body Matters: Exploring the Materiality of the Human Body*', *Journal of the Royal Anthropological Institute*, 27: 1027–8.

Joyce, P. (2010). 'What is the social in social history?', *Past & Present*, 206(1): 213–48.
Laqueur, T. (1990). *Making Sex: Body and Gender From the Greeks to Freud* (Cambridge, Mass.: Harvard University Press).
Lewis, M. (2002). *Urbanisation and Child Health in Medieval and Post-medieval England: An Assessment of the Morbidity and Mortality of Non-adult Skeletons from the Cemeteries of Two Urban and Two Rural Sites in England (AD 850–1859)* (Oxford: Archaeopress).
Leatherman, T. and Goodman, A. (2020). 'Building on the biocultural syntheses: 20 years and still expanding', *American Journal of Human Biology*, 32: e23360.
Lucas, G. (2012). *Understanding the Archaeological Record* (New York: Cambridge University Press)
Magnússon, S. G. and Szijártó, I. M. (2013). *What Is Microhistory? Theory and Practice* (New York: Routledge).
Mant, M. (2016). 'Slips, trips, falls, and brawls: fractures of the working poor in London during the long eighteenth century' (PhD dissertation, McMaster University).
Mant, M. L. and Holland, A. J. (2019). *Bioarchaeology of Marginalized People* (London: Academic Press).
Marshall, Y. and Alberti, B. (2014). 'A matter of difference: Karen Barad, ontology and archaeological bodies', *Cambridge Archaeological Journal*, 24(1): 19–36.
Merleau-Ponty, M. (1945; 2012). *Phenomenology of Perception*, trans. D. A. Landes (Abingdon: Routledge).
Meskell, L. (2004). *Object Worlds in Ancient Egypt: Material Biographies Past and Present* (Oxford: Berg).
Mytum, H. (2010). 'Ways of writing in post-medieval and historical archaeology: Introducing biography', *Post-Medieval Archaeology*, 44(2): 237–54.
Owsley, D. W., Bruwelheide, K. S., Barca, K. G., Reidy, S. K. and Fleskes, R. E. (2018). 'Lives lost: What burial vault studies reveal about eighteenth-century identities', in P. K. Stone (ed.), *Bioarchaeological Analyses and Bodies: New Ways of Knowing Anatomical and Archaeological Skeletal Collections* (Cham: Springer), pp. 111–45.
Pilloud, S. and Louis-Courvoisier, M. (2003). 'The intimate experience of the body in the eighteenth century: Between interiority and exteriority', *Medical History*, 47(4): 451–72.
Pluciennik, M. (2002). 'Art, artefact, metaphor', in Y. Hamilakis, M. Pluciennik and S. Tarlow (eds), *Thinking Through the Body. Archaeologies of Corporeality* (Boston, Mass.: Springer), pp. 217–32.
Porter, R. (2001). 'History of the body reconsidered', in P. Burke (ed.), *New Perspectives on Historical Writing*, 2nd edn (Cambridge: Polity Press), pp. 233–6.
Roper, L. (2010). 'Beyond discourse theory', *Women's History Review*, 19(2): 307–19.
Ruberg, W. (2020). *History of the Body* (London: Red Globe Press).
Rublack, U. (2013). 'Matter in the material renaissance', *Past & Present*, 219(1): 41–85.
Schouwenburg, H. (2015). 'Back to the future? History, material culture and new materialism', *International Journal for History, Culture and Modernity*, 3(1): 59–72.

Schrader, S. A. and Torres-Rouff, C. (2021). 'Embodying bioarchaeology', in C. M. Cheverko, J. R. Prince-Buitenhuys and M. Hubbe (eds), *Theoretical Approaches in Bioarchaeology* (London: Routledge), pp. 15–27.

Siena, K. (2019). *Rotten Bodies: Class and Contagion in Eighteenth-century Britain* (New Haven and London: Yale University Press).

Smail, D. L. (2007). *On Deep History and the Brain* (Berkeley: University of California Press).

Sofaer, J. R. (2006). *The Body as Material Culture: A Theoretical Osteoarchaeology* (Cambridge: Cambridge University Press).

Saul, F. P. (1972). 'The human skeletal remains of Altar de Sacrificios: An osteobiographic analysis', *Papers of the Peabody Museum*, 63(2): 3–123.

Stodder, A. L. and Palkovich, A. M. (eds) (2012). *The Bioarchaeology of Individuals* (Gainesville: University Press of Florida).

Szreter, S. and Mooney, G. (1998). 'Urbanization, mortality, and the standard of living debate: New estimates of the expectation of life at birth in nineteenth-century British cities', *The Economic History Review*, 51(1): 84–112.

Tarlow, S. (2011). *Ritual, Belief and the Dead in Early Modern Britain and Ireland* (Cambridge: Cambridge University Press).

Tilley, C., Keane, W., Kuchler, S., Rowlands, M. and Spyer, P. (eds) (2006). *Handbook of Material Culture* (London: Sage).

Tilley, L. and Oxenham, M. (2011). 'Survival against the odds: Modelling the social implications of care provision to seriously disabled individuals', *International Journal of Palaeopathology*, 1(2): 35–42.

Wahrman, D. (2008). 'Change and the corporeal in seventeenth- and eighteenth-century gender history: Or, can cultural history be rigorous?', *Gender & History*, 20(3): 584–602.

Wesp, J. K. (2015). 'Bioarchaeological perspectives on the materiality of everyday life activities', *Archaeological Papers of the American Anthropological Association*, 26(1): 139–48.

White, C. (2014). *The Materiality of Individuality: Archaeological Studies of Individual Lives* (New York: Springer).

Witmore, C. (2014). 'Archaeology and the new materialisms', *Journal of Contemporary Archaeology*, 1(2): 203–46.

Zuckerman, M. K. and Armelagos, G. J. (2011). 'The origins of biocultural dimensions in bioarchaeology', in S. C. Agarwal and B. A. Glencross (eds), *Social Bioarchaeology*. (Chichester: Wiley-Blackwell), pp. 15–43.

# 1

# Archives of embodiment: body and experience in the archaeological and historical record

*Karen Harvey*

Despite a growing interest in 'embodiment', historians of the body rarely consider the extant material remains of their subject, remains which are the objects of study within the discipline of bioarchaeology (in North America) or osteoarchaeology (in the United Kingdom). This chapter seeks to contribute to a discussion about how historians and other scholars might examine the archaeological (and particularly bioarchaeological record) and the historical record together in order to better understand the embodied experiences of people in the past. The archaeologist Sarah Tarlow has articulated an important distinction that is at work in both disciplines: focusing on human remains, she says, archaeologists necessarily examine 'the *material rather than the experiencing* body' (Tarlow, 2011: 8). Overcoming this apparent distinction between the material and the experiencing body, by uniting skeletal and documentary records, is now an ambition shared by many archaeologists and historians. To both reconstruct the experiencing body as a material body and to interpret the material body as an experiencing body is a considerable challenge, though, and one that requires the expertise of scholars in both disciplines. This chapter offers new ways to study past embodied experiences as an outcome of the material, social and cultural by drawing on the bioarchaeological, material and historical record. Focusing on two non-elite individuals from the north of England between 1793 and 1849 – James Simpson and Ann Purvis – it draws on the rich but also incomplete evidence to reconstruct their lives as lived.

In so doing, the chapter explores how we can align the work of bioarchaeologists and historians of the body, attending to their respective research questions, approach and data, in ways that avoid either discipline becoming a mere illustration of or supplement to the other. I propose that one way in which this can be achieved is to begin with instances where our data converge on the same person or topic, whether those data are derived from the physical archive of human remains, the material archive of the archaeological record, or the historical archive of visual, written or material documents. In bringing both the bioarchaeological and historical record into play, each has the potential to reinforce as well as to lead the other. On occasion, too, the evidence, methods and findings of bioarchaeology and history can be in tension. It is in exploring those very tensions, I argue, that new knowledge about the embodied experience of men and women in the eighteenth and nineteenth centuries can often arise. The archive of embodiment – of the experience of having and of being a physical body – is constituted from both the archaeological and historical record.

Archaeologists and historians have the past in common, yet the challenge of uniting them in a study of past embodiment is considerable given that concrete disciplinary differences certainly exist. It is useful to acknowledge these, at least from the perspective of a trained professional academic historian. First, chronology: historians tend to work across much shorter time frames than archaeologists. Second, scale: archaeologists have an interest in populations, accessed via large bodies of data, whereas historians (certainly those who work on the body and are usually trained in social or cultural history) tend to work on relatively smaller communities and often single individuals and their specific lives. Third, data: as captured by the archaeologist John Moreland, 'archaeologists study objects, historians study words' (Moreland, 2001: 8), often in the form of written historical documents. Fourth, while both archaeologists and historians are trained in rigorous evidence-based methodologies, scholars in these disciplines generally have contrasting interpretive approaches to their evidence. This is particularly pronounced when considering the approaches of bioarchaeologists (trained in scientific methods) and social and cultural historians of the body. Archaeologists, and particularly those dealing with material human remains, have a low level of comfort with a high level of inference from the evidence.[1] Social and cultural historians, in contrast, often apply a range of interpretive skills to examine the unwritten meanings in their sources. Embedded in the interpretive practice of social and cultural historians is a high level of comfort with a high level of inference from the evidence. Admittedly, these are general differences which apply to a lesser and greater extent for individual scholars and pieces of scholarship. Yet, combining archaeology and history in a study of embodiment requires us to become cognisant of the emphases that arise in those disciplines out of these differences; of where our research methods and customary types of data both converge and diverge. Before embarking on the two case studies that form the heart of this chapter, I wish to explore the commonalities and distinctions between these disciplines by discussing four key terms or concepts: the material body, experience, biography and identity.

## The material body

The study of material culture has been driven by a 'material turn' in the academy that has impacted both archaeologists and historians. Archaeologists have, of course, always focused on the material record, yet Dan Hicks has described how archaeology and anthropology experienced what he calls 'a Material-Cultural Turn' (Hicks, 2010). In the area of the human body, archaeology has moved from a dominant approach to the body as a product of discourse (often relying on Foucault) to one that sees 'the body as the phenomenological center of experience' (Bulger and Joyce, 2013: 68). Work on embodiment in archaeology has often proceeded without attention to the body itself, but instead to representations of the body or the spaces through which the body has moved (Bulger and Joyce, 2013: 68–85). The broader archaeological interest in bodies as a site of lived experience grounded in bioarchaeology is actually relatively recent, representing a shift away from 'the disciplinary poles of biology and culture' in favour of 'theories of embodied practice' (Hamilakis *et al.*, 2002: 7, 8). Joanna Sofaer insists that 'the body is never pre-social' (Sofaer, 2006: 74). For Sofaer, treating the body as material culture signals that the physical body is a product of both 'social action and biology together' (Sofaer, 2013: 231). Importantly, this requires 'work combining bioarchaeological and ethnographic or historical information' (Sofaer, 2006: 237). Such are the demands of studying what I have called elsewhere, the 'the socio-materiality of the body' (Harvey, 2020: 138).

For historians, the material turn has meant dedicated work with material objects, sometimes exclusively or predominantly; history as a discipline is no longer based on written texts. The focus on culture and meaning, alongside the material, tracks the similar developments in archaeology (Harvey, 2017). One of the distinguishing features of historians' approaches to material culture is their object-driven rather than object-centred approaches. History is not an object-based discipline: historians' questions are about the contexts, uses and meanings of objects – not the objects themselves. This emphasis is driven by historians' commitment to experience, the second concept I wish to highlight.

## Experience

Ultimately, historians' interest in objects stems from a desire to access experience (Harvey, 2017). History is the discipline of past experience: historians aim to situate their objects (material, visual or written) in a context in order to reconstruct experience (comprised from ideas, feelings, relationships, structures and other factors). Through their interpretive actions they step through their inanimate documents to produce an account of the once living. The impulse to move through the object to experience is heightened when that object is the human body: as skeletal remains, their inadequacy as a record of lived experience is startling, yet they are also traces of a once living embodied person and contain information about that life that is invariably impossible to acquire in any other way. The human body as a 'document' or an 'object' is, of course, quite a different proposition to a ceramic punch bowl, a pair of velvet breeches or a fire surround. These skeletal remains were once not the inanimate objects they are now. In recognition of this, bioarchaeologists have carefully attended to the ethics of their work (DeWitte, 2015). For historians, the nature of the body as physical object means that their aim to move through these remains to a reconstruction of that person's lived experience is heightened. After all, and as discussed in the Introduction to this volume, for many historians the body contains the subject and the self; it is the very fact of this material subject that defines human experience, or 'embodiment'.

Experience is illusive; past experience even more so. Examining experience is a contentious process and necessarily requires that the scholar in any discipline extends further than the evidence strictly permits (Scott, 1991). In this extension of analysis through or past the evidence, researchers employ contrasting practices of interpretation and modes of writing, both of which might include creative or imaginative steps. This is accentuated because experience is intrinsically diachronic. Historians seek to attend to lives that were lived and experienced in time. In this process, historians use narrative to plot the discrete moments of experience that are registered in the historical record, which they then link together using their disciplinary knowledge and skills. It is especially at these links that historical interpretation invariably takes place.

## Biography

Bioarchaeologists also seek to use skeletal remains to reconstruct lives lived. The third key term or concept – biography – is central to these endeavours and exemplifies some of the shared interests of scholars in the two disciplines. The term 'osteobiography' has been used to refer to the study of a whole life course through human remains, thus creating a biography for those human remains. In John Robb's study of Neolithic Italy, osteobiography refers to 'the study through human skeletons of the biography as a cultural narrative' and comprises the cultural meanings of life events and the study of the remains after death (Robb, 2002: 160). Applying ageing techniques to skeletal remains, for example, allows the archaeologist to plot a person's osteobiography over the life course, aligning these with cultural meanings of particular life stages found in other evidence (Robb, 2002: 161). In this instance, the biography does not refer to an individual's life experiences but a broader cultural narrative. A different variation of biography, drawing on bioarchaeology, has been proposed by the medieval historian Robin Fleming. Fleming insists on the value of skeletal remains for historians' reconstruction of the biographies of those medieval men and women who left no trace in the written record. Fleming's study of a seventh-century woman who died around the age of 20 years with leprosy, 'Eighteen' (the number given to the remains by archaeologists and chosen by Fleming as the moniker), situates the remains in the context of population-level data about early medieval Britain. Fleming's conclusion is that the numbers are important and, combined with the individual information, these data tell us things especially about individuals such as Eighteen. Such evidence will 'betray the human cost of things often written about by historians as impersonal and faceless trends' (Fleming, 2006: 47). As Fleming writes elsewhere, this supplements a medieval history of Britain that is so often devoid of 'living, breathing human beings' (Fleming, 2009: 607). As she writes, 'Skeletons, first and foremost, are the remains of individuals, who, while living, had hopes and sorrows all their own. These were people with individually aching knees and their very own sore shoulders' (Fleming, 2006: 29).

In attempting to bridge the disciplinary gap it is important to avoid simplistic characterisations of other disciplines, particularly in relation to the term 'biography'. Historians would baulk at the suggestion that their discipline provides 'textual biographies' by arranging key facts and dates, that 'the textual record tends to be static and closed' and that their sources are 'random textual citations' which provide details that are external to a person's experience, compared to a skeletal record which can in turn provide 'more complex or nuanced a portrait' of a person's life (Robb *et al.*, 2019: 28, 29). In fact, biography has long been regarded as 'an inferior form of history' (Sardica, 2013: 384). Reconstructing through written documents the events of an individual's life can occlude the wider cultural and social structures, and the power relationships, that have patterned experience. Nevertheless, an insistence on the lives of (especially non-elite) individuals, rather than large populations, through a practice we could call 'biography', 'social history' or perhaps 'life reconstruction', is a commitment shared between archaeologists and historians.

## Identity

This commitment is consonant with a focus on identity, the fourth key term or concept. Arguably, it is here that the interests of the two disciplines come into closest proximity. Expressed as an 'archaeology of personhood' (Fowler, 2004) or an 'archaeology of a socially contextualised self', in archaeology such an approach examines the distinctive and lived social identity of the individual, 'the experiences, expectations, and rights a person derives from ascribed and achieved statuses or identities' (Clark and Wilkie, 2006: 337). Rather than a choice of either approach or form of data, searching for this lived social identity is best achieved by 'textually informed archaeologies' (Marshall, 2013: 207). Such an even-handed combination of archaeology and history is promoted by Megan Perry, who underlines historical bioarchaeology as a 'uniquely inter- and intra-disciplinary approach', and one which should include 'the relationship between human biological data and information derived from other historical and archaeological sources that exemplify a contextualised bioarchaeological study' (Perry, 2007: 488). Perry draws out the commonalities and conflicts between different datasets on particular communities within the Roman and Byzantine Near East, exposing the possible motivations of ancient writers in the process.

## Interrogating archives of embodiment for the eighteenth and nineteenth centuries

Combinations of archaeology and history are not new; synergies clearly emerge around these four concepts of the material body, experience, biography and identity. Yet, significantly, all of the work cited so far concerns prehistory or the pre-modern (medieval) past. For post-medieval Britain, the period covered by this book, it is also established practice for bioarchaeological analysis to draw upon parish records, census data and other historical evidence to provide context for archaeologies of burial sites and skeletal remains. A small but growing body of published work on a range of non-elite population groups exploits these techniques. In work on admissions to London general hospitals over the long eighteenth century, for example, Madeleine Mant has utilised written and bioarchaeological material to reconstruct the working lives of the labouring poor (Mant, 2020). Rebecca Gowland's study of twenty-one unidentified adolescent pauper apprentices in North Yorkshire demonstrated how these bodies had been shaped by poverty, both before and after birth, contributing to our understanding of the lived experiences of poverty (Gowland, 2018). Studies of eighteenth- and nineteenth-century individuals, rather than large populations, have also been undertaken. One instructive study of the burial vault at Darnall's Chance House, in Maryland, built in c.1741–2 by the Scottish merchant James Wardrop and his wife Lettice Lee, examined both the bioarchaeological and historical record. Even here, though, while there are extensive records for the house and its inhabitants and the skeletons were aged quite precisely, only three of the adults out of a total of nine individuals could be identified with some certainty. The study was able to comment on the experiences of people of genteel rank, the social practices in recording (or not) children's births in a context of high infant mortality, and the importance of kin relationships that were observable in the burial of Lee's siblings in the vault (Owsley *et al.*, 2018). Yet, the authors are left to surmise whether the woman at the centre of the burials is, in fact, Lettice Lee. Connecting the specific bioarchaeology of the remains to the lived experiences of a named individual is frustratingly eluded. Even for a period of British history that has an apparent surfeit of both archaeological and historical evidence, overcoming the distinction between the material and the experiencing body remains a challenge.

This chapter extends this existing scholarship, underpinned by the aforementioned concepts of the material body, experience, biography and identity. It builds on work begun during a pilot project in which bioarchaeologists and historians of the body worked together to identify collections of skeletons from the eighteenth and nineteenth centuries with surviving associated historical records which would sustain research on co-designed topics.[2] The pilot developed a template for research – 'from skeletal biography to social biography' – designed to connect the population-level studies of skeletal collections to both general historical and specific biographical research. This method included record linkage of bioarchaeological information and historical documents (parochial records and other sources) for any named individuals in archaeological collections, which allowed for in-depth case studies. It was therefore also a requirement of the collections that the skeletal remains could be identified (from grave goods such as a coffin plate, for example) and traced in the historical record and that they were in a sufficiently good condition to be the subject of detailed osteological analysis. Of the six sites initially considered, together holding 791 skeletons, only three sites held remains that could be named from the archaeological record. The 546 skeletons from these three sites included thirty-eight named individuals and five where likely or partial names were detectable. These are low proportions: just 4.93% of the individual bodily remains in all six surveyed collections were fully identifiable (Swales, 2016). Furthermore, only two of these sites had associated accessible parish records of baptisms, marriages and burials (arguably the most useful initial historical documents initially): Carver Street, Sheffield 1806–1855 and St Hilda's Church, Coronation Street, South Shields 1818–1855. These sites gave rise to a set of case studies, including the chapters on history of maternity (Craig-Atkins and Fissell, this volume: Chapter 2) and impairment or disability (Newman and Turner, this volume: Chapter 7) in this collection. This chapter focuses on the individuals that could be clearly named and that survived in a good enough condition for osteological analysis. Only three individuals met these criteria (James Simpson, Jane Prince and Ann Purvis), out of an original possible 791 (less than 0.4% of the total sample). As Jane Prince had an indeterminate date of death in the archaeological record, she was judged potentially difficult to find in the historical record. This chapter thus focuses on James Simpson and Ann Purvis to explore the interdisciplinary practices drawing on bioarchaeology and history undertaken by an historian of the body drawing on bioarchaeological data and approaches.

### Risk, youth and masculinity: James Simpson (1815–34)

The experiences of young men in the British past were profoundly shaped by gender and the patriarchal nature of their society. Young men – blessed with the privileges of manhood and not yet having acquired the status of householder – could enjoy considerable license (Shepard, 2006: 93–125). Yet, manhood brought with it anxieties to conform to (and juggle) the patriarchal expectations of self-control, strength and independence, ultimately expressed in the ability to sustain and successfully manage a household of which one was head (Harvey, 2012; Shepard, 2000). For the consolidating middle class, their young men were the future (Barker, 2008; Davidoff and Hall, 2002: 416–49). It was into this world that James Simpson was born on 26 December 1815. He was the first son of Robert and Rebecca (neé Blacktin) Simpson (then aged 24 and 20 respectively), who had been married less than a year when their son arrived. Robert hailed from Wirksworth in Yorkshire, while Rebecca had been born in Cheshire. They were married on 19 January 1814 at Sheffield Parish Church, and it was in this town that they went on to have their ten children. Their youngest child, Rebecca, was born in 1839, when her mother was 44, following the loss of three children all aged 3 years or less in the previous five years. Just four of their ten children outlived them (one boy and three girls).

Robert and Rebecca's migration to Sheffield occurred during a momentous transformation in the town. Like other northern towns such as Leeds and Manchester, Sheffield experienced a dramatic increase in population and huge changes to its urban environment during the period 1780–1830 (Barker, 2004). This both reflected and impacted a changing economy and social structure. Dominated by the metal industry, early nineteenth-century Sheffield witnessed considerable deprivation. Most of the metal production took place in small workshops in which artisanal craftsmen were prominent; yet, by 1844 Friedrich Engels used the Sheffield grinders as an exemplary case of the degraded English proletariat (Engels, 1892). However, alongside the grinders, cutlers and steel workers in Sheffield were many other trades and these became greater as a proportion of the population as the Sheffield economy diversified to accommodate the growing middling-sorts there and in the region (Barker, 2004: 181; Hey, 1998). Robert Simpson was a currier and leather cutter, taking the material that had already been transformed from skin to leather through the tanning process and preparing this into the appropriate state for those who would make the leather goods (be they shoes, saddles or gloves). Such trades had previously been organised into guilds, but these struggled to maintain control of manufacture and such companies were in abeyance by the early nineteenth century (Rusbridge, 2019: 19–20, 99). Simpson carried on this trade for many years and was evidently successful. From 1825 until 1846, for example, he paid for his entries in a series of trade directories (Gell, 1825). By the time James entered his teens, his father's respectability in the town was well established. In 1832, he was named as a trustee to a local coach maker, Robert Robinson (*Sheffield Independent*, 14 January 1832). In 1836, Robert was named as one of two trustees for Samuel Barker the boot and shoemaker from Sheffield, along with another currier (*Perry's Bankrupt Gazette*, Saturday 5 November 1836). His reputation amongst the leather trades extended further, and in 1840 he was trustee for a wood turner, William Lee (*Sheffield Independent*, 23 May 1840).

James Simpson died, aged 18, on 15 March 1834. He left behind seven siblings, four aged less than 10 years old and four of them girls. It is the tin coffin plate that allowed archaeologists to identify this as James Simpson's burial: a tin plate (rather than the more common iron) also suggests a degree of wealth (Swales, 2016: 5). The nature of James' burial underscores the relative financial security of this young family. He was buried at Carver Street Methodist Chapel in Sheffield, on 18 March 1834, and his interment cost £2 12s 6d (Chapel Keeper's funeral book). Subsequently, the family were able to install a gravestone to memorialise James, along with three of his siblings who had died in the intervening three and a half years (see Figure 1.1).[3] This material culture chimes with the status of this early nineteenth-century artisan's family.

The Simpsons were also members of the thriving Methodist community of early nineteenth-century Sheffield. Methodism was well-established across Yorkshire, but its vibrancy in Sheffield may have been what attracted Robert and Rebecca, or their families (Wolffe, 2008). Looking back from 1835, one writer remembered the 'extraordinary revival of religion in Sheffield' that took place from 1794–6, part of a national expansion in nonconformity (Rigg, 1835: 608; Watts, 1995). The Carver Street Chapel was built in 1804 and generated 'much talk' on its construction (Holland, 1823: 792). Though northern Methodism is often associated with the industrial workers,

Figure 1.1 The Simpson gravestone at Carver Street Chapel.

town-centre chapels attracted 'wealthy and influential' members in 'easy circumstances' (Rigg, 1835: 609). Carver Street was 'one of the largest and most handsome' and became more successful than the existing Norfolk Street chapel for a time, eventually leading to a split amongst the Sheffield Methodists in 1831 (Rigg, 1835: 608, 610). By the time of James Simpson's death, there were thirty-two Methodist ministers and nearly 12,000 members operating in the extensive Sheffield Circuit (Rigg, 1835: 607). This Methodist context meant that James was likely to have been well-educated. By 1823, one Methodist Sunday school in the town had forty-seven members (Holland, 1823: 794). There were at least three Methodist day-schools in Sheffield, in addition to a school of the National Society dedicated specifically to the education of poor boys and girls; the Carver Street Chapel fostered very close relationships with several of these schools, with its own school room opening in the yard in 1834 (*Carver Street Methodist Church*, 1955: 7; Rigg, 1835: 610; Wooler, 2016: 48).

Class is buried deep within the body. The status and prosperity of Rebecca and Robert's household is not only evident in the material culture of James Simpson's burial but also within the material remains of his body. His bodily remains indicate that he was well nourished and had not experienced lasting disease, perhaps suggesting the advantages of rank. James Simpson's body is, at least in its current state, fairly unremarkable. Though an initial report indicated that the skeleton was relatively complete, in fact a significant minority is missing and many elements (for example, all the ribs) are incomplete. Nevertheless, apart from post-mortem damage to the left fibula and sacrum, the only notable pathology in these skeletal remains concerns the mandible: there is a small cavity on the left second molar (Campanacho, 2017a: 4). The partial evidence of James Simpson's physical remains indicate a body free from chronic disease with no responses indicative of environmental stress or trauma.

The cause of James' death remains unknown. Given the absence of significant parts of the skeleton, it is possible that he died from a major trauma to his torso, perhaps as a result of accident or assault. A second possibility is acute infectious disease. It is important to note that there were three bodies in this grave. Though it is not clear to whom the third body belonged, we do know that the 18-year-old James was buried with his much younger brother, William, who died less than three weeks later the day after his 3rd birthday, on 8 April 1834. The remains of William were in too poor a condition to sustain a full skeletal analysis. Yet the coincidence of their deaths in quick succession, and the lack of a cause of death detectable from James' skeleton, might indicate infectious disease as a cause of death. The historical record provides no evidence to support either possibility. Local newspapers for that spring, summer and autumn do not report any major accidents or assaults, no coroner or court inquest into such incidents, nor any widespread disease at this time.

The attempt to connect the archaeological skeletal record for James Simpson with the historical written record produces just three direct meeting points: a record of his birth and baptism and of his death and burial in the parish registers, along with the record of the internment cost in the Methodist Chapel Keeper's funeral book. No other record can be found for this young man. He was too young to have established himself in trade or to have created a business. He was almost certainly working. The eldest child and the eldest son in a family where there were several younger siblings, James would have shouldered a considerable responsibility to work. It is highly likely that at the time of his death he was assisting his father, just as his younger brother John was listed as an assistant to his currier father in the census of 1841. James was too young to have married and established his own family. He was also too well behaved to have done anything sufficiently disorderly or criminal to make the local or national newspapers. So we do not know how he died and we know very little about how he lived.

Both the bioarchaeological and the historical record for James Simpson appear to bespeak silence, yet these are only silences if we are searching for a particular pathology or social event. In fact, we are able to reconstruct a rich and quite specific context for this young man. James benefited from having a skilled father who lived and worked at home at his own business. Though Robert would eventually face periods of financial difficulty, his business was still advertised in the trade directory of 1846 (*Slaters 1846 Directory*). This context of the comfort and security experienced by a respectable family we can observe in the skeletal remains; James' burial and remains indicate clearly the advantages of class.

Yet, as the oldest son and an important potential economic contributor to the household economy, James' death was perhaps a significant factor in his father's apparent downward trajectory towards insolvency. By the directory of 1849, Robert was no longer listed and in summer 1850 he was reported as 'out of business' (bankrupt) and a 'prison case', being held in jail for debt. This last newspaper report noted that he had moved from Brook Hill to Change Alley, though had previously been on Market Street. This was evidence of his precarity and also of the newspaper's desire to identify him for readers (*Sheffield Independent*, 1850). Imprisonment for debt was not unusual for a tradesman, however; nor did it mean an inevitable decline for the entire family (Paul, 2019). Indeed, some of Robert's children went on to have some considerable success. This was especially notable for the girls. Two of his three daughters who survived until adulthood – Emma and Rebecca – remained unmarried and enjoyed successful careers as teachers, Emma becoming principal of the private day school in Sheffield at which they both taught by 1881, and the women also served as landladies to clerical and professional lodgers (1881 Census). Emma and Rebecca both lived until the age of 75; their elder sister, Mary, died aged 82. This longevity amongst the women was in stark contrast to the sons of Rebecca and Robert. In addition to the loss of James and William in 1834, the family buried George Henry at Carver Street just one week after his 1st birthday on Christmas Eve 1837, later losing their youngest remaining son Robert aged 23 on Christmas Eve 1850 (Yorkshire Burials, PR-138-2-24; PR-138-2-15).[4] John, the only son who lived until adulthood, was a clerk, though he predeceased his three sisters when he died aged 59 in the Sheffield Union Workhouse. The life expectancy of the women in the Simpson family outstripped that of the men.

James Simpson's remains might suggest physical health and resilience. Yet we contend with the fact of his death. Only five from a total of thirty-eight males excavated from Carver Street died between the ages of 18 and 26 years. Overall, 13% of the adult males died as young adults compared with 7/29 or 24% women; thus, James Simpson's death does not appear to be part of a landscape of the inflated risks of mortality to young men in this town (McIntyre and Willmott, 2003: 38). Moreover, burial registers for Sheffield from 1831–55 suggest that there is an underrepresentation of older adults amongst the skeletal remains excavated from the Carver Street burial ground, which means that the skeletal sample consistently underestimates life expectancy for young adults by over 20% (McIntyre and Willmott, 2003: 41). Life expectancy at birth in Sheffield in the 1840s was 32 years; cemetery records from 1860–2 suggest life expectancy for manual workers was 32.5, compared to 47.1 for professional and managerial workers (McIntyre and Willmott, 2003: 40; Szreter, 2005: 186). Indeed, had he died three months earlier James would have been classed as an adolescent (13–17 years in the Carver Street excavation) (McIntyre and Willmott, 2003: 36). As Lewis points out, children whose remains fall into the hands of bioarchaeologists are exceptional because they are a minority of non-survivors (Lewis, 2007: 186–7). As a young man who died shortly after his 18th birthday, James is unusual. He may have been a victim of the many accidents which took place in increasingly mechanised manufacture and for which there was no established legal framework for compensation until the end of the century (Bronstein, 2008; Moses, 2018). As noted earlier, James might also have succumbed to an infectious disease invisible in his skeletal remains. His death might also be placed within a broader context of the specific risks inherent in being a young man in early Victorian England. The risks to young men were highly gendered. Women certainly behaved violently and were the victims of violence, but violence was embedded in working-class manly sociability in ways that would have simply been unacceptable for most women, and certainly women from the skilled rank from which James Simpson hailed. Whether playful or murderous, fighting amongst young working-class men was learned from an early age and 'could be seen as a normal, even playful part of young men's lives' (Carter Wood, 2004: 79). Juvenile crime was a pressing issue in this society (Shore, 1999). Indeed, historical records indicate that men habitually committed violent criminal acts more frequently than women (Kesselring, 2015; Walker, 2009: 25). Though there are lively debates about how gender impacted the nature of criminal activity, levels of indictment and prosecution, and forms of punishment – plus considerable regional variation – Peter King has demonstrated that the proportions of female offenders indicted across a range of regional and national courts remained fairly consistent in the period 1750–1850, with a national average of 17.31% in 1834–8 (King, 2009: 222). For non-felonies (misdemeanours), women were probably a higher proportion (23.9 % of the prison population held for assault in London in 1816, for example) (King, 2009: 219).

Where scholars have compared the historical records of crime with the skeletal evidence, the same pattern emerges. In one dataset including coroners' records from 1232–1452, women were recorded as victims of violent acts

13.3% of the time and as perpetrators 4.4% of the time), while skeletal records from the same period show that men's bodies displayed fractures at twice the rate of women, though these data vary considerably between different towns and urban and rural locations (Grauer and Miller, 2017). In her study of the admissions records of the Royal London Hospital and skeletal remains from eighteenth- and nineteenth-century London, Madeleine Mant has found a far greater proportion of men present with fractures in the hospital and skeletal record (74.1% and 84.5% respectively) (Mant, 2016: 48). Interestingly, male admissions to hospital peak in the 18–30 years age bracket; in contrast to the comparable peak for women in the 41–50 years age bracket (Mant, 2016: 51–4). In a more recent study including data from a larger sample of London hospitals, men comprised 77.4% of all cases of fracture (Mant, 2020: 456). Though this difference may be down to a number of influential cultural and social factors, the risks of fracture in young men's lives is striking. Elsewhere, Mant shows that in the eighteenth and nineteenth centuries men were twice as likely to have multiple fractures than women, one aspect of the 'accident hump' in men between the ages of 20 and 50 observable in many societies (Mant, 2019: 10, 11). The majority of these fractures were not explained by intentional violence or other criminal activity, and Mant convincingly argues that most multiple fractures were the result of a range of accidental factors in urban settings or working environments. Arising from social, cultural or economic factors, younger men's bodies appear to have been particularly at risk of damage. James Simpson's skeletal remains suggest the advantages and the promise of his class, but his death demonstrates the combined risks of gender and age for young middle-class men in the early nineteenth century.

### Vulnerability, care and older women: Ann Purvis (*c*.1793–1849)

Middle age was reputedly a challenging time for women in Georgian Britain. The loss of visible youth was particularly damaging for a woman's social esteem and it often came at the same time as retirement from work and the end of a woman's reproductive life: this is perhaps why the process of ageing for women was seen as most pronounced around menopause than in frail old age, even though old age in general was often placed at 60 years of age (Ottaway, 2004: 41; Vickery, 2013). Yet, historians of older women also insist on their varied experiences, often shaped profoundly by class, and the 'period of unprecedented freedom and autonomy' that was enjoyed by many (Botelho and Thane, 2001: 5). Ann Purvis, who was buried aged 56 years at the Anglican church of St Hilda's in South Shields on 17 October 1849, prompts a reconsideration of the experiences of middle-aged women in this period. Ann was then living half a mile away on Shadwell Street, the most northerly thoroughfare skirting the edge of the South Shields promontory and running behind the quays at the mouth of the River Tyne. In contrast to the wider and more attractive commercial roads, the street that followed the line of the shore was 'narrow, crooked and inconvenient' (Parson and White, *History, Directory & Gazetteer of Durham & Northumberland*, 1827: 284). It was in a house on this street that, in 1841, Ann was listed as aged 45 and living in the household of William Purvis, a pilot on Shadwell Street (*Census Returns of England and Wales*, 1841). On the night of the census, the 70-year-old William and the 45-year-old Ann were accompanied in the house by the 15-year-old John Purvis. Deciphering the relationships between these three from the historical documents is not straightforward. Family relationships were not provided in the census, and women's marital status only recorded if a woman was the head of household. William had previously been married to Isabella Skipsey in 1792, and together they had several sons (but no daughters); Isabella died aged 36 and was buried on 25 June 1809 (Bishop's Transcripts, Durham University Library). William may have subsequently married Ann, because although no record of their marriage can be found, the brief notice of her death in the newspaper did identify her as William's widow (*The Newcastle Courant*, Friday 19 October 1849). Parish records do not record a John, son of William and Ann Purvis. They do, however, record a John Purvis born in June 1826 at South Shields, to the pilot John Skipsey Purvis and Mary Purvis, and a John born to William's son Andrew and his wife Thomasine in 1822 (*England Births & Baptisms 1538–1975*). John was certainly related to William (Wallace, 2018: 1–2). Whatever the precise relationship between the elderly man, middle-aged woman and teenage boy on the evening the census was taken in 1841, we can be sure they were close relations.

The vast majority of the families in South Shields were employed in trade, manufacture or handicraft (Wallace, 2018: 5). Women must have worked because they were the majority of the population. In South Shields, Ann was one of around nearly 9,000 inhabitants, of whom over 5,000 or 59% were women. The sex ratio of South Shields was characteristic of ports such as Portsmouth, Hull and Bristol, which had sex ratios of 70, 82 and 81:100 (male:female) respectively (Butler, 2012: 132). The wider Tyne area may not have seen the growth in population witnessed in other towns in the early nineteenth century, but the sudden demand for coal meant that the town had seen considerable population growth in the 1820s (Butler, 2012: 58–9). The expansion in coal and growth in the population meant that traffic on the Tyne River also increased. In the early nineteenth century, South Shields was a thriving port town, thronged with shipyards, dry docks, roperies and collieries. As a result, one commentator wrote, 'there are usually about 500 vessels lying at one time' (Parson and White, 1827: 283). Such an environment sustained many pilots – 120 sea pilots and 40 river pilots according to this writer – whose job it was to guide ships in and out of the mouth of the River Tyne, to help them negotiate their way along the crowded river (often from aboard the vessel), and to notify the Pilot Office of the arrival and departure of vessels (Parson and White, 1827: 283). William Purvis was himself a pilot, and father to several pilots. Pilots were licensed by Trinity House in Newcastle, and their highly respected work sustained the safety, health and legality of commercial shipping into England's ports (Mackenzie, 1827: 679–88; *To Masters of Ships*), though the South Shields Pilot Office was located on Shadwell Street (Wallace, 2018: 8). The job of pilot was skilled and, in the context of a port, a high-status occupation. A trade directory of 1828–9 listed only six pilots in South Shields, none of them Purvis', but by 1834 no less than seven Purvis men (including William) were listed in this occupation (Pigot & Co, 1828: 179; Pigot & Co, 1834: 43).

In addition to his job as pilot, William at one time rented a pub and beer shop which extended from Shadwell Street down to the river (*Newcastle Journal*, 17 March 1838). Given that William would have been out on the shore or the water at various times of the day, it would have been entirely in keeping with women's working patterns if Ann had not only worked in the pub and shop but also taken responsibility for their day-to-day operation. The census records no occupation for her, as wives' occupations were not required in the 1841 census (Higgs, 1987: 63). Yet we know that in the early nineteenth century, large proportions of women – around 40% of those listed in trade directories – worked in food and drink, dealing or shopkeeping, and by the 1851 census the extensive employment of women in 'dealing' was given as 38% (Barker, 2006: 62–7; Higgs, 1987: 75; Shoemaker, 1998: 188). Even greater numbers of women's work in these sectors would have been hidden behind their husband's or father's occupations. It is almost certain that as the younger of the two adults in the house, but as the only woman, Ann also fulfilled the demanding housewifery and care duties required by the inhabitants, not least for the 70-year-old William who was to die in 1843 from 'decay'.

Ann's skeletal remains suggest that at this time she would have been experiencing some infirmities herself. The skeleton of Ann Purvis is not well preserved, yet several observations can be made from its analysis (see Figure 1.2). We know that she suffered considerable tooth loss, with clear signs of decay caused by poor dental hygiene and/or sugary foods, as well as poorly developed teeth as a result of childhood disease or malnutrition. In fact, Ann only had three remaining teeth at the time of her death (Campanacho, 2017a: 2). Signs of periosteal reaction in both femurs and one tibia

Figure 1.2 Skeletal remains of Ann Purvis.

(caused by stress to and overuse of muscles or by infection) were virtually healed at the time of death, and were thus related to her earlier life. She showed signs of degenerative joint disease in her second cervical vertebra (in the neck) which may have been age related (Campanacho, 2017a: 3). It was impossible to detect if this spinal degenerative joint disease was more widespread because all other vertebrae were missing (Campanacho, 2017b: 3). However, Ann's humerus (in the upper arm) also displayed degenerative changes, in this case formation of new bone at the joint margins known as osteophytes (Campanacho, 2017b: 13). This joint disease may have caused Ann aches and pains. At 56, and with bodily markers widely recognised as symptoms of ageing in the eighteenth century, Ann would have certainly been regarded as an older person. Of the thirty individuals in the St Hilda's sample who were identified as adult women and assigned an age at death, ten were in the 45+ bracket (the other groupings were: 18–25 years (five), 26–35 years (seven), 26–45 years (one), 36–45 years (six), 36–45+ (one)) (Raynor *et al.*, 2011: 45). In the context of these data, then, Ann's death was not an anomaly. We do not know how she died: neither the burial register nor the newspaper announcement of her death provide any details (nor did the register give a cause of death for the other twelve people listed as having died in South Shields that week).

At the point of her death in October 1849, Ann Purvis was still living in Shadwell Street. We do not know if she was living alone, with the younger John Purvis, or perhaps with one of William's three sons from a previous marriage who also lived on the street. Yet, with the death of William, in the house on Shadwell Street in October 1843, we can imagine that Ann may have been left somewhat vulnerable as an unprotected ageing spinster or widow. Older women's susceptibility to poverty, especially if alone, has been well established (Thane, 1978: 33; Thane, 2000: 193, 271–2). Women lived longer, had more restrictive work opportunities and lower wages when in work; they had lower rates of remarriage and arguably suffered in a cultural context where old women were vilified much more viciously than old men. No records survive that record Ann independently at work and she may have resorted to support from others.

By the turn of the nineteenth century, the system of poor law provision for the elderly was patchy and stagnating, as well as being relatively less generous in the north (King, 2000: 147, 191; Ottaway, 1998). The detrimental impact of the New Poor Law on the elderly was considerably delayed and in the 1840s over half of women over their mid-60s received Poor Law support, a gendered pattern replicated in many counties (Goose, 2005; Thomson, 1984a: 267; Thomson 1984b). In 1851 Northumbria, for example, the sex ratio (male to female) of indoor relief via the workhouse was 81:100 and for outdoor relief it was 30:100; the English average was 97 and 45 respectively (Goose, 2005: 372–3). Yet, at 56, Ann may have been too young to fall into the category of the elderly (those over their mid-60s) widely considered bound for community support though the Poor Law (Thomson, 1984a: 267). Aside from poor relief, the facilities for healthcare and treatment were limited. Only 4.7% of the admissions to the Newcastle Infirmary in 1851 were from South Shields, no doubt because of the cost of travel along the River to Newcastle on top of the cost of admission (Butler, 2012: 138). South Shields town had a dispensary on East King Street from 1821 supplying the poor with free medical and surgical aid, along with a Society for the Relief of the Indigent Sick (established in 1818) under the auspices of which women would visit the homes of the poor (Parson and White, 1827: 280). By 1875, the dispensary alone listed 4146 patients (Whitfield, 2016). In principle, Ann may have also been able to access the support of Trinity House in Newcastle, which licensed the pilots on the Tyne. In addition to housing twenty-five pensioners in their alms house, it provided for up to 100 out-pensioners receiving between £5 and £7 per annum, though being located in Newcastle it was again unlikely she would have accessed this (MacKenzie, 1827: 687). Work and access to the well-documented systems of neighbourly support amongst her respectable artisan family and kin were likely to have been Ann's strategies for survival (Hindle, 2004: 15–95).

The material culture of Ann Purvis' burial is pertinent here. Ann's skeletal remains are identifiable because of the survival of her coffin breastplate. The predominant use of iron coffin decoration at St Hilda's suggests the working-class nature of the community buried here (Swales, 2016: 11). Ann's breastplate was the only one that was complete: two angels held palm fronds above a draped urn and winged cherub, the latter representing the departed soul (Raynor *et al.*, 2011: 87). Ann's wooden coffin was also more elaborate than the others unearthed from St Hilda's. The coffin lid was edged with tin which had been punched into a decorative pattern, while the interior of the coffin featured copper upholstery studs (Swales, 2016:

11). Ann's coffin was therefore more ornate than burials close by at St Hilda's, yet still modest compared to middle- and upper-ranking assemblages from the same period (Raynor et al., 2011: 89–90). This might align with what we know about the social status of Ann's head of household, William, but it is not the burial an historian would expect for a poor and vulnerable older woman in the 1840s. Arguably, it is also in tension with the state of Ann's body. While it is difficult to be precise about the chronology of her dental deterioration or skeletal lesions, Ann's skeletal remains suggest her possible exposure to malnutrition or hard labour or other physical challenges. The material culture of Ann's burial disrupts the bioarchaeological record and encourages us to rethink past experiences of ageing (Appleby, 2010). It is indicative of Ann Purvis' community status and the care with which she was treated.

In this way, Ann's skeleton provides evidence of material embodiment, of a life lived, that is missing from the documentary record. Both the historical and archaeological record for Ann Purvis are incomplete. These patchy patterns of survival suggest the existence of historic patriarchy and the challenges with which women daily wrestled. Aligning these partial archives exposes an apparent tension between the body as a material object on the one hand, and the body as experienced on the other. The physical processes of ageing, and the marking of biological age on the skeleton, do not correlate consistently with social status or social identity in the past. Indeed, social status and social identity are not consistently recorded in the physical body (Appleby, 2010). As Sofaer has commented, 'the notion of social age – what it means and how it is understood – is not well articulated in relation to skeletal remains' (Sofaer, 2011: 290). In coupling the material, documentary and archaeological records for Ann Purvis, we disrupt the conclusion that Ann may have experienced a reduced social status according to the interaction of her age, gender, marital status, class and compromised bodily state. A poor older woman with physical infirmities and no husband, Purvis was certainly vulnerable, but she was also firmly held within networks of family and kin.

## Conclusions

The archive of embodiment encompasses both the archaeological and historical record. It allows scholars from different disciplines to combine their methods to reconstruct the experiencing body as a material body and to interpret the material body as an experiencing body. In so doing, scholars are enabled to expose both the commonalities and conflicts between the data and our interpretation of these. This can produce new knowledge about the lived experiences of non-elite individuals in the past that would otherwise simply be inaccessible. The information generated through bioarchaeology is unrivalled. From the perspective of the history of the body it offers us 'history from the inside' (Robb *et al*, 2019: 29). Historical documents can provide incomparable evidence of quotidian social relationships, structures of thought and shared meanings. Combining the data and approaches of these two disciplines does not restore anything approaching a full account of the lives of men and women like James Simpson or Ann Purvis: as non-elite individuals, so much of their individual experience remains frustratingly out of reach. Nevertheless, bringing them together is the most productive way of accounting for all the many facets of the past that have comprised lived experience and the condition of being a thinking, feeling and embodied person.

## Acknowledgements

Though this is a single-authored chapter, the work has also drawn on the research of Vanessa Campanacho, Diana Swales and Hannah Wallace, and the expert advice and guidance of Elizabeth Craig-Atkins.

## Notes

1 This contrasts with a common characterisation of the two disciplines, in which historical written sources have been seen as the more reliable for meaning, but it accords with the traditional view of archaeology as struggling to sustain analyses of social and spiritual life. See John Moreland, *Archaeology and Text* (2001), p. 13.
2 'The Material Body: An Interdisciplinary Study in History and Archaeology' (British Academy Small Grant SG151375; 2015–2018).
3 The gravestone was for four siblings, also for Sarah Ann and George (Dec. 1837). The inscription reads:

Sacred/ to the memory/ of James the son of Robert/ and Rebecca Simpson/ who departed this life/ March 20th? 1834, aged 18 years./ Also William their/ son who departed this life/ April 8th 1834, aged 3 years/ Also Sarah Ann, their/ daughter who departed this life May 26th 1835?/ aged 1 year and 8 months/ Also of George Henry, their/ son who departed this life/ December 21st 1837 aged 1 year.

From: www.findagrave.com/memorial/146601899/james-simpson (accessed 3 August 2023).
4 On George Henry see PR138-2-24; Yorkshire Burials, Find my Past. On Robert see PR-138-2-15; Yorkshire Burials, Find my Past.

# References

## Primary sources

Bishop's Transcripts, Durham University Library, DDR/EA/PBT/2/227. Find my Past: www.durhamrecordsonline.com/ (accessed 10 July 2019).
*Carver Street Methodist Church, Sheffield: Third Jubilee Handbook, 1805–1955* (1955).
Chapel Keeper's funeral book, Non-Conformist burials, Carver Street Chapel (Wesleyan Methodist), Sheffield Archives: NR1021.
*Census Returns of England and Wales, 1841*: The National Archives of the UK (TNA). Accessed via www.ancestry.co.uk (accessed 10 July 2017).
Gell, R. (1825). *A General & Commercial Directory of Sheffield and its Vicinity* (Manchester). Accessed via 'Historical Directories of England and Wales', University of Leicester: http://specialcollections.le.ac.uk/digital/collection/p16445coll4 (accessed 30 June 2020).
*Pigot and Co's National Commercial Directory for 1828–9* (1828) (London: J. Pigot & Co). Accessed via *Historical Directories Online* (accessed 5 March 2021).
*Pigot and Co's National Commercial Directory for Durham, Northumberland and Yorkshire, 1834* (1834). (London: J. Pigot & Co). Accessed via *Historical Directories Online* (accessed 5 March 2021).
*Slaters' Directory of Sheffield* (1846).
*To Masters of Ships, and Pilots: A Digest of the Provisions, Penalties &c. of the Pilots' Act ... Made by the Corporation of Trinity House of Deptford Strond* (1810) (London: S. Smith).

## Newspapers and periodicals

*The Newcastle Courant* (1849). Friday 19 October. Accessed via *British Library Newspapers: Part I: 1800–1900* (Gale Cengage) (accessed 10 July 2019).
*Newcastle Journal* (1838). Saturday 17 March.
*Perry's Bankrupt Gazette* (1836). Saturday 5 November.
*Sheffield Independent* (1832). Saturday 14 January.
    (1840). Saturday 23 May.
    (1850). Saturday 29 June.

## Secondary sources

Appleby, J. E. P. (2010). 'Why we need an archaeology of old age, and a suggested approach', *Norwegian Archaeological Review*, 43(2): 145–68.
Barker, H. (2004). 'Smoke cities': northern industrial towns in late Georgian England', *Urban History*, 31(2): 175–90.
Barker, H. (2006). *The Business of Women: Female Enterprise and Urban Development in northern England 1760–1830* (Oxford: Oxford University Press).
Barker, H. (2008). 'Soul, purse and family: middling and lower-class masculinity in eighteenth-century Manchester', *Social History*, 33(1): 12–35.

Botelho, L. and Thane, P. (eds) (2001). 'Introduction', *Women and Ageing in British Society since 1500* (Abingdon and New York: Routledge).

Bronstein, J. L. (2008). *Caught in the Machinery: Workplace Accidents and Injured Workers in Nineteenth-Century Britain* (Stanford: Stanford University Press).

Bulger, T. J. and Joyce R. A. (2013). 'Archaeology of embodied subjectivities', in D. Bolger (ed.), *A Companion to Gender Prehistory* (Chichester: Wiley), pp. 68–85.

Butler, G. A. (2012). 'Disease, medicine and the urban poor in Newcastle-upon-Tyne, c. 1750–1850' (PhD dissertation, Newcastle University).

Campanacho, V. (2017a). 'Osteobiographical Report – Identified Skeletal Remains: CS472 – Ann Purvis and Carver Street 1093 – James Simpson' (Sheffield, unpublished report).

Campanacho, V. (2017b). 'Anthropology Recording Form for Ann Purvis' (Sheffield, unpublished report).

Carter Wood, J. (2004). *Violence and Crime in Nineteenth-century England: the Shadow of our Refinement* (London; New York: Routledge).

Clark, Bonnie J., and Laurie A. Wilkie (2006). 'The prism of self: gender and personhood', in S. M. Nelson (ed.), *Handbook of Gender in Archaeology* (Lanham, MD: AltaMira), pp. 333–364.

Davidoff, L. and Hall, C. (2002). *Family Fortunes: Men and Women of the English Middle Class, 1780–1850*, revised edn (London and New York: Routledge).

DeWitte, S. N. (2015). 'Bioarchaeology and the ethics of research using human skeletal remains', *History Compass*, 13(1): 10–19.

Engels, F. (1892). *The Condition of the Working-Class in England in 1844*, trans. F. K. Wischnewetzky (London: Allen & Unwin).

Fleming, R. (2006). 'Bones for historians: Putting the body back into biography', in D. Bates, J. Crick and S. Hamilton (eds), *Writing Medieval Biography, 750–1250: Essays in Honour of Frank Barlow* (Woodbridge: Boydell & Brewer), pp. 29–48.

Fleming, R. (2009). 'Writing biography at the edge of history', *American Historical Review*, 114(3): 606–14.

Fowler, C. (2004). *The Archaeology of Personhood: An Anthropological Approach* (London: Routledge).

Goose, N. (2005). 'Poverty, old age and gender in nineteenth-century England: The case of Hertfordshire', *Continuity and Change*, 20(3): 351–84.

Gowland, R. (2018). '"A Mass of Crooked Alphabets": The construction and othering of working-class bodies in industrial England', in P. K. Stone (ed.), *Bioarchaeological Analyses and Bodies: New Ways of Knowing Anatomical and Archaeological Skeletal* Collections (Cham: Springer), pp. 147–63.

Grauer, A. L. and Miller, A. G. (2017). 'Flesh on the bones: A historical and bioarchaeological exploration of violence, trauma, sex and gender in medieval England', *Fragments: Interdisciplinary Approaches to the Study of Ancient and Medieval Pasts* 6: 38–79.

Hamilakis, Y., Pluciennik, M. and Tarlow, S. (2002). 'Introduction', in Y. Hamilakis, M. Pluciennik and S. Tarlow (eds), *Thinking through the Body. Archaeologies of Corporeality* (Boston, Mass.: Springer), pp. 1–22.

Harvey, K. (2012). *The Little Republic: Men and the House in Eighteenth-Century Britain* (Oxford: Oxford University Press).

Harvey, K. (2017). 'Introduction', in K. Harvey (ed.), *History and Material Culture: A Student's Guide to Approaching Alternative Sources*, 2nd edn (Routledge, Abingdon), pp. 1–26.
Harvey, K. (2020). 'One British thing: A history of embodiment: Ann Purvis, ca.1793–1849', *Journal of British Studies*, 59(1): 136–9.
Hey, D. (1998). *A History of Sheffield* (Lancaster: Carnegie).
Hicks, D. (2010). 'The material-cultural turn. Event and effect', in D. Hicks and M. C. Beaudry (eds), *Oxford Handbook of Material Culture Studies* (Oxford; New York: Oxford University Press).
Higgs, E. (1987). 'Women, occupations and work in the nineteenth century censuses', *History Workshop Journal*, 4(3): 17–38.
Hindle, S. (2004). *On the Parish?: The Micro-politics of Poor Relief in Rural England c. 1550–1750* (Oxford: Clarendon).
Holland, J. (1823). 'Memoir of Mr. Samuel Hill, Late of Sheffield-Park', *The Wesleyan-Methodist Magazine*, 2(12): 790–6.
Kesselring, K. J. (2015). 'Bodies of evidence: Sex and murder (or gender and homicide) in early modern England, c. 1500–1680', *Gender and History*, 27(2): 245–62.
King, P. (2009). *Crime and Law in England, 1750–1840: Remaking Justice from the Margins* (Cambridge: Cambridge University Press).
King, S. (2000). *Poverty and Welfare in England, 1700–1850* (Manchester: Manchester University Press).
Lewis, M. E. (2007). *The Bioarchaeology of Children: Perspectives from Biological and Forensic Anthropology* (Cambridge: Cambridge University Press).
Mackenzie, E. (1827). *A Descriptive and Historical Account of the Town and County of Newcastle-upon-Tyne*, vol. 1 (Newcastle upon Tyne: Mackenzie and Dent).
McIntyre, L. and Willmott, H. (2003). *Excavations at the Methodist Chapel, Carver Street, Sheffield*, Report 507.2 (Sheffield: ARCUS, unpublished report).
Mant, M. (2016). '"Readmitted under urgent circumstance": Uniting archives and bioarchaeology at the Royal London Hospital', in M. Mant and A. Holland (eds), *Beyond the Bones: Engaging with Disparate Datasets* (Amsterdam: Elsevier), pp. 37–60.
Mant, M. (2019). 'Time after time: individuals with multiple fractures and injury recidivists in long eighteenth-century (c. 1666–1837) London', *International Journal of Paleopathology*, 24: 7–18.
Mant, M. (2020). 'A little time woud compleat the cure': Broken bones and fracture experiences of the working poor in London's General Hospitals during the long eighteenth century', *Social History of Medicine*, 33(2): 438–62.
Marshall, Y. (2013). 'Personhood in prehistory: a feminist archaeology in ten persons', in D. Bolger (ed.), *A Companion to Gender Prehistory* (Chichester: Wiley), pp. 204–25.
Moreland, J. (2001). *Archaeology and Text* (London: Duckworth Academic).
Moses, J. (2018). *The First Modern Risk: Workplace Accidents and the Origins of European Social States* (Cambridge: Cambridge University Press).
Ottaway, S. (1998). 'Providing for the elderly in eighteenth-century England', *Continuity and Change*, 13(3): 391–418.

Ottaway, S. (2004). *The Decline of Life: Old Age in Eighteenth-Century England* (Cambridge: Cambridge University Press).
Owsley, D. W., Bruwelheide, K. S., Barca, K. G., Reidy, S. K. and Fleskes, R. E. (2018). 'Lives lost: What burial vault studies reveal about eighteenth-century identities', in P. K. Stone (ed.), *Bioarchaeological Analyses and Bodies: New Ways of Knowing Anatomical and Archaeological Skeletal Collections* (Cham: Springer), pp. 111–45.
Parson, W. and White, W. (1827), *History, Directory & Gazetteer of Durham & Northumberland*, vol. 1 (Leeds: W. White).
Paul, K. T. (2019). *The Poverty of Disaster: Debt and Insecurity in Eighteenth-century Britain* (Cambridge: Cambridge University Press).
Perry, M. A. (2007). 'Is bioarchaeology a handmaiden to history? Developing a historical bioarchaeology', *Journal of Anthropological Archaeology*, 26(3): 486–515.
Raynor, C., McCarthy, R. and Clough, S. (2011). *Coronation Street, South Shields, Tyne and Wear. Archaeological Excavation and Osteological Analysis Report* (Lancaster: Oxford Archaeology North).
Rigg, J. (1835). 'Methodism in Sheffield', *The Wesleyan-Methodist Magazine*, 14(08): 606–612.
Robb, J. (2002). 'Time and Biography: Osteobiography of the Italian Neolithic lifespan', in Y. Hamilakis, M. Pluciennik and S. Tarlow (eds), *Thinking Through the Body: Archaeologies of Corporeality* (New York: Kluwer Academic/Plenum Publishers), pp. 153–71.
Robb, J., Inskip, S. A., Cessford, C., Dittmar, J., Kivisild, T., Mitchell, P. D., Mulder, B., O'Connell, T. C., Price, M. E., Rose, A. and Scheib, C. (2019). 'Osteobiography: The history of the body as real bottom-line history', *Bioarchaeology international*, 3(1): 16–31.
Rusbridge, T. B. S. (2019). 'The culture of materials and leather objects in eighteenth-century England' (PhD dissertation, University of Birmingham).
Sardica, J. M. (2013). 'The content and form of "conventional" historical biography', *Rethinking History*, 17(3): 383–400.
Shoemaker, R. B. (1998). *Gender in English Society, 1650–1850: The Emergence of Separate Spheres* (London: Longman).
Sofaer, J. R. (2006). *The Body as Material Culture: A Theoretical Osteoarchaeology* (Cambridge: Cambridge University Press).
Sofaer, J. R. (2011). 'Towards a social bioarchaeology of age', in S. C. Agarwal and. B. A. Glencross (eds), *Social Bioarchaeology* (Oxford: Wiley-Blackwell): pp. 285–311.
Sofaer, J. R. (2013). 'Bioarchaeological approaches to the gendered body', in D. Bolger (ed.), *A Companion to Gender Prehistory* (Chichester: Wiley): pp. 226–43.
Scott, J. W. (1991). 'The evidence of experience', *Critical Inquiry*, 17(4): 773–97.
Shepard, A. (2000). 'Manhood, credit and patriarchy in early modern England c. 1580–1640', *Past & Present*, 167: 75–106.
Shepard, A. (2006). *Meanings of Manhood in Early Modern England* (Oxford: Oxford University Press).

Shore, H. (1999). *Artful Dodgers: Youth and Crime in Early Nineteenth-Century London* (London: Boydell & Brewer & Royal Historical Society).

Swales, D. (2016). 'The material body: An interdisciplinary study in history and archaeology information on potential case study sites' (Sheffield, unpublished report).

Szreter, S. (2005). *Health and Wealth: Studies in History and Policy* (Woodbridge: Boydell & Brewer).

Tarlow, S. (2011). *Ritual, Belief and the Dead in Early Modern Britain and Ireland* (Cambridge: Cambridge University Press).

Thane, P. (1978). 'Women and the poor law in Victorian and Edwardian England', *History Workshop Journal*, 6: 29–51.

Thane, P. (2000) *Old Age in English History: Past Experiences, Present Issues* (Oxford: Oxford University Press).

Thomson, D. (1984a). '"I am not my father's keeper": Families and the elderly in nineteenth century England', *Law and History Review*, 2(2): 265–86.

Thomson, D. (1984b). 'The decline of social welfare: Falling state support for the elderly since early Victorian times', *Ageing and Society*, 4(4): 451–82.

Vickery, A. (2013). 'Mutton dressed as lamb? Fashioning age in Georgian England', *Journal of British Studies*, 52(4): 858–86.

Walker, G. (2009). *Crime, Gender and Social Order in Early Modern England* (Cambridge: Cambridge University Press).

Wallace, H. (2018). 'Ann Purvis (1793?–1849) St. Hilda's, South Shields' (Sheffield, unpublished report).

Watts, M. (1995). *The Dissenters II: The Expansion of Evangelical Nonconformity* (Oxford: Clarendon).

Whitfield, W. (2016). *The Dispensaries: Healthcare for the Poor Before the NHS* (London: Bloomsbury).

Wolffe, J. (2008). 'The 1851 census and religious change in nineteenth-century Yorkshire', *Northern History*, 45(1): 71–86.

Wooler, F. (2016). 'Educating the workers of Sheffield in the 18th and 19th centuries: St Luke's National School, Garden Street, Sheffield', *Industrial Archaeology Review*, 38(1): 47–58.

# 2

# Marking maternity: integrating historical and archaeological evidence for reproduction in the late eighteenth and early nineteenth centuries

*Elizabeth Craig-Atkins and Mary E. Fissell*

Like so many disused urban churchyards in England, St Hilda's in South Shields succumbed to the pressures of urbanisation and redevelopment. A 2006 developer-funded excavation in advance of construction work on Coronation Street yielded an unexpected finding: a cluster of fetal and perinatal remains. Such a finding is surprising in at least two ways: first, the bodies of unbaptised infants, whether stillborn or live births, were not supposed to be buried in such a graveyard. Only the remains of those who had been christened should have been interred in consecrated ground (Houlbrooke, 1998). Second, in the lower levels of the cemetery, these remains were grouped together in a space dominated by such graves, rather than being buried in family plots, as was the norm (Tarlow, 2010: 108). This chapter explores a range of historical possibilities for this striking finding, thus identifying and examining an array of themes common to the archaeology of childhood and history of reproduction and the emotions to which a unified approach has yet to be taken. In doing so, we raise broader questions about interdisciplinary working and demonstrate the significant value of close collaboration between historians and archaeologists in studies of the material and experiencing body. We present a novel, effective model of co-working and offer justification for others to adopt our approach to integrating historical and archaeological sources.

The assemblage from St Hilda's church would not be startling were it found in Ireland, where a significant number of so-called cilliní were dedicated to the interment of what seem to have been unbaptised infants and children (Finlay, 2000; Murphy, 2011a; 2011b). In the period under study, both Protestant and Catholic Churches in Ireland followed the same burial rules as in England: no unbaptised individuals could be buried in consecrated ground. The Irish repurposed prehistoric monuments and disused structures or dedicated specific plots for the burial of unbaptised infants and children, but also adults of unknown baptismal status (Finlay, 2000: 409). This created what we might call sites of vernacular consecration, a concept we will return to later in our discussion of the evidence from St Hilda's. However, no burial sites comparable to the Irish cilliní are known in England. In some cases, fetal remains are recovered from within the pelvic cavities of adult female skeletons, suggesting contemporaneous death during pregnancy or childbirth.[1] Rarely, burials of fetuses, perinates and infants have also been encountered in locations outside consecrated ground in England (Cherryson et al., 2012: 122; Heighway and Bryant, 1999: 200; Nowakowski and Thomas, 1992; Tarlow, 2010; Whitworth, 1994: 136). These examples have never been discussed collectively, but in combination suggest that there may have been specific cultural practices in response to the deaths of the youngest individuals that the archaeological evidence has yet to fully reveal.

This chapter argues that situating the St Hilda's assemblage in a larger social and cultural history of death rituals and fetal and perinatal loss provides useful contexts for interpreting the skeletal remains. While an understanding of the legal codes governing burial is helpful, more significant are scattered stories of individuals contravening or contesting those rules, which afford glimpses of the meanings of death and burial for people whose beliefs and attitudes are otherwise unknown. These small stories may challenge casual assumptions about the significance of infant loss for working-class families who experienced high rates of infant mortality. Similarly, from an archaeological perspective, consideration of the information that can be obtained from such skeletal remains, alongside funerary and burial evidence, enriches and problematises this inquiry through its illumination of the actions taken by the living in response to those deaths.

Explaining the presence of fetal and perinatal remains in eighteenth and nineteenth century burial sites is challenging; by and large, unbaptised individuals, especially the very young, were not interred in consecrated ground, but were buried or simply abandoned in out of the way places (Tarlow, 2010: 52). While rules about christening have always been stretched by midwives administering emergency baptisms, or local vicars baptising newly deceased infants to ensure proper burial, fetal remains invoke different contexts: the deaths of women during pregnancy, stillbirth, induced abortion and infanticide (Tomkins, 2010, see esp. 210). Such histories are not often combined, but primary sources suggest that re-constructing a reproductive history that considers all the potential pathways to the burial of such remains is productive. In this chapter we bring both historical and archaeological methods to bear upon the site of St Hilda's, exploring what we are calling the *fields of force* within which it was constituted.

## St Hilda's church cemetery

A small part of the southern section of the cemetery of St Hilda's church, South Shields, was excavated in 2006 prior to its destruction during the construction of a supermarket (Raynor *et al.*, 2011) (see Figure 2.1). The church occupied the southern edge of the market square in the rapidly industrialising town. Its Coronation Street burial ground appears to have been the only churchyard serving the community of South Shields during

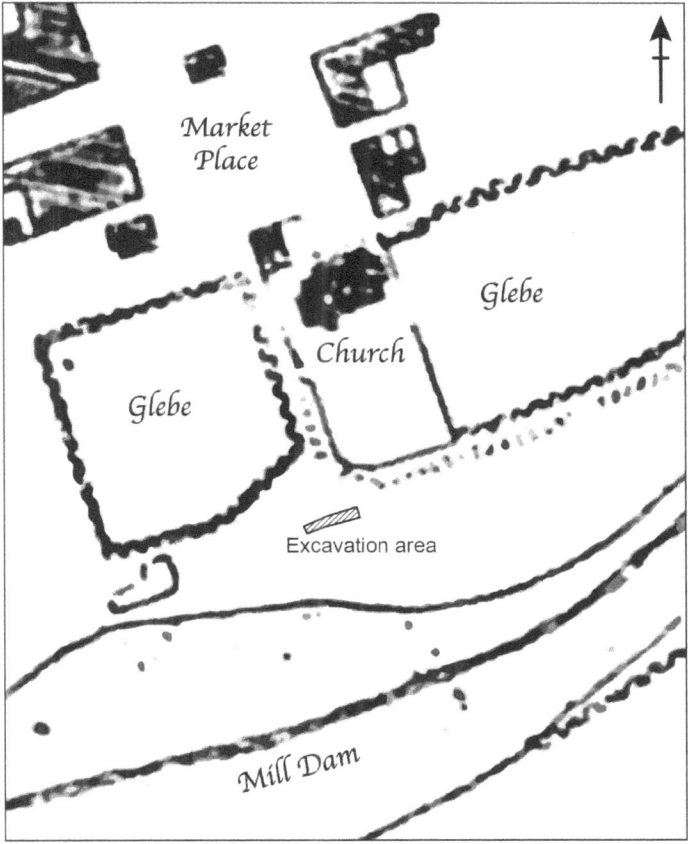

**Figure 2.1** Location of St Hilda's church and the surrounding town of South Shields as represented on Richardson's map of 1768 and Fryer's map of 1773. The area of excavation which revealed the fetal and perinate group discussed in this chapter is overlain.

the late eighteenth and early nineteenth centuries, the time period from which the archaeological evidence dates. The cemetery excavations revealed two distinct chronological phases of burial, split by a period during which the over-full cemetery was built up with a substantial quantity of new earth. The lower burials date from the latter quarter of the eighteenth century to 1818 and the upper burials from 1818 to just beyond the cemetery's closure in 1855, with burial finally ceasing completely around 1860 (Raynor et al., 2011: 30, 98).

The excavated area was 70 m south of the church, which still stands. During the early phase of burial this land was beyond the southern boundary of the cemetery as indicated on contemporary maps (Fryer, 1773; Raynor et al., 2011: 99; Richardson, 1768), but was still used for a substantial number of burials. The western area of this lower burial group was dominated by the interments of fetuses and perinates. At the time of excavation and reporting in 2011, such a concentration of burials was described as unprecedented in Britain (Raynor et al., 2011: 6), and indeed there are many unusual aspects of this burial group. In total, thirty-four burials of fetuses and perinates were excavated from thirty-three plots (see Figure 2.2). In no cases were these burials accompanied by adult female remains, suggesting all were postpartum. In eight instances, it appears that plots were intentionally reused for one or more additional burials of fetuses and perinates, suggesting graves were sufficiently visible to facilitate identification and reuse. The vast majority of burials were made in individual wooden containers. Given the estimated ages at death of the remains and their location beyond the contemporary cemetery boundary, this burial cluster was interpreted by the excavators as unbaptised infants, for whom burial within the cemetery proper was not legitimate (Raynor et al., 2011: 98). However, the archaeological evidence of these graves is entirely inconsistent with their being covert burials. Rather, we suggest that the intention was to provide normative funerary rites to the perinates, with concomitant investment in planning and ceremony. The clustering did not continue after work to raise the cemetery between 1816–18. At this point the cemetery boundary was also extended, so that the excavated area was now within its periphery, at which point the burials of older children and adults began to appear frequently in this location. What had formerly been, we argue, a site informally consecrated through local practices now became part of the officially consecrated churchyard.

Unusually, from 1798, St Hilda's parish burial records include age at death; occupation of male head of household (burials of women and children were listed by husbands' or fathers' occupations); and, occasionally, causes of death, providing data about mortality and economic structures in South Shields (Durham Record Office, EP/SS.SH 1/78 Register of burials, 19 May

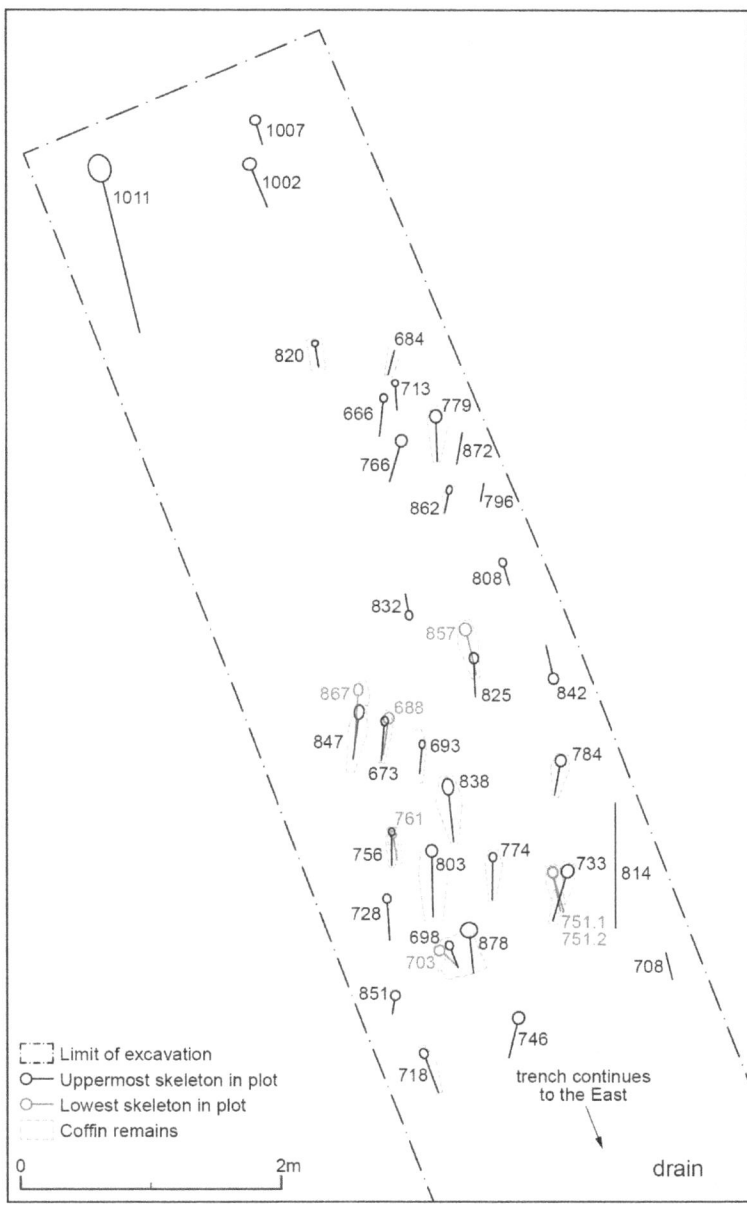

Figure 2.2 Plan of the lower level of the western section of the excavated area, indicating the locations of human skeletal and coffin remains.

1785–30 October 1799). We used the 167 burial records from January to September 1798 to create a snapshot view of the parish. A smallpox epidemic marked the last quarter of 1798, so those months were not included. This was a maritime economy; of the sixty-seven entries that listed occupation, thirty-six, or over half, were of burials whose wage-earners worked in shipping, including twenty-three 'mariners', a few shipwrights, a sailmaker and five 'trimmers', the men who distributed cargo, especially coal, on board a ship as it was loaded. By contrast, only three gentleman and eight artisanal occupations, including blacksmith, clockmaker, cordwainer, joiner and watchmaker, were listed.

Age at death statistics indicate the hazards of infancy in South Shields: thirty-eight out of 167 burials were of infants less than 1 year old; another thirteen were between 1 and 2 years old; 31% of all burials were for children under 2. However, neonatal and perinatal burials were under-represented by comparison to the archaeological sample discussed here; just under 5% of burials were for babies under a month old. If a South Shields resident survived childhood, they might live to an old age; 10% of burials were for those aged 80 years and above. Consumption (pulmonary tuberculosis) was far and away the biggest killer listed; of the thirty-three burials that listed cause of death, nineteen, or 58% were due to consumption. People in their 30s, 40s and 50s, of all occupations, succumbed to the disease. Fever, dropsy and smallpox were the other diseases listed, suggesting that perhaps the parish clerk had a particular concern with these ailments.

## Disciplinary lenses

In exploring the meanings of these remains, this chapter poses methodological questions about how bioarchaeology and the history of medicine might inform each other. While these questions have been debated between us as a result of our work on the case study of St Hilda's church, they have a wider resonance for our disciplines. We have identified what we call the *handmaiden problem*.[2] Many collaborations put one or other discipline into a helper role, called upon to explain some facet of the other discipline's project, creating epistemological problems by concealing the knowledge-making practices that generated that 'helper' knowledge. One discipline's 'results' are stripped of information about their making, transformed into facts, and mobilised to explain part of the other discipline's project. Much of the subtlety, the soft spaces where further research might interrogate knowledge-making practices as well as knowledge itself, is made to disappear.

We propose a different model: our disciplines function as equals in a mutually devised project. Each of us has had to reflect on disciplinary biases and habits of mind, and how we frame what the 'other' discipline does. As we worked together, it became clear that different disciplinary training led us to see sources and problems in different ways, differences that have been productive. In what follows, we will offer a series of brief sketches of the kinds of differences to which we refer, and then dive deeper into the assumptions each of us brought to our work. Most of the chapter has been fully co-written, the result of many productive cross-disciplinary conversations that probed deeper disciplinary assumptions as well as interpretive strategies. Our collaboration worked in part because neither of us felt the need to defend customary disciplinary practices, but, rather, to explain and illustrate how they worked for the other scholar. To underline the ways in which our respective disciplines sometimes differ, we indicate which of us is 'speaking' when discussing such moments of productive difference and dialogue.

We noticed that Fissell moved immediately from human remains to issues of motherhood and reproduction; the bones were quickly embedded in a social matrix. Such a move is not surprising; not only has she been working on the history of gender and reproduction for a long time, but also history might have little to say about such perinatal individuals as *individuals* (Fissell, 2004a; Fissell, 2017). Craig-Atkins's focus initially rested on the fetal and perinatal remains. Her first consideration was to obtain data from the bones, evaluating this at the individual and group level. Next, she was concerned with the funerary context – how and where the individuals had been buried. Her approach tackled the material evidence first, and, as a result of the physically bounded nature of the material body, began with the individual. Additional layers of interpretation and enquiry rested on what Julienne Rutherford (2017: 15) has called 'the spatiotemporal complexity of fetal experience'. As a consequence of biological and social interconnectivity, the fetal and perinatal skeleton reflects the experiences of its mother, including maternal nutrition, rearing behaviour and stress exposure (Rutherford, 2017: 18). Similarly, the creation of social identity for perinates and stillbirths is complex and relational, connected by its making to mother, father and society (Ellis, 2020: 188). Identifying whether women have borne children from their skeletal remains is highly problematic (McFadden, 2020), and it is rarely possible to pair infant skeletons with those of their mothers.[3] Therefore, for bioarchaeologists, the skeletal remains of fetuses, perinates and infants offer a more direct route to studying maternity than the remains of women themselves. Moreover, as a result of their heightened susceptibility to environmental stressors, the youngest members of any group offer a sensitive proxy for the health of an entire population, not just childbearing women (Satterlee Blake, 2017).

We brought different assumptions to the language used to describe the remains. Craig-Atkins was mindful of biologically accurate and comparable terminology (see Buckberry, 2018: 56–7). Prioritising a standardised biological basis for terminology (e.g. Gowland, 2006: 143–4; Lewis, 2007: 2; Sofaer, 2005: 121–4), the terms *fetus*, *perinate* and *infant* were used to reflect stages of physiological development.[4] In most cases, we simply cannot determine the gestational status of any individual set of remains. A skeleton of the same developmental stage – for example 36 gestational weeks (GWS) – might be the remains of a stillborn fetus, or a low-birthweight newborn, or even the result of a very late-term abortion (Lewis, 2007: 84). We agreed that using terms linked to skeletal development makes clear the limits of our knowledge. Words like *baby* and *mother* were used rarely, but could be deployed when conveying the socially constructed implications of these biological identities. Fissell was concerned about the emotive connotations of such words.

Fissell: Over the past three decades, the history of medicine has taken a social – and then a cultural – turn, much like the larger discipline of history (Craig-Atkins and Harvey, this volume: introduction; Fissell, 2004b). Such turns may seem implicitly antithetical to the science-based discipline of bioarchaeology, as in the case of so-called retrospective diagnosis (Arrizabalaga, 2002; Mitchell, 2011; Packard, 2016; Wilson, 2000). For many historians of medicine, Fissell included, knowing what people in the past *really* died of can seem like a form of historical blindness. In this case the word *really* means 'using modern medical diagnostic categories'. There is nothing inherently wrong with doing so, but for a cultural historian, it can seem like an empty form of precision that might occlude the very things that we are exploring. Cultural historians are much more interested in understanding how historical actors made sense of their experiences; indeed, how that making sense was a significant part of their lived experience.

Craig-Atkins: Early twentieth-century osteological research was undertaken largely by medically trained scholars and thus privileged the identification of biological characteristics and diagnosis of diseases categorised in contemporary medicine. Theoretical frameworks which engage explicitly with the material body and experiencing body, and the body as both a biological and cultural object, have since created a more nuanced context within which osteologists have situated their research (Craig-Atkins and Harvey, this volume: introduction). This has manifested in the integration of skeletal remains into archaeologies of gender, disability and care. In a practical sense, biological data obtained from human remains form a strand of evidence used in the interpretation of cultural practice (Gowland and Knüsel, 2006), and conceptually archaeologists theorise material bodies as physical objects which interact reflexively with their cultural contexts (Sofaer, 2005). Bone and tissue are plastic materials, which respond and adapt to both internal and external environments. Thus, the physical body is shaped by lifestyle and behaviour, access to the resources it needs to grow and maintain itself and exposure to disease, all of which result from the choices made (or enforced upon) the living person by their social and physical environment and then influence subsequent choices they make during their lifetimes. For societies who did not document their experiences, or for which only some sectors of society did, one of our main sources of evidence for physical experience will always remain the body itself. To say that the biological is not the sum total of personal experience should not be to deny the reality of physically embodied experiences. Historians, too, emphasise that their actors' subjective experiences were grounded in their physical bodies (Craig-Atkins and Harvey, this volume: introduction).

While there is much more that both of us could say about the ways in which our disciplinary perspectives intersect and divide on the subject of the body, we have arrived at some shared understandings. Both bones and texts serve as proxies for what we really want to know, which is how people lived in their bodies, experienced their lives through them, and how bodies were created and re-created through contextually contingent understandings. The two disciplines speak eloquently on different things, and each offers insights that the other cannot. When set side by side, they offer up productive tensions and challenges.

## The fields of force which shaped the St Hilda's burials

A useful analytic will bring both disciplines to the table in an equal way; here we do that by arguing that three intersecting fields of force shaped the archaeological record at St Hilda's. First, perinatal mortality rates were high; many women experienced miscarriage, stillbirth or neonatal death; many children did not live beyond their first few weeks. Second, people at all social levels highly valued what they saw as a decent burial, but the costs of burials could be problematic, especially for perinatal loss. Third, in the absence of reliable forms of contraception, and changing patterns in the way that the law dealt with unwed motherhood, unwanted pregnancies must have been fairly frequent, perhaps resulting in the burial of fetal and perinatal remains at St Hilda's.

Sources for this study include newspaper stories about a range of reproductive issues, often linked to criminal cases. The period in which burials took place, estimated to be 1780–1860, was one in which newspapers boomed, aided by new steam-powered printing presses after 1810 and rising literacy rates. Not only were there more stories in more newspapers, but also from the 1840s, England was gripped by a moral panic about infant life. Exposés mushroomed in the press on topics such as baby-farming, infanticide and burial clubs. Baby-farms were, at best, day-care for infants; women working in factories could not combine childcare with work as they had done before in their homes. At worst, baby-farms were passive infanticide, infants so neglected that they died. Burial clubs were insurance for the costs of burial and were common in working-class communities. Middle-class observers argued that clubs were financial incentives to infanticide. While rarely substantiated, such claims made sensational news, fuelled by class prejudice (Hunt, 2006; Thorn, 2003). This panic created a density of primary sources, which may conceal continuities over the longer nineteenth century. Our working assumption is that many practices documented in these mid-century sources were longer-term, more gradual developments, but only became more visible at mid-century in this panic fuelled both by newspaper growth and a new demographic imperative spurred by the advent of the Registrar-General's office (Higgs, 2004).

Similarly, there are interpretive issues with the archaeological data arising from differential survival and preservation in the funerary record. First, the excavations at St Hilda's uncovered only a tiny area of a much larger cemetery and so cannot provide a representative sample of the dead from this population. Given the highly unusual demographic make-up of this cemetery population created by the perinatal burial group, we cannot reliably compare age-specific mortality patterns between St Hilda's and other contemporary cemeteries. Second, the nature of archaeological chronologies is to collapse decades and generations – we cannot reflect on how many of the individuals excavated were alive at any one time, or pinpoint their dates of death, nor match up familial groups of perinates and the women who bore them.

## Infant mortality

Infant mortality rates were substantial in pre-modern Britain, often reaching the magnitude of 150–175 per 1000 live births, and, broadly speaking, these rates remained largely unchanged throughout the nineteenth century (Garrett, *et al.*, 2006). In the period of the burials at St Hilda's, mortality in places like South Shields was shaped by conflicting developments. On the one hand, longer-term gradual improvements in health and hygiene, and modest improvements in midwifery training, had a small positive effect on perinatal mortality (Smith and Oeppen, 2006; Woods, 2009). On the other, the twin forces of industrialisation and urbanisation made these mushrooming cities much less healthy places to live than the towns that preceded them.

Women and children, our focus here, experienced these stresses in multiple ways: poor diets, overcrowding, exposure to industrial pollution, harmful labour practices and other similar factors impinged upon their health. The deterioration of general health in industrial populations is plentifully evidenced in their skeletons (Floud and Harris, 1997; Roberts and Cox, 2003).[5] During the mid-nineteenth century in London, disparities in body size were more pronounced among poorer women than men (Ives and Humphrey, 2017) and in poorer women than wealthier women (Hughes-Morey, 2016). Industrial period infants and children were also small for their age (Hodson and Gowland, 2019; Ives and Humphrey, 2017; Newman et al., 2019). Chronic diseases related to nutrition, immune health and lifestyle also increased; scurvy, rickets and tuberculosis, for example, being identified more frequently in skeletal remains following industrialisation (Brickley et al., 2007; Ives, 2017; Lewis, 2002a; 2002b). Notably, cases of rickets and scurvy among individuals under six months of age at death suggest either early cessation of breastfeeding, to the significant detriment of the infant's metabolic health, or that breastfeeding women were passing their own deficiencies on to their dependent infants (Hodson and Gowland, 2019; Newman, 2019; Satterlee Blake, 2017: 46). While the broader picture of the health implications of these dual developments – urbanisation and industrialisation – has long been known, the remains uncovered at St Hilda's paint a more specific picture of the way that these costs were paid by the very youngest and, by implication, their mothers.

During fetal development, observation and measurement of the formation and fusion of different hard tissues enable us to assign age to a skeleton with an accuracy of a few weeks (Cunningham et al., 2016) and thus generates a foundation of data from which to build a critical understanding of their short lives. This process is particularly accurate when based on formation and eruption of deciduous teeth (Al Qahtani, 2014) or dimensions of the base of the skull (Hodson, 2018). Long bone length is a less accurate proxy for chronological age, being affected by environmental factors to a greater extent than the former methods. As a result, a dental age in advance of age assessed from long bone development is commonly used as a marker of exposure to physiological stress, both during early life and in the womb (Halcrow et al., 2017: 97–8).

The age at death distribution for the fetal and perinatal individuals from the lower burial group at St Hilda's is presented in Figure 2.3. The burials include the remains of several who died at or before 28 weeks gestation. Four have an age at death below 24 weeks, the range classified today as late miscarriage. However, these youngest individuals have been assigned an age based solely on femoral development, and therefore may be older if exposed to physiological stress *in utero*. An additional five individuals aged

58   *The material body*

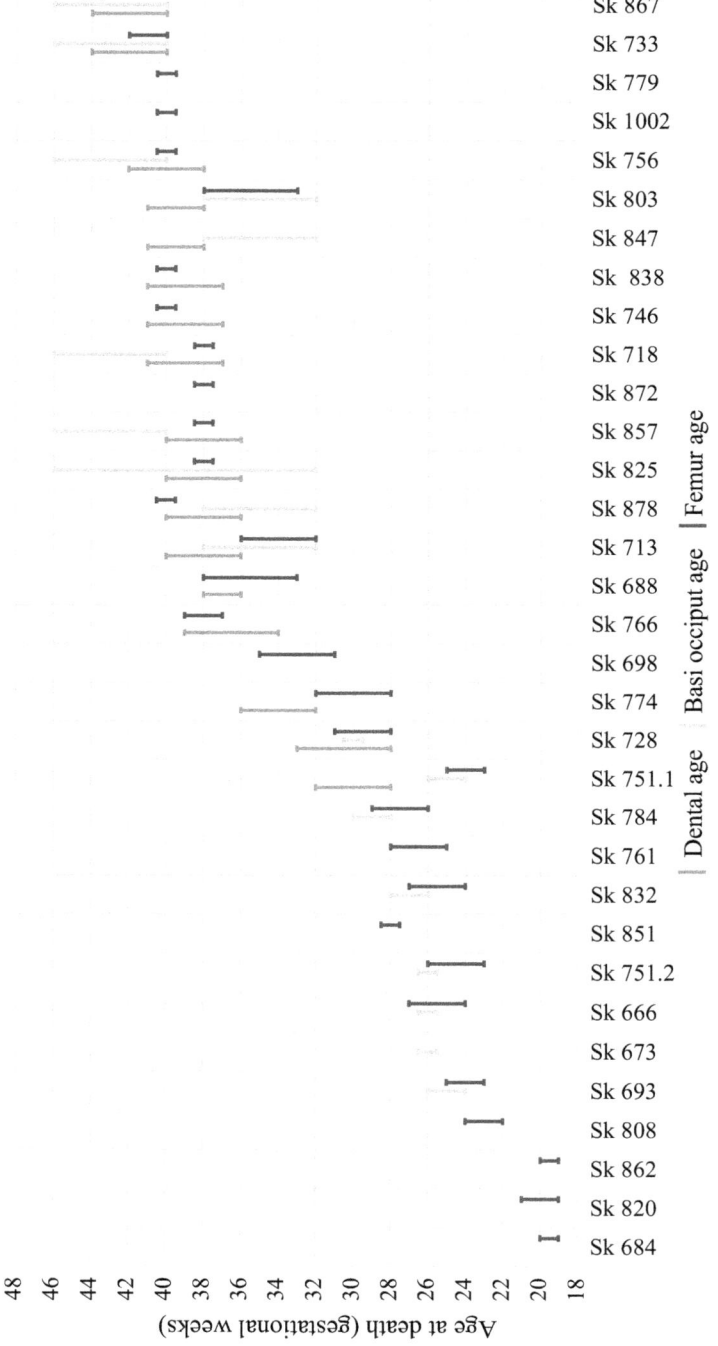

Figure 2.3 Age at death distribution of the fetal and perinatal individuals from St Hilda's based on dental development (Al Qahtani et al., 2010), basi occiput dimensions (Scheuer and McLaughlin Black, 1994) and femoral length (Kiserud et al., 2017; Scheuer et al., 1980). Four fetal/perinatal individuals are omitted from this chart as none of the required skeletal elements could be assessed (Sks 703, 796, 842, 1007).

24–28 weeks have age estimates based on the *basi occiput* (part of the base of the skull), which has been argued to be a reliable marker of chronological age (Hodson, 2018). Notable among this group are skeletons 751.1 and 751.2 who were interred together in the same grave and were likely twins. One of the pair has a dental age significantly in advance of the skeletal ages attributed to both individuals, suggesting the twins were both small for their gestational age as well as born prematurely: like today, not an unlikely outcome of multiple pregnancy (Giorgione et al., 2021). Today, fetuses under 28 weeks gestation would be assigned to the latter half of the second trimester of pregnancy. The end of that trimester is the point at which a modern fetus would be considered viable without extensive medical care. It is highly unlikely that any of these premature individuals survived for long following their births and the group probably includes a number of stillbirths.

The remaining perinates died between the ages of $c.28$–37 gestational weeks (fetal) and $c.38$–45 gestational weeks (perinatal).[6] It is not possible using the available resolution of osteological analysis to make any assumptions about whether the majority were born alive or stillborn, nor how long they lived had they been born alive (Halcrow et al., 2017).[7] It is conceivable that the large group of individuals from St Hilda's aged between $c.37$–40 weeks are both small-for-gestational-age and full term; however, the parity seen between dental, occipital and femoral age in many cases does not appear to reflect significant exposure to *in utero* stress.

Prematurity is a key factor in perinatal death today, alongside asphyxia, infection and birth defects (Halcrow et al., 2017; WHO, 2020). More than 90% of extremely preterm babies (less than 28 weeks) born in low-income countries die within the first few days of life (WHO, 2018) and birth between 28–36 GWS also results in increased risk of infant death (Kramer et al., 2000). Premature birth can also indicate poor health and/or nutritional stress in the mother, as can the delivery of small-for-gestational-age babies (Halcrow et al., 2017: 87). Perhaps the women who bore these perinates struggled with poverty, but poor urban maternal health was not restricted to the lowest socioeconomic classes (Hodson, 2018).[8]

In modern Western culture, with at-home pregnancy tests and early scans, it can be difficult to imagine just how uncertain pregnancy determination was in earlier times (Bell and Fissell, 2021). Quickening, the moment in pregnancy where women start to notice *in utero* fetal movements, was often the key indicator, although not fool proof (Gowing, 1997). Crucially, it made the determination of pregnancy a private matter for the woman concerned. Before the 1830s, when the use of the stethoscope was adopted in British obstetrics, no medical practitioner could be certain of a pregnancy before the actual delivery. Today, quickening usually occurs around 18–20 weeks, but women who have already experienced pregnancy may report fetal movements up to four weeks earlier, presumably as a result of familiarity (Engstrom, 1985). As the youngest individual from St Hilda's was unlikely to be less than 20 weeks at death,[9] it is plausible that all the pregnant women had experienced quickening and were aware of their pregnancies. This consideration has implications for the experiences of, and responses to, the deaths of the perinates from St Hilda's, whose remains were buried with care and attention – a topic to which we will return.

From the historical record, maternity care may have been a scarce resource in South Shields, which suggests another kind of contextual explanation for the high proportion of perinatal remains at Coronation Street. South Shields' infant mortality rates in 1851 were 191, substantially above even the 151 recorded for Tyneside and Wallsend, directly across the river from South Shields; some southern rural districts had rates below 100.[10] South Shields had 4.6 doctors per 10,000 people, half the rate of the neighbouring Westoe district and a quarter of that in wealthy districts like Bath and central London.[11] The most significant medical practitioner, however, is more difficult to locate in the historical record: midwives were well known in their communities but were not usually registered and often did not list themselves in local directories.

Midwifery provision may have improved somewhat in the century from 1750 to these 1851 figures; a number of Newcastle charities and a hospital provided new forms of care. Across the river from South Shields, a Lying-In Charity had provided midwifery care and childbed linens from 1761 onwards to poor women in Newcastle and Gateshead. By 1806, the charity claimed that it had delivered 5883 women and improved the quality of midwifery care (*The Newcastle Courant*, Saturday 1 March 1806). A charitable lying-in hospital founded in Newcastle in 1761 offered a course of lectures on midwifery in 1824 (Mackenzie, 1827; *Newcastle Courant*, Saturday 28 August 1824). Such provision of charitable care and new forms of education is characteristic of English midwifery improvement in the later eighteenth and early nineteenth centuries. Further local research is needed in Tyneside and Durham archives to better illuminate the shape of maternity provision in South Shields, but it is clear that poverty shaped many women's reproductive lives.

Newspaper accounts privileged the exceptional, so must be read with care, but they tell stories about severe deprivation with a lack of adequate obstetric care. In 1843, Margaret Wheatley, a 22-year-old single woman who lived in central Newcastle, died after four days in labour. She had sent for a midwife, but could not afford the 2s 6d fee, so the midwife did not assist. Instead, a neighbour attended her. Wheatley refused to send for the relieving officer (the local Poor Law official), who could have paid for medical attendance. An autopsy concluded that her life might have been saved had she had proper medical care (*The Newcastle Courant*, Friday 29 December 1843). There's a deeper story here than just the tragic consequences of lacking 2s 6d for the midwife. The 1834 New Poor Law had radically changed the situation of women like Wheatley. Over the eighteenth and into the nineteenth century, many English communities tacitly accepted premarital sex, so long as marriage followed if pregnancy ensued (Adair, 1996). Unmarried poor women could expect considerable social pressure to name the father of their child; indeed, midwives had long been expected to interrogate such women whilst they were in labour. Once a father had been identified, the Poor Law authorities chased him for child support; they also covered the cost of a midwife and usually that of a month's lying-in. In other words, there was support for young unmarried women pregnant in a failed lead-up to marriage.

After 1834, this whole structure changed. The so-called 'Bastardy Clause' of the New Poor Law absolved the fathers of responsibility and punished mothers by threatening to incarcerate them in the workhouse. Workhouses were seen, with some justification, as prisons for poverty, and Wheatley may have wanted to avoid such incarceration. Working-class activists protested the gender and class politics of the Bastardy Clause. An indignant article in the *Newcastle Journal* only a day after the report on Wheatley's death bemoaned 'the folly, wickedness, and depravity' of the Bastardy Clause (*Newcastle Journal*, Saturday 30 December 1843). The article's indignation was about both the financial burden of unwed motherhood, and the way the law encouraged men to avoid the consequences of their sexual acts.

Further scholarship is needed on how this law actively re-configured kinship and gender relations, but at minimum we need to note that adequate maternity care might be out of reach for a poor woman, and that the situation of poor unmarried pregnant women became much worse after 1834. It is clear that infant mortality was a problem experienced widely, and this affected the women of South Shields disproportionately. Such experience will have given rise to the need to dispose of the bodies of many perinates in this community, leading to the second field of force: burial practices provided to perinates.

## *The financial burden of decent burial*

It is often assumed that high infant mortality rates meant that infant life was not highly valued in the past. Missing evidence for burial of perinates at some archaeological sites has led to conclusions that 'it is likely stillbirths and neonates were frequently buried singly outside the normal places of human burial' (Tarlow, 2010: 52). This observation does not imply that infant life was not valued. However, funerary responses to infant mortality were distinct from those associated with older children and adults, which suggests differences in attitudes surrounding their deaths. In contrast, historical sources are virtually unanimous about the importance placed upon a decent burial across all classes in late-eighteenth- and nineteenth-century Britain (Gittings, 1998; Litten, 1991; 1998; Strange, 2005). While historical evidence abounds for funerary practices for children, we have much less about their younger counterparts. The St Hilda's site affords us an unusual opportunity to see how the 'decent burial imperative' functioned when the deceased was a perinate, in particular regarding the use of grave furnishings such as coffins and the location of burials.

Waterlogged conditions in the lower levels of burial at St Hilda's, which were cut into the silts of the Mill Dam, facilitated the survival of organic materials so that coffins associated with the fetal and perinatal burial group were especially well preserved (Raynor *et al.*, 2011: 84). The best-preserved coffin was that of skeleton 820, an individual of *c.*21–23 GWS (Sk 819, BG 822). Butt joints secured with nails fixed the various panels into a rectangular container 0.23m long and 0.15m wide, but the timber was very roughly hewn and workmanship was poor – the excavators described the box as 'crudely hammered together' (Raynor *et al.*, 2011: 84). Vertical internal grooves suggest that the box was originally subdivided, and therefore served another purpose before being used as a coffin. Indeed, seven of the other coffins used for fetuses and perinates at St Hilda's appear to be reused boxes, as opposed to purpose-built coffins (Raynor *et al.*, 2011: 85).[12]

Anecdotal historical evidence suggests that use of box coffins was widespread, an example of what historians call an 'economy of makeshift' (Hufton, 1974). In Edwardian Manchester, for example, it was routine to ask shopkeepers for old soapboxes for infant burials. In Baltimore and Lyon, perinatal remains were found in just such repurposed boxes (Hardwick, 2020: 169–200; Hemphill, 2012: 442; Oman, No date: 9; Roberts, 1976: 85). At the same time, the economy of makeshift indicated by the repurposing of commercial boxes as coffins also suggests the economic hardship that decent burial posed for the working classes. Much of the textual evidence for working-class attachment to infants dates from later autobiographies and oral histories, so that the archaeological record here makes it clear that such practices date back to the eighteenth century (Ross, 1993).

A second way that funeral expenses could be curtailed is through reuse of coffins for more than one body. There is evidence for this practice in two of the lower burials at St Hilda's: the burial of possible twins 751.1 and 751.2 in plot 26 and skeletons 673 (25–27 GWS) and 688 (36–38 GWS) in what was probably a single coffin in plot 16 (Raynor et al., 2011: 34). However, in neither case is cost-saving the only explanation. Familial connection might be a compelling reason for the burial of the former in a single coffin, and cannot be ruled out in the latter, which, although unlikely to be twins, may have been born to related women. The reuse of plots is seen in other cases without reusing coffins; for example, in plot 22, skeletons 756 (38–42 GWS) and 761 (27–29 GWS) are buried in the same grave, but in two separate coffins – one a reused box and the other a single-break form.[13]

The burials at St Hilda's are contemporary with the heyday of eighteenth- and nineteenth-century elaborate funerary practices, during which the use of coffins and various grave inclusions was common (Hoile, 2018; Litten, 1991; 1998; Swales, 2011). Even among the poor, for whom financial restrictions would have been great, the importance of providing a funeral and decent burial was such that many risked financial hardship to provide the best burial possible (Hurren and King, 2005; Richardson, 2000: 167–9; Strange, 2005). Most adult coffins at Coronation Street were purpose-built containers of the single-break form. Fourteen preterm individuals and nine perinates were also buried in single-break coffins, suggesting there was both desire and availability of small purpose-built coffins (Raynor et al., 2011: 85). The evidence for burials of some perinates in purpose-built coffins suggests that the wider standards of decent burial also applied to such interments, although not all burials were able to meet these standards.

## Burial location

Graveyards were sanctified ground in which only those who had been baptised could be buried; at least in theory. Our working hypothesis is that the lower burial group, with its abundance of fetal and perinatal remains, may not have been sanctified ground before the 1816–18 relevelling and expansion of the churchyard (Raynor et al., 2011: 98). We suggest that unwritten custom was to use this area which adjoined sanctified ground as burial space for those perinates who had not been baptised. The gradual accumulation of perinate burials could thus have served as a form of vernacular consecration of this land, its purpose reinforced and legitimised through its use.

There is limited but nonetheless tantalising evidence of such vernacular consecration in post-medieval England beyond St Hilda's. At Lanercost Priory, Cumbria, four burials of 'stillborn or newly-born infants' based on their skeletal size and an additional two small, but empty, graves were dug into the demolition layers of the Priory. They were located in an undocumented burial area, interpreted as unbaptised infants excluded from the main cemetery (Whitworth, 1994). At St Oswald's, Gloucester, a group of eighteenth- and nineteenth-century burials made within the ruins of the Priory, beyond the official area of burial, included three perinates (Rogers, 1999: 232). At Jedburgh Abbey, in the Scottish borders, a group of fifteen post-monastic burials included three children, one of whom was less than 1 year, possibly a perinate. Grave-digging in this phase was noticeably haphazard and was interpreted as resulting from being outside official control (Lewis and Ewart, 1995: 129–30, 152). The latter two groups included older children and adults, although they have still been interpreted as excluded from consecrated ground on the basis of factors including baptismal status.

The burials of perinates and, perhaps, stillbirths at Coronation Street can be interpreted as the result of cross-cutting imperatives for working-class families in South Shields. On the one hand, there is evidence that such families sought a decent burial for even the youngest dead. However, such desires were confounded by the relatively high costs of burial, sometimes remedied by an ambiguity about when a newborn attained full personhood; some neonates were buried as stillbirths to save money. Stillbirths seem to have occupied an even more liminal status, neither treated in the same way as neonates nor completely distinct from them. Clear rules about interment in a churchyard – only those who had been baptised were eligible – turn out to be rather more ambiguous in practice.

There is clear anecdotal evidence from the 1870s and 1890s about the desire for churchyard burial for infants and children, even when unaffordable or unsanctioned. In 1876, workmen found the remains of a child in a fish basket that had been deposited in a Liverpool cemetery by dropping it over the boundary wall. In 1889, another workman found a box with infant remains hidden in the same cemetery's shrubbery. Two months later, another unofficial burial of an infant in a wooden box was found (Strange, 2005: 243–4). Working-class families often carried burial insurance on children to help defray the costs of a decent burial. But a newborn who died shortly after birth was unlikely to have been added to a burial policy in time. In 1842, Thomas Wakley had testified to a Select Committee that a poor person could not be buried for less than 10s, a substantial sum for a working family (Burying The Dead In Towns, 1842). In the same year, a Select Committee heard from a surgeon in Leeds about a grave that contained an additional body of a child 'said to be illegitimate' buried without a coffin; seemingly not an uncommon finding (Q2510 Select Committee on Interments X PP, 1842). While these families may not have been able to afford a proper burial, they sought an approximation of one by interring the bodies of their infants in a cemetery; we cannot know with what forms of ritual.

Stillbirths were perhaps even more challenging for poor families, and, as we will see, sextons recognised this hardship and tried to ameliorate it. In 1891, three women, somewhat the worse for alcohol, were seen hiding in some shrubbery in a Liverpool cemetery and it was discovered that they had hidden a small cardboard box with the body of a stillborn infant (Strange, 2005: 244). In Newcastle in November 1866, two boys found a cardboard box with the remains of a female infant, buried in a quarry. An inquest was held because of suspicion of infanticide. A stranger and sadder story emerged. The superintendents of two cemeteries – the new form of non-churchyard burial grounds developed mid-century – testified that three women had come to them seeking to bury an infant on the previous Sunday evening. One testified that they had carried the very same box the boys had discovered. However, the women had neither the burial fee nor a certificate backing up their claim that the infant had been stillborn, and so both superintendents turned the women away. By Friday's inquest, the women could not be identified, and the verdict 'found dead' was returned (*The Newcastle Daily Journal*, Saturday 3 November 1866). These new cemeteries often include un-consecrated ground so that Nonconformists could avoid burial in Anglican ground; we know of no research that explores the use of such ground for the interment of stillbirths, but this story suggests such sites may have been used for such. Nor were stillbirths registered until 1927, so the certificate seems to have been one from the midwife or doctor who attended the birth rather than a formal death certificate (*The Newcastle Courant etc*, Friday 30 September 1859).

This story has haunted our historical imaginations as we worked on the project. The narrative beautifully illustrates the paradoxes of perinatal loss. On the one hand, such loss, to judge by the evidence from St Hilda's, could be sorely felt, and addressed by means of the same funerary rituals as the loss of any other individual. However, stillborn infants were neither insured nor were they eligible for burial in a churchyard as they were not baptised, presenting both issues about personhood (was this an individual who should be given full funerary rites?) and a material problem of how to deal with such fetal remains (Mooney, 1994). In Tynemouth in 1851, for example, a soldier and his comrade were seen digging a small grave in a yard; after investigation an inquest was held. It emerged that the soldier's wife had given birth to a stillborn child and the father was preparing its grave; a midwife testified that the baby had been born dead prematurely, and thus the case was not about concealing an infanticide as authorities had feared (*The Newcastle Courant etc*, Friday 23 May 1851). Perhaps many other such tiny graves were dug that did not excite concern.

Rich textual evidence shows that midwives were the crucial figures involved in solving the problem of disposing of a perinatal body, often in alliance with sextons or cemetery workers. The latter often helped out by covertly interring perinatal remains in an adult coffin or grave. Thomas Wakley heard testimony in an 1859 inquest that it was commonplace for sextons to inter stillbirths in the coffins of unrelated adults, no one the wiser (*The

*Era*, Sunday 25 September 1859). Wakley assumed that this practice concealed countless infanticides, which he characteristically described as 'hundreds upon hundreds of murdered children lying in the cemeteries and grave-yards of the metropolis'; but from another perspective, it was a way that sextons might help working-class families cope with the high costs of burial (*The Newcastle Courant etc*, Friday 30 September 1859). The 1840s career of a London midwife and abortion provider suggests that not only stillbirths were interred secretly in churchyards with sextons' help. This midwife buried aborted fetuses in cardboard boxes, claiming they were stillbirths, with what must have been the connivance of sextons (*The Morning Post*, Saturday 30 September 1848; Mooney, 1994). The tone of reporting on this detail of the testimony implies that such burial practices for stillbirths were commonplace.

In nineteenth-century cemeteries, differences in burial costs for a stillborn infant versus live-born could be significant, and midwives conspired with families to cut costs. A Staffordshire midwife, for example, testified that she routinely certified infants who had lived for up to four days as 'stillborn' to save burial costs. A Birmingham midwife routinely signed stillbirth certificates for newborns and carried their bodies to the sextoness at a local cemetery (Strange, 2005: 240–3). While much of this evidence emerged in a late-century context where doctors were concerned about false certificates disrupting the collection of vital statistics, there is little reason to believe that such practices did not have a longer history.

In other words, it seems that it was common practice for midwives and sextons to attempt to mitigate the high costs of burials for perinates by clandestinely interring them in other coffins and charging the families a fraction of the cost of a burial. This custom may have been centuries old. The antiquary W. J. Thoms recorded a superstition that a stillborn buried clandestinely in a grave meant good luck for the legitimate burial; that individual was believed to ascend straight to heaven (Henderson, 1866: 5–6; Thoms, 1859: 172). Archaeological evidence consistent with this practice is not uncommon, but often challenging to interpret. Burials of women with perinates in their arms were excavated from nineteenth-century graves in Methodist cemeteries at Carver Street, Sheffield and Darwen, Lancashire, and there are six examples of adults buried with perinates at St Martin's-in-the-Bull-Ring in Birmingham (Buteux and Cherrington, 2006: 27; Gibson and Griffiths, 2011: 27; McIntyre and Willmott 2003: 26). These situations are commonly interpreted as women and infants who died in childbirth but may also reflect the practice of avoiding burial fees (either in cases of maternal and infant death or where an infant was buried with someone else) or even hiding infanticides as Wakley had feared (Cherryson *et al.*, 2012: 122).

The complex archaeological record at St Hilda's paints a picture of a community desiring to afford the best burials they could manage for even the youngest dead. Funerary practices in South Shields acknowledged loss and attempted, via ritual, to knit up the community, to re-make it again around the loss of even its youngest members. But burial costs were high, and families employed a range of strategies to contain costs when the loss was perinatal or a stillborn. Some of the evidence of these strategies comes from reading against the grain in cases such as the abortionist interring fetal remains, or the complaints of middle- and upper-class commentators about how economic limitations pushed the poor to circumvent the law by concealing births, committing infanticide or using abortifacients. While such moral concerns cannot be taken at face value, they highlight the very real reproductive pressures felt by many women, which we argue were often in contradiction with the 'decent burial' imperatives sketched in this section.

## Unwelcome and unwanted pregnancy

The large proportion of Coronation Street burials of remains of less than 28 GWS leads us to the context of unwanted as well as wanted (or at least accepted) pregnancies. The third 'field of force' that may structure this assemblage is the lack of effective contraception, made even more problematic by the erosion of older customs that accepted premarital sex in contexts in which pregnancy resulted in community pressure to marry, or at minimum, guarantees of child support from fathers. As mentioned above, with the advent of the so-called Bastardy Clause, women faced substantial reproductive pressures. Nor were unwanted births limited to unmarried women; many a working-class family simply could not feed another child. The historical record suggests that women responded to these pressures with a mix of abortion, passive and active neonaticide, and baby-farming, or outsourcing infant care. Midwives played crucial roles in many aspects of these vexed pregnancies.

Here we bring together evidence, largely taken from newspapers, about problem pregnancies and the various solutions women found to address them. The clandestine nature of solutions to unwanted pregnancy often renders them archaeologically and historically invisible, but on rare occasions, such actions become hyper-visible in the historical record when reported in newspapers or prosecuted in courtrooms. Such evidence provides potential contexts for the assemblage from St Hilda's. This discussion emphasises that the apparent silence on subjects such as contraception, abortion and infanticide in the archaeological record does not mean they were insignificant to the lives of eighteenth- and nineteenth-century people.

Methodologically, this third field of force moves us in a different direction. In our discussions of perinatal mortality and of the burial imperative, archaeological and historical evidence often seem to line up, to function in what we can call an additive way. For example, the archaeological evidence of coffins integrates well with a large array of textual sources that show that even quite poor people worked hard to avoid the ignominy of a parish burial. However, for the third field of force – unwanted pregnancy – historical and archaeological evidence do not match up well; they seem to speak past each other or even to be in contradiction. Rather than understanding this gap as a problem, we see it as profoundly productive. We argue that this gap can be interpreted as a pointer to the complex situation of young children in early and mid-nineteenth-century working-class English culture. As we will see, in a world in which reliable contraception was largely unknown, many a pregnancy may have been unwelcome. Infants were paradoxically both highly valued and often unwanted.

On the continent, a network of foundling hospitals offered desperate mothers an anonymous way to surrender an infant that they could not keep, but for women in South Shields no such option existed; even the foundling hospital in London was neither anonymous nor simple. Sometimes infants were left at a place where they would be found promptly; in 1867 Mr Pearson, a South Shields butcher, found a carefully wrapped-up baby on his butcher's block (*The Leeds Times*, Saturday 12 January 1867)! Other infants were neglected or abandoned in ways that led to their deaths. Newspapers frequently reported on the bodies of infants. For example, the body of a five-day-old girl was found by two schoolboys wrapped in a cloth under the parapet of Tyne Bridge. At the inquest the surgeon declared that the child had been delivered by a skilled midwife or medical man, but was unable to determine cause of death (*Newcastle Courant*, Friday 6 September 1861). In 1857, at Shotley Bridge, southwest of Newcastle, an infant girl's body was found in a stream but on this occasion, keen detective work identified the alleged mother, tracing her train journey in detail. She was charged with infanticide and bound over for trial (*Newcastle Guardian, and Tyne Mercury*, Saturday 28 February 1857). Subsequently, despite being described as the mother of eight illegitimate children, and thus not a witness likely to be granted much moral authority, 44-year-old Catherine Hemsley was acquitted due to insufficient evidence (*Newcastle Guardian, and Tyne Mercury*, Saturday 7 March 1857). The newspaper account is too sparse to help us interpret how a jury reached what may seem a surprising verdict.

Undoubtedly, some of the newspaper reporting of such cases was amplified by the mid-century moral panic about infant life, but many a story of an unwanted pregnancy resulting in perinatal mortality is similar in form to those a century or more earlier. Women working as domestic servants were vulnerable to their masters' sexual advances. As Laura Gowing has illuminated for the seventeenth century, such women were likely to conceal or deny their pregnancies and find themselves accused of infanticide (Gowing, 1997; 2003). Similar cases were frequently reported in nineteenth-century Newcastle newspapers. For example, Ann Anderson, a domestic servant, died in 1842 from a massive dose of arsenic, probably taken to procure an abortion. While the mistress of the house tried to claim that a fellow servant had been the father, testimony at the trial revealed that Anderson had told a friend that it had been the master (*Newcastle Journal*, Saturday 12 February 1842; see also *Newcastle Courant*, Friday 18 July 1873; *Newcastle Daily Journal*, Monday 25 February 1867).

The medical and legal situation for women such as Anderson who wished to avoid pregnancy was dire. Middle-class couples began to practise family limitation from the 1850s, if not earlier, but not so working-class ones (Banks, 1969). At the same time, abortion had become much more perilous legally. From 1803, Lord Ellenborough's Act made abortion or attempted abortion after quickening punishable by death – later modified to transportation, or a prison term if before quickening (Keown, 2002). Despite the legal consequences, abortion continued to be widely used, at least to judge by the many advertisements for abortifacients published in newspapers (Ryan, 1837: 881; Taylor, 1846: 592–4). While the medical profession maintained a studious silence on all aspects of family limitation, newspapers offered a plethora of pills offering abortifacients in barely concealed phrases about restoring female regularity (McLaren, 1978: 78–89). Judging by newspaper accounts, arsenic must have been used frequently by women as an abortifacient, sometimes with fatal results (Whorton, 2010; *The Northern Liberator*, Saturday 30 March 1839). Where drugs did not work, there were, it seems, an array of midwives, surgeons and other practitioners offering surgical abortions.

Women in the South Shields area were certainly no strangers to abortion. Midwives were often the obvious people to whom women turned when they found themselves with an unwanted pregnancy; while little is known about her, a midwife was hanged in Newcastle in 1781 when a woman died as a result of the abortion she had performed (*British Evening Post*, 27–29 November 1781; see later references such as *The Newcastle Courant*, Friday 28 December 1860). In 1862, another young Newcastle woman, described as working as a servant 'at a spirit bar', sought help from a midwife with an unwanted pregnancy. First Jane Ann Irving took medicine provided by Ann Milburn. When that did not work, Catherine Grecian, another midwife, came over from Sunderland and performed a surgical abortion. When Irving later sickened, her mother taxed her with her suspicions, and the story was out (*The Newcastle Courant*, Friday 12 December 1862).

An extraordinary series of advertisements placed in Newcastle newspapers for over 30 years reveal an Edinburgh midwife who offered Newcastle women solutions to unwanted pregnancies. In 1803 Mrs Laidlaw told readers that she would *'receive lying-in Women who wish Concealment'* – italicising the phrase for emphasis. Laidlaw offered a range of services: milk, night nurses and even the promise 'to relieve the Parents altogether' for a 'Sum of Money'. Decades later, she claimed 42-years' experience, although her advertisement had become a little more discreet (*The Newcastle Courant*, Saturday 9 July 1803; *The Newcastle Courant etc.*, Saturday 5 August 1820; *The Newcastle Courant etc.*, Saturday 12 May 1827). Mrs Laidlaw advertised in Newcastle newspapers for over three decades, suggesting that her services were in local demand, although probably beyond the means of most women. Nor was any woman likely to travel to her from Newcastle merely for a routine delivery.

Textual evidence from the Newcastle region suggests a huge, submerged number of women seeking to end a pregnancy or rid themselves of an unwanted infant. Disposal of the remains of terminated pregnancies was highly varied, from disposal with refuse to attempts to provide a decent burial, sometimes clandestinely. Traces of these practices may appear in the archaeological record, albeit in a form indistinguishable from the burials of neonates or stillbirths. In other cases, the sites chosen prevented survival of evidence, and/or may yet remain concealed. Therefore, this topic is both significant and highly charged in archaeology; it is both highly emotive and characterised by tenuous evidence (Scott, 1997). Indeed, only in extremely rare cases can the osteological record speak on the issue of unwanted children: where physical abuse left severe injury, which is difficult to evidence conclusively (Wheeler *et al.*, 2013) or where suggestive excavated evidence can be combined with historical context. For example, the excavation of a nineteenth-century privy shaft in the Five Points district of New York City revealed three perinates – two aged around 40 weeks at death and the third 20–22 weeks (Crist, 2005). The context implies clandestine, perhaps casual, disposal, and their ages at death implicate miscarriage, stillbirth, abortion or infanticide. Five Points was associated with prostitution, so that combining the historical and archaeological records offered rare evidence to explore reproductive choices faced by nineteenth-century working women.

Given the potentially dire legal consequences of abortion or infanticide, we will never be able to determine the full extent of incidence, but documentary evidence suggests it was substantial. Such evidence is subtractive; that is, it cannot simply be added to the archaeological evidence to make a unitary analysis. Rather, it serves as a powerful counterpoint to the churchyard at St Hilda's, making those burials – and the care with which they were performed – stand out against a tapestry of reproductive crisis.

In the largely patriarchal culture of early nineteenth-century England, working men achieved full maturity only upon becoming fathers and heads of their own households, but in such an economically tempestuous period, sustaining fatherhood could be precarious. Female domestic servants were sexually preyed upon by masters, or sought to pressure them into marriage, while many young women continued to engage in what they thought were premarital sexual relations, only to be abandoned by their partners when they fell pregnant. It was, in sum, a reproductive economy full of peril. What may not be visible in St Hilda's churchyard are the testimonies to that peril.

## Conclusions

In this project we have attempted to integrate historical and archaeological evidence to consider multiple pathways that might have led to the burial of a group of fetuses and perinates in one northern industrial community and illuminate, through this, the reproductive experiences of women whose children did not survive beyond birth. We have also reflected upon the process of collaborative working across disciplines, devising a new way of understanding and harnessing our complementary expertise as a historian and an archaeologist as we collaborated on researching and writing this chapter. In so doing we have identified what we call the 'handmaiden problem' and sought to avoid it. We have glimpsed a world where reproduction was a risky and dangerous process. While medical care was available, it was often insufficient and inaccessible. Nevertheless, considerable effort and expense were expended to afford decency and respect in response to infant death, sometimes with compromises involving 'economies of makeshift'. We have also identified examples of concealment, unwanted pregnancies and means of ending them accessible to many but increasingly viewed with disapprobation by lawmakers, which often remain largely invisible in historical and archaeological records.

At times, our evidence has been contradictory, much like the issues we have been investigating. It is clear from the archaeological record that the 'decent burial imperative' extended to the very youngest members of the community. At the same time, historical evidence suggests that the ability to provide such burials was limited; women carrying a small box from site to site, frustrated at every turn, or sneaking into a churchyard at night to perform a clandestine burial. Equally, such imperatives – and the emotional attachments we infer from them – were clearly not afforded every pregnancy or perinate. For many women, pregnancy was crisis; the reproductive landscape of late-eighteenth through mid-nineteenth-century England was perilous. Lacking contraceptive means, stigmatised and punished by the

'Bastardy Clause' of the New Poor Law, some women used desperate means to ensure they did not become mothers. Combining historical and archaeological evidence has highlighted this paradox, where pregnancy and infant life was highly valued in some settings and the source of desperation in others.

The integration of our disciplinary evidence and perspectives has thus opened up new avenues of inquiry and illuminated aspects of past lived experience that might otherwise be invisible. It has enabled us to offer a deeper insight into the circumstances that resulted in archaeologically unprecedented evidence for the burial of a cluster of fetuses and perinates beyond the boundary of the late-eighteenth- to early nineteenth-century burial ground at St Hilda's church, South Shields. These graves, which we argue represent a focus of vernacular consecration, have been explored through intersecting fields of force shaped by high infant mortality, the moral imperative of decent burial and women's experience of pregnancy, birth and motherhood, and a new layer of complexity and nuance has been introduced to the reproductive experiences of eighteenth- and nineteenth-century women.

## Acknowledgements

With thanks to collections managers at the Department of Archaeology, University of Sheffield (Sophie Newman, Tegid Watkins and Nina Maaranen) for access to the skeletal remains from St Hilda's and to Diana Swales, Sophie Newman and Delaney Mitchell for their archive osteological data which facilitated identification of fetal and infant individuals. Thanks are also due to John Bennet for comments on a draft of this chapter. The authors are incredibly grateful for the opportunity to meet and work together provided by the British Academy-funded 'The Material Body: An Interdisciplinary Study in History and Archaeology' (British Academy Small Grant SG151375; 2015–2018).

## Notes

1 Examples contemporary with St Hilda's include Chelsea Old Church, London where two fetal and one perinatal individual were excavated in total. Two of these were located within the pelvic cavities of women (Cowie et al., 2008). At St Martin's-in-the-Bull-Ring there were nine fetal individuals, five of whom were recovered from the pelvic area of females (Brickley, 2006). There can be some doubt whether burials where fetal and perinatal remains are found in the pelvic cavity represent death during pregnancy and childbirth or result from the fall of the remains of the smaller individual into the pelvic cavity of the female

during decomposition, which would be possible had the fetal/perinatal remains been laid above the adult in the grave.
2   Critical scholarship of archaeology's contributions to the study of the past has described the subject as 'handmaiden to history' (Perry, 2007), reflecting the tendency for historical narratives to be seen as more legitimate, truthful and complete than those obtained from physical evidence, including the human skeleton.
3   Mother/infant pairs can be identified in the archaeological record using ancient DNA evidence, which remains prohibitively expensive for many research projects, coffin plate evidence, which is rare for perinates or mother/perinate pairs (Hoile, 2020: 66, 79), or, considerably more tenuously, when a female and infant are buried in the same grave.
4   Assigning chronological age is complicated by the fact that archaeological data provide only proxies for this variable: biological age, the stage of physiological development of the skeleton; and social age in the form of evidence of how an individuals' maturity was interpreted within their social and cultural context. A lack of agreed standards for age thresholds across different archaeological projects has made explicitly defining age categories in each new scholarly work a necessity. In this chapter, fetus = conception to $c.$37 gestational weeks (GWS), perinate = $c.$38–45 GWS, infant = $c.$45 GWS–1 year of age (Halcrow et al., 2017), but specific age ranges in gestational weeks are always used where possible to avoid ambiguous generalisation.
5   However, see Gowland and colleagues (2018) for evidence that eighteenth- and nineteenth-century rural populations were not necessarily 'healthier'.
6   Not discussed here are a further five individuals from the lower burial group aged over 46 weeks at death. These are Sk 756 6 months, Sk 590 6–12 months, Sk 586 7 months–1 year and Sk 678 11–12 years, and Sk 593 over 12 years. Three adults were also buried in this area of the cemetery, one at the south-western and two at the north-eastern extent of the perinate group. The adults are not discussed here, but if this site is analogous to the Irish cilliní, they may be individuals who had not been baptised, or whose baptismal status was unknown.
7   However, there are techniques that can help distinguish stillborn infants from live births based on the absence or presence, respectively, of gut bacteria which then affects the process of decomposition in archaeologically visible ways (Booth, 2016). This technique is destructive, requiring sectioning of bones to create histological sections and has not yet been undertaken at St Hilda's.
8   Hodson noted that the middling sort in London experienced higher rates of growth disruption during childhood than the poorest individuals in addition to high rates of pathological lesions.
9   Our reassessment revised that presented in the site report, where skeleton 862 is assessed as 16–18 GWS (Raynor et al., 2011: 105) to $c.$21–23 GWS.
10  'Infant Mortality' CAMPOP, *Populations Past – Atlas of Victorian and Edwardian Population* www.populationspast.org/imr/1851/#10/54.9409/-1.6342 (accessed 24 May 2018).

11  'Doctors' CAMPOP, *Populations Past -Atlas of Victorian and Edwardian Population* www.populationspast.org/doc/1851/#9/51.4437/-0.8913 (accessed 24 May 2018).
12  Four are from the lower burials, associated with skeletons 820 (21–23 GWS), 862 (21–23 GWS), 825 (36–40 GWS) and 761 (27–28 GWS) and three are from the later burials among the upper levels, i.e. not from the fetal and perinatal burial group.
13  Single-break coffins are an elongated kite shape with flattened top and bottom points – the classic six-sided shape of many modern coffins.

## References

### Primary sources

Burying The Dead In Towns, HC Deb 08 March 1842 vol 61 cc281–3; https://api.parliament.uk/historic-hansard/commons/1842/mar/08/burying-the-dead-in-towns (accessed 7 June 2021).
Fryer, J. (1773). Plan of South Shields, North Shields and Tynemouth.
Richardson (1768). Plan of the Townships of South Shields & Westoe, in the county of Durham.
Select Committee on Interments X, Q2510 PP 1842, https://babel.hathitrust.org/cgi/pt?id=hvd.32044106496045&view=1up&seq=512&q1=%22Robert%20Baker%22 (accessed 7 June 2021).

### Newspapers and periodicals

*British Evening Post* (1781). 'Country News' 27–29 November.
*The Era* (1859), 'Unprotected State of Infantine Life.—Important Investigation'. Sunday 25 September.
*The Leeds Times* (1867). Saturday 12 January.
*The Morning Post* (London, England) (1848). Saturday 30 September.
*The Newcastle Courant* (1803). 'Advertisements & Notices'. Saturday 9 July.
   (1806). 'Advertisements & Notices'. Saturday 1 March.
   (1820). 'Advertisements & Notices', Saturday 5 August.
   (1824). 'Advertisements & Notices' Saturday 28 August.
   (1827). 'Advertisements & Notices', Saturday 12 May.
   (1843). 'London, Thursday, Dec. 28'. Friday 29 December.
   (1851). 'Police Intelligence'. Friday 23 May.
   (1859), 'Daily and Periodical Press', Friday 30 September.
   (1860) 'Executions at Durham'. Friday 28 December.
   (1861). 'Coroners' Inquests', Friday 6 September.
   (1862). 'Re-Opening of Chester-Le-Street Parish Church'. Friday 12 December.
   (1873). 'Durham Assizes', Friday 18 July.
*Newcastle Daily Journal* (1866). 'News'. Saturday 3 November.
   (1867) 'Northumberland and Newcastle Spring Assizes'. Monday 25 February.

*Newcastle Guardian, and Tyne Mercury* (1857). 'Child Murder at Berry Edge'. Saturday 28 February.
——— (1857). 'Durham Spring Assizes'. Saturday 7 March.
*Newcastle Journal* (1842). 'Case of Poison Adjourned Inquest' (1842). Saturday 12 February.
——— (1843). 'Local & General Intelligence' Saturday 30 December.
*The Northern Liberator* (1839). 'Weekly Gossip'. Saturday 30 March.

### Secondary sources

Adair, R. (1996). *Courtship, Illegitimacy, and Marriage in Early Modern England* (Manchester: Manchester University Press).
Al Qahtani, S. J., Hector, M. P. and Liversidge, H. M. (2014). 'Accuracy of Dental Age Estimation Charts: Schour and Massler, Ubelaker, and the London Atlas', *American Journal of Physical Anthropology*, 154(1): 70–8.
Al Qahtani, S. J., Liversidge, H. M., Hector, M. P. (2010). 'Brief communication: The London atlas of tooth development and eruption', *American Journal of Physical Anthropology*, 142(3): 481–90.
Arrizabalaga, J. (2002). 'Problematizing retrospective diagnosis in the history of disease', *Asclepio*, 54(1): 51–70.
Banks, J. A. (1969). *Prosperity and Parenthood: A Study of Family Planning Among the Victorian Middle Classes* (London: Routledge & Paul).
Bell, S. and Fissell, M. E. (2021). 'A little bit pregnant? Productive ambiguity and fertility research', *Population and Development Review*, 47(2): 505–26.
Booth, T. J. (2016). 'An investigation into the relationship between bacterial bioerosion and funerary treatment in European archaeological human bone', *Archaeometry*, 58(3): 484–99.
Brickley, M. (2006). 'The people: Physical anthropology', in M. Brickley, S. Buteux, T. Adams and R. Cherrington (eds), *St Martin's Uncovered: Investigations in the Churchyard of St. Martin's-in-the-Bull-Ring, Birmingham, 2001* (Oxford: Oxbow Books), pp. 90–151.
Brickley, M., Mays, S. and Ives, R. (2007). 'An investigation of skeletal indicators of vitamin D deficiency in adults: Effective markers for interpreting past living conditions and pollution levels in 18th and 19th century Birmingham, England', *American Journal of Physical Anthropology*, 132: 67–79.
Buckberry, J. (2018). 'Techniques for identifying the age and sex of children at death', in S. Crawford, D. M. Hadley and G. Shepherd (eds), *The Oxford Handbook of the Archaeology of Childhood* (Oxford: Oxford University Press), pp. 55–70.
Buteux, S. and Cherrington, R. (2006). 'The excavations', in B. M. Brickley, S. Buteux, T. Adams and R. Cherrington (eds), *St Martin's Uncovered: Investigations in the Churchyard of St. Martin's-in-the-Bull-Ring, Birmingham, 2001* (Oxford: Oxbow Books), chapter 3.
Cherryson, A. K., Crossland, Z. and Tarlow, S. (eds) (2012). *A Fine and Private Place: The Archaeology of Death and Burial in Post-Medieval Britain and Ireland*, Leicester Archaeology Monograph 22 (Leicester: University of Leicester).

Crist, T. (2005). 'Babies in the privy: Prostitution, infanticide and abortion in New York City's Five Points District', *Historical Archaeology*, 39(1): 19–46.

Cunningham, C., Scheuer, L. and Black, S. (2016). *Developmental Juvenile Osteology*, 2nd edn (London: Academic Press).

Ellis, M. A. B. (2020). 'Still life: A bioarchaeological portrait of perinatal remains buried at the Spring Street Presbyterian Church', *Historical Archaeology* 54(1): 184–201.

Engstrom, J. (1985). 'Quickening and auscultation of fetal heart tones as estimators of the gestational interval: A review', *Journal of Nurse-Midwifery*, 30(1): 25–32.

Finlay, N. (2000). 'Outside of life: Traditions of infant curial in Ireland from cillín to cist', *World Archaeology*, 31(3). 407–22.

Fissell, M. E. (2004a). *Vernacular Bodies: The Politics of Reproduction in Early Modern England* (Oxford: Oxford University Press).

Fissell, M. E. (2004b). 'Making meaning from the margins: The new cultural history of medicine', in J. Warner and F. Huisman (eds), *Medical History: The Stories and their Meanings* (Baltimore: Johns Hopkins Press), pp. 364–89.

Fissell, M. E. (2017). 'Remaking the maternal body in England, 1680–1730', *Journal of the History of Sexuality*, 26(1): 114–39.

Floud, R. and Harris, B. (1997). 'Heath, height, and welfare: Britain, 1700–1980', in N. Steckel and R. Floud (eds), *Health and Welfare During Industrialization* (Chicago: The University of Chicago Press), pp. 91–126.

Garrett, E., Galley, C., Shelton, N. and Woods, R. (2006). 'Infant mortality: A social problem?', in E. Garrett, C. Galley, N. Shelton and R. Woods (eds), *Infant Mortality: A Continuing Social Problem* (Aldershot: Ashgate), pp. 3–14.

Gittings, C. (1998). *Death, Burial and the Individual in Early Modern England* (London: Routledge).

Giorgione, V., Briffa, C., Di Fabrizio, C., Bhate, R. and Khalil, A. (2021). 'Perinatal outcomes of small for gestational age in twin pregnancies: Twin vs. singleton charts'. *Journal of Clinical Medicine*, 10(4): 643–52.

Gowing, L. (1997). 'Secret births and infanticide in seventeenth-century England', *Past and Present*, 156: 87–115.

Gowing, L. (2003). *Common Bodies: Women, Touch, and Power in Seventeenth-Century England* (New Haven: Yale University Press).

Gowland, R. (2006). 'Ageing the past: Examining age identity from funerary evidence', in R. Gowland and C. Knüsel (eds), *Social Archaeological of Funerary Remains* (Oxford: Oxbow Books), pp. 143–54.

Gowland, R., Caffell, A. C., Newman, S., Levene, A. and Holst, M. (2018). 'Broken childhoods: Rural and urban non-adult health during the Industrial Revolution in northern England (eighteenth–nineteenth centuries)', *Bioarchaeology International*, 2(1): 44–62.

Gowland, R. and Knüsel, C. (2006), *Social Archaeological of Funerary Remains* (Oxford: Oxbow Books).

Gibson, M. and Griffiths, J. (2011). *Readearth Primitive Methodist Chapel, Readearth Road, Darwen, Lancashire* (Lancaster: Oxford Archaeology North, unpublished report).

Halcrow, S. E., Tayles, N. and Elliott, G. E. (2017). 'The bioarchaeology of fetuses', in S. Han, T. K. Betsinger and A. B. Scott (eds), *The Anthropology of the Fetus: Biology, Culture, and Society* (New York: Berghahn Books), pp. 83–111.
Hardwick, J. (2020). *Sex in an Old Regime City* (Oxford: Oxford University Press).
Heighway, C. M. and Bryant, R. (1999). *The Golden Minster: The Anglo-Saxon Minster and Later Medieval Priory of St Oswald at Gloucester* (Oxford: Council for British Archaeology).
Hemphill, K. M. (2012). '"Driven to the commission of this crime": Women and infanticide in Baltimore, 1835–1860', *Journal of the Early Republic*, 32: 437–61.
Henderson, W. (1866). *Notes on the Folklore of the Northern Counties of England and the Borders* (London: Longmans, Green, and Co.).
Higgs, E. (2004). *The Information State in England: The Central Collection of Information on Citizens Since 1500* (Houndmills, Basingstoke, Hampshire: Palgrave Macmillan).
Hodson, C. M. (2018). 'Stressed at birth: Investigating fetal, perinatal and infant growth and health disruption' (PhD dissertation, Durham University).
Hodson, C. M. and Gowland, R. (2019). 'Like mother, like child: Investigating perinatal and maternal health stress in post-medieval London', in R. Gowland and S. Halcrow (eds), *The Mother-Infant Nexus in Anthropology: Small Beginnings, Significant Outcomes* (Cham: Springer), pp. 39–64.
Hoile, S. (2018). 'Coffin furniture in London c. 1700–1850: The establishment of tradition in the material culture of the grave', *Post-Medieval Archaeology*, 52(2): 210–23.
Hoile, S. (2020). 'Death, time and commerce: Innovation and conservatism in styles of funerary material culture in 18$^{th}$–19$^{th}$ century London' (PhD dissertation, University College London).
Houlbrooke, R. (1998). *Death, Religion, and the Family in England, 1480–1750* (Oxford: Clarendon Press).
Hufton, O. H. (1974). *The Poor of Eighteenth-Century France 1750–1789* (Oxford: Clarendon Press).
Hughes-Morey, G. (2016). 'Interpreting adult stature in industrial London', *American Journal of Physical Anthropology*, 159(1): 126–34.
Hunt, A. (2006). 'Calculations and concealments: Infanticide in mid-nineteenth century Britain', *Victorian Literature & Culture*, 34(1): 71–94.
Hurren, E. and King, S. (2005). '"Begging for a burial": Form, function and conflict in nineteenth-century pauper burial'. *Social History*, 30(3): 321–41.
Ives, R. (2017). 'Rare palaeopathological insights into vitamin D deficiency rickets, co-occurring illnesses, and documented cause of death in mid-19th century London, UK', *International Journal of Paleopathology*, 23: 76–87.
Ives, R. and Humphrey, L. (2017). 'Patterns of long bone growth in a mid-19th century documented sample of the urban poor from Bethnal Green, London, UK', *American Journal of Physical Anthropology*, 163(1): 173–86.
Keown, J. (2002). *Abortion, Doctors and the Law: Some Aspects of the Legal Regulation of Abortion in England from 1803 to 1982* (Cambridge: Cambridge University Press).

Kiserud, T., Piaggio, G., Carroli, G., Widmer, M., Carvalho, J., Neerup Jensen, L. *et al.* (2017) 'The World Health Organization fetal growth charts: A multinational longitudinal study of ultrasound biometric measurements and estimated fetal weight', *PLoS Medicine* 14(1): e1002220.

Kramer M. S., Demisse, K., Yang, H., Platt, R. W., Sauve, R. and Liston, R. (2000). 'The contribution of mid and moderate preterm birth to infant mortality', *Journal of the American Medical Association*, 284: 834–49.

Lewis, J. and Ewart, G. (1995). *Jedburgh Abbey: The Archaeology and Architecture of a Border Abbey* (Society of Antiquaries Scotland: Edinburgh).

Lewis, M. E. (2002a). *Urbanisation and Child Health in Medieval and Post-Medieval England. An Assessment of the Morbidity and Mortality of Non-Adult Skeletons from the Cemeteries of Two Urban and Two Rural Sites in England* (AD 850–1859), BAR British Series 339 (Oxford: Archaeopress).

Lewis, M. E. (2002b). 'Impact of industrialisation: Comparative study of child health in four sites from medieval and post-medieval England (A.D. 850–1859)', *American Journal of Physical Anthropology*, 119: 211–23.

Lewis, M. (2007). *The Bioarchaeology of Children: Perspectives from Biological and Forensic Anthropology* (Cambridge, Cambridge University Press).

Litten, J. (1991). *The English Way of Death: The Common Funeral Since 1450* (London: Hale).

Litten, J. (1998). 'The English funeral 1700–1850', in Cox, M. (ed), *Grave Concerns: Death and Burial in England 1700–1850*, Council for British Archaeology research report 113 (York: Council for British Archaeology), pp. 3–16.

Mackenzie, E. (1827). 'Medical establishments: The lying-in hospital and charities', in *Historical Account of Newcastle-Upon-Tyne Including the Borough of Gateshead*, pp. 517–22. British History Online, www.british-history.ac.uk/no-series/newcastle-historical-account (accessed 4 June 2018).

McFadden, C. (2020). 'Parturition markers and skeletal sex estimation', in A. Klales (ed.), *Sex Estimation of the Human Skeleton: History, Methods and Emerging Techniques* (London: Academic Press), pp. 131–46.

McIntyre, L. and Willmott, H. (2003). *Excavations at the Methodist Chapel, Carver Street, Sheffield*, Report 507.2 (Sheffield: ARCUS, unpublished report).

McLaren, A. (1978). *Birth Control in Nineteenth-Century England* (New York: Holmes & Meier).

Mitchell, P. (2011). 'Retrospective diagnosis and the use of historical texts for investigating disease in the past,' *International Journal of Paleopathology*, 1: 81–8.

Mooney, G. (1994). 'Still-births and the measurement of urban infant mortality rates c. 1890–1930', *Local Population Studies*, 52: 42–52.

Murphy, E. M. (2011a). 'Children's burial grounds in Ireland (cilliní) and parental emotions toward infant death', *International Journal of Historical Archaeology*, 15(3): 409–28.

Murphy, E. M. (2011b). 'Parenting, child loss and the cilliní of post-medieval Ireland', in M. Lally and A. Moore (eds) *(Re)thinking the Little Ancestor: New Perspectives on the Archaeology of Infancy and Childhood* (Oxford: Archaeopress), pp. 63–74.

Newman, S. (2019). 'North and south: A comprehensive analysis of non-adult growth and health in the industrial revolution (AD 18th–19th C), England' (PhD dissertation, University of Durham).
Newman, S. L., Gowland, R. L. and Caffell, A. C. (2019). 'North and south: A comprehensive analysis of non-adult growth and health in the Industrial Revolution (AD 18th–19th C), England'. *American Journal of Physical Anthropology*, 169: 104–21.
Nowakowski, J. A. and Thomas, C. (1992). 'Tintagel churchyard excavations 1991', *Cornish Archaeology*, 3: 131–34.
Oman, E. (No Date). *Salford Stepping Stones* (Swinton: N. Richardson).
Packard, R. M. (2016). '"Break-bone" fever in Philadelphia, 1780: Reflections on the history of disease', *Bulletin of the History of Medicine*, 90(2): 193–221.
Perry, M. (2007). 'Is bioarchaeology a handmaiden to history? Developing a historical bioarchaeology', *Journal of Anthropological Archaeology*, 26(3): 486–515.
Raynor, C., McCarthy, R. and Clough, S. (2011). 'Coronation Street, South Shields, Tyne and Wear: Archaeological Excavation and Osteological Analysis Report' (Lancaster: Oxford Archaeology North, unpublished report).
Richardson, R. (2000). *Death, Dissection and the Destitute*, 2nd edn (Chicago: University of Chicago Press).
Roberts, C. A. and Cox, M. (2003). *Health and Disease in Britain: From Prehistory to the Present Day* (Gloucester: Sutton Publishing).
Roberts, R. (1976). *A Ragged Schooling: Growing up in the Classic Slum* (Manchester: Manchester University Press).
Rogers, J. (1999). 'Burials: The human skeletons', in C. Heighway and R. Bryant (eds), *The Golden Minster: the Anglo-Saxon Minster and Later Medieval Priory of St Oswald at Gloucester* (York: Council for British Archaeology), pp. 229–46.
Ross, E. (1993). *Love and Toil. Motherhood in Outcast London, 1870–1918* (New York: Oxford University Press).
Rutherford, J. (2017). 'The borderless fetus: Temporal complexity of the lived fetal experience', in S. Han, T. K. Betsinger and A. B. Scott (eds), *The Anthropology of the Fetus: Biology, Culture, and Society* (New York: Berghahn Books), pp. 15–33.
Ryan, M. (1837). 'Observations on criminal abortion', *London Medical and Surgical Journal* 2: 881.
Satterlee Blake, K. A. (2017). 'The biology of the fetal period: Interpreting life from fetal skeletal remains', in S. Han, T. K. Betsinger and A. B. Scott (eds), *The Anthropology of the Fetus: Biology, Culture, and Society* (New York: Berghahn Books), pp. 34–58.
Scheuer, J. L., Musgrave, J. H. and Evans, S. P. (1980). 'The estimation of late fetal and perinatal age from limb bone length by linear and logarithmic regression', *Annals of Human Biology*, 7(3): 257–65.
Scheuer, L. and McLaughlin-Black, S. (1994). 'Age estimation from the pars basilaris of the fetal and juvenile occipital bone', *International Journal of Osteoarchaeology*, 4: 377–80.
Scott, E. (1997). 'Introduction: On the incompleteness of archaeological narratives', in J. Moore and E. Scott (eds), *Invisible People and Processes: Writing Gender*

*and Childhood into European Archaeology* (Leicester: Leicester University Press), pp. 1–12.

Smith, R. and Oeppen, J. (2006). 'Place and status as determinants of infant mortality in England, c.1550–1837', in E. Garrett, C. Galley, N. Shelton and R. Woods (eds), *Infant Mortality: A Continuing Social Problem* (Aldershot: Ashgate), pp. 53–78.

Sofaer, J. R. (2005). *The Body as Material Culture: A Theoretical Osteoarchaeology* (Cambridge: Cambridge University Press).

Strange, J-M. (2005). *Death, Grief and Poverty in Britain, 1870–1914* (Cambridge: Cambridge University Press).

Swales, D., O'Neill, R. and Willmott, H. (2011). 'The hidden material culture of death: Coffins and grave goods in late 18th- and early 19th-century Sheffield', in C. King and D. Sayer (eds), *The Archaeology of Post Medieval Religion* (Woodbridge: Boydell), pp. 215–32.

Tarlow, S. (2010). *Ritual, Belief and the Dead in Early Modern Britain and Ireland* (Cambridge: Cambridge University Press).

Taylor, A. S. (1846). *A Manual of Medical Jurisprudence* (London: J. Churchill).

Thoms, W. J. (1859). *Choice notes from 'Notes and Queries': Folk Lore* (London: Bell and Daldy).

Thorn, J. (2003). *Writing British Infanticide: Child-Murder, Gender, and Print, 1722–1859*. (Newark: University of Delaware Press).

Tomkins, A. (2010). 'Demography and the midwives: Deliveries and their dénouements in North Shropshire, 1781–1803', *Continuity & Change*, 25(2): 199–232.

Wheeler, S.M., Williams, L., Beauchesne, P. and Dupras, T. L. (2013). 'Shattered lives and broken childhoods: Evidence of physical child abuse in Ancient Egypt', *International Journal of Paleopathology*, 3(2): 71–82.

Whitworth, A. M. (1994). 'Lanercost Priory excavations in 1994', *Transactions of the Cumberland and Westmorland Antiquarian and Archaeological Society*, 98(2): 133–44.

WHO (2018). 'Preterm birth', www.who.int/mediacentre/factsheets/fs363/en/ (accessed 2 November 2020).

WHO (2020). 'Newborns: Improving survival and wellbeing', www.who.int/en/news-room/fact-sheets/detail/newborns-reducing-mortality (accessed 2 November 2020).

Whorton, J. C. (2010). *The Arsenic Century: How Victorian Britain was Poisoned at Home, Work and Play* (Oxford: Oxford University Press).

Wilson, A. (2000). 'On the history of disease-concepts: The case of pleurisy', *History of Science*, 38(3): 121, 271–319.

Woods, R. (2009). *Death Before Birth: Fetal Health and Mortality in Historical Perspective* (Oxford: Oxford University Press).

# 3

# Embodying the history of shoes: footwear and gender in Britain, 1700–1850

*Matthew McCormack*

John Gay's satirical poem 'Trivia: Or the Art of Walking the Streets of London' (1716: 2–3) described the many hazards that the pedestrian might encounter and how best to avoid them. It began by advising the reader on appropriate footwear:

> Let firm, well-hammer'd Soles protect thy Feet
> Thro' freezing Snows, and Rains, and soaking Sleet.
> Should the big Laste extend the Shoe too wide,
> Each Stone will wrench th' unwary Step aside:
> The sudden Turn may stretch the swelling Vein,
> Thy cracking joint unhinge, or Ankle sprain;
> And when too short the modish Shoes are worn,
> You'll judge the Seasons by your shooting Corn.

Well-made shoes protected feet against the elements, as well as other contemporary urban dangers mentioned in the poem, such as mud, overflowing gutters and the contents of chamber pots. They were therefore essential apparel for the early-Georgian *flâneur*. As Gay reminds us, however, ill-fitting shoes hold dangers of their own, resulting in injuries, accidents and medical complaints. Other items of clothing impact on the human body but shoes do so in a unique way. Shoes have to bear the body's entire weight and the considerable stresses imposed by walking, while supporting the delicate structure and sensitive skin of the foot. Furthermore, the forces imposed on shoes leave an indelible impression of their wearer, giving an insight into the shape, size and motions of their bodies. No other garment does this. Footwear therefore has the potential to tell us a great deal about the human body.

This chapter makes a case for an embodied history of shoes, which thinks about shoes as material articles that had a close and reciprocal relationship with past physical bodies, allowing the historian to shed new light on both. To date, histories of gender and the body have had little to say about the history of shoes, and vice versa. Shoe history is a relatively self-contained field, which has traditionally focused on curation and design. Recent historical work on consumption has explored the social and cultural history of shoes, but the focus tends to be on shoes themselves rather than what they tell us about the bodies of their wearers (Riello, 2006; Riello and McNeill, 2006; Semmelhack, 2017). The one historical field that has systematically thought about shoes as objects that relate to bodies is archaeology. For example, studies of footwear remains have demonstrated changing patterns of wear over a long period or across social classes, suggesting differences in the way that people walked (Anderson, 2017; Trujillo-Menderos, 2014). Alternatively, evidence of human bones has allowed archaeologists to speculate about the nature of footwear where no such evidence has survived (Mays, 2005). In general, shoes retrieved from archaeological digs are in poor condition: leather is only preserved in specific conditions, so the evidence tends to be scraps that are heavily decayed and very fragile (Veres, 2005).

This study will instead focus on examples of footwear from museum collections. The condition of these vary, but particular attention has been paid to worn examples as it is these that tell us most about the bodies of their wearers. Because of the significance of damage and wear, curators are more sensitive to it in relation to shoes than to other garments, and tend not to privilege 'perfect' examples over worn ones, nor carry out restoration to 'repair' them. Because of shoes' vital practical function, it is important to engage with them as objects in order to get a sense of their materiality. Studying their shape, weight, texture and flexibility gives an insight into what they would have been like to wear, and examining patterns of wear on the soles, heels and uppers tells us about their wearer. So, whereas the current study of material culture encompasses a range of approaches – including the subjective, the emotional and the economic – this study will prioritise the practical physicality of the object itself. As Ulinka Rublack has argued, material articles like shoes need to be studied as 'real-life objects in use' (2013: 85).

The particular focus of this study will be footwear from Britain from the early eighteenth to the mid-nineteenth centuries. Historians often identify the 'long' eighteenth century as a key period of change in gender relations, whereby masculine and feminine roles respectively diverged into 'separate spheres' of public life and domesticity (Vickery, 1993). In the Enlightenment, social roles were justified in terms of new understandings of the body and the self (Wahrman, 2004). According to Thomas Laqueur, a flexible 'one sex' vision of the body (where men and women shared a common body governed by the four humours) was replaced by a 'two sex' body (where men and women had utterly different physiologies that equipped them for separate social roles) (1990: 8). This model has been much debated: for example, Barbara Duden has shown how the language of the humours persisted, in a way that may have had little to do with Galenic medicine (2013: 54). Thinking about shoes in relation to embodied masculinity and femininity therefore offers a critical perspective on some dominant narratives of the period.

This period has also been chosen because the method of manufacture was broadly consistent before the introduction of sewing machines, new materials and new welting techniques in the 1840s. Large-scale mechanisation came late to the shoe industry, which tended to take place in workshops, small factories and private houses. Before mass production drove down costs, shoes were sewn by hand and were very labour intensive. They were therefore a significant purchase and working people would typically only have owned one or two pairs, in fairly generic styles. Museum shoe collections tend to be skewed in class and gender terms, since it is the finer or more decorative examples that were more likely to have been kept. Men's shoes were typically plainer than women's, and working people wore their shoes until they could no longer be repaired and then discarded them (so their shoes are more likely to be recovered by archaeologists). More women's shoes are therefore preserved in museums than men's, and more elite than plebeian; but by using four major shoe archives, this study has attempted to locate a representative range of footwear across the social classes.[1]

As well as using material evidence from museums, this chapter will explore writings from the time about feet and footwear. Some of this writing is medical, often by writers who were keen to establish chiropody[2] as a respectable medical discipline, and who were anxious to distance themselves from the corn doctors and barbers who were notorious for butchering people's feet: Lewis Durlacher paraded his credentials as 'Surgeon-Chiropodist to Her Majesty the Queen and the Royal Family' (1850: frontispiece). Other writings focus on clothing, but these too were concerned with health and hygiene: a novel and distinctive focus for the eighteenth century. This scientific emphasis might appear neutral, but Peter McNeil and Giorgio Riello argue that it continued the centuries-old debate about the expense and morality of fashion, and that shoes were 'at the center of such debate' (2005: 194). Attention is also paid to life writing, in order to get an insight into how people from the time articulated their experience of wearing shoes.

The chapter will begin by thinking about the impact that the body has upon shoes, and the way in which the body is therefore visible in worn footwear. As well as providing historians with concrete, physical evidence of the wearer, this also highlights the very individual relationship that people have with their shoes, something that is perceptible in a range of cultural practices across our period. It is also revealing to think about the requirements that shoes have to fulfil and the materials that they are made from in order to achieve this. The focus will then be reversed, as the chapter thinks about the impact of shoes upon the body. It will explore how the design of shoes affects the experience of wearing them, and the influence that this has upon the wearer's bodily health, posture and mobility.

## The impact of the body on shoes

Shoes commonly bear tell-tale signs of their owner. Look at the insole of any used pair of shoes and you will likely see the outline of a footprint, with indentations marking where the heel, midfoot and toes have exerted repeated pressure on the sole. The term 'footprint' is commonly used today to signify the impact of human activity, but in the case of shoes this literal footprint is a record of a human being. In addition to the footprint, wear to the sole and heel provide evidence of how the wearer moved in their shoes, and stretches in the upper record the outline of their foot. Shoes in museum collections rarely come with a provenance, and although it is possible to infer things about the owner from the design of the shoe, patterns of wear are often the only direct record we have of them. For example, we do not know who owned these wellington boots in Northampton Museum (see Figure 3.1): their style dates from around 1820 and the quality of the materials and workmanship tells us that the owner was well-to-do. By studying the boot, however, we can see that it has stretched in order to mould to the foot. Wellingtons like this were made of supple leather and were bespoke articles, since before the availability of elastic they had to fit exactly, but it was fashionable in this period to wear tight boots in order to give the impression of slender feet. To judge by the stretching – which extends beyond the outline of the sole – and also by the long cut that has been made to the leg in order to get them on and off, this pair were made too small. The owner could afford to wear footwear that fitted, but chose not to in order to achieve a certain appearance.

Footwear therefore has a unique relationship with its owner. Bespoke footwear is directly manufactured for a particular owner, but even shoes that were made in generic sizes gradually mould to the foot through wear and adaptation. Proverbs attest to the common identification of shoes with their wearer. To 'step into another man's shoes', to 'walk a mile in their shoes' or to 'wait for dead men's shoes' suggest that shoe and owner are synonymous (Demello, 2009: 251). The ghostly outline of the absent foot has encouraged various cultures to identify the worn shoe with the soul of its original owner. Impromptu monuments of empty shoes can convey loss,

Figure 3.1 Wellington boots, 1800–25.

and soldiers who looted boots from the fallen on the battlefield would leave their own worn-out pair as a mark of respect (Semmelhack, 2017: 320, 120). The folk practice of concealing shoes within the house in order to protect it against evil spirits suggests that the shoe magically retains the power of its owner (Houlbrook, 2013). As June Swann notes, the shoe is 'the only garment we wear which retains the shape, the personality, the essence of the wearer' (1996: 56). Many people resisted buying shoes second hand for this reason, a practice that was often regarded as being unlucky. Contemporaries also highlighted the medical dangers of wearing used shoes, which retained bodily traces of their former owner: Christian Struve warned that a boy contracted scarlet fever 'by wearing the boots of a patient labouring under that disease' (1802: 343–4). Writers like this showed little sympathy for working people who had no choice but to wear second hand or cast-offs.

In practice, shoes were often acquired used due to their expense (Richmond, 2013: 91).

The structure of the human foot places certain requirements upon shoes. Humans are bipeds, so place the entire weight of their bodies upon their feet. Primates have an opposable big toe, but as human feet are just used for walking, their toes have shortened and have largely lost the ability to grab (Fernandes et al., 2018). Human feet are plantigrade, since humans stand and walk on flat feet rather than upon their toes. Their feet therefore developed an arch, to bear the weight of their bodies and the forces imposed by locomotion. The renowned surgeon Sir Charles Bell eulogised that 'there is nothing more beautiful than the structure of the human foot'. He praised its structure in architectural terms:

> The foot has in its structure all the fine appliances you see in a building. In the first place, there is an arch … so that, instead of standing, as might be imagined, on a solid bone, we stand upon an arch composed of a series of bones, which are united by the most curious provision for the elasticity of the foot; hence, if we jump from height directly upon the heel, a severe shock is felt; not so, if we alight upon the ball of the great toe, for there an elasticity is formed in the whole foot, and the weight of the body is thrown upon this arch, and the shock avoided. (Hall, 1847: 96–7)

In total, the foot consists of twenty-six bones, thirty-three joints and dozens of ligaments. When stressed in the right way, they can withstand great forces, but the foot is also extremely fragile at certain points and angles. (England football fans may remember how their hopes in the 2006 World Cup hinged on the fourth metatarsal in Wayne Rooney's right foot.) For this reason, shoes should ideally offer a measure of protection and support in their uppers as well as their soles.

Shoes therefore have to fulfil various requirements. These requirements are exacting and often in opposition to one another, so shoe manufacture has historically been a very complex and skilled business. Shoes have to endure great forces and yet also protect a sensitive and vulnerable part of the body. They therefore have to be strong and hardwearing, at the same time as being soft and flexible. Additionally, they have to be waterproof. Gay reminds us that shoes protect us against the elements, and Richard Weekes wrote to his brother in October 1801 to suggest that he 'wear a flannell waistcoat. gett a pair of Buck boots. directly and wear them. for the wet weather is coming on' (Ford, 1987: 53). For this reason, shoes have historically been manufactured from leather. With the exception of wooden clogs, all of the examples examined here were leather shoes. Even fine silk brocade shoes for indoor wear were based upon leather, with a layer of fabric on top (see Figure 3.2).

Figure 3.2 Slip-on men's shoe, 1700.

Leather is strong, durable, flexible, breathable and waterproof. Before the vulcanisation of rubber in the 1840s, and the later invention of petrochemical plastics, any material article that required these properties was typically made from it. William Nisbet noted that the 'materials of which the shoe is formed' are fundamental to its design:

> The substance, along with softness and pliancy, should possess the particular quality of excluding moisture. Leather is generally preferred, and by preparing it with a composition of oil, wax and turpentine, till the leather is fully saturated, it becomes impervious to the access of the wet of any kind. Thus by a shoe ... made of a soft, pliable material, rendered impervious to moisture, an easy motion of the whole foot will be permitted. (1801: 32)

Leather has these properties because of its origins in skin. Leather is essentially a by-product of the meat industry and shoe leather tended to be made from cowhide (Riello, 2007). After butchering, the flesh and hair are removed and the leather is soaked, dried and stretched. The tanning process alters the protein structure in the leather, to make it more durable and retard putrefaction. It remains a changing organic material, however, and needs to be 'fed' with polish if it is going to retain its flexibility, impermeability and longevity, not to mention its shiny appearance. Eighteenth-century household manuals abounded with recipes for bootblack, and servants spent much of their time polishing shoes: one gentleman lamented that his refused to do it anymore until they got a pay rise, 'wh. measure we were obliged to come into' (Ford, 1987: 218). Given the expense of shoes in this period, it was essential that they were maintained so as to last as long as possible. Because they were made from skin, shoes – and other leather articles like breeches and waistcoats – became a kind of second skin to the wearer, raising the question of where the boundaries of the body begin and end (Festa, 2005: 48). Moulding to the body and complementing the function of the wearer's own skin, the wearing of shoes was fundamentally an embodied experience.

A further characteristic of the wearer's skin that impacts on the shoe is its tendency to sweat. The combination of moisture, acid and heat darkens the leather, so sweat marks are visible on shoes in museum collections. This provides a lasting physical trace of their wearer and potentially biological material: there is a large forensic literature on how to obtain biological traces from clothing, although this decreases with the age of the object (Sterzik *et al.*, 2018). Alison Fairhurst notes that sweat also damaged the shoe, causing leather to curl at the edges and the glue to degrade (2018: 34). Georgians believed that sweat had a corrosive effect on skin – which of course includes leather – but they were more concerned about its effect on the body than the shoe. A 1797 treatise on healthy clothing noted that 'there is not a greater and more important emunctory [that is, an organ with an excreting function] in the whole human system than the feet' and that 'free perspiration from the feet' was essential (Anon., 1797: 15, 17).

Eighteenth-century medicine was still informed by the ancient humoral understanding of the body, which conceived of a fluid economy that needed to be regulated by purging in order to stay healthy. A chiropody treatise of 1785 blamed corns on 'obstructed perspiration' – rather than what we would today identify as a protective layer of hard skin formed in response to the rubbing of the shoe – since trapped sweat becomes 'so acrid and corrosive as to occasion the most painful inflammations' (Low, 1785: 31, 29). As Kevin Siena notes, blockages that caused fluids to stagnate 'provided common explanations for early modern diseases' (2019: 21). Despite the sweat and smell of feet, another writer cautioned against bathing them too frequently, since 'it is apt to attract a greater flow of humours to the spot, and thus increase, perhaps bring on, a morbid perspiration' (Anon., 1818: 208).

For this reason, much medical writing on feet focused on socks, not so much for their ability to prevent blisters, but for the breathability and dryness of their material. Cotton socks, oddly, were universally condemned for their tendency to absorb sweat, 'thus confining the feet in a bath of cold perspirable matter' (Anon., 1818: 214). Furthermore, 'cotton saturated with the sweat of the feet (and cotton can contain more than linen), soon rots'. Instead, wool was recommended. Podiatric writers lauded wool for its ability to prevent 'humidity and smell' (Anon., 1797: 16, 18). Soldiers who had to march long distances were issued with woollen socks, and the many treatises on foot health that appeared during the First World War continued to recommend them (Webb-Johnson, 1916: 28–9). This suggests that a concern with healthy perspiration outlived the humoral body, as we can see in this treatise of 1847:

> The pedestrian well knows the difference on a long day's walk, between a cotton or linen stocking and one of wool; he knows that the former soon becomes hard, damp and chilly, with the moisture of the foot, whereas the latter enables him to bear fatigue, defends the foot from the friction of the shoe, secures it from blisters, and in every way ministers to his comfort. (Hall, 1847: 129)

Note how the intrepid pedestrian who could endure a 'long day's walk' was conceived of in the masculine: podiatric writers tended to adopt a masculine universal unless specifically talking about women, assuming that only men would need to wear shoes for a utilitarian purpose.

As well as being strong, flexible and sweaty, feet are also delicate. Whereas walking barefoot hardens the sole, this does not happen when the foot is shod. Shoes therefore create a self-fulfilling prophecy: wearing shoes makes the foot soft and delicate, which in turn means that shoes have to be worn to protect this vulnerable extremity. Writers at the time noted that 'feet are peculiarly exposed to injury from the delicacy of the skin' (Hall, 1847: 103). In particular, this delicacy was described in terms of the nerves. Nisbet noted that feet, like the hands, 'are endowed with much sensibility, by the large share of nerves they visibly possess. In covering them, therefore, particular regard should be had that no interruption take place to these purposes of nature'. Shoes should therefore possess 'pliancy' and allow the wearer to feel what they are coming into contact with (1801: 31). This abundance of nerves also explained the pain caused by ill-fitting footwear and the complaints that resulted from them. Corns led to the 'desiccation of the nervous *fibrialle* of the skin; and the pain they communicate is like that which we experience in walking with gravel or small stones in our shoes' (Low, 1785: 34).

As we have seen, this emphasis on the nervous body coexisted with an older vision of the body, which excreted and rotted. This is important for the history of gender, since the supposed decline of the humoral body is often central to accounts of how gender roles diverged over the course of the eighteenth century. The embodied history of shoes shows how multiple visions of the body existed alongside one another in the eighteenth century, and that these had a practical and physical dimension as well as a theoretical medical one. This approach therefore offers a critical perspective on some of our key narratives of gender change in this period.

## The impact of shoes on the body

Shoes are unique among garments in that they support the whole body. As well as affecting the feet and the legs, their role in absorbing shock, bearing weight and enabling mobility impact upon body parts higher up such as the hips, the spine, the shoulders and the neck. Contemporary medical writings emphasised that ill-fitting footwear, and the complaints they caused, were a factor in the body's general health. As Durlacher explained, 'these local complaints, when neglected, injure the general system by preventing the body from obtaining that natural and indispensable exercise, so conducive to health'. He therefore urged that patients seek the 'proper attention' of a professional chiropodist, rather than cutting their feet with 'razors, knives and other unwieldy instruments' (1850: x).

Choice of footwear affects the body's entire posture and gait. A 1792 translation of the German Bernhard Faust's *Catechism on Health* by the Scottish physician James Gregory emphasised the importance of the foot's natural structure for standing and walking:

> Q. 108. What is the form of the human foot?
>
> A. At the toes it is broad, the heel small, and the inside of the foot is longer than the outside.
>
> Q. 109. Why does it take this form?
>
> A. That a man may walk and stand with ease and firmness, and move his body freely.

The writer was not just using the masculine universal here: he was specifically describing the way that patrician men were expected to stand and move in this period. The next question concerned the type of shoe that should facilitate this, and the answer was one that has 'the same form as the foot' (1797: 35). At the time of writing, this was a pointed remark, since shoes did *not* take the form of the foot, as we will see. Even half a century later, Durlacher bemoaned that choice of footwear was impairing people's mobility:

> Few adults possess that firmness of step and ease of walking which Nature intended, in consequence of the confined and compressed condition in which their feet have been placed, by the unyielding material and bad shape of their shoes; the consequence is, that the natural spring and muscular action of the foot are lost, and they are deprived of the assistance that would be rendered by the action of the toes in progression. (1850: 18–19)

Placing 'Nature' in opposition to fashion and the trappings of civilisation was a common trope in these writings. On the one hand, this was characteristic of the Enlightenment; on the other, it expressed anxieties about modernity itself.

Studying texts like these and shoes themselves helps us to understand how people walked in the past. McNeil and Riello argue that attitudes and practices around walking changed over the eighteenth century. The early eighteenth-century city was not easy to move around and there are few references to urban walking (2005: 178). Patrician men's shoes from this period are either for indoor wear (see Figure 3.2) or for riding: stiff, high-heeled boots were ideal for the stirrups but unwieldy for walking (McCormack, 2017). Walking was therefore for plebeians, whereas Gay notes that those who could afford it travelled by horse, carriage or sedan chair (1716: 28–9). Changes to the urban environment over the course of the century, however, made walking a more viable and pleasurable pursuit. The parks, promenades, squares and pavements of the urban renaissance facilitated urban walking. Diaries from the second half of the eighteenth century by the likes of John Wilkes (Eagles, 2014) and James Boswell (Pottle, 1950) record how often they travelled around the metropolis on foot. From the later eighteenth century, men's footwear became more suitable for perambulation. Heels lowered, soles were more flexible, and the leather was thinner and more supple (see Figure 3.3). As well as a different type of shoe, walking on hard pavements required a different type of walk: Durlacher noted that persons from the country noted that 'they suffer more from corns when in the town, owing probably to the flat surface of the pavement causing an equal degree of pressure, to which they had not previously been accustomed' (1850: 13).

Figure 3.3 Men's shoe, 1828.

Walking was not universally accessible, however. The increasing normativity of walking among late-Georgian men – facilitated by new styles of footwear such as the wellington boot – highlighted the many people in contemporary society who were not able to walk easily for reasons of disability, illness or age. As the chiropodist D. Low blithely noted:

> The blessing of being able to *walk* is seldom much regarded but by those to whom, from whatever cause, that blessing has been denied. By the most trifling accident to the feet ... we may be forced to forgo this noble exercise; and exercise which is of all others the most productive of pleasure to man, and of which the neglect cannot but prove essentially injurious to his bodily health, as well as to the animal spirits, which regulate all his functions. (1785: ix)

The writer evokes a noble and vigorous image of the masculine body. The bodily ideal of the late-Georgian man was tall, with shapely and strong legs, and of erect but easy posture. The 'accomplishments' of the polite man including dancing, riding and fencing – activities that required a strong but supple body (McCormack, 2011). If men's shoes were becoming more suitable for these muscular activities, women's shoes were going in the opposite direction. By the close of the eighteenth century, shoes for respectable women were light and flimsy, signalling their suitability for domestic roles. If, as Karen Harvey argues, citizenship was becoming 'embodied' in this period, then shoes serve only to highlight how citizenship was being assigned along gendered lines (2015: 821).

Low continued that the causes of foot complaints that impede walking were clear: 'the use, or rather abuse, of shoes' (1785: x). The rest of this chapter will therefore focus upon the ways in which contemporary writers critiqued the design of shoes, in terms of their negative impact upon the body. Much of this concern focused on children, since their growing bodies were particularly susceptible to becoming malformed by inappropriate footwear. Philippe Ariès (1962) famously argued that, over the course of the early modern period, children ceased to be regarded as little adults and childhood came to be seen as a special life stage. This particularly applied to their dress: writers since Locke emphasised that children should wear loose clothing, to 'Let Nature have scope to fashion the Body as she thinks best' (1693: 10). Faust argued that young children should be dressed in a loose frock and that their shoes should be formed to the shape of their feet. They should not wear heels, since they 'cause the back tendon to shrink and impede the free and easy motions of the body in walking and running'. He continued:

> When children are suffered to walk much, and are bare-footed, they acquire an easy and steady pace. Little children ought not to wear shoes before the eighteenth month; if they do, the soles must be thin and soft, that they may learn to walk easily and well. Boots ought not be worn by children. (1797: 37)

Figure 3.4 Children's pumps, c.1830.

Infants should therefore go barefoot, or wear shoes that were sufficiently soft that they would not malform their delicate growing feet (Struve, 1802; Underwood, 1805). Surviving examples of children's shoes largely bear out these principles. A box of children's shoes in the Museum of Leathercraft dating from the early nineteenth century are of fine manufacture, indicating their elite origins (see Figure 3.4). The leather is notably soft, with supple soles and soft fabric linings. Although the lefts and rights were made the same, the soft leather easily stretched to the shape of the foot. In terms of style, they are strikingly similar to women's shoes of the time. As with petticoats, girls never left them, whereas the transition to masculine youth was often marked by the ceremonial presentation of a first pair of boots (Semmelhack, 2017: 95).

Footwear writers had several objections to contemporary footwear, in terms of the injurious effect it had on the body. Often it simply did not fit. Few could afford bespoke footwear and those who could not had to make do. Margo Demello notes that, for much of European history, 'most people were accustomed to wearing shoes that did not really fit their feet' (2007: 283). In the military, shoes for privates were produced in bulk in a range of sizes: this was the origin of standard sizing, and thence the mass ready-to-wear market, where the consumer had no contact with the producer (Riello, 2006: 212). Prior to this, however, if one wanted shoes to fit well then they had to be made to measure. J. Sparkes Hall bemoaned that shoemakers use 'some old misshapen pieces of wood, that perhaps did service to their fathers and grandfathers' instead of using proper lasts. He urged that everyone 'who wishes to be comfortably fitted, should have a pair of lasts made expressly for his own use' – something that would have been accessible only to the wealthy (1847: 108, 104). Easy mobility in shoes was therefore the preserve of those who could afford footwear that fitted, suggesting that different classes moved differently.

We can get an insight into the bespoke relationship in the correspondence of Hampton Weekes, a surgeon at St Thomas's Hospital. His correspondence with his family in Sussex reveals an intense interest in dressing well and making a good appearance in London society. In October 1801 he was particularly concerned with acquiring a good pair of boots. He repeatedly asked his father to arrange for the local shoemaker, John Randell, to make him a pair of 'buck boots' and, not being there in person, specified them at great length in his letters: 'If you were to desire him to make me a pair, stiff in the Leg & pretty high up, long in ye. foot with seams on each side of the Leg instead of behind'. A subsequent letter included a sketch of the style he desired: his ability to describe what he wanted in visual and anatomical terms possibly owed something to his occupation. He continued, 'Now for buck boots, crimping at the instep is quite out of fashion, neither do they have any tongues at the instep quite plain, & stiff Legd, tell Randles to make them round toed & rather long in the Foot than my last Shoes for they were too short'. A week later he urges, 'be pleased to send them soon, for I have walked to day almost upon my Toes it being so very dirty'. Alas, his father replied on 18 November: 'Randles has declind making your buck boots says he dont know how therefore wish you to get a strong pair in London tell them they must be stout and the Soal good' (Ford, 1987: 55, 61, 74, 77). Getting shoes in the size, style and fit that you wanted was therefore a lengthy and complex business, involving detailed knowledge of the product and its vocabulary, and a two-way relationship with the producer.

As well as being the wrong size, footwear writers complained that shoes were the wrong shape. Virtually all shoes produced in the seventeenth and eighteenth centuries were straight lasted. Shoe historians are undecided about the reason for this: Swann suggests that the manufacturing process for heeled shoes lent itself to straight lasts with squared toes, and that this continued until shoes with lower heels became fashionable at the end of the eighteenth century (1986: 32). Others argue that they were simply quicker to produce (Wilson, 1969: 186), or were a conscious fashion choice

(Anderson, 2017: 178). Either way, straight lasting exercised medical writers on feet and footwear throughout the eighteenth century and beyond. Several treatises included images of a human foot superimposed on a straight lasted sole, protruding beyond its edges in order to demonstrate the lack of fit (Gregory, 1797: plate 2). Shoes should have 'the true shape of the foot, which at the toes is broad, the heel small, and the length of the inside is greater than the outside. They should be made from two lasts, as the shape of the feet indicates.' Only by wearing these 'natural shaped shoes' would foot complaints such as corns be cured (Anon., 1797: 19–20). In the meantime, most people continued to wear straights, and soldiers were ordered to swap their shoes daily to prevent them wearing unevenly, so they would last longer (Cuthbertson, 1768: 135). This was contrary to the medical advice, which urged people never to do this (Nisbet, 1801: 32). After about 1790, shoes were increasingly lasted to the right and left feet, but this did not necessarily mean that they fitted better. In this period, it was fashionable for men and women alike to have the appearance of small feet, so shoes were commonly worn too small. As we have seen, this is visible in stretching and damage in shoes in museum collections. This was accompanied by a shift from wide to pointed toes. 'Square toes' became an insult to suggest that somebody was old-fashioned (Anon., 1818: 96).

The fashion for tight, short, pointed shoes was blamed for a wide range of foot complaints in the early nineteenth century, including corns, calluses, blisters and bunions. Samuel Cooper noted that corns 'are usually owing to wearing tight shoes, and consequently women and genteel persons are more frequently afflicted than the lower classes' (1815: 145). Bunions or 'onions' were so called because of the spherical swelling on the joint of the great toe. They were blamed on 'the wearing of shoes too short, and with a narrow sole, so that the feet are subjected to an undue degree of pressure' (Durlacher, 1850: 65). In modern terms, hallux valgus is caused by a misalignment of the first metatarsal and the proximal phalanx, by forcing the big toe inwards (Trujillo-Menderos *et al.*, 2014: 590). Paleopathologists have reported high prevalences of hallux valgus in pre-modern populations who wore pointed, high-heeled footwear, and that it is also an outcome of female footwear today (Mafart, 2007: 166–70).

Footwear in the eighteenth and early nineteenth centuries came in for so much criticism that writers repeatedly evoked the value of going barefoot. As well as being recommended for children, walking barefoot was lauded for its naturalness, in contrast with the unnaturalness of wearing restrictive footwear. Some writings take an ethnographic turn at this point, lauding the noble savage 'who never wear[s] shoes', who has much greater mobility and can use their toes to perform 'delicate operations' (Anon. 1797: 18–19). These sources exhibit a tension between admiring this ability and curiosity at the different bodies of other races. Edward Swaysland suggested that the 'Hindoo shoemaker' does not himself wear shoes, so he can use his feet as 'auxiliary hands' to assist his labours (1905: 14). As one chiropodist argued:

> Without shoes, the most delicate feet, far from being injured by fatigue, would be more and more hardened and invigorated by it; and for the truth of this remark, let us turn our eyes to various countries yet uncivilised, in which the *luxury* of wearing a SHOE is still unknown, and in which is likewise still unknown the *pain* which results from a CORN.

Here we see not just a critique of shoes but of modern civilisation in general, where the 'tyrant FASHION' requires Britons to wear shoes that are uncomfortable and emasculating (Low, 1785: xi). Arguably, this particularly applies to men, since Christopher Forth argues that modern masculinity revolves around a fundamental tension: as men become 'civilised' they become detached from the conditions of struggle that constitute authentically 'masculine' habits and practices (2008: 4–5). Luxury was often accused of corrupting the body politic in the eighteenth century by rendering men weak and effeminate, and sapping their native qualities of independence and public spirit (Carter, 1997). Shoes help us to understand how this process could be seen as directly corrupting the *physical* body, by impairing men's mobility, hardness and physical health.

Shoes therefore give us a fundamental insight into gender and the ways in which it was embodied in the Georgian period. Bodies impacted on footwear, providing a lasting record of that body that is unsurpassed by any other physical source, bar human remains themselves. And as we have seen, footwear impacted on bodies, affecting their posture and mobility, and causing a range of ailments. Writings from the time reveal an intense interest in the close relationship between shoes and bodies. Whereas some of this writing is blandly practical, it is also evident that there were important political agendas in the background: to create chiropody as a respectable medical profession; to justify the roles of the sexes and their relative position in society; and to grapple with the contradictions of consumerism and Western modernity. Shoes therefore supported not only the physical body, but a whole host of contemporary ideologies.

## Acknowledgements

I would like to thank museum curators for giving me access to their collections, in particular Rebecca Shawcross at Northampton Museum and Elizabeth Semmelhack at the Bata Shoe Museum, Toronto. I am grateful for feedback on this chapter from Tim Reinke-Williams and the volume editors, and also from audiences in Birmingham, Edinburgh and Liverpool.

## Notes

1 A total of seventy-six items of footwear (singles and pairs) have been consulted from the Bata Shoe Museum (Toronto), The Museum of Leathercraft (Northampton), the UK's national shoe collection (Northampton Museum and Art Gallery) and the National Army Museum (store at Stevenage).
2 Until recently, physicians in Britain who specialised in feet were known as chiropodists. The term podiatrist is more commonly used today, which is more in line with international usage.

## References

Anderson, V. (2017). 'Old shoes in a new perspective – fashioning archaeology'. *Fashion Practice*, 9(2): 168–82.

Anon. (1797). *On Clothing* (Manchester).

Anon. (1818). *The Art of Preserving the Feet; Or, Practical Instructions for the Prevention and Cure of Corns, Bunnions, Callosities, Chilblains, &c.* (London).

Ariès, P. (1962). *Centuries of Childhood: A Social History of Family Life*, trans. Baldick, R. (New York: Vintage).

Carter, P. (1997). 'An "effeminate" or "efficient" nation? Masculinity and eighteenth-century social documentary', *Textual Practice*, 11(3): 429–44.

Cooper, S. (1815). *Practice of Surgery: Being an Elementary Work for Students and a Concise Book of Reference for Practitioners* (Hanover).

Cuthbertson, B. (1768). *A System for the Complete Interior Management and Economy of a Battalion of Infantry* (Dublin).

Demello, M. (2009). *Feet and Footwear: A Cultural Encyclopedia* (Oxford: Greenwood).

Duden, B. (2013). 'Fluxes and stagnations: a physician's perception and treatment of humours in Baroque ladies', in P. Horden and E. Hsu (eds), *The Body in Balance: Humoral Medicine in Practice* (New York: Berghann), pp. 53–68.

Durlacher, L. (1850). *A Concise Treatise on Corns, Bunions and the Disorders of the Nails* (London).

Eagles, R. (ed.) (2014). *The Diaries of John Wilkes, 1770–1797* (Oxford: Boydell and Brewer).

Fairhurst, A. (2019). 'Eighteenth-century women's shoes: a valuable historical resource', *Costume*, 53(1): 20–42.

Fernandes, P. J., Mongle, C. S. and Leaky, L. (2018). 'Evolution and function of the hominin forefoot', *Proceedings of the National Academy of Sciences of the United States of America*, 115(35): 8746–51.

Festa, L. (2005). 'Personal effects: wigs and possessive individualism in the long eighteenth century', *Eighteenth-Century Life*, 29(2): 47–90.
Ford, J. (ed.) (1987). *A Medical Student at St Thomas's Hospital, 1801–1802: The Weekes Family Letters* (London: Wellcome).
Forth, C. (2008). *Masculinity in the Modern West: Gender, Civilization and the Body* (Basingstoke: Palgrave).
Gay, J. (1716). *Trivia: Or the Art of Walking the Streets of London* (London).
Gregory, J. trans. (1797). *The Catechism of Health: Selected and Translated from the German of Dr Faust* (Edinburgh).
Hall, J. S. (1847). *The Book of the Feet: A History of Boots and Shoes...* (New York).
Harvey, K. (2015). 'Men of parts: masculine embodiment and the male leg in eighteenth-century England', *Journal of British Studies*, 54(4): 797–821.
Houlbrook, C. (2013). 'Ritual, recycling and recontextualisation: putting the concealed shoe into context', *Cambridge Archaeological Journal*, 23(1): 99–112.
Laqueur, T. (1990). *Making Sex: Bodies and Gender from the Greeks to Freud* (Cambridge Mass.: Harvard University Press).
Locke, J. (1693). *Some Thoughts Concerning Education* (London).
Low, D. (1785). *Chiropodologia, Or, A Scientific Enquiry into the Causes of Corns, Warts, Onions and other Painful or Offensive Cutaneous Excrescences* (London).
Mafart, B. (2007). 'Hallux valgus in a historical French population: paleopathological study of 605 first metatarsal bones', *Joint, Bone, Spine*, 74(2): 166–70.
Mays, S. A. (2005). 'Paleopathological study of hallux valgus', *American Journal of Physical Anthropology*, 126(2): 139–49.
McCormack, M. (2011). 'Dance and drill: polite accomplishments and military masculinities in Georgian Britain', *Cultural and Social History*, 8(3): 315–30.
McCormack, M. (2017). 'Boots, material culture and Georgian masculinities', *Social History*, 42(4): 461–79.
McNeil, P. and Riello, G. (2005). 'The art and science of walking: gender, space and the fashionable body in the long eighteenth century', *Fashion Theory*, 9(2): 175–204.
Nisbet, W. (1801). *A Practical Treatise on Diet, And on the Most Salutary and Agreeable Means of Supporting Lift and Health, by Ailment and Regimen* (London).
Pottle, F. (ed.) (1950). *Boswell's London Journal, 1762–1763* (New Haven: Yale University Press).
Richmond, V. (2013). *Clothing the Poor in Nineteenth-Century England* (Cambridge: Cambridge University Press).
Riello, G. (2006). *A Foot in the Past: Consumers, Producers and Footwear in the Long Eighteenth Century* (Oxford: Oxford University Press).
Riello, G. (2007). 'Nature, production and regulation in eighteenth-century Britain and France: the case of the leather industry', *Historical Research*, 81(211): 75–99.
Riello, G. and McNeil, P. (eds) (2006). *Shoes: A History from Sandals to Sneakers* (London: Berg).
Rublack, U. (2013). 'Matter in the material Renaissance', *Past and Present*, 219: 41–85.
Semmelhack, E. (2017). *Shoes: The Meaning of Style* (London: Reaktion).

Siena, K. (2019). *Rotten Bodies: Class and Contagion in Eighteenth-Century Britain* (New Haven: Yale University Press).

Sterzik, V., Hinderberger, P., Panzer, S. and Bohnert, M. (2018). 'Visualizing old biological traces on different materials without using chemicals', *International Journal of Legal Medicine*, 132(1): 35–41.

Struve, C. (1802). *A Familiar Treatise on the Education of Children, During the First Period of their Lives* (London).

Swann, J. (1986). *Shoes* (London: Batsford).

Swann, J. (1996). 'Shoes concealed in buildings', *Costume*, 30: 56–69.

Swaysland, E. (1905). *Boot and Shoe Design and Manufacture* (Northampton).

Trujillo-Menderos, A., Arnay-de-la-Rosa, M., González-Reimers, E. and Ordóñez. A. C. (2014). 'Hallux valgus among an 18th century population of the Canary Islands', *International Journal of Osteoarchaeology*, 24: 590–601.

Underwood, M. (1805). *A Treatise on the Diseases of Children* (London: Mathews), vol. 3.

Veres, M. (2005). 'Introduction to the analysis of archaeological footwear', *Australian Historical Archaeology*, 23: 89–96.

Vickery, A. (1993). 'Golden age to separate spheres? A review of the categories and chronology of English women's history', *The Historical Journal*, 36(2): 383–414.

Wahrman, D. (1994). *The Making of the Modern Self: Identity and Culture in Eighteenth-Century England* (New Haven: Yale University Press).

Webb-Johnson, C. (1916). *The Soldier's Manual of Foot Care and Foot Wear* (London: Dryden).

Wilson, E. (1969). *A History of Shoe Fashions* (London: Pitman).

# 4

# 'The Corporation of Corpse-stealers': archaeological and historical evidence of bodysnatching in early eighteenth-century London

*Robert Hartle*

The subject of bodysnatching – specifically, the trade in corpses stolen for anatomical dissection – has long interested historians (Abbott, 2006; Bailey, 1896; Bailey, 1991; Ball, 1928; Cole, 1964; Fido, 1988; Guttmacher, 1935; Lennox, 2016; MacPhail, 1914). Archaeologists have also studied the subject, bringing together material and documentary sources, with a focus on grave protection (physical measures to prevent disturbance) and osteological evidence of surgical training and dissection (Fowler and Powers, 2012; Kausmally, 2015; Mitchell, 2012; Mytum and Webb, 2018). Nevertheless, the extensive literature from both historians and archaeologists has, predominantly, examined the period when bodysnatchers became commonly called 'Resurrectionists' – between the Murder Act of 1752, which gave courts the power to provide anatomists the bodies of hanged murderers, and the Anatomy Act of 1832, which effectively ended the practice of bodysnatching by providing legal access to the unclaimed corpses from hospital, prison or workhouses. Bodysnatching in earlier periods has received comparatively little attention.

The prevailing historiographical representation of early British bodysnatchers holds that they were surgeon/anatomists themselves (or, more commonly, their pupils), having supplied their own material from at least the late sixteenth century by illegally acquiring cadavers at the gallows. In her seminal work, *Death, Dissection and the Destitute*, Ruth Richardson suggested churchyards raids were almost commonplace in London by the 1720s, citing a contemporary guide to the city, which satirically observed:

> the Corporation of Corpse-stealers, I am told, support themselves and Families very comfortably; and that no-one should be surpris'd at the Nature of such a Society, the late Resurrections in St. Saviours, St. Giles's and St. Pancras'

Church-yards, are memorable Instances of this laudable Profession. (Anon, 1725: 47–8; 1728 reprint cited in Richardson, 2001: 55)

However, it has long been thought impossible to place and date the inception of churchyard bodysnatching with any precision (Ball, 1928: 72; Richardson, 2001: 55–7), and few authors have attempted to characterise the early years of the practice with detail. Guttmacher made the seemingly unsupported claim that all early bodysnatching was done secretly and on a small scale (1935: 13), and Cole believed it engendered no significant public alarm or protest in England until the second half of the eighteenth century (1964: 11, 93). The transition of bodysnatching into a trade and the commodification of the corpse – with anatomists as consumers only, supplied by a new stratum of professional thieves (mostly sextons and gravediggers) – was, it is also argued, probably an uneven and piecemeal process, not fully complete before the mid-eighteenth century (Fido, 1988: 21; Guttmacher, 1935: 13; Moore, 2006: 86–7; Richardson, 2001: 55–7). Whilst some authors have cited a limited number of reported incidents of churchyard bodysnatching and a few examples of prosecutions in London between 1720 and 1750 (e.g., Linebaugh, 1975: 71; Moore, 2006: 71, 80, 87; Richardson, 2001: 54–5), others have perpetuated a misconception that there were no prosecutions for bodysnatching in the city until the late eighteenth century (Bailey, 1991: 21; Cole, 1964: 11).

Although the question of why sourcing cadavers from gallows transitioned to churchyard bodysnatching has long been confidently attributed to the convergence of problematic cadaver supply and increased demand in the early eighteenth century, other basic questions about the chronology, methods and beneficiaries of early bodysnatching are still not satisfactorily answered. That so little about this period is known is largely attributable to two factors. First, bodysnatchers were by necessity circumspect and disinclined to keep potentially self-incriminating records. Therefore, surviving written records mostly represent occasions when perpetrators were detected or caught. Second, available evidence is scattered, problematically fragmented, subjective or indirect, making it more challenging to work with in isolation. However, new evidence which emerged in 2015 has prompted the present wider interdisciplinary re-examination of corpse stealing during the first quarter of the eighteenth century. Archaeological excavations of the 'New Churchyard', Liverpool Street, London, by Museum of London Archaeology (MOLA) for Crossrail Ltd recovered physical evidence of early eighteenth-century grave protection. The site also had a history of bodysnatching: the corpse of a patient from St Bartholomew's Hospital had been stolen from the New Churchyard in 1717 to be dissected in Oxford. Contemporary records identified those involved, including gravedigger Joseph Bowen, who stole the corpse, and medical men behind the theft, led by a surgeon named John Kersey (Hartle, 2017).

Building on existing knowledge, this chapter will align the New Churchyard evidence with extensive new documentary research (particularly drawing on newspapers and apprenticeship, hospital, criminal and parish records). It will demonstrate that the prevailing historiographical representation of early British bodysnatching, particularly in London, requires considerable revision. This chapter will first discuss the New Churchyard evidence and consider the professional, social and legislative context of bodysnatching in early eighteenth-century London and Oxford. It will then discuss the earliest known cases in England and provide the first identification of a network of bodysnatchers – the so-called 'Corporation of Corpse-stealers' – demonstrating how they established a churchyard bodysnatching *modus operandi* in London which was a trade from the outset, and show that their exposure set judicial precedent and excited public outcry far earlier and wider than previously recognised. Last, this chapter will demonstrate how these early activities may have promulgated the practice and influenced later bodysnatching in London and beyond.

## The New Churchyard: archaeological evidence

Established in 1569 for municipal use, the non-parochial 'New Churchyard' (later 'Bedlam' or 'Bethlem') saw *c.*25,000 interments before closing in 1739. From 1700 it was predominantly used by the prisons of Ludgate and Poultry Compter, and the hospitals of Bethlem and St Bartholomew's. During the 2011–15 excavation, the historic theft of bodies was perhaps indicated by the discovery of eleven empty coffins, but this could not be stated with confidence due to widespread disturbance from intercut graves. However, one burial (Figure 4.1) provided compelling evidence for bodysnatching; not through the removal of a corpse from a grave, but instead through the protective measures designed to prevent this. The skeleton had been encased in sand that filled an undecorated wooden coffin, stone slabs had been placed on the coffin lid, and rubble was scattered in the grave fill. Had they attempted to steal the body, would-be bodysnatchers, needing to work quickly and quietly post-interment, would have found re-digging the grave laborious and the corpse effectively anchored into the coffin (and, by extension, the ground).

The earliest responses to bodysnatching would have included digging graves deeper and simple security measures such as guards, locking churchyard gates and raising walls. By the mid-eighteenth century, executed criminals also occasionally had their corpses buried with quicklime to make them

Figure 4.1 Burial [3999]/[4000], 0.5 m scale.

unfit for dissection (Bailey, 1991: 28). Anti-Resurrectionist measures recorded for the late eighteenth to early nineteenth century include close parallels to the New Churchyard burial: grave fills were compacted or had obstructions placed within them – such as rubble, branches or straw – and coffin lids were covered by stones (Hartle, 2017: 73–4; *Derby Mercury*, 25 March 1829, p. 4). Although scant, there is archaeological evidence of more sophisticated measures developed after the 1790s, including iron coffins, mortsafes and 'coffin collars' (Hartle, 2017: 69–75; Mytum and Webb, 2018).[1] The latter anchored the corpse to the coffin. However, the early date of New Churchyard burial appears archaeologically unprecedented.

Stratigraphy suggests a post-1700 date for the New Churchyard burial, when the site was becoming densely packed, and the closure of the ground provides a *terminus ante quem* of March 1739. The skeleton belonged to an adolescent aged *c.*16 years at time of death and of indeterminate sex. Osteological analysis showed a possible healed blunt force trauma injury on the skull and widespread tuberculosis (TB) – a possible cause of death (Hartle, 2017: 222–3). Unfortunately, the individual is unidentifiable because the New Churchyard had no burial register and the grave no breastplate or gravestone.

### Supply and demand: cadavers in early eighteenth-century London and Oxford

Founded in 1540, the Barber-Surgeons' Company still regulated surgery in the City of London (to a radius of seven miles) at the turn of the eighteenth century. London had no university or medical schools and, whilst physicians were typically university educated, surgeons trained under apprenticeship. For the surgical education of their members and apprentices, the Barber-Surgeons' Masters and Stewards of Anatomy also gave four lectures annually at their hall, where additional lectures could be conducted to broader audiences subject to permission and invitation (Young, 1890). However, the Barber-Surgeons' influence on education was waning and it was London's two public hospitals – St Bartholomew's and St Thomas's (Figure 4.2) – that offered the broadest experience for aspiring surgeons and physicians alike. Staff at both trained apprentices but the three surgeons of St Thomas's also took short-term paying pupils (limited to three each in 1703) (Lawrence, 1996: 117; Wilson, 1992). Additionally, increased demand began fostering a small but burgeoning market of supplementary private lectures outside the Surgeon's Hall. The first verifiable private lecturers to offer courses on human and comparative anatomy in London were: Bernard Connor (1666?–98), who lectured at Oxford in 1696 before repeating his course at St Martin-in-the-Fields, Westminster, in 1697 (*Post Man and Historical Account* [*PMHA*], 11–14 January 1697), p. 2); George Rolfe (born *c.*1680, *fl.*1728), who lectured with 'human subjects' at the Surgeon's Hall in 1701, before lecturing at his house in Chancery Lane, Holborn, in 1704–6 and

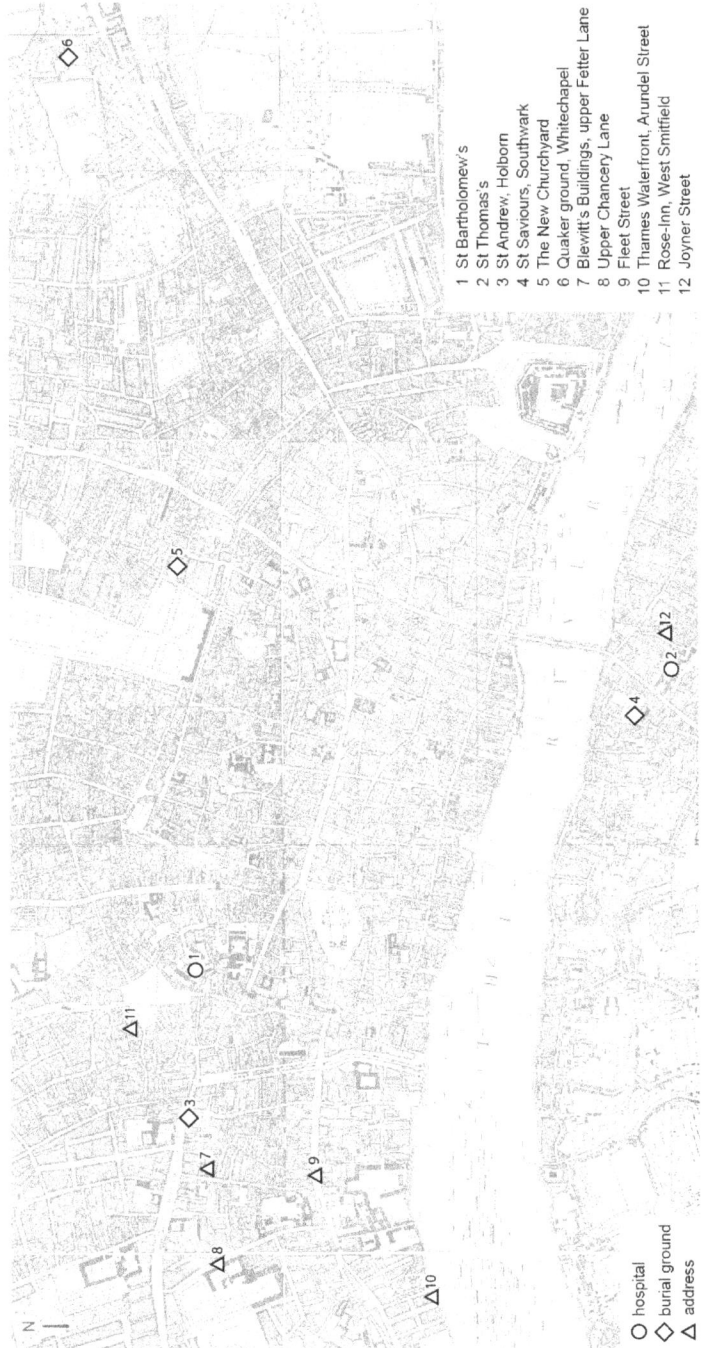

Figure 4.2 Key locations mentioned in this chapter, plotted on Rocque's map of London, 1746.

1713; and James Douglas (1675–1742), who lectured in 1706 at Fleet Street. Connor used animal vivisection and dissection and it is unknown if Rolfe used human remains outside the Surgeon's Hall, but Douglas used animals, preparations and 'fresh' human subjects if available (Douglas, 1707: 209–11; Peachey, 1924: 11–13).

The demand for human remains created by these activities meant problems with cadaver supply were endemic. Whilst occasional insights came from autopsy, this procedure was still not widely accepted, and was usually restricted to cause of death and subject to family permission and hospital regulation (Harley, 1994). For the purposes of dissection, the only universally available lawful source of cadavers was those willing to sell or bequeath their own bodies. Nevertheless, although condemned criminals and others are known to have sold their corpses in the early eighteenth century, such sales were extremely rare and financially motivated rather than altruistic. Bequests were almost unheard of.[2]

Instead, the principal supply was granted by Crown and legislature: the Barber-Surgeons were allowed the bodies of four criminals per annum executed at Tyburn and the Royal College of Physicians could also claim up to six from executions within London, Middlesex or Surrey. However, although dissection of these bodies outside the halls and jurisdiction of the Barber-Surgeons and Royal College was proscribed, this meagre provision nevertheless met intra-professional competition from as early as the late sixteenth century, from unauthorised anatomists who 'begged' or bribed executioners (South, 1886: 231–3). By the beginning of the eighteenth century, when this increasingly left officials with warrants empty handed at the gallows, supply problems were exacerbated by the increasing violence of the 'mob': friends, relatives or well-wishers who aimed to rescue and secure the remains of the executed for 'decent' burial (Linebaugh, 1975). Prevailing public antipathy is evident in this anonymously authored epigram, which illustrates the perceived repugnance and ignominy of dissection, as well as a mistrust of medical practitioners:

> *To the Physitions upon a Dissection,*
> Trouble not yourselves, ye Butchering Fools,
> Our Bodies want not your dissecting Tools,
> For he that takes your Drugs, and Poisnous Stuffs,
> I'll swear be Anatomiz'd enough.
> (*Diverting Post*, 23–30 June 1705, p. 9)

This unprecedented combination of professional and lay interference forced the Barber-Surgeons and Royal College to expend considerable resources asserting their corporate rights during the first decades of the eighteenth century. As a result, unofficial acquisitions became increasingly conspicuous. The Barber-Surgeons were particularly quick to issue formal complaints:

unauthorised anatomists risked £10 fines and rescuers were prosecuted (Linebaugh, 1975).

An almost identical situation prevailed in Oxford. The first Reader in Anatomy was founded at the university in 1624 and medical students were obliged to attend their lectures.[3] Despite the professors showing little inclination to conduct their anatomical duties in the early eighteenth century, practical instruction nevertheless underwent a short revival led by aspiring students and deputies (Robb-Smith and Sinclair, 1950: 10–11, 18–26). A Charter of Charles I (1636) allowed the Reader the bodies of anyone executed within twenty-one miles of the city following the spring Assizes. However, executions were rare and, as in London, official acquisitions became increasingly confrontational. In 1714, John Bellers (1654–1725) wrote: 'it is not easy for the students to get a body to dissect at Oxford, the mob being so mutinous to prevent their having one' (Robb-Smith and Sinclair, 1950: 12, 24).

### Early evidence of bodysnatching in England: finding other sources of cadavers

Events of 1700 to 1715 support the established assertion that early bodysnatching was conducted directly by the medical profession itself. Three incidents involving students, discussed below, give the earliest clear evidence of how cadavers acquired at the gallows of London and Oxford were beginning to be supplemented by other illicit methods in this period, including churchyard bodysnatching.[4]

One of these incidents involved William Stukeley (1687–1765), who studied medicine at the University of Cambridge (Matric. 1704, M.B. 1709) and attended Rolfe's London lectures in 1706. His memoirs recalled how, while home in Holbeach, Lincolnshire, in February 1708, he and a local Cambridge graduate had exhumed the corpse of a man who had committed suicide and been buried 'in the highway'. They then dissected it and displayed the skeleton. Although Stukeley noted how, 'The Country people were strangely alarm'd at this unusual Operation' (Commentary 1720, in Lukis, 1882: 43), he faced no apparent legal consequences.

Four years earlier there had been an attempt at bodysnatching from a churchyard in Oxford. On 11 January 1724, Oxford antiquarian Thomas Hearne (1678–1735) wrote in his diary of an incident which had occurred twenty years earlier:[5]

> a pretty young Woman being buried in St. Peter's Ch. Yard in the East, search was made in the night time for her body, but they mistook her Grave, & took up one Goody Beacham, an old Woman who had been Bed-maker of Edm. Hall [St. Edmund Hall]. This old Woman they had convey'd out of the Church

Yard but being some way or other disturbed as they were going along, thy drop'd her, and set her in her shrewd, bolt upright, just under Edm. Hall against the Wall, where (before day) in the Morning she, being seen, frighted some People, who knew nothing of the Matter. (Rannie, 1907: 156–7)

Hearne, who lived and was educated at St Edmund Hall (Vertue, 2004), is perhaps a firsthand witness, but his account appears corroborated by burial registers: the 'pretty young Woman' was probably Katherine Wallis, spinster, buried 14 January 1704, and 'Goody [Goodwife] Beacham' was Elizabeth Beacham, widow, the next person to be buried two days later (Burials of St. Peter-in-the-East).[6]

In London, only months earlier, the 'young men' of St Thomas's had been caught dissecting dead patients (Minute Books of the Grand Committee, 27 October 1703). No punishment was noted but apprentices and pupils were pointedly prohibited from dissecting patients again, whilst staff surgeons, who had been forbidden from 'dismembering' dead patients as early as 1670, required strict authorisation thereafter. Although a case of bodysnatching, there is no evidence the corpses were acquired post-burial. Exhumations, however, may not have been difficult. Although St Thomas's required all patient burials to be coffined by 1700, they buried paupers en masse in graves not fully backfilled between interments (Parsons, 1934: 104, 129, 135, 149, 186–7, 231). Evidence from recent archaeological excavation of circa late-seventeenth-century patient burials from St Thomas's did not demonstrate bodysnatching but did reveal both mass burial and surgical interventions, including medical waste (amputated limbs) and at least one example of post-mortem modification indicative of dissection (Miles, forthcoming).

### Identifying the 'Corporation of Corpse-stealers' and the emergence of churchyard bodysnatching in London

Surgeon John Kersey – the instigator of the theft of a St Bartholomew's patient from the New Churchyard in 1717 – has been almost entirely overlooked by history.[7] However, by identifying Kersey, this chapter reveals his role in early churchyard bodysnatching in London and, by extension, allows the first detailed examination of the early eighteenth-century 'Corporation of Corpse-stealers'. As this section suggests, evidence points not to St Bartholomew's but, instead, reveals a network of aspiring young medical men, including Kersey, who were educated at St Thomas's and pursued careers as private anatomy lecturers.

Born c.1687, Kersey was the son of publisher and lexicographer John Kersey (1657–1720).[8] His apprenticeship began on 1 June 1703 under the surgeon and embalmer Thomas Greenhill (*fl*.1698–1732 (Davidson, 2004)),[9] but transferred to St Thomas's surgeon Simon Rideout on 6 April 1709 (Register of apprentices bindings [RAB]: /002: 430; Register of freedom admissions [RFA]: 35; Court minute book [CMB]: 82).[10] Kersey would have assisted Rideout in all aspects of his hospital and private practice, and attended lectures at the Surgeon's Hall, but he also joined a small student fraternity, including William Cheselden (1688–1752) (Cope, 1953), who began his apprenticeship at St Thomas's in 1703 (the same year patient dissections by pupils were banned); and Stukeley, who, after his own body-snatching foray, supplemented his studies at Cambridge by becoming a pupil at St Thomas's between August 1709 and May 1710. Stukeley's memoirs recalled how the juniors of St Thomas's socialised with the wider medical community in coffee houses and taverns but also formed their own informal learned societies. Kersey was probably among a group of 'young Physicians & Surgeons' formed by Stukeley, who met weekly to lecture among themselves and occasionally 'dissected som' part or other' (Commentary 1720, in Lukis, 1882: 46).

By the end of 1710, Stukeley had left St Thomas's and London, and Cheselden had completed his apprenticeship. Stukeley ultimately found his niche as clergyman and antiquarian, but Cheselden quickly established his medical reputation by immediately embarking on two lucrative and prestigious ventures: private lectures at his home and the publication of his highly influential *Anatomy of the Human Body* (1713).[11] Cheselden's achievements are widely documented; however, the role of St Thomas's in fostering early entrepreneurial anatomy lecturing has hitherto not been fully recognised. Cheselden was only the first of a series of men educated at St Thomas's in the 1700s and 1710s to undertake such work. Kersey was the second and completed his apprenticeship on 3 June 1712.[12] Although Kersey's professional activities are not documented until 1717 (see below),[13] it seems probable he initially worked with Cheselden,[14] whose 1713 syllabus certainly indicates at least one unidentified partner (Cheselden, 1713: 270) (Figure 4.3).

Cheselden, Kersey and their peers would have had little or no access to cadavers while studying at St Thomas's. Although occasional cadavers may have been acquired via extra-mural employment,[15] ignoring recent hospital restrictions on patient dissection risked expulsion. However, establishing successful lecturing careers required marketable courses, for which a reliable provision of cadavers was advantageous, since the alternatives – drawings, models, casts and animals – were, by themselves, increasingly considered inadequate. It is known Cheselden initially used 'executed bodies' from Tyburn (Cheselden, 1713), as many had done before him, but this arrangement became unviable in 1714. Cheselden was reprimanded that year by the Barber-Surgeons for frequently taking Tyburn bodies without authorisation

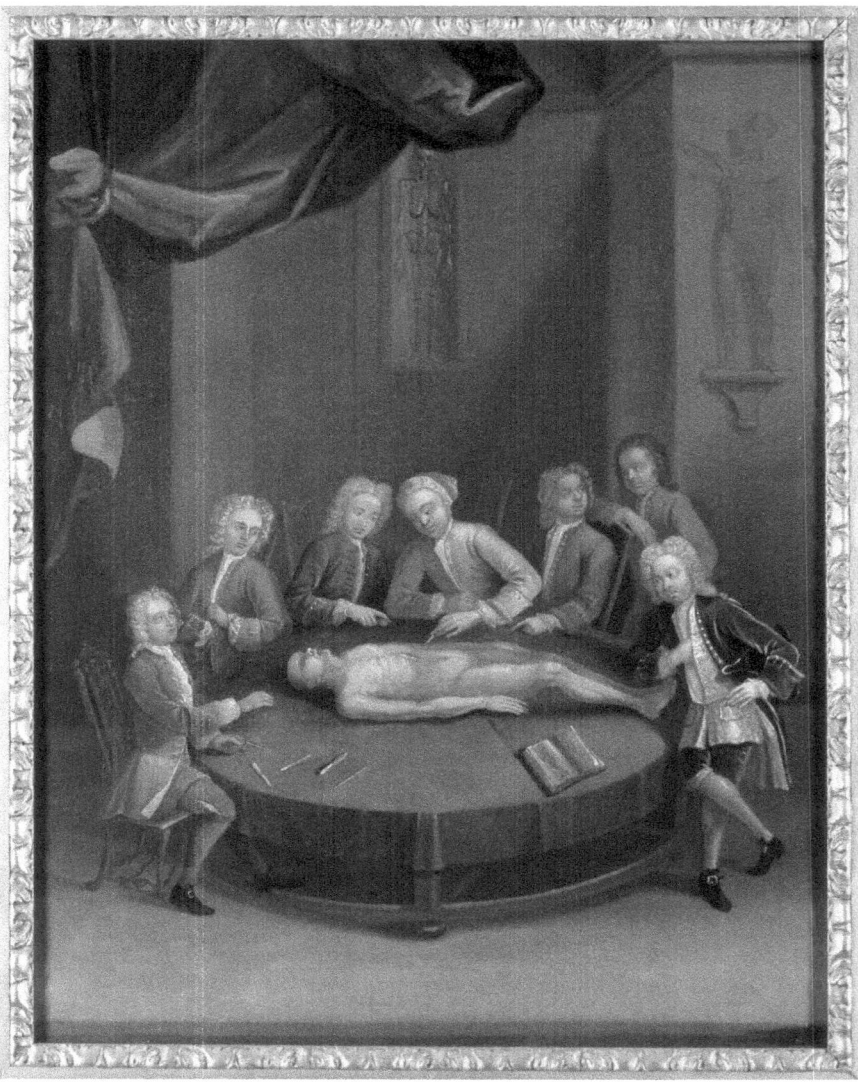

Figure 4.3 William Cheselden giving an anatomical demonstration to six spectators in the anatomy-theatre of the Barber-Surgeons' Company, London. Oil painting, c.1730/1740.

and for competing with official lectures at the Surgeons' Hall. He responded by promising to cease his private lectures, but would, in later life, bitterly condemn the restrictions placed on private dissection by the Barber-Surgeons, which he considered deliberately stifled the education and advancement of young surgeons (Le Dran, 1749: 472). Cheselden's reprimand is widely cited in histories of bodysnatching but was more significant than has been appreciated. Members of the Barber-Surgeons, such as Cheselden and Kersey, were subject to the full scrutiny and jurisdiction of the Company. For them the 1714 reprimand appears to have been a watershed. Thereafter the students and alumni of St Thomas's sought what they were denied – professional freedom and cadavers – and found new routes to both in London and Oxford.

There appears to be no further evidence of churchyard bodysnatching in Oxford until 1749 (*Kentish Weekly Post or Canterbury Journal* [*KWPCJ*], 22–25 March 1749, p. 2) and the practice probably faltered in the city (Boston and Webb, 2012).[16] Instead, the university became reliant on visiting lecturers with cadavers sourced from London. In 1710, anatomist D. Lavater of Zurich was forced to lecture on osteology at the Ashmolean Museum because he had no corpse to dissect, having failed to 'obtain' one from London (Robb-Smith and Sinclair, 1950: 24). With his private lecturing in London hindered and his application for two St Thomas's staff positions in 1714–15 unsuccessful, it is conceivable Cheselden sought work in Oxford, possibly assisted by Kersey. Cheselden was perhaps the unidentified London surgeon who Thomas Hearne records conducted the dissection of 'a woman' at the Clarendon Building, Oxford, on 15 May 1715 (Rannie, 1901: 59).[17] Cope suggests that others supplied Cheselden with Tyburn corpses that season, but that the supply was again interrupted: Cheselden's former master, James Ferne (d.1741, St Thomas's surgeon, 1703–41), was himself reprimanded by the Barber-Surgeons' on 21 April 1715 for taking cadavers out of the Surgeon's Hall without authorisation (Cope, 1953: 10).

The earliest recorded cases of bodysnatching outside of the gallows in England (above) suggest occasional, opportunistic or ad hoc forays. However, by 1716, with the dead of St Thomas's protected and the monopoly on supply from execution sites now more effectively enforced, the men of St Thomas's progressed to what must have seemed the easiest, most circumspect and sustainable method of cadaver procurement: theft from burial grounds by proxy. By this time, Flemish anatomist Andreas Vesalius (1514–64) had probably inspired generations of British anatomists to adopt a direct approach to bodysnatching. Vesalius had taken bodies from the gallows but also, by his own admission, kept 'bodies taken from graves' in his bedroom, and he had encouraged students to follow his example (O'Malley, 1964: 114, 222). Kersey clearly admired Vesalius, demonstrating his vocation by baptising his first son 'John Vesalius Kersey' (Baptisms of St Andrew, Holborn, 14 December 1718).[18] However, Kersey and his peers may have also looked to anatomists in seventeenth-century Paris, who had set a precedent for delegating the theft itself to corruptible gravediggers (Guerrini, 2015: 22–3; Harding, 2002: 115–16).

The three earliest recorded cases of churchyard bodysnatching in London suggest the practice emerged in the city during the 1710s. Exploring these cases chronologically allows, for the first time, a detailed account of its early *modus operandi*. Most (if not all) of these thefts were undertaken by men linked with St Thomas's and include the 1717 New Churchyard incident.

An incident in 1716 represents the first known example of churchyard bodysnatching in London. It demonstrates the early public and legal response and shows how the practice was a trade in London from inception, with both consumers and suppliers. On 11 November 1716, a man learned that his wife's corpse had been exhumed the night after its burial in the Quaker ground, Whitechapel (see Figure 4.2) and 'carry'd to a Hospital in Southwark'. The burial register shows the corpse belonged to Sarah Shepherd (formerly Stiver, née Hoe) who died of 'consumption' (TB) aged 41 on 9 November (Library of the Religious Society of Friends [LRSF], London, Quarterly Meeting of London and Middlesex [QMLM]: Burials 1699–1723, Devonshire House, fol.566). Mr Shepherd organised a search of the hospital but, despite obtaining a warrant, was denied full access by a 'person of authority'.[19] When the corpse was returned to Mr Shephard in a coffin on 16 November it had been dissected: 'us'd after a barbarous Manner', the *Weekly Packet* reported (17–24 November 1716, p. 3).

A general ignorance of bodysnatching appears to have still been prevalent in London – the *Stamford Mercury* commented that the Quaker community was 'much surpriz'd at such a barbarous and inhuman Treatment' (22 November 1716, p. 7). The Devonshire Meeting, who oversaw the Whitechapel ground, responded by authorising £10 for a prosecution to 'prevent such Practices for the future'. Their gravedigger, Michael Holmes, was swiftly dismissed after his son, John, was linked to the crime, committed to Newgate and examined before the Lord Mayor.[20] However, John Holmes was discharged and his employer, 'one Griffiths', was arrested. Described as a 'Savage Creature' who 'made it his Business to treat with Sextons and Grave-Diggers, to purchase dead bodies', Griffiths had paid Holmes and an unidentified coachman 10s and 6s, respectively (*Stamford Mercury*, 29 November 1716, pp. 6–7).[21]

Unfortunately, no more can be said about 'Griffiths' (including his first name) or who he supplied. Although the *Weekly Packet* noted he was to be tried at the next session of the Old Bailey (17–24 November 1716, p. 3), records for his prosecution – perhaps the first of its kind in London – do not seem to survive. Moreover, no surgeons appear to have been named or prosecuted for their involvement, so their identity and that of the 'Hospital in Southwark' cannot be proved. However, the only Southwark hospitals at that time were St Thomas's and Lock Hospital (located on the outskirts of Southwark). The incident was not noted in its official records but St

Thomas's, with its history of teaching and surgical operations, would seem far more likely to have sourced a cadaver for anatomical study than the latter, a smaller institution which treated venereal disease. The involvement of Cheselden could be suggested but is equally unprovable. Cheselden is known to have restarted his lectures in London during that winter (1716/17).[22] Although the location of these lectures was not recorded, the institutional status of St Thomas's could have offered him a venue sheltered from the Barber-Surgeons.[23]

The second case demonstrates a clear connection with St Thomas's, a continuity of the *modus operandi* and the early establishment of legal precedent. It involved a man called William Childers, who died of 'consumption' in St Bartholomew's and was buried in the New Churchyard on 10 or 11 April 1717. Gravedigger Joseph Bowen exhumed his corpse at 11 pm, placed it in a sack, and bent it double into a hamper. It was delivered to the Rose Inn, West Smithfield (see Figure 4.2), and sold to John Kersey and two 'young surgeons' for one guinea. However, the landlady became suspicious and surreptitiously searched the hamper after one man said it contained wine, while another claimed it held Westphalia hams. The men were detained under suspicion of murder but released after incriminating Bowen, explaining that Childers had died a natural death and was to be anatomised in Oxford (*Weekly Journal or British Gazetteer* [*WJBG*], 20 April 1717, p. 5; *Stamford Mercury*, 25 April 1717, p. 8; *Evening Post*, 4–7 May 1717, p. 3; *Weekly Packet*, 4–11 May 1717, p. 3; *Weekly Journal or Saturday's Post* [*WJSP*], 1 June 1717, p. 3).

Childers was one of 207 St Bartholomew's patients who died between March 1717 and March 1718 (Butler, 1740: 27) but his identity is unclear because no record exists of his burial (or reburial).[24] It is conceivable the skeleton discovered in 2015 – an adolescent *c.*16 years old with widespread TB, of indeterminate sex – was Childers, had he married very young and the burial was his reinterment.[25] However, given the New Churchyard's association with St Bartholomew's and the prevalence of TB victims among the hospital's dead,[26] a more plausible scenario (albeit equally unprovable) is that the skeleton belonged to another St Bartholomew's patient buried after Childers. Perhaps remembering the theft of April 1717 and being too poor to arrange burial elsewhere, friends or family could have brought basic materials to the funeral to protect the body.

One of the 'young surgeons' with Kersey was probably his new apprentice,[27] but the other is identified within a letter to Thomas Hearne from John Woodward (1665–1728), dated 30 March 1717. Woodward enquired: 'There went thither [London to Oxford] lately young Surgeons, Mr Kersey and Mr Brathwaite, to teach a course of Anatomy. How have they acquitted themselves?' (Rannie, 1902: 35). Thomas Brathwaite (or Braithwaite) was just 21 years old and was related to prominent families from Westmorland, Hampshire and Kent (Betham, 1805: 496–7; Lane-Poole, 2004).[28] Still an apprentice, his master was not Kersey but St Thomas's surgeon William Dickinson.[29] The wording of Woodward's question could suggest that if Kersey had previously lectured at Oxford, then this was the first course read by him, with Brathwaite, his junior, presumably acting as demonstrator.[30]

How many corpses Kersey's group stole in 1717 is unclear, but more than one was probably required. Despite courses being conducted by necessity in the colder seasons, without modern refrigeration, they would have been usable for only short periods. When the group were arrested in mid-April, they were probably completing a course started in early to mid-March. Moreover, although their syllabus does not survive, courses commonly comprised lectures over many weeks and were generally repeated over the autumn–spring anatomy season (September to May).[31] Circumstantial evidence could indicate the group used multiple corpses and churchyards. First, Thomas Abraham, gravedigger of Kersey's own parish (St Andrew, Holborn), was 'detected of several misdemeanours' in mid-April. Accused of 'robbing the dead and other enormities [...] most sacrilegiously practised', he was dismissed on 23 April (Vestry minute books). Bodysnatching was not explicitly recorded, and no details were revealed publicly; however, the timing and link to Holborn seem an unlikely coincidence and suggests Abraham could have been another employee of Kersey. Second, a bag containing a 'murder'd child' and 'heads of two others' was found on the Thames waterfront near Arundel Street on 12 April (*Evening Post*, 11–13 April 1717, p. 2). It is tempting to speculate this was an attempt by Kersey's group to destroy evidence, since the discovery was made not far from Kersey's home (Figure 4.2) and immediately followed their arrest and release.

St Bartholomew's records show the impoverished Mrs Childers requested their help to prosecute all those involved.[32] Kersey's group avoided indictment, probably due to their social status and connections.[33] However, an Old Bailey jury found Bowen 'guilty of the Indictment' on 1 May 1717, after hearing evidence from witnesses at the funeral and the Rose Inn. Bowen was fined of 40s, plus fees (costs) and whipped from Newgate to Smithfield Bars on 29 May 1717. The court thought this punishment 'condign [fitting, deserved]' and, having recently seen similar crimes (presumably in 1716, above), commented: 'he and his Fraternity are grown such common Disturbers, that the Dead can't rest quietly in their Graves for 'em' (Old Bailey Proceedings Online [OBPO], LL ref: t17170501–35).

Since records from 1716 do not survive, Bowen's trial is perhaps the earliest surviving example of a bodysnatching prosecution in London (and Britain) and demonstrates the early establishment of judicial precedent. First, no medical practitioner would be prosecuted in London for their part in bodysnatching until the late eighteenth century; instead, it would continue to be their employees who were punished. Second, the crime of bodysnatching continued to be considered a misdemeanour and not a felony. Punishments would, therefore, remain relatively lenient and included whipping, fines and short prison sentences, rather than harsher punishments such as deportation or death. Although the records of this case do not document the rationale behind the sentencing, it probably paralleled well-documented late-eighteenth-century cases, which did not recognise bodysnatching as 'theft'. Common law, it was argued, held that the dead body (or parts thereof) was *nullius in bonis* (among the property of no person) and therefore could not be 'owned'. Thus, an indictment for theft only occurred if 'property' was also taken, such as a shroud or coffin.[34] There remained no statute against stealing a corpse;[35] instead, bodysnatching was cognisable in a criminal court as a great indecency, *contra bonos mores* (against good morals).[36]

There is no evidence of Kersey professionally after April 1717. Continuance of his work perhaps left no record, but it is more probable that his career faltered, not because of public exposure, but due to familial tragedy and ill-health. The years 1719 and 1720 saw the deaths of his first son and father respectively, and Kersey himself died in February 1723 (Burials of St Andrew, Holborn: 21.04.1719, 07.02.1720 and 26.02.1723, respectively; Will of John Kersey, 1720).[37] However, Brathwaite's career continues to illustrate the bodysnatching activities of the men of St Thomas's. In the winter of 1717/18, he may have formed a new partnership with another recent alumnus of St Thomas's, Joshua Symonds (1694?–1731). Symonds had succeeded Cheselden as apprentice to Ferne at St Thomas's and completed his apprenticeship there in late 1716 (Peachey, 1924: 19). In late 1717, Symonds published a syllabus for a course of thirty human anatomy lectures aimed at students (Symonds, 1717). The syllabus did not record the venue but a letter to Hearne dated 9 November 1717 suggests he had taken Kersey's place in Oxford. Dr Richard Mead (1673–1754), physician of St Thomas's Hospital, wrote: 'Mr. Simmonds, a surgeon [...] who comes [from London to Oxford] to give a course of Anatomy to your young students' (Rannie, 1902: 105). As will now be discussed, Brathwaite certainly received bodies stolen from a churchyard in London that winter.

The third earliest London case involved a woman buried at 9 pm on 11 February 1718 in St Saviours, Southwark (see Figure 4.2). By 11 pm, gravedigger William Dod and soldier George Gambol had exhumed her corpse, stripped it and squeezed it into a hamper by breaking her neck and back. It was carried to the nearby home of a surgeon of St Thomas's, described as a 'lusty fat man' (Anon, undated). However, the men forgot the address (*WJBG*, 15 February 1718, p. 5). One account recorded that they ran away after knocking at the wrong door (*Original Weekly Journal*

[*OWJ*], 8–15 February 1718, p. 5), another that they were challenged by a maid (*WJSP*, 15 February 1718, p. 4), and another that the hamper was left unattended while they 'made water' and then discovered by a gentleman who raised the alarm (Anon, undated). The deceased – described as a 60-year-old midwife whose son was a cooper – was probably Catherine Worrell (née Simonds).[38] While her body was reclaimed by family after being 'exposed to public view' at St Thomas's (*WJSP*, 15 February 1718, p. 4), other concerned citizens excavated St Saviours' burial grounds to search for loved ones. Many of those buried in the previous six weeks were found missing from their graves.[39]

An anonymous angry letter responding to the incident was published in the *Original Weekly Journal* (15–22 February 1718, p. 4). It demonstrates awareness of bodysnatching had markedly increased since 1716, but that the antipathy was equally strong:

> Sir, the sudden Resurrection of the Dead in Southwark, is become the general Subject of Conversation, and has render'd Death far more Frightful and Terrible to some People, than ever it was described. And I fear our Teachers will now find a hard Tuggon't to perswade People to submit so tamely to it as formerly; seeing that neither common Humanity, the strongest Elm, nor even the Grave are capable of Protecting the most Pious Mortal, after he has left these Transitory Mansons, from falling into the Hands of some Galenian Butcher or other, to be Scarified in such a Manner, as would make a Bailiff, a Hangman, or a Hussar almost Tremble, at the sight of him.

The letter also reveals an awareness of the transactional relationships involved, referring to 'Sexton, or Grave Digger, standing Proxie's at the Cart-Tail', and branded surgeons:

> Wretches who deserve Tyburn, or at least an Oates's Punishment [pillory and whipping], for Tempting such Necessited Rascals to become Accessaries, to a Fact that a Turk would be Astonish'd to hear of; and of which, such falsely Stile themselves Christians, ought Justly to be Asham'd of Committing.

Although the sexton, Dod and their families were all carried before a Magistrate, only Dod was detained. Gambol was arrested later but gave King's evidence, testifying he had been paid 5s 'porteridge' and that Dod was paid 30s for each child under 2 years old and one guinea per adult (*OWJ*, 8–15 February 1718, p. 5). Awaiting trial in Marshalsea prison, Dod was protected from the 'Clamour of the Thieves in that Prison, who pretend to be much Honester Fellows, because they only robb the Living' (*Stamford Mercury*, 20 February 1718, p. 10). Sentenced at the Kingston assizes soon after, his punishment seems to have followed the precedent set in 1717: he was fined six nobles (£2) and given two years' imprisonment (*OWJ*, 29 March 1718–5 April 1718, p. 4). St Thomas's distanced itself from scandal through a newspaper advertisement in which they publicly insisted the 'Person' responsible was a 'Teacher of Anatomy on his own Account' and denied any association with him (*Post Boy*, 13–15 February 1718, p. 2). An internal inquiry, however, attributed the thefts to Brathwaite, after bodies were found at his lodgings in Joyner Street, Southwark (Figure 4.2). Brathwaite again avoided prosecution but, having already been previously rebuked for bringing unauthorised guests to the wards, was dismissed from his apprenticeship and refused entry to the hospital (Minute Books of Courts and Committees [MBCC], 26.03.1718).

Nevertheless, although Brathwaite was publicly presented as fully culpable, the large number of corpses reportedly stolen that winter seems excessive for the needs of just one teacher. Indeed, there is evidence Brathwaite was scapegoated for the activities of others. The autobiography of Alexander Monro (1697–1767) records that he studied surgery and dissection with Cheselden in London from early 1717 to spring 1718. During this time, Monro claimed he was 'furnished with more [bodies] than with the utmost Application he could make use of' (Erlam, 1954: 81). He did not explain their source publicly but recorded the dates and descriptions of eight corpses he dissected between 5 August 1717 and 18 January 1718 (six children (boy and girls) between 'some months old' and 7 years old, a man *c.*26–27 years old and a woman 'over 60' (Commonplace Book)). Although a precise correlation is impossible because of limited biographic detail, potential matches can be found for all these individuals among the burial register of St Saviours. Monro recalled how these bodies were dissected by a 'Society of young Gentlemen', who 'undertook to give Lectures in Their turns on different Organs',[40] and how, by early 1718, he had enough material to make numerous anatomical preparations to send home to his father (Erlam, 1954: 81; Guerrini, 2006).

## The influence and legacy of early churchyard bodysnatching

Although it is beyond the scope of this chapter to fully assess the influence of early churchyard bodysnatching in both London and beyond, this section serves to demonstrate that its legacy was both long lasting and wide ranging. Churchyard bodysnatching persisted during the 1720s and perhaps intensified. Yet, while private anatomy courses began to flourish in London during this period, evidence of the practice of bodysnatching during this decade is rarer. The careers of Thomas Brathwaite and others offer some clues about why this was and demonstrate the ongoing demand for cadavers.

Expelled from St Thomas's, Brathwaite continued his education under London surgeon Richard Lee, completing his apprenticeship on 22 October

1719 (Freedom Admission Papers, /0402–0408). However, Brathwaite also returned to Oxford in early 1719. Using a London newspaper, he advertised a course on human and comparative anatomy to be conducted in the 'public schools' of Oxford in March 1719, for which he claimed forty-two students had already subscribed (*Daily Courant*, 2 March 1719, p. 2). Brathwaite was to demonstrate and his new partner, Christopher Furneaux (1693–1730) of Exeter College, would read the lectures.[41] Although Brathwaite perhaps continued working with Furneaux in Oxford into the 1720s,[42] it seems more probable he gained his next employment in London with Scottish surgeon John Douglas (d.1743), brother of Dr James Douglas (Bevan, 2008). From late 1719 to early 1723, John Douglas performed private practical anatomy lectures for students, with an emphasis on the dissection of human subjects (Douglas, 1719; Peachey, 1924: 22). Douglas had been a pupil at St Thomas's in *c.*1715–16 (Cheselden, 1723: vii) and been made foreign brother of the Barber-Surgeons in 1717. He clearly knew Brathwaite; they had been contemporaries at St Thomas's and in later life Douglas described Brathwaite as an 'ingenious Surgeon, and accurate Anatomist' (1735: 44). Another indication of an association or friendship between the two men is the venue of Douglas's lectures. Records show the house was located a few doors from Kersey's house in Fetter Lane (see Figure 4.2) and that Brathwaite continued the lease of the same property from 1724 (Land Tax Assessment Books [LTAB], /62, 71, 74, 77, 80, 83, 86, 89; Anon, 1728: 146).

Brathwaite's career, however, was not a long one. He took an apprentice in 1725[43] but died of an unknown cause in the summer of 1730 (Will of Thomas Brathwaite, PROB 11/640/275, dated 17.05.1730, proved 30.10.1730).[44] An auction of his belongings to benefit his family[45] included: an 'anatomy in wax', instruments of midwifery, surgery and dissection, a syllabus, medical books and 'Anatomical Preparations and Curiosities, not commonly to be met with'. The latter included the hymen from a 22-year-old woman executed at Tyburn, three boxes of bones, one box of 'anatomical preparations injected', an 'old man's head', an embryo in spirits, three fetuses (dried and in spirits) and one fetus in utero (Payne, 1731: 114–15). As well as being indicative of a lecturing career supported by illicit procurement, these items may suggest specialism in obstetrics and midwifery. Indeed, Brathwaite's only known publication was a pamphlet which criticised his rival, St Andre, and others for their credulity over the fraudulent rabbit births of Mary Toft (Brathwaite, 1726; Harvey, 2020).

Between 1719 and 1727 there are four known incidents of bodysnatching in London, but none can be linked to a surgeon or hospital (Hartle, 2017: 268; *Daily Journal* (London), 17 February 1727, p. 2). Douglas and/or

Brathwaite may have been responsible, but the London market in private anatomy lecturing was becoming more crowded: Swiss physician Nathaniel St Andre (1680?–1776) initially lectured with 'Mr. Martin' (see note 23) from 1718 and later alone until 1726; and Peter Coltheart, foreign brother of the Barber-Surgeons, lectured in Covent Garden, 1721–6. Cheselden was appointed assistant surgeon at St Thomas's in 1718 and surgeon in 1719, in place of Brathwaite's former master, Dickinson (recently deceased), but also lectured privately with Francis Hauksbee (1687–1763) between 1720–2 at Fleet Street. Whether Hauksbee, Coltheart and Cheselden had access to cadavers in this period is unrecorded, but St Andre was able to source preparations and supplied students with human skeletons (*PMHA*, 6–8 March 1718, p. 2, and 11–13 September 1718, p. 2; *Daily Courant*, 21 November 1719, p. 4, and 5 October 1721, p. 4; Lawrence, 1996: 180–5; Peachey, 1924: 8–24).

Churchyard bodysnatching had clearly become a national practice by the mid-1720s. On 11 January 1724, Oxford antiquarian Thomas Hearne (1678–1735) noted in his diary that it was 'common practice nowadays for young Physicians to rob Church Yards [...] many Clarks, as 'tis said, in London, & other great Places, being confederate with [them]' (Rannie, 1907: 156–7). In Scotland this had developed broadly in parallel: suspicion of bodysnatching from a grave in Edinburgh was documented in 1678 and an allegation of the same recorded in 1711 (Richardson, 2001: 54); and four apprentice surgeon-apothecaries of Perth were fined for bodysnatching in October 1718 (Warrants of Decreets). However, the practice proliferated in and around Edinburgh from the mid-1720s, following Monro's appointment as foundation Professor of Anatomy at the university.[46] Although there is no evidence the alumni of St Thomas's – specifically, Cheselden, Kersey, Brathwaite, Symonds and Douglas – ever lectured at Cambridge, it is certainly possible one or more of them did, and there are clear links between London, St Thomas's and early bodysnatching in Cambridgeshire. Cambridge students are known to have studied concurrently in London[47] and George Rolfe, the early London lecturer, was the university's first Professor of Anatomy, 1707–28. Rolfe is said to have neglected his duties, but anatomical teaching did occur during his tenure and into the 1730s. The university opened its first anatomy school in 1716 and, as at Oxford, it was common contemporary practice to supplement college teaching with private lectures (Rolleston, 1932). Although a sixteenth-century Royal grant allowed the university the bodies of two executed criminals annually for dissection, additional bodies were sought via a clause in the Physicians Bill in 1724.[48] After the clause was rejected, five incidents of churchyard bodysnatching were reported in and around Cambridge between 1725 and 1732 (*Caledonian*

*Mercury*, 1 April 1725, p. 1; *Ipswich Journal or Weekly Mercury* [*IJWM*], 1–8 October 1726, p. 3; *KWPCJ*, 7–11 February 1730, p. 2 and 12 April 1732, p. 4), and the university was compelled to publish an ordinance against the practice by its students and graduates in 1731 (Peachey, 1924: 3, 13).

In London, during the decades following Brathwaite's death in 1730, medical training and lecturing became increasingly common within hospitals (including St Thomas's), private extra-mural anatomy tuition proliferated and bodysnatching persisted. Two prominent anatomy lecturers of this period had close links with Oxford. First, Edward Nourse (1701–61), son of an Oxford surgeon, who was apprenticed at St Bartholomew's in December 1717 and advanced to staff surgeon by 1745. He lectured at his house from 1729 and then at St Bartholomew's from 1734 (Moore, 2004). Second, Frank Nicholls (1699?–1778) who matriculated undergraduate in 1714 at Exeter College, Oxford, and would have been a pupil of Furneaux and probably an auditor of Kersey, Brathwaite and Symonds. Nicholls was lecturing at Oxford by *c*.1721 and was Professor of Anatomy at Oxford by the time he first lectured in London in 1727 (Guerrini, 2008; Robb-Smith and Sinclair, 1950: 26–31).

For Cheselden, the 1730s and 1740s brought significant professional success, placing him as arguably the most eminent British surgeon of his generation. We may suspect Cheselden, Nourse and Nicholls all sourced cadavers through the practice of bodysnatching but evidence is generally lacking or circumstantial.[49] Nevertheless, although anatomists advertising London lectures during the 1700s to 1730s had refrained from promising access to human remains, those of the 1740s were more explicit about its availability (Lawrence, 1996: 183). Some among the next generation of lecturers were irrefutably incriminated in churchyard bodysnatching. The private lectures of surgeon Sir Caesar Hawkins (1711–86), for example, who had trained in London in the 1720s, were linked to bodysnatching in 1736 (Hartle, 2017: 269). Only the previous year he had been appointed surgeon to St George's Hospital, where he would have worked alongside Cheselden, who had joined the hospital's surgical staff in 1733. However, it is William Hunter (1718–83) and his brother John Hunter (1728–93) who are most notable – and who became somewhat notorious (see Figure 4.4). In 1749, the year he became pupil to Cheselden, John Hunter avoided prosecution after being arrested in possession of a corpse stolen from a Westminster churchyard (Chaplin, 2009: 61). From the mid-eighteenth century, the Hunters were at the forefront of a burgeoning of private anatomical instruction in London through the establishment of the first private anatomy schools, but they also helped transform bodysnatching from a trade into an industry (Moore, 2006).

Figure 4.4 A nightwatchman disturbs a body-snatcher who has dropped the stolen corpse he had been carrying in a hamper, while the anatomist runs away. Etching with engraving by W. Austin, 1773.

## Conclusions

Introducing a lecture to students in c.1780, William Hunter observed that anatomy was the basis of surgery, but that it also familiarised 'the heart to a kind of necessary Inhumanity' (St Thomas's Hospital Manuscript 55: 182v, quoted in Richardson, 2001: 31). This clinical dispassion, exemplified by bodysnatching, came into conflict with both the individual grief and general moral repugnance of the lay populace. The New Churchyard archaeology is a rare physical manifestation of contemporary antipathy toward bodysnatching but also the undocumented anxiety of bereavement.

This chapter shows that this antipathy was a response to a well-organised network of bodysnatchers. The *modus operandi* of the early churchyard bodysnatching which they established in London shows that it was a trade from the outset. The dead body was already objectified within the surgical fraternity by the end of the seventeenth century, but to the men of St Thomas's it was an anonymous material commodity to be bought and sold.

It is clear that the practice of churchyard bodysnatching excited a public outcry far earlier and wider than previously recognised: the archaeological evidence from the New Churchyard is the material manifestation of the outrage visible in print culture. As this chapter discussed, bodysnatching quickly became an early newspaper sensation. Widely considered tantamount to both spiritual and physical violation, the earliest known prosecutions in London for churchyard bodysnatching probably set judicial precedent. Those who conducted the thefts themselves were vilified at the time but have not been adequately considered by historians until now. Among the surgeons of the period, Cheselden achieved a far longer lasting legacy than most of his peers, including two key figures in the history of early bodysnatching, Thomas Brathwaite and John Kersey. Brathwaite had some limited posthumous status as a luminary[50] and published at least once, but neither he nor Kersey gained any accoutrements of surgical eminence: hospital appointments, patronage, fellowships or eponymic recognition. Bodysnatching in the early eighteenth century does not appear to have necessarily partnered professional success. Nevertheless, while corpses could be a commodity and a conduit to professional prestige and personal fortune, difficulties in obtaining bodies for the purpose of research and teaching meant that the wider adoption of churchyard bodysnatching was arguably a necessary mechanism underpinning surgical advancement for over a century. Much is owed to the entrepreneurial efforts of junior members of London's medical elite, a small group of men educated at St Thomas's, as well as those they bribed to steal on their behalf who were, together, the 'Corporation of Corpse-stealers'.

## Acknowledgements

Although the research for this chapter was part of a personal and self-funded project, the author would like to thank his MOLA colleagues for their advice and help during the writing and publication process, particularly Susan Wright, David Bowsher, Juan Jose Fuldain Gonzalez and Tracy Wellman. The author would also like to thank Karen Harvey and Elizabeth Craig-Atkins for inviting him to write this chapter and for their invaluable guidance, constructive comments and enthusiasm.

## Notes

1 Extensive evidence from this period has recently been found at St James's Chapel, Hampstead Road, London, excavated by MOLA Headland Infrastructure (MHI) for HS2 (Hartle, 2022).
2 Charles Smith, a dwarf, sold his body to a surgeon in *c.*1725, receiving 6d a week until his death in 1735 (*Derby Mercury*, 18 December 1735, p. 4); a

'Whimsical Lawyer' bequeathed his body for dissection in 1729, on condition his remains were preserved and displayed (*IJWM*, 12–19 April 1729, p. 4), as did philosopher Robert Greene (1678?–1730) (Vian, 1890); Richard Ellis, of Colonel Kirkes's regiment, was whipped and court-martialled in 1725 after attempting to sell his pregnant wife, dead or alive, to Edinburgh's anatomists (*Mist's Weekly Journal*, 8 May 1725, p. 2).

3 Four Lent term dissection lectures (January–March), by the Reader and his appointed surgeon, and three Michaelmas term osteological lectures (October–December) (Ayliffe, 1714, Vol. 2: 111–12 and 189–90).

4 Possible earlier evidence for the movement of illicitly acquired cadavers or their disposal after dissection includes: a mutilated corpse found in a shallow grave near Tyburn in September 1697 – the *Post Man and the Historical Account* suggested that it was one of the 'Malefactors last Executed there, which was begg'd by a private Chirurgeon' (28–30 September, 1697, p. 2); a child's corpse found abandoned in a coffin in the churchyard of St Dunstan, Stepney, in April 1700 – the 'very dismal Spectacle' had signs of dissection, including dismemberment, craniotomy and organ removal (*London Post with Intelligence Foreign and Domestick* [*LPIFD*], 1–3 April 1700, p. 2); and a case in the Custom House, Dublin, in September 1700, discovered to contain a corpse in a coffin dated 1698. A 'gentlewoman' had paid to transport it from London, claiming it contained 'old Clothes for her Friend' (*Flying Post or the Post Master* [*FPPM*], 14–17 September 1700, p. 2). This could have simply been a mix up with repatriated remains; alternatively, they were perhaps stolen, covertly transported and sourced for an anatomical skeleton.

5 Robb-Smith and Sinclair (1950: 24) imprecisely dated this incident to *c.*1710.

6 The incident was later recorded in an epigram attributed to 'Dr. H—n' (Hodges and Reeve, 1749: 190).

7 There appears to be no mention of Kersey in any secondary sources, except recognition of his existence in Wallis and Wallis (1988: 203).

8 His parents, John Kersey and Juliana Owen, married 16.02.1686 (Marriages of St Bride Fleet Street); Juliana Kersey bur. 28.04.1745 (Burials of St Michael Cornhill); Wallis, 2004.

9 Greenhill conducted autopsies and espoused embalming for teaching anatomy and anatomical preparations. Ironically, Greenhill also stressed the importance of funeral practices, considered the 'want of a burial to be a Punishment and a Curse', and noted the 'Infamy and Disgrace of the Dead bodies being denied burial' (1705a: 3–5, 118; 1705b).

10 John Kersey senior perhaps secured his son's career – a 'John Kersey' was subscriber to Greenhill's work (1705a). Rideout was appointed surgeon in 1691 and was elected Barber-Surgeons' Steward of Anatomy in 1708 (Parsons, 1934: 125; MBCC, 28.04.1714; CMB: 9).

11 Lecturing was particularly profitable, since students commonly each paid several guineas to attend, and audiences could be large (Guerrini, 2004).

12 See note 10.

13 From 1713 Kersey lived with his parents at the 'Surgeon's Arms', Blewitt's Buildings, Fetter Lane (LTAB, /42, fol.28, /47, fol.28, /59, fol.27, /65, fol.24; *Post*

*Boy*, 24–26 October 1717, p. 2) and married Rebecca Taylor on 14 February 1716 (Parish registers of St James, Clerkenwell).

14 Mirroring the Barber-Surgeons' 'Masters' and 'Stewards of Anatomy', traditional format involved a 'Reader', who read/led the lecture, and 'Demonstrator', who dissected (Kausmally, 2015: 48; Young, 1890: 362). Kersey was perhaps 'Demonstrator' to Cheselden's 'Reader'.

15 In 1742 the *London Evening Post* (30 September 1742–2 October 1742, p. 2) reported on material evidence of bodysnatching in London found, remarkably, in the church of St Michael, Southampton, when an old burial was disturbed for a new grave. Marked 'Edward Serle, Gent, 1711', the wooden coffin contained only clothes stuffed with animal bone and wool. Serle, it was said, had been buried in Southampton 'with his Ancestors, pursuant to his Desire'. Despite a 'Grand Funeral', it was thought his body had been sold to anatomists in London. Although bodysnatching cannot be substantiated, Edward Serle and his burial seemingly existed. 'Edward Serle' (or Searl), resident of All Hallows London Wall, London, died aged 60 in 1711 and his burial was registered on 18 December 1711. At St Michael, Southampton, 'Mr Searle' was buried 'in ye Church' on 26 December 1711. The All Hallows register does not distinguish intra- and extra-parochial burials; therefore, the former date could reflect the coffin leaving London and the latter its burial in Southampton. If the interpretation of theft was correct, an embalmer may be strongly suspected, since transporting a body in a wooden coffin to Southampton would have required embalming to mitigate unpleasant putrefaction during transit. Having trained under Greenhill, Kersey may have had opportunities, both during or after his apprenticeship, to develop the close professional relationships with undertakers necessary to bribe them or substitute corpses, with or without their connivance.

16 Hearne notes the event of 1704 left an impression and increased burial within churches because of its perceived security (Rannie, 1907: 156–7).

17 The cadaver may have been Mary Skip, the only women recently hanged at Tyburn (highway robbery, 11.05.1715, OBPO, OA17150511).

18 His other children probably included Mary, bapt. 26 November 1716 (Baptisms of St Andrew, Holborn) and John, bapt. 10 October 1720 (Parish registers of St James, Clerkenwell).

19 Sarah Shepherd married John Stiver, 11 January 1695 (QMLM: Marriages 1690–1700, Devonshire House, fol.267), who died January 1700 (QMLM: Burials 1699–1723, Devonshire House, fol.4), then married Peter Shepherd, 28 January 1700 (Parish registers of St Dunstan, Stepney).

20 Michael Holmes was dismissed, and his replacement was ordered in future to dig graves six foot deep and backfill promptly. News spread to the Peel Meeting, who oversaw the Chequer Alley burial ground, near Bunhill Fields. They let adjoining properties and feared their poorer tenants might be 'prevailed upon' to steal corpses. It was ordered these tenants be replaced by Quakers and gates locked at night (Devonshire House Monthly Meeting Men's minutes (regular), Vol. 3, 1707–27: 219–20, 239; Devonshire House Monthly Meeting Men's minutes (adjourned), Vol. 4, 1707–30: 156, 173, 175, 237, 243, 295; Peel House Monthly Meeting Men's minutes (regular), Vol. 4, 1709–17, 29 tenth month [Nov] 1716).

21 Holmes was perhaps recruited because he had already committed a similar crime. A week earlier a 'John Holms' of St Mary, Whitechapel, had been branded for stealing the shroud from a corpse, although on that occasion it was noted 'No Notice taken of the Corps' (OBPO, LL ref: t17161105-78).

22 Thomas Secker (1693–1768) studied in London during that winter and attended 'Courses of Anatomy with Mr Cheselden' (Greaves and Macauley, 1988: 7).

23 Two other men advertised courses in their London homes, 1715–18, but there is no evidence either used cadavers: 'Mr Martin' in Northumberland Court, Charing Cross (*PMHA*, 10–12 April 1716, p. 2; 16–18 August 1716, p. 2; 15–17 August 1717, p. 2; 14–16 November 1717, p. 2; 6–8 March 1718, p. 2); and Hosea Fiquel (d.1736), an army surgeon, English by nationalisation, who lectured in Leicester Fields, 1715–16 (*Evening Post*, 1–3 December 1715, p. 2; *Daily Courant*, 3 November 1716, p. 3; Will of Hosea Fiquel, PROB 11/680/328, proved 12.10.1736; Wallis and Wallis, 1988: 45).

24 By 1717, the New Churchyard was used for those buried at the cost of the hospital (paupers or unclaimed dead). However, the death and burial registers of St Bartholomew's do not survive before 1762 and 1744, respectively (Harding, 2002: 94–5; Maitland, 1756: 986; Moore, 1918). This has created a large void in the historic record because a burial register was never kept at the New Churchyard. Patient burials transferred to St Giles, Cripplegate, following the closure of the New Churchyard and indicate how heavily used the latter must have been by St Bartholomew's: 178 patient burials (noted 'B.H.') were recorded by St Giles 3 March 1739–28 February 1740 – *c.*51% of the 349 patients who died in the hospital during approximately the same period (Burials of St Giles, Cripplegate; St Bartholomew's Hospital, Minutes of the Board of Governors [MBG], SBHB/HA/1/11, 1734–48: 231, 255, 337, 357, 368–9 and 372).

25 Childers was probably reburied in the New Churchyard. No record of his reburial appears to exist elsewhere.

26 Consumption killed 38% of the patients buried 3 March 1739–28 February 1740 (Burials of St Giles, Cripplegate).

27 John Whiten (RAB:/003: 184 (04.12.1716)).

28 Baptised 4 May 1695 (Baptisms of St Martin-in-the-Fields), son of John Brathwaite (*fl.*1699, deceased by 1712), Stationer, and Sylvestra Brathwaite (née Cooke, 1669–1740).

29 Dickinson had been appointed in May 1714, in place of Kersey's former master, Rideout (deceased), and had recently been elected a Steward of Anatomy (Dickinson, 1901: 116; Parsons, 1934: 160, 167; MBCC: 08.04.1719; CMB: 15.08.1717). Brathwaite's apprenticeship had not begun under Dickinson (RFA: 104; CMB: 210) but under army surgeon Latimer Ridley on 7 October 1712. It was discharged on 11 February 1713 and transferred to Dickinson because Ridley had falsely claimed Freedom of the Barber-Surgeons.

30 Visiting surgeons required permission from the incumbent Chancellor or Vice-Chancellor of Oxford to lecture (Ayliffe, 1714, Vol. 2: 153; Robb-Smith and Sinclair, 1950: 24). Brathwaite's connections may have proved useful – his uncle, Thomas Brathwaite (1660?–1720), had been Vice-Chancellor of Oxford,

1710–12 (Will of Doctor Thomas Brathwaite, PROB 11/575/455, proved 31 August 1720; Foster, 1891: 172).
31  Cheselden's course of 1713, for example, lasted two months, repeated 1 September 1713, 1 November 1713, 12 January 1714 and 12 March 1714 (Cheselden, 1713).
32  Her forename was not recorded (MBG, SBHB/HA/1/09, 1708–19: 169r and 169v).
33  Brathwaite's family may have supplied legal advice, representation and influence: his maternal uncle, Richard Cooke, and his mother's cousin, John Marsh (d.1753), were both barristers-at-law (Burke and Burke, 1847; Roberts, 1933: 246).
34  See indictments of 1777 and 1788 (Anon, 1832: 204–9; Dobie, 1829: 156–60; *Public Advertiser*, 31 January 1789).
35  Except for witchcraft, a felony 1604–1735 (Guttmacher, 1935: 363).
36  Occasionally also associated with charges of trespass.
37  Kersey's wife, Rebecca, died in 'ye Hospital' in 1725 (Burials of St Andrew, Holborn: 30.03.1725).
38  Buried 26 April 1706. Widow of John Worrell, distiller, and mother of Thomas Worrell (bapt. 4 December 1687), carpenter's apprentice (Parish registers of St Saviours, Southwark; Parish registers of St Katherine by the Tower; Freedom Admission Papers [FAP], /0301–0306: 04.09.1705).
39  One source recorded thirty missing (Anon, undated) and another recorded twenty-five children and thirteen adults missing (*OWJ*, 8–15 February 1718, p. 5). This represents approximately 30 to 40% of the ninety-five individuals buried by St Saviours 1 January–10 February 1718 (*c*.fifty-one children, forty-four adults (Parish registers of St Saviours, Southwark)). These thefts probably reflect a typical disproportionate targeting of women and children. Hearne noted in 1724: 'tis for young people, especially young, Women, that they [bodysnatchers] generally seek' (Rannie, 1907: 156–7). Such bias addressed a key problem with contemporary lawful supply – relatively few women were condemned to execution. Pregnant women and young children were never knowingly executed (Chaplin, 2009: Appendix 2).
40  Probably a continuation of the society founded by Stukeley a decade earlier. According to Monro, the group also included physician William Rutty (1687–1730) (Morgan 1730: 427) and physician and man-midwife James Douglas (1675–1742) (Erlam, 1954).
41  Furneaux, son of a vicar of Torrington, Devon, matriculated undergraduate in 1710, Fellow 1713, B.A. 1715, M.A. 1718 and B.Med 1719 (Foster, 1891: 540; Howard, 1877: 195–6).
42  Details of Furneaux's later life are mostly lacking. He was described as 'Professor of Anatomy' when listed by Jebb as a subscriber (1722: 572). In 1721, he forcefully claimed a corpse from the Oxford gallows to dissection at Exeter College, despite the man's parents wanting a funeral and attending the execution with a coffin (Robb-Smith and Sinclair, 1950: 26).
43  Richard Austin (Apprenticeship Books, IR1/11/12, 16.09.1725), possibly the same 'Richard Austin' who studied operations as St Thomas's pupil from October 1725 to February 1726 (Wilson, 1992).

44  What killed Kersey and Brathwaite at relatively young ages (*c.*36 and *c.*35, respectively) is unrecorded but may have been occupational. In 1779, surgeon Peter Clare noted links between disease, putrefaction and the dissection room, and observed that many aspiring anatomists 'died unheard of in early life' (Clare, 1779: 118–20). Although the transmission of infectious diseases from cadavers was poorly understood in the early eighteenth century, the risk was recognised. In 1727, the *WJBG* noted how anatomist practices 'the barbarous Custom of digging up human Bodies after their Decent Interment' manifested dangerous 'contagious Distempers' (22 April 1727, p. 2). In November 1729, the deaths of four unidentified surgeons from 'goal fever' were linked to a dissection at St Bartholomew's. The subject, Hester Morgan, was dying of the disease when executed at Tyburn (*Ipswich Journal*, 22–29 November 1729, p. 3 and 20–27 December 1729, p. 4). There is no indication Kersey and Brathwaite targeted specific corpses. Indeed, their subjects probably placed them at greater risk because the anonymity of bodysnatching masked cause of death. Sarah Shepherd and William Childers (1716 and 1717, above), for example, both died of 'consumption'. During his education in London, Monro dissected the suppurated lungs of a man who had died from TB and, after scratching his hands, was lucky to survive a dangerous infection (Erlam, 1954: 81).

45  Brathwaite married his last master's daughter, Mary Lee, and the couple had a son (Will of Richard Lee, PROB 11/700/501, proved 26 February 1740).

46  Bower suggests Monro initially relied on corpses procured from London (1817: 176)

47  For example, Stukeley and William Rutty (see note 40).

48  Stukeley supported this and attended the House of Lords when the Bill was debated (Commentary 1720, in Lukis, 1882: 73–4).

49  See Cheselden's possible involvement in 1716 and 1718, above. Direct evidence against Cheselden, however, is perhaps limited to his own candid admission in *Osteographia* (1733: Table 43) that one skeletal specimen was dug 'out of a grave', for which he was strongly chastised by John Douglas: 'if Mr CHESELDEN dug it out of a grave himself, or set any body else about it, he ought to have kept that part of the story to himself; because People are too apt to suspect and surmise such things, without being told them in so publick a manner' (Douglas, 1735: 36).

50  John 'Chevalier' Taylor (1703?–72) credited 'Hunter, Nicols, Monro, Brathwaite' for teaching him anatomy (Taylor 1761: 47).

# References

### Primary sources

Apprenticeship Books, TNA, IR1.
Baptisms of St Andrew, Holborn, LMA, P82/AND/A/001/MS06667/007–008.
Baptisms of St Martin-in-the-Fields, Westminster Archives.
Burials of St Andrew, Holborn, LMA, P69/AND2/A/010/MS06673/008.

Burials of St Giles, Cripplegate, LMA, P69/GIS/A/002/MS06419/017.
Burials of St Michael, Cornhill, LMA, P69/MIC2/A/003/MS04063/002.
Burials of St Peter-in-the-East, Oxfordshire Family History Society, Oxford, PAR213/1/R1/5.
Commonplace book, MS M165: 261–263, Medical Library, University of Otago.
Court minute book (CMB), Worshipful Company of Barber-Surgeons, 1707–31, LMA, CLC/L/BB/B/001/MS05257/007.
Freedom Admission Papers (FAP), LMA, COL/CHD/FR/02
Land Tax Assessment Books (LTAB), LMA, CLC/525/MS11316.
Marriages of St. Bride Fleet Street, LMA, P69/BRI/A/005/MS06540/002.
Minutes of the Board of Governors (MBG), St Bartholomew's Hospital Archives.
Minute Books of Courts and Committees (MBCC), St. Thomas's Hospital, www.londonlives.org (accessed 30 June 2022).
Minute Books of the Grand Committee, St. Thomas's Hospital, LMA, H01/ST/A/006/004.
Old Bailey Proceedings Online (OBPO) www.oldbaileyonline.org, version 7.2, (accessed 5 May 2017).
Parish registers of St Dunstan, Stepney, LMA, P93/DUN/269.
Parish registers of St James, Clerkenwell, LMA, P76/JS1/008.
Parish registers of St Katherine by the Tower, LMA, CLC/199/TC/004/MS09661.
Parish registers of St Saviours, Southwark, LMA, P92/SAV/3005–6.
Register of apprentice bindings (RAB), Worshipful Company of Barber-Surgeons, 1672–1707, LMA, CLC/L/BB/C/008/MS05266.
Register of freedom admissions (RFA), Worshipful Company of Barber-Surgeons, 1707–32, LMA, CLC/L/BB/C/006/MS05265/004.
Vestry minute books, St Andrew, Holborn, LMA, P82/AND/B/001/MS04251/002:17.
Warrants of Decreets, Perth and Kinross Archives, B59/26/8/25/bundle 8.
Will of John Kersey, 1720, LMA, Archdeaconry Court of London, MS 9052/39/182.
Wills, TNA, Prerogative Court of Canterbury, PROB 11.

### Newspapers and periodicals

*The British Chronologist* (1775), Vol. 2 (London).
*Caledonian Mercury* (1725).
*Daily Courant* (1716–19).
*Daily Journal* (1727).
*Derby Mercury* (1735–1829).
*Diverting Post* (1705).
*Evening Post* (1715, 1717).
*Flying Post or The Post Master (FPPM)* (1700).
*Ipswich Journal or Weekly Mercury (IJWM)* (1726–29).
*Kentish Weekly Post or Canterbury Journal (KWPCJ)* (1749).
*London Evening Post* (1742).
*London Post with Intelligence Foreign and Domestick (LPIFD)* (1700).
*Mist's Weekly Journal* (1725).

*Original Weekly Journal (OWJ)* (1718).
*Post Man and Historical Account (PMHA)* (1697–1718).
*Post Boy* (1717–18).
*Public Advertiser* (1789).
*Stamford Mercury* (1716–18).
*Weekly Packet* (1716).
*Weekly Journal or British Gazetteer (WJBG)* (1717–27).
*Weekly Journal or Saturday's Post (WJSP)* (1717–18).

### Secondary sources

Abbott, G. (2006). *Grave Disturbances: A History of the Body Snatchers* (Kent: Eric Dobby Publishing).
Ayliffe, J. (1714). *The Antient and Present State of the University of Oxford, Vols.1 and 2* (London).
Anon. (undated). *A full and true account of thirty dead bodies of Men Woman and Children, that was taken out of one of the burying grounds belonging to St. Mary Overs …* (London: British Library General Reference Collection 74/1851.c.10.(37.)).
Anon. (a German Gentleman) (1725). *A View of London and Westminster: Or, the Town Spy* (London).
Anon. (1728). *An account of the election of members of parliament for the City of London in the year 1727* (London).
Anon. (1832). *Legal Examiner*, Vol. 1 (London).
Bailey, J. (1896). *The Diary of a Resurrectionist, 1811–1812* (London).
Bailey, B. (1991). *The Resurrection Men* (London: Time Warner Books).
Ball, J. (1928). *The Sack-'em-up Men* (Edinburgh: Oliver and Boyd).
Betham, W. (1805). *The Baronetage of England*, Vol. 5 (London).
Bevan, M. (2008). John Douglas (d.1743), in *Oxford Dictionary of National Biography (ODNB)* www.oxforddnb.com/view/article/7907 (accessed 2 August 2019).
Brathwaite, T. (1726). *Remarks on A Short Narrative of an Extraordinary Delivery of Rabbets* (London).
Boston, C. and Webb, H. (2012). 'Early medical training in Oxford', in P. Mitchell (ed.), *Anatomical Dissection in Enlightenment England and Beyond* (Farnham: Ashgate), pp. 43–67.
Bower, A. (1817). *The History of the University of Edinburgh*, Vol. 2 (Edinburgh).
Burke, J., and J.B. Burke (1847). *Burke's Genealogical and Heraldic History of the Landed Gentry*, Vol. 2 (London).
Butler, J. (1740). *Sermon Preached Before the Right Honourable the Lord-Mayor, the Court of Aldermen, the Sheriffs, and the Governors of the several Hospitals of the City of London, at the Parish Church of St. Bridget, on the Monday in Easter-Week* [15 April], *1740* (London).
Chaplin, S. (2009). 'John Hunter and the "Museum Economy", 1750–1800' (PhD dissertation, King's College London).
Cheselden, W. (1713). *The Anatomy of the Humane Body* (London).

Cheselden, W. (1723). *Lithotomus Castratus; Or Mr. Cheselden's Treatise on the High Operation for the Stone* (London).
Clare, P. (1779). *An Essay on the Cure of Abscesses by Caustic and on the Treatment of Wounds and Ulcers* (T. Cadell).
Cole, H. (1964). *Things for the Surgeon* (London: Heinemann).
Cope, Z. (1953). William Cheselden, 1688–1752 (Edinburgh, London: Livingstone).
Davidson, L. (2004). 'Greenhill, Thomas (*fl.*1698–1732)', in *ODNB* www.oxforddnb.com/view/article/11428 (accessed 2 July 2019).
Dickinson, W. (1901). *Record of the Lambert-Dickinson Family* (Flushing: Dickinson).
Dobie, R. (1829). *The history of the united parishes of St. Giles in the Fields and St. George Bloomsbury* (London).
Douglas, J. (1707). *Myographiae comparatae specimen* (London).
Douglas, J. (1719). *A syllabus of what is to be perform'd in a course of anatomy, chirurgical operations, and bandages …* (London).
Douglas, J. (1735). *Animadversions on a Late Pompous Book, Intituled, Osteographia…* (London).
Erlam, H. (1954). *Alexander Munro (Monro), primus …* (Wellcome Library RAMC/804).
Fido, M. (1988). *Bodysnatchers: A History of the Resurrectionist* (London: Weidenfeld and Nicolson).
Foster, J. (1891). *Alumni Oxonienses: The Members of the University of Oxford, 1500–1714*, Vols 1 and 2 (Oxford).
Fowler, L. and Powers, N. (2012). *Doctors, Dissection and Resurrection Men* (London: MOLA Monograph Series 62).
Greaves, R. and Macauley, J. (1988). *The Autobiography of Thomas Secker, Archbishop of Canterbury* (Lawrence: University of Kansas Press).
Greenhill, T. (1705a). Νεκροκηδεία *or The Art of Embalming* (London).
Greenhill, T. (1705b). 'An account of a person deceased of a Scirrhous Tumor in his Breast', *Philosophical Transactions of the Royal Society*, 24(300): 2009–11.
Guerrini, A. (2004). 'Anatomists and entrepreneurs in early eighteenth-century London', *Journal of the History of Medicine and Allied Sciences*, 59(2): 219–39.
Guerrini, A. (2006). 'Alexander Monro "Primus" and the Moral Theatre of Anatomy', *The Eighteenth Century*, 47(1): 1–18.
Guerrini, A. (2008). Nicholls, Francis [Frank] (bap. 1699?, d.1778), in *ODNB* www.oxforddnb.com/view/article/20109 (accessed 2 July 2019).
Guerrini, A. (2015). *The Courtiers' Anatomists: Animals and Humans in Louis XIV's Paris* (Chicago: University of Chicago Press).
Guttmacher, A. (1935). 'Bootlegging Bodies: A history of bodysnatching', *Bulletin of the Society of Medical History of Chicago*, 4: 353–402.
Harding, V. (2002). *The Dead and Living in Paris and London: 1500–1670* (Cambridge: Cambridge University Press).
Harley, D. (1994). 'Political post-mortems and morbid anatomy in seventeenth-century England', *Social History of Medicine*, 7: 1–28.
Hartle, R. (2017). *The New Churchyard: From Moorfields Marsh to Bethlem Burial Ground, Brokers Row and Liverpool Street* (London: Crossrail Archaeology Series 10).

Hartle, R. (2022). 'St James's Gardens post-excavation assessment' (London, unpublished MHI report).
Harvey, K. (2020). *The Imposteress Rabbit Breeder* (Oxford: Oxford University Press).
Hodges, J. and Reeve, W. (1749). *Joe Miller's Jests: Or, the Wits Vade-mecum* (London).
Howard, J. J. (ed.) (1877). *Miscellanea Genealogica et Heraldica*, Vol. 2 (London).
Jebb, S. (1722). *Aelii Aristidis Adrianensis Opera Omnia...* (Oxford).
Kausmally, T. (2015). 'William Hewson (1739–1774) and the Craven Street Anatomy School – Anatomical teaching in the 18th century' (PhD dissertation, University College London).
Lane-Poole, S. (2004). 'Braithwaite, John (1696–1740)', in *ODNB* www.oxforddnb.com/view/article/3233 (accessed 3 July 2019).
Lawrence, S. (1996). *Charitable Knowledge: Hospital Pupils and Practitioners in Eighteenth-Century London* (Cambridge: Cambridge University Press).
Le Dran, H. (1749). *The operations in surgery of Mons. Le Dran . . . with remarks . . . by William Cheselden* (London).
Lennox, S. (2016). *Bodysnatchers: Digging Up The Untold Stories of Britain's Resurrection Men* (Barnsley: Pen and Sword History).
Linebaugh, P. (1975). 'The Tyburn riots against the surgeons', in D. Hay, P. Linebaugh, J. G. Rule, E. P. Thompson and C. Winslow (eds), *Albion's Fatal Tree: Crime and Society in Eighteenth-Century England* (London: Pantheon Books), pp. 65–118.
Lukis, W. (ed.). (1882). *The Family Memoirs of the Rev. William Stukeley, M.D.*, Surtees Society, Vol. 73 (London).
MacPhail, A. (1914). 'Body-snatchers, and after: A plea for anatomy', *St Bartholomew's Hospital Journal* (1913–14): 112–19.
Maitland, W. (1756). *The History and Survey of London from its foundation to the present time*, Vol. 2 (London).
Miles, A. (forthcoming). *Dancing in the Rigging: A Burial Ground of St Thomas's Hospital, Southwark, Excavations at Shard Place, 2014–17* (London: MOLA Studies Series).
Mitchell, P. (ed.) (2012). *Anatomical Dissection in Enlightenment England and Beyond* (Farnham: Ashgate).
Moore, N. (1918). *The History of St Bartholomew's Hospital*, Vol. 2 (London: C. Arthur Pearson).
Moore, N. (revised by Bevan, C.) (2004). 'Nourse, Edward (bap. 1701, d.1761)', in *ODNB* www.oxforddnb.com/view/article/20375 (accessed 31 July 2019).
Moore, W. (2006). *The Knife Man* (London: Random House).
Morgan, J. (1730). *The New Political State of Great Britain* (London).
Mytum, H. and Webb, K. (2018). 'Body snatchers and mortsafes: An archaeology of fear', in Mytum, H., and Burgess, L. (eds), *Death across Oceans: Archaeology of Coffins and Vaults in Britain, America, and Australia* (Washington, D.C: Smithsonian Books), pp. 227–48.
O'Malley, C. (1964). *Andreas Vesalius of Brussels, 1514–1564*, University of California Press.

Parsons, F. (1934). *The History of St Thomas's Hospital*, Vol. 2 (London: Methuen & Co).

Payne, T. (1731). *A catalogue of the libraries of the Reverend and learned Thomas Brathwaite, D.D. Late Warden of Winchester-College, and Vice-Chancellor of Oxford. And His Late Nephew, Tho. Brathwaite, Surgeon and Anatomist* (London).

Peachey, G. (1924). *A Memoir of William and John Hunter* (Plymouth: Brendon).

Rannie, D. (ed.). (1901). *Remarks and Collections of Thomas Hearne: Vol. 5 (1 December 1714–31 December 1716)*, Oxford Historical Society, Vol. 42.

Rannie, D. (ed.). (1902). *Remarks and Collections of Thomas Hearne: Vol. 6 (1 January 1717–1 May 1719)*, Oxford Historical Society, Vol. 43.

Rannie, D. (ed.). (1907). *Remarks and Collections of Thomas Hearne: Vol. 8 (23 September 1722–9 August 1725)*, Oxford Historical Society, Vol. 50.

Richardson, R. (2001). *Death, Dissection and the Destitute*, 2nd edn (Chicago: University of Chicago Press).

Roberts, R. (ed.) (1933). *Calendar of Inner Temple Records*, Vol. 4, 1714–50.

Robb-Smith, A. and H. Sinclair (1950). *A History of the Teaching of Anatomy in Oxford* (Oxford: Oxford University Press).

Rolleston, H. (1932). *The Cambridge Medical School* (Cambridge: Cambridge University Press).

South, J. (1886). *Memorials of the Craft of Surgery in England* (London).

Symonds, J. (1717). *Syllabus Partium Corporis Humani* (London).

Taylor, J. (1761). *The history of the travels and adventures of the Chevalier John Taylor*, Vol. 1 (London).

Vertue, G. (2004). 'Hearne, Thomas (bap. 1678, d.1735)', in *ODNB* www.oxforddnb.com (accessed 5 August 2023).

Vian, A. (1890). 'Greene, Robert (1678?–1730)', in S. Lee and L. Stephen (eds), *Dictionary of National Biography (DNB), 1885–1900: Vol. 23* (London: Smith, Elder & Co.), p. 74.

Wallis, P. and Wallis, R. (1988). *Eighteenth Century Medics* (Newcastle-upon-Tyne: Project for Historical Biobibliography).

Wallis, R. (2004). 'Kersey, John, the elder (bap. 1616, d.1677)', in *ODNB* www.oxforddnb.com/view/article/11428 (accessed 2 July 2019).

Wilson, P. (1992). '"Sacred sanctuaries for the sick": Surgery at St Thomas's Hospital 1725–26', *The London Journal*, 17(1): 36–53.

Young, S. (1890). *The Annals of the Barber-surgeons of London* (London: Blades, East & Blades).

# 5

# Who smokes anymore? Documentary, archaeological and osteological evidence for tobacco consumption and its relationship to social identity in industrial England, 1700–1850

*Anna M. Davies-Barrett and Sarah A. Inskip*

It has been argued that tobacco was the first truly global commodity (Gately, 2001). The arrival of Europeans in the Americas resulted in the widespread distribution of the plant through colonial and imperialistic expansion. Port books and tax records show that after arriving in Europe in the sixteenth century, in just 200 years, American tobacco had virtually traversed the globe and generated enormous wealth for Western states; it was the impetus for the earliest colonies and a significant actor in the emergence of the slave trade. As tobacco spread, it became entangled with everyday life, both through its incorporation into pre-existing rituals and contexts (especially those that already involved intoxicants (Withington, 2011)), and through the formation of entirely new practices and behaviours. This necessitated the emergence of new tobacco etiquette and material culture, such as pipes, cutters, snuffboxes and tobacco jars (McShane, 2022).

In the late sixteenth and early seventeenth centuries, tobacco was brought into England in small quantities. In 1603, just 25,000 lbs were imported (Goodman, 1993: 59). However, within decades, imports had increased exponentially, and tobacco prices had fallen, making the product easily available to all members of society (Taylor, 2018: 40). By 1700, 38 million lbs arrived in various ports across the country (Goodman, 1993: 59). This could equate to enough for every inhabitant of England to have a pipeful a day (Shammas, 1990: 78, table 2). Although used as a medicine in pills, drinks and ointments, tobacco was largely consumed in clay pipes, which remained the predominant mode for consumption until the late nineteenth century. Snuff-taking emerged initially among elites at the end of the eighteenth century (Hughes, 2003) and gradually filtered down to the rest of society, while the cigar did not become popular in England until the nineteenth century.

Despite a diverse range of sources that attest to tobacco culture in industrial England, research on tobacco history has been dominated by economic historians who have used trade and taxation sources (e.g. for England: MacInnes, 1926; Shammas, 1990). The reliance on these led to large gaps in our knowledge of the social components of tobacco use, such as who used it, why and what its effects were on the body. Further, more recent narratives about tobacco use are mostly drawn from the perspectives of middle- to upper-class white, 'literate' men, especially from urban centres. One way to reassess current narratives is to take a multidisciplinary approach and draw on the various sources of evidence for tobacco use that exist for England.

In this chapter, we aim to bring various strands of information together for the first time to create an interdisciplinary perspective on tobacco and tobacco use in three different communities in England (Barton-upon-Humber, central London and Coventry) from 1700 to 1850. We focus on how embodied experiences (as described by Craig-Atkins and Harvey, this volume: introduction) of tobacco use were strongly tied up with different and intersecting aspects of identity – especially occupation, gender and class – using a combination of population-level and individual case study analyses. First, we present trends drawn from historical research and artistic representations to explore social perceptions of tobacco consumption. We follow with data derived from archaeological clay pipe assemblages from the regions of interest, which provide information on the identities of smokers and their smoking practices in different contexts. We then present results of the analysis of evidence for tobacco use in archaeological human skeletal remains, providing direct population-level impressions about exactly who was using tobacco and how. Finally, we combine historical and osteobiographical approaches in a case study of Sarah Green, an identified woman from Coventry, to explore how aspects of her identity may have intersected to affect her choice to consume tobacco.

Using various forms of evidence, we demonstrate that age, class, gender, ethnicity and regional and cultural backgrounds may have all affected the ways in which people experienced tobacco consumption. In particular, we identify a disconnect between documentary evidence for consumption of tobacco as a predominantly male social practice, and osteoarchaeological evidence for a large proportion of women also consuming, perhaps in the privacy of their own homes. Also evident is that class and occupation were likely dictators of the ways in which tobacco was consumed, and that the association of certain tobacco consumption practices with specific social groups within the media was used to marginalise these same people. While each strand of evidence (historical, archaeological, osteological) can contribute unique perspectives about tobacco use, together they can capture the complexity of this history and provide a broader consideration of tobacco consumption in relation to social identity during the industrial period in England. Using this approach, we are able to show how the social, the material and the body itself can combine to provide embodied experiences of groups often overlooked in historical contexts (Craig-Atkins and Harvey, this volume: introduction).

## Regions of study

Prior to presenting relevant historical, archaeological and osteological evidence, it is important to outline a brief history of the three regions chosen to represent different English communities, since this is integral to contextualising their tobacco use practices. Barton-upon-Humber (Barton) is a medieval market town in Lincolnshire situated just 5 miles south-west of Hull, on the southern banks of the Humber Estuary. Until the nineteenth century, Barton was small, with between one and two thousand residents (Barton on Humber Branch Workers' Educational Association [BHBWEA], 1978) who were mostly dependant on agricultural work. During rail expansion in the early 1800s, which saw the population double, occupations and businesses in the town became more varied, serving local needs (Rodwell, 2011: 8). Most of these roles were manual, with 29% of men employed in farming, and 38% of women in domestic services; there was also a large portion of men (around 22%) and some women in shopkeeping and trading, while just 5% of men were recorded as being within 'professional' occupations (e.g. solicitors, clergymen) (BHBWEA, 1978: 36, table 2). In the 1850s, nearly 80% of residents were born in Lincolnshire. Of the remaining individuals, only 1.7% ($n = 68$) were from outside England, of which nearly all were from the home nations or Ireland (BHBWEA, 1978: 5). At Barton, excavations of St Peter's Church between 1978 and 1984 yielded around 2,800 burials dating from AD 950 to 1855 (Waldron, 2007). Of these, 141 adult individuals dating to phase A (1700–1850) were analysed in the current study.

In the eighteenth and nineteenth centuries, London became the biggest town in the world (Schwarz, 1992), and was at the centre of a global trading network. It was highly cosmopolitan, attracting migrants, merchants, investors and scholars from across the globe. It was also highly stratified, housing the country's richest and some of its poorest communities, with the West End being wealthier than the East. St James's, the church from which our skeletal material originates, was located along Piccadilly in the boundaries of Westminster City. It was a particularly busy thoroughfare through London and was home to some of the wealthiest families in the city. However, the area of central London also had many poor (Besant and Mitton, 1902; Boulton and Schwarz, 2011). Communities within the city were socially and occupationally diverse, with many skilled and unskilled labourers – most of whom were involved in all kinds of manufacturing, service sectors or dealing, and 'middling classes' – including tradesmen, shopkeepers and professionals (Schwarz, 1992: 11, 51). Between 2017 and 2019, construction for HS2 resulted in the excavation of St James's Gardens in Euston, the area used as a cemetery for St James's, Piccadilly. The cemetery was in use between 1788 and 1853 and is one of the largest industrial period cemetery excavations to have ever taken place in the UK, with over 10,000 burials recovered, as recorded in the (unpublished) Mace Dragados & HS2 (2022) *Report – St James's Gardens Post-Excavation Assessment*. A sample of 281 complete adult individuals were analysed from four different burial areas believed to correspond to a range of socioeconomic statuses, from high to low. Thus, the sample from St James's Gardens reflects a variety of occupations and lifestyles.

Once an exceptionally prosperous medieval town, Coventry suffered a decline in the early post-medieval period. However, it went on to become an industrialised city, helped first by the construction of a canal, and then by the arrival of the railway in the 1830s (Soden, 2003). Although previously famous for cloth, Coventry became important in the silk ribbon weaving trade (Stephens, 1969) and later the watch making industry (Trickett, 2006). The weaving and ribbon trades provided jobs for thousands of residents. The city had a high number of small workers' houses and was densely crowded. It is reported that the wealthy preferred not to live within the city, but did enter for entertainment (Stephens, 1969). By the mid-nineteenth century, there was a large number of Irish migrants, who worked in the local industries (Prendergast, 2019). Excavated between 1999 and 2000, the post-medieval burial ground of Holy Trinity Church, located on the former site of the Cathedral of St Mary's in the centre of Coventry, yielded 1,706 skeletons, the vast majority of which were buried between *c.*1776 and 1850 (Soden, 2000). This assemblage included several historically documented individuals, identified from their coffin plates. The cemetery contained a mixture of low status and some more wealthy members of the town. Just over 100 skeletons were retained and are now held by the University of Leicester, and a total of seventy-nine adult skeletons were available for analysis in the current study.

## Historical sources

In this section, we examine the available historical evidence and previous historical research into the social perspectives of tobacco use. The aim is to identify if and how tobacco may have related to various components of identity, including gender, class, social status and age. Social historians have addressed the gap in our knowledge about tobacco culture in England using diverse sources containing information reflective of people's ideas, thoughts and perceptions about tobacco and tobacco use from the late sixteenth to twentieth centuries. Sources include poems, plays, songs, satires, paintings, pamphlets, criminal proceedings, learned writing and (etiquette) books, of which relevant examples have been presented here.

Tobacco arrived in England both as a disease panacea and as an intoxicant. While for the former it seems to have been recommended as a medicinal remedy for common ailments in both men and women (see Gardiner, 1610; Pauli, 1746; Vaughen, 1602), the very first English pipe users were men; the habit was introduced by those in male occupations (sailors, adventurers, merchants, sojourners) (Lemire, 2018). Initially, tobacco was expensive, limiting its use to those that could import it or afford to buy it. Working (2022) and Withington (2007) show how tobacco use and smoking in company had a key role in elite identity construction in seventeenth-century England. It demonstrated associations with exploits in the 'New World' and was key in politics and negotiation, becoming strongly intertwined with elite male sociability (see Withington, 2007; Working, 2022). By the mid-seventeenth century, tobacco's popularity had increased among all men, as can be observed in multiple types of sources from the period. Male consumption of tobacco features strongly in poetry and plays (McCullen, 1968). There are contemporary references to excessive consumption of tobacco, especially in taverns (e.g. Pauli, 1746: 18), which were key sellers of the product (McShane, 2022). Male drinkers with tobacco pipes are frequently depicted in satire in eighteenth- and nineteenth-century London (Roman, 2022). The masculine nature of public pipe smoking can be further demonstrated through the review of historical documentation on assaults and homicides where tobacco pipes were used as a weapon, which were overwhelmingly committed in drinking establishments and by men that had them to hand (Inskip and Muir, 2023). Many anecdotes from the period begin with a man smoking a pipe in a drinking house (e.g. Whitely, 1888: 15, 18, 60).

In the late seventeenth and eighteenth centuries, the emergence of polite society and new rules around civility and bodily control resulted in a shift in manners and etiquette around tobacco use. Hughes (2003: 66) and Tullett (2019) both argue that smoking was becoming discouraged in some public spaces, increasingly seen by historical commentators as impolite and as a habit of the lower classes (e.g. Hartley, 1860). Snuff, fashionable in French courts, became popular among elite English groups at this time. This, it was argued, fit better in polite society as it was smokeless and removed the need for frequent expectoration (Hughes, 2003: 68). It became fashionable in London and potentially the most generic form of tobacco use in the country (Goodman, 1993: 93). Snuff, Tullett (2019: 150) argues, was not without its problems when it came to politeness and bodily control; instead of encouraging salivation, it caused sneezing and nasal ejections which resulted in dirty handkerchiefs and soiled clothing. It eventually fell out of fashion, with pipe smoking re-emerging strongly in the nineteenth century (Goodman, 1993: 93). At this time, new and more expensive types of pipes made of meerschaum, and later brier, emerged. Cigar smoking, which was long associated with the Spanish, also became popular with upper-class males. By this time, tobacco consumption habits had become so intertwined with social status that Hilton (2000: 17–18) shows that, in reference to Sherlock Holmes, you could tell what status a man was by the way he consumed his tobacco. How to smoke correctly was also frequently a subject in male etiquette books (e.g. Day, 1840; Hartley, 1860) and the pursuit of tobacco consumer knowledge was an important part of gentlemanly connoisseurship (Hilton, 2000: 28–9). High-status men socialised in their smoking rooms and refrained from public smoking, which was associated with lower-class males.

There is far less written about the use of tobacco by women; their lives were rarely the subject of written discourse, and fewer of their writings have survived. This had led to the impression that they did not consume much tobacco. Nevertheless, McShane (2021) shows there is evidence that women frequently consumed tobacco and suggests that this evidence has been overlooked due to the assumption that consumption was of the male sphere and the fact that it did not fit with narratives of eighteenth- and nineteenth-century female domestication and politeness. In fact, Goodman (1993: 61) argues that prior to the nineteenth century, there is little evidence to support the idea that smoking was a particularly gendered activity in England (although see Lemire, 2018: 758). For instance, travellers' diaries indicate that women were likely to have been smoking and chewing tobacco in England (Penn, 1901: 79–81) and Teare (1798: 9) discussed washerwomen who needed to smoke as much as soldiers, sailors and other labouring men. However, it is possible that regionality played a part. McShane (2021: 30; 2022: 7) highlights how female smoking was universally accepted in areas with strong maritime and tobacco trade connections, such as in the West Country.

However, by the eighteenth century there is significant commentary to support the idea that it was not considered desirable for women to smoke (McShane, 2021). Importantly, Rowley (2003: 181) argues that if tobacco smoking was a strongly male exploit, it was automatically unwomanly. Evidence for this attitude is found within poetry, plays, satire and news reporting. Pipe-smoking women were often labelled with 'undesirable' or 'unfeminine' characteristics. In several satirical prints, such as Rowlandson's 'St Giles Courtship' (1799) and 'Sea Stores' (1812), women looking to solicit men or in promiscuous positions were depicted with pipes (Inskip and Muir, 2023). In an assessment of four assault cases where women used pipes as an *ad hoc* weapon, all were committed by lower-class women and details suggest that in two cases they were possibly soliciting men (Inskip and Muir, 2023). The association between pipe smoking and women from ethnic minorities may have also painted the practice as something 'exotic' or 'other' (e.g. Chatterjee, 2022), or worked to further marginalise ethnic groups by associating them with the disreputable activity of pipe smoking and associated 'undesirable' behaviours (Figure 5.1). These perceptions of female smoking did not change until the early twentieth century, when the mass-produced cigarette emerged on the market and tobacco companies identified the untapped potential of women consumers (Hilton, 2000).

Older women were also subject to commentary, such as the woman in Cruikshank's (1807) 'Smoking a Parson!!'. They were often portrayed as poor and/or eccentric or having masculine attributes. Inquisitions into the deaths of four older women do point to habitual pipe use. During an inquisition into the death of a 70-year-old pauper woman, who was 'very fond of her tobacco pipe,' from Southwark, London, she was labelled as a 'peculiar old woman' (Anon., 1898). *The Lancet* reports on the death of Phoebe Randal, a smoker of over 20 years who burnt to death after her bedclothes caught fire from her pipe (Anon., 1857). The pipe was often given to her by her husband 'freely' as it was the 'only comfort she had' as she suffered from significant ill health. Mary Clues (52 years old) from Coventry (Wilmer, 1774), and Grace Pett (about 60 years) from Ipswich (Anon., 1744) also burnt to death with the inquisitions recording their long-standing habits of smoking a pipe at bedtime, with both recorded as intoxicated before their demise. Importantly, the latter three cases highlight habitual pipe smoking in the privacy of the home.

While female smoking was apparently frowned upon in polite society in the eighteenth and nineteenth centuries, snuffing – which is not associated with spitting, blackened teeth and smoke – was more acceptable and became popular with elite women in the first part of the eighteenth century. McShane (2022: 36), who draws upon diaries, snuff boxes and print discourse, suggests that social commentary on snuffing focused more on how snuff was taken, and that criticism was levelled at those that used it immoderately. McShane (2022) goes on to say how, unlike pipe users, female snuffers were depicted more favourably in media.

Historical evidence suggests that tobacco was used by all sections of society; however, perceptions about the way in which it should be used fluctuated with time. What emerges strongly from this research is that, by

**Figure 5.1** Two prostitutes bargaining with a naval man. Thomas Rowlandson's *Sea Stores*, 1812.

the eighteenth century in England, social norms around tobacco use, especially that of the pipe and cigar, appeared to be highly gendered and interconnected with socioeconomic status and class (Goodman, 1993; Hilton, 2000; Hughes, 2003; McShane, 2022). Despite this, much of our evidence pertains to London and metropolitan areas. We still know little about rural women's use beyond the fact that diaries highlighted by McShane (2022) indicate they were consuming it. Thus, perceptions of who was consuming tobacco and how are perhaps distorted by materials that focus on polite society and the urban elite.

## Clay tobacco pipes

Clay tobacco pipes are one of the most common finds on historical archaeological sites (Lemire, 2018). The style and make of a pipe, the inclusion of decoration or motifs, its manufacturer and provenance and the spread of different types within an assemblage can all provide information about the people who were using them. This section will consider archaeological pipe assemblages from four different areas of London, followed by Barton and Coventry to further contextualise pipe usage in these areas and the identities of those using them.

In England, London dominated the clay-pipe-making industry in the first part of the seventeenth century and remained a leading producer until the twentieth century (Oswald, 1967). By 1750, there were also large centres of industry in the regions of York, Hull, Bristol and Chester (Oswald, 1967: 6). As English pipe production was subject to codes and regulations from the seventeenth century, we have a significant amount of information from historical records about pipes, their makers, designs and marks. This information has been used by archaeologists to date contexts and sites and to help reconstruct trading networks (e.g. Cortes Bárcena, 2013). However, pipes are under-exploited as a source of information about smoking culture (Cessford, 2001). The fact that pipes were generally cheap, were diverse in quality and form and used publicly makes them an ideal medium to explore facets of society, such as identity and class. Davey (1981) demonstrates how the types and quality of pipes varied between high-status occupants of Norton Priory and those nearby at Chester, while Hartnett (2004) uses tobacco pipes and historical records to assess local agency in colonial Ireland. Archaeological science has also enabled archaeologists to assess residues from pipes, with new approaches revealing what substances have been smoked (Raffety et al., 2012) and the genetic sex of the users (Schablitsky et al., 2019).

Thousands of clay pipes have been excavated across London, and, while few reports consider their meaning beyond typology and dating, studies have been useful in demonstrating differences between social groups in terms of the types of pipes present and how they were used. At St James's Gardens, thirty clay pipes were recovered from the cemetery, with twenty associated with burials. Pearce (2022) examined the pipes and identified that most of these were typical of London, with one French import. Unstratified material from the cemetery produced six mid-nineteenth-century pipes, including a floral decorated pipe, one claw pipe, one with raised thorns, one possibly associated with a local public house and a French pipe of a befeathered woman's head. Of pipes found in burials, three had red wax on the mouthpiece, thought to prevent the clay from sticking to and damaging people's lips. There were two pipes with masonic symbols, one with generic leaf seams and another with distinctive oak leaf decoration. The mixed nature of the assemblage may reflect the diverse nature of those interred at the cemetery and those visiting it. The decorative range of the pipes, and the presence of two with masonic imagery, suggests that they may have acted for their user as a means to signify aesthetic preferences and associations with certain groups in a city with an incredibly diverse populace. Interestingly, all the pipes found within burials were recovered from the second and third cemeteries, thought to represent the working class and middling sorts. This could suggest that pipe smoking was an important element of identity for these groups, important enough for pipes to potentially be included within burials.

In terms of the lower echelons of London society, Pearce (2007) examined clay pipes from three privies from a group of terraces on Regents Street, in Limehouse – situated in the dockland area of the city, and from a row of terraces from the Minories at Goodmans Yard, Whitechapel (Ritchie and Miles, 2011). Although some of the pipes from the Minories are a little earlier than those at Limehouse, the pipes at both sites are mostly without decoration and are not of high quality; the earlier pipes at the Minories have limited evidence for milling or burnishing, a technique used until the early eighteenth century on higher quality pipes. However, at both sites it is possible that some of the pipes might have had longer stems, which may have been more expensive (Cessford, 2001; Pearce, 2007). All contexts contained local London pipes. This suggests that individuals from these two locations may have preferred locally made pipes, either because they were easy to obtain from local establishments such as taverns, inns or theatres, sometimes free with drinks, or because they were cheaper to procure. Ritchie and Miles (2011) noted that some pipes at both sites were used heavily; even though they were generally disposable, certain pipes continued to be used for some time, possibly demonstrating that they were favoured by their user. While there was much similarity in the pipes between the three Limehouse privy contexts, Pearce (2007) also noted subtle quality and stylistic differences between contexts. This suggests that while people in the area used similar pipes, tastes and/or means varied between inhabitants living closely together.

We can contrast the findings from the Minories and Limehouse with those found in the moat area at the Tower of London (Higgins, 2004), a high-status site. While some of the earliest pipes date to the early to mid-seventeenth century, the majority came from the late seventeenth to the mid-nineteenth century from local London makers. In this assemblage there was a great range of variation in pipe types and manufacturers. Here we find three more unusual pipes, one each from Bristol and Chatham, and one pipe possibly from France or Italy (Higgins, 2004: 242). Higgins suggests that it is difficult to be sure whether this reflects the mobile nature of the soldiers based at the tower, or provisioning at a high-status site (Higgins, 2004: 242). Many of the pipes were decorated and some of the earliest pipes were burnished to a high quality. In terms of decoration, a high number of pipes had armorial motifs. While these have been associated with taverns and inns (Pearce, 2007), and a tavern was very close to the Tower, Higgins (2004) suggests that variations in their form suggests they possibly came from a range of sources.

There is much less information about clay pipes from Barton, but the first recorded pipe maker in Hull, established by 1644 (Watkins, 1979), is just five miles from the town. Sixty-seven clay pipe stem fragments and twelve bowl parts were recovered from excavations of the cemetery at St Peter's Church. The date range of the identifiable fragments ranged from the mid/late seventeenth century through to the nineteenth century. These fragments were consistent with pipes made in Hull, but may also have been procured from nearby Nottingham and Lincoln (Mann, 2011). Only one pipe had decoration: swags of drapery and leaves along the stem (Mann, 2011). Excavations on Maltby Lane found two mid–late seventeenth-century pipes (Trott, 2011), while four fragments from Dam Road were also likely to be locally made pipes (Taylor, 2008). A single Prince of Wales pipe was found somewhere in Barton, although no information is provided for its context (Le Cheminant, 1981). Without more extensive work on clay pipes in the area, the information that can be gleaned is limited. In general, it seems that people in the town preferred local or regional pipes, perhaps reflecting the more insular nature of the small town. The lack of decoration could indicate that, unlike in larger more diverse populations, pipes were not used as a priority means of expressing facets of identity.

Excavations at Much Park Street, at the centre of Coventry's industrial heart, revealed an assemblage of 221 clay pipe fragments that date mostly from the late seventeenth to the nineteenth century. These were associated with a well, demolition layers of a ribbon factory, and terraced housing (Hylton, 2016), which was described as dilapidated by the 1800s (Prendergast, 2019: 76). Unlike Barton and the assemblages from Limehouse and the Minories, there was greater variation in the pipes represented, despite the fact that they were recovered from an apparently poor district. This included glazed/painted stems, decorated pipes with possible association to taverns (plume and feathers, and anchors), a pipe with rouletting, a leaf decorated stem, a bowl being held by a claw and a bowl in the form of a basket. Whitely (1888: 78, 90) recounts that the Horse and Jockey pub on the corner of Much Park Street was the meeting place of the 'dilettante of the city' and the Rose Inn was a meeting place of the well-to-do. The theatre was also not far away. Although the community at Much Park Street included many that laboured in the factory, and from the nineteenth century included many Irish immigrants (Prendergast, 2019), a mixed community may be in the vicinity of the street which could explain the diversity in pipes. Despite the street's Irish connections, none of the pipes had decorations associated with Ireland, such as those presented by Hartnett (2004).

## The osteological evidence

The analysis of evidence for tobacco use in archaeological human skeletal remains, alongside an estimation of biological sex and age – and contextual information from the burial ground, can provide the only direct information about exactly who was consuming tobacco within a specific population. Here, we describe the two distinctive characteristics of the dentition that have been used as evidence of prolonged or habitual tobacco consumption. We follow with the results of analysis of three skeletal samples from our regions of interest, to further investigate how osteological evidence can provide information on the variation of tobacco use by sex, age, location and status.

The first type of evidence available from the skeleton is the 'pipe-notch', a characteristic semi-circular abrasion caused by habitual clenching of the teeth around the stem of a clay pipe while smoking (see Figure 5.2). The presence of these dental abrasions is well known in post-medieval skeletal populations from various countries (Geber and Murphy, 2018; Inskip *et al.*, 2023; Ubelaker, 1996; Walker and Henderson, 2010), but they are inconsistently recorded and reported. It should also be noted that the formation of pipe-notches represents the use of a specific abrasive clay pipe stem, while tobacco consumption was likely to have taken place in a variety of

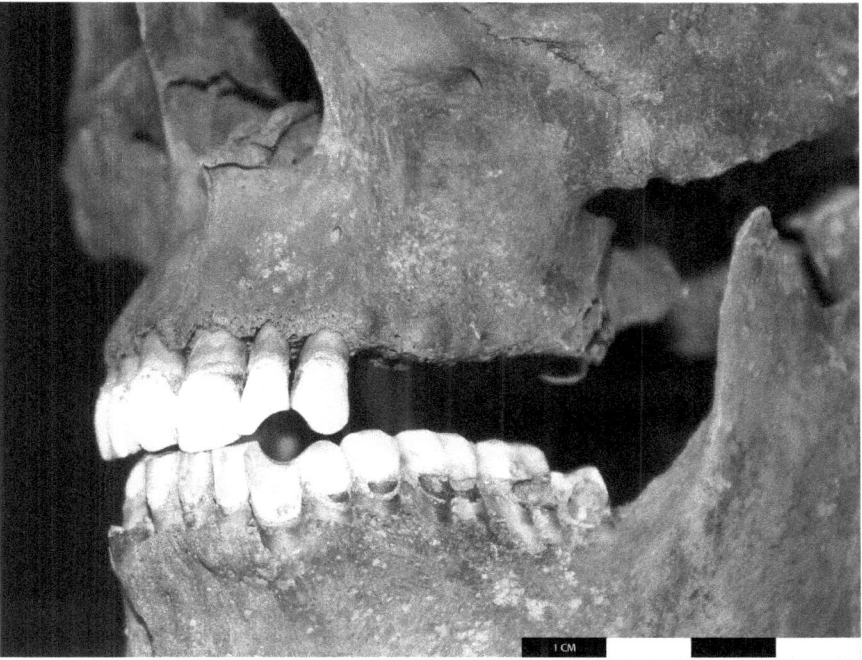

**Figure 5.2** Circular pipe-notch in the left dentition of a middle adult male caused by abrasion of the enamel surfaces by the habitual smoking of a clay pipe (PSN208, Sk134130, St James' Gardens).

forms, including via the taking of snuff and the smoking of cigars, cigarettes and the use of less abrasive pipe stems/mouthpieces.

Therefore, the second form of evidence – tobacco staining on the lingual (inner-facing) surfaces of the teeth – can potentially provide greater information on tobacco consumption, outside of specific pipe usage. This evidence consists of the adhesion to the tooth of a substance of variably light brown to black colour (see Figures 5.3 and 5.4). While little is known about the process, the adherence of tobacco staining to the lingual aspects of the teeth is likely to be highly variable. A number of factors could influence its formation, including the type of tobacco consumed, the means by which it is consumed, the oral biome of the person consuming it and their oral hygiene routine (if any), the types of food and drink consumed and the use of the mouth for other purposes (e.g. its use occupationally as a third hand/tool). There does appear to be a strong correlation between pipe-notch formation and lingual staining (Walker and Henderson, 2010); however, other sources

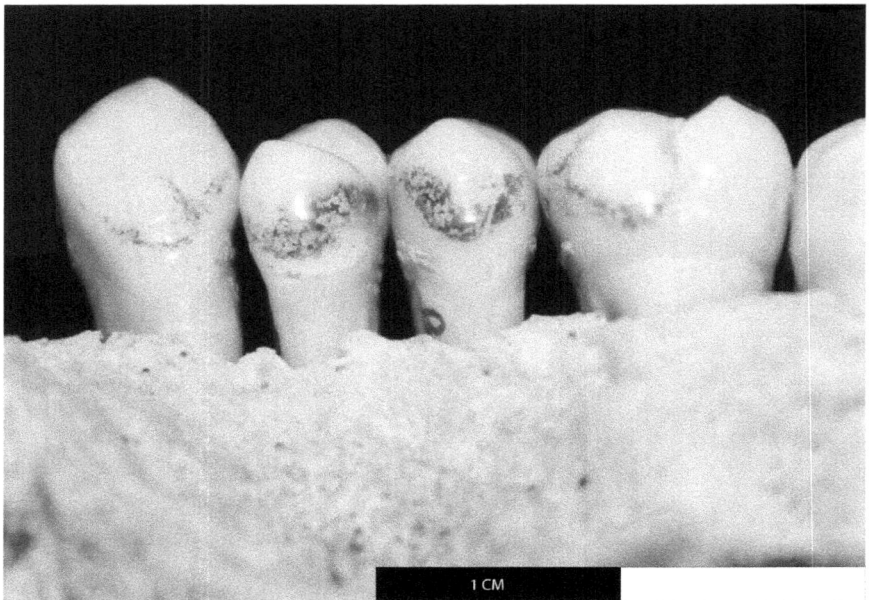

Figure 5.3 Staining caused by tobacco smoking on the lingual (inner-facing) surfaces of the upper left canine, premolars, and first molar of a young adult possible male (PSN157, Sk1963, Barton-upon-Humber).

could potentially contribute to the staining of the teeth, such as the inhalation of other forms of smoke or consumption of tea, coffee or other discolouring substances during life. Additionally, tobacco staining should not be confused with preserved soft tissue or other organic adhesions to the teeth occurring post mortem, nor with calculus deposits (which may also be stained a brown colour due to tobacco consumption). Generally, differentiation of this substance from other sources can be made by observing the typical characteristics of this kind of staining: a very thin coating which is not raised from the tooth surface, a 'cracked ink' or 'dry riverbed' appearance to the substance (see Figure 5.4), and its location predominantly on the lingual surfaces. Combining staining with pipe-notches will provide a minimum estimate of tobacco consumption use within a population.

Very few studies have attempted to present prevalence rates of smoking in different populations, despite the fact that known smoking status can provide opportunities for the investigation of trends in tobacco consumption and its relationship to various diseases in the past. There have been some exceptions, however. Walker and Henderson (2010) analysed the adult population of St Mary and St Michael Cemetery, London (1843–54), and

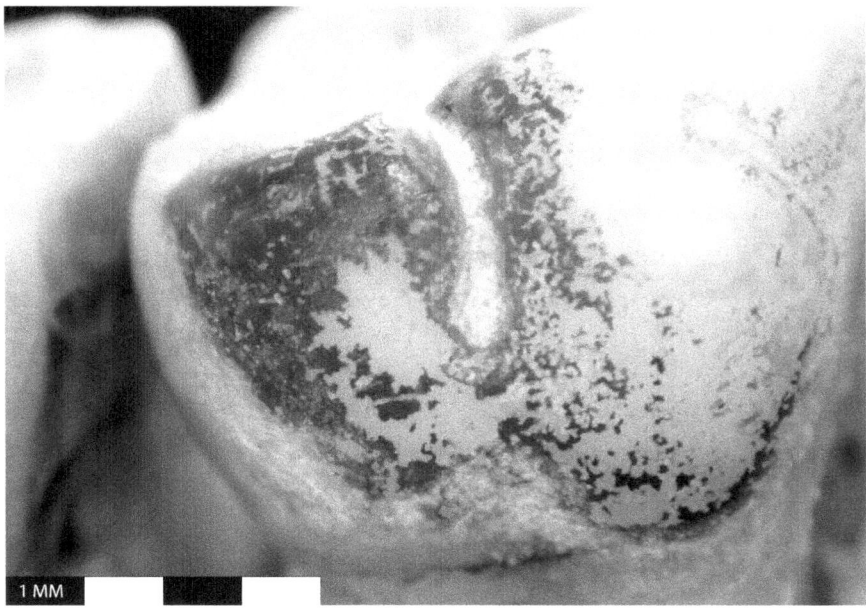

**Figure 5.4** Magnified image of lingual staining on the upper right first molar of an older adult female (PSN25, Sk417, Holy Trinity Church).

found a significantly higher prevalence of notches (39.6% males, 2.9% females) and lingual staining (25.9% males, 3.9% females) in males. Geber and Murphy (2018) found higher rates of pipe-notches in an Irish population from Kilkenny Union Workhouse (1847–51) – 60.7% in males, 28.6% in females – but did not investigate the prevalence of lingual staining. Geber and O'Donnabhain (2020) have since provided further data from a solely male Irish prison population at Spike Island (1860–83), which presented with a pipe-notch prevalence of 77.3%. Inskip *et al.* (2023) found that 97% of males with observable dentition in a Dutch population from Beemster (eighteenth and nineteenth century) had pipe-notches. Here we assess notches and staining from our sites at Barton, Coventry and central London for comparison with historical and archaeological sources. We recorded the prevalence rates of evidence for smoking in three separate categories:

1. *Prevalence of pipe-notches:* All available dentition were observed for pipe-notches. This type of wear is typically seen on the incisors, canines and premolars at the intersection between two teeth. For this reason, these teeth were divided into nine 'sites', consisting of a pair of neighbouring teeth, in both the upper and lower dentition (see Figure 5.5). The presence or absence of a pipe-notch within an individual was recorded

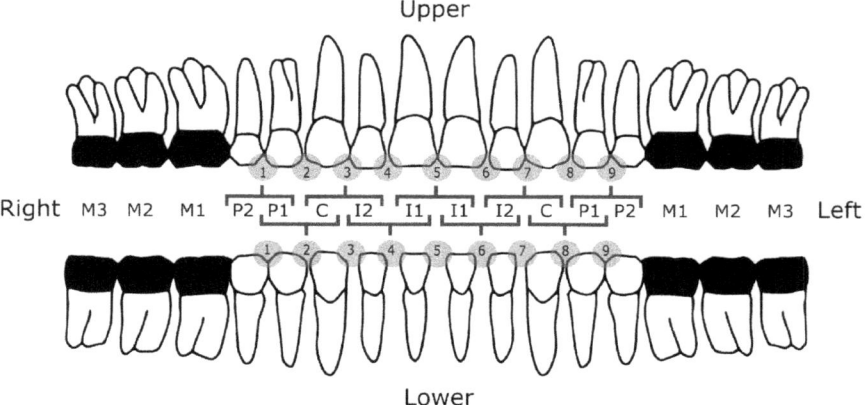

**Figure 5.5** The anterior dentition is divided into nine 'sites' (circles), made up of the intersection between two teeth. At least one of either the corresponding upper or lower sites, consisting of both teeth, for all nine sites must be present for the accurate observation of a pipe-notch. Molars (black) were not recorded for pipe notches since the pipe stem is very unlikely to be in contact with these teeth due to their position at the back of the mouth.

if all nine sites were represented by at least one upper or lower pair, in which both teeth within the pair were present. If at least one site was absent in both the upper and lower dentition, a score of unobservable was attributed to the individual, as a pipe-notch may have been present but could not be accurately observed.

2. *Prevalence of lingual staining:* All available dentition were observed for lingual staining. To be included, at least 25% (eight of thirty-two) of lingual surfaces had to be observable. If not, then a score of unobservable was attributed to the individual. If any dentition presented with discolouration to the tooth surface with the characteristics typical of lingual staining, then the individual was scored as present for staining.
3. *Total prevalence of evidence for smoking:* The total prevalence of individuals with any evidence for smoking was calculated. A score of present was attributed to any individual who demonstrated evidence for a pipe-notch and/or lingual staining.

### Age and sex estimation

Age and sex estimates for each individual were established using standard osteological methods (Brickley, 2004: 23–4, fig. 9a; Brooks and Suchey,

1990; Bruzek, 2002; Buikstra and Ubelaker, 1994: 18–20; Cunningham *et al.*, 2016; Falys and Prangle, 2015; İşcan *et al.*, 1984a, 1984b, 1985; Klales *et al.*, 2012, after Phenice, 1969; Lovejoy *et al.*, 1985). Adult individuals were categorised into one of the following age categories: young adult (20–34 years), middle adult (35–49 years), old adult (50+ years), or unknown adult (20+ years). Each individual was also placed in one of the following sex estimation categories: female, male or unknown.

*Evidence of tobacco use, sex and age*

A total of 470 adults (20+ years) with estimated sex were analysed. Due to absences of dentition or unobservability of tooth surfaces, 49.8% (234/470) of the sample were excluded, of which many were old adults who had significant tooth loss in life. Of the remaining 236 individuals with observable dentitions, 57.6% (136/236) of the sample presented with evidence for smoking, in the form of a pipe-notch and/or lingual staining (Table 5.1).

Evidence for pipe smoking, in the form of pipe-notches, was strongly associated with males. A total of 45.2% (57/126) of males with observable dentition demonstrated evidence of pipe-notches, while only three middle adult females (5.1%, 3/59) presented with a pipe-notch. In males, an increase in the prevalence rate of pipe-notches is observable with increased age, rising progressively from 40.4% in young adults, to 47.5% in middle adults, to 50% (9/18) in the oldest age category. This is unsurprising given that it takes time to develop pipe-notches.

The lack of pipe-notches in females does not, however, mean that women were not tobacco users. A total of 28% (35/125) of females presented with lingual staining (in comparison to 51.2% in males). The total prevalence of females with overall evidence for smoking (which required a stricter inclusion criteria of a greater number of observable teeth) was even higher at 42.9% (36/84; 65.8% in males), indicating a significant proportion of females may have consumed tobacco in some form. It is difficult to assess differences in the prevalence of smoking in females in different age categories due to the reduced sample size, particularly in the old adult age category, in which only seven individuals within the entire observable female sample fell. However, a very large proportion of older women were smokers (85.7%, 6/7).

Evidence for smoking was present in all age groups, with a rise in prevalence in later age groups in both males and females. The presence of notches and staining in the young adults suggests that many individuals were likely to have been smoking in adolescence, if not sooner. The higher prevalence in

Table 5.1 Prevalence rates of evidence for smoking in populations from Coventry, Barton and London. Prevalence rates are presented in three groups: rate of pipe-notches; rate of lingual staining; rate of pipe-notches and/or lingual staining combined.

| Population | Sex | Adult age | Pipe-notch | Lingual staining | Pipe-notch and/or lingual staining |
|---|---|---|---|---|---|
| Holy Trinity Church, Coventry | Female | Young | 0% (0/5) | 14.3% (1/7) | 16.7% (1/6) |
| | | Middle | 0% (0/3) | 25% (2/8) | 40% (2/5) |
| | | Old | - (0/0) | 100% (1/1) | 100% (1/1) |
| | | Unknown | - (0/0) | 50% (1/2) | 100% (1/1) |
| | | Total | 0% (0/8) | 27.8% (5/18) | 38.5% (5/13) |
| | Male | Young | 0% (0/4) | 20% (1/5) | 25% (1/4) |
| | | Middle | 36.4% (4/11) | 46.7% (7/15) | 71.4% (10/14) |
| | | Old | 50% (1/2) | 60% (3/5) | 100% (3/3) |
| | | Unknown | - (0/0) | - (0/0) | - (0/0) |
| | | Total | 29.4% (5/17) | 44% (11/25) | 66.7% (14/21) |
| | Total | | 20% (5/25) | 37.2% (16/43) | 55.9% (19/34) |
| St Peter's Church, Barton-upon-Humber | Female | Young | 0% (0/9) | 15.4% (2/13) | 22.2% (2/9) |
| | | Middle | 20% (1/5) | 15.4% (2/13) | 33.3% (2/6) |
| | | Old | - (0/0) | 100% (2/2) | 100% (2/2) |
| | | Unknown | - (0/0) | 0% (0/1) | - (0/0) |
| | | Total | 7.1% (1/14) | 20.7% (6/29) | 35.3% (6/17) |
| | Male | Young | 50% (6/12) | 50% (7/14) | 61.5% (8/13) |
| | | Middle | 14.3% (1/7) | 33.3% (5/15) | 50% (5/10) |
| | | Old | 75% (6/8) | 54.5% (6/11) | 77.8% (7/9) |
| | | Unknown | 0% (0/1) | 0% (0/2) | 0% (0/1) |
| | | Total | 46.4% (13/28) | 42.9% (18/42) | 60.6% (20/33) |
| | Total | | 33.3% (14/42) | 33.8% (24/71) | 52% (26/50) |

## Who smokes anymore? 151

| | | | | | |
|---|---|---|---|---|---|
| St James's Gardens, London | Female | Young | 0% (0/16) | 30% (12/40) | 50% (12/24) |
| | | Middle | 12.5% (2/16) | 32.1% (9/28) | 45.5% (10/22) |
| | | Old | 0% (0/1) | 50% (3/6) | 75% (3/4) |
| | | Unknown | 0% (0/4) | 0% (0/4) | 0% (0/4) |
| | | Total | 5.4% (2/37) | 30.8% (24/78) | 46.3% (25/54) |
| | Male | Young | 41.9% (13/31) | 63.6% (21/33) | 61.1% (22/36) |
| | | Middle | 56.1% (23/41) | 52.9% (27/51) | 70.6% (36/51) |
| | | Old | 25% (2/8) | 62.5% (5/8) | 66.7% (6/9) |
| | | Unknown | 100% (1/1) | 33.3% (1/3) | 100% (2/2) |
| | | Total | 48.1% (39/81) | 56.8% (54/95) | 67.3% (66/98) |
| | Total | | **34.7% (41/118)** | **45.1% (78/173)** | **59.9% (91/152)** |
| Total | Female | Young | 0% (0/30) | 25% (15/60) | 38.5% (15/39) |
| | | Middle | 12.5% (3/24) | 26.5% (13/39) | 42.4% (14/33) |
| | | Old | 0% (0/1) | 66.7% (6/9) | 85.7% (6/7) |
| | | Unknown | 0% (0/4) | 14.3% (1/7) | 20% (1/5) |
| | | Total | 5.1% (3/59) | 28% (35/125) | 42.9% (36/84) |
| | Male | Young | 40.4% (19/47) | 55.8% (29/52) | 58.5% (31/53) |
| | | Middle | 47.5% (28/59) | 48.1% (39/81) | 68% (51/75) |
| | | Old | 50% (9/18) | 58.3% (14/24) | 76.2% (16/21) |
| | | Unknown | 50% (1/2) | 20% (1/5) | 66.7% (2/3) |
| | | Total | 45.2% (57/126) | 51.2% (83/162) | 65.8% (100/152) |
| | Total | | **32.4% (60/185)** | **41.1% (118/287)** | **57.6% (136/236)** |

older adults is likely due to the accumulation of evidence for smoking over a lifetime.

*Evidence for tobacco use, location and status*

Overall prevalence rates of smoking in both males and females were similar between populations, ranging from 52% at St Peter's Church, Barton-upon-Humber, to 59.9% at St James's Gardens, London. This suggests that regardless of location, at least half the population were using tobacco in some form or other in this period. Prevalence rates of lingual staining ranged from 33.8% (24/71) at Barton, to 37.2% (16/43) at Coventry, to 45.1% at London (78/173). There were also variations in the prevalence of pipe-notches, with the population from Coventry presenting the lowest prevalence (20%, 5/25), and higher rates within the populations from London (34.7%, 41/118) and Barton (33.3%, 14/42). This indicates that, while smoking may have been no less popular in any one population, methods of consumption within those populations may have varied based on fashions, preferences and practicalities.

Within the population from St James's Gardens, it was possible to further investigate prevalence rates of smoking according to socioeconomic status (Table 5.2). Differences in the prevalence of lingual staining and pipe-notches can be observed in males among different socioeconomic groups. While males from the group with the highest socioeconomic status present with the lowest prevalence of pipe-notches (22.2%, 2/9), this group also presents with the highest prevalence of lingual staining (64.7%, 11/17). The prevalence rate for overall evidence of smoking within males with the lowest socioeconomic status presented the lowest result, at 50% (9/18), lower than in males from other status groups where rates ranged from 58.6% to 80%. A smaller observable sample size in females made it difficult to determine differences among socioeconomic status groups. However, while lingual staining did not tend to vary among socioeconomic groups (ranging from 24.1% to 38.5%) in females, the overall prevalence rate for evidence of smoking in the middle-high status group was considerably lower (26.9%, 7/26) than in other status groups, which ranged from 44.4% in the high-status group to 80.0% in the low-status group. Interestingly, one of only three women to demonstrate evidence for a pipe-notch was of high socioeconomic status, which is surprising considering the reduced number of pipe-notches observed in men in this status group. Differences in prevalence rates among socioeconomic groups from St James's Gardens could be due to a host of factors, including reduced sample sizes, but also supports historical observations of variations in social norms and identity signifiers within different social strata, as well as access to resources, such as types of smoking paraphernalia.

Table 5.2 Prevalence rates of evidence for smoking in different status groups, ranging from high to low, from St James's Gardens, London.

| Population | Sex | Status group | Pipe-notch | Lingual staining | Pipe-notch and/or lingual staining |
|---|---|---|---|---|---|
| St James's Gardens, London | Female | High | 16.7% (1/6) | 27.3% (3/11) | 44.4% (4/9) |
| | | Middle-high | 0% (0/21) | 24.1% (7/29) | 26.9% (7/26) |
| | | Middle-low | 0% (0/8) | 38.5% (10/26) | 71.4% (10/14) |
| | | Low | 50% (1/2) | 33.3% (4/12) | 80% (4/5) |
| | Male | High | 22.2% (2/9) | 64.7% (11/17) | 75% (12/16) |
| | | Middle-high | 44% (11/25) | 52% (13/25) | 58.6% (17/29) |
| | | Middle-low | 61.3% (19/31) | 62.2% (23/37) | 80% (28/35) |
| | | Low | 43.8% (7/16) | 43.8% (7/16) | 50% (9/18) |
| | Total | High | 20% (3/15) | 50% (14/28) | 64% (16/25) |
| | | Middle-high | 23.9% (11/46) | 37% (20/54) | 43.6% (24/55) |
| | | Middle-low | 48.7% (19/39) | 52.4% (33/63) | 77.6% (38/49) |
| | | Low | 44.4% (8/18) | 39.3% (11/28) | 56.5% (13/23) |

## Case study: Sarah Green of Much Park Street, Coventry

As well as providing population-level information, a careful consideration of the different types of evidence available can also provide a greater understanding of individual embodied experiences. In this section, we use osteobiographical information and historical data of an identified woman with lingual staining, to explore the ways in which different components of her identity may have intersected to affect her choice to consume tobacco. Analysis of the dentition of PSN25 (Sk417), an older adult (50+ years) female from Holy Trinity Church, Coventry, demonstrated unusually heavy lingual staining on the upper molars (Figure 5.6). The woman was identified as Sarah Green from her coffin plate. Her death certificate indicates that she died in 1847, aged 62 years, from 'fever and convulsions'. Census data from 1841 placed Sarah on Much Park Street, Coventry, sharing a household with her husband(?) John Green, 75, a shoemaker; Sarah Green, 19, a silk winder; Catherine Green, 17, a 'filler'; George Green, 13 and Ellen Ward, 2. At the time of the 1841 census, Sarah was a 'nurse'. This term could encompass a broad range of occupations, including nursemaid or midwife,

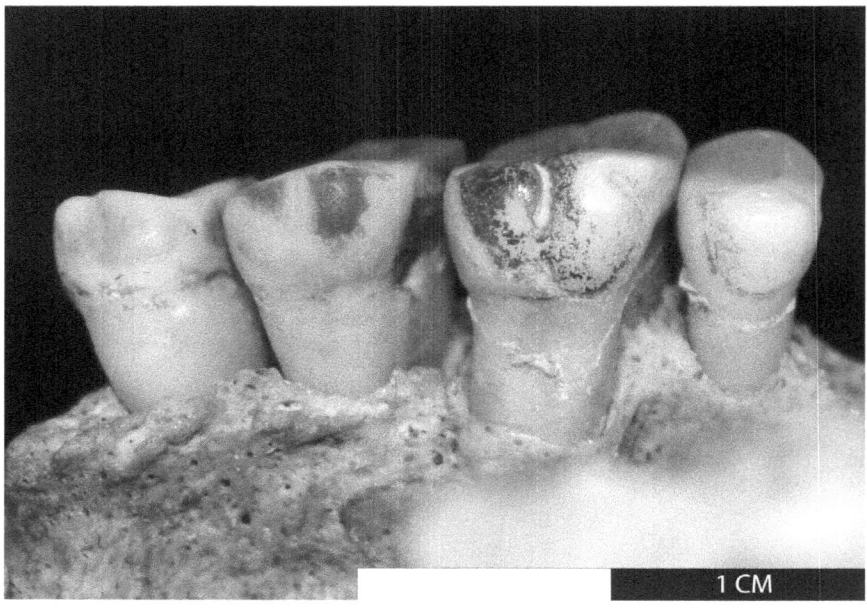

Figure 5.6 Heavy lingual staining on the upper right dentition of Sarah Green (PSN25, Sk417), an older adult female buried within the post-medieval burial ground for Holy Trinity Church, Coventry.

but may be referring to the role of a domiciliary nurse: a working-class woman who visited and cared for the sick, particularly the poor, within their own homes (Denny, 1999). Many of Much Park Street's inhabitants, located in the centre of the city, were involved in the silk ribbon trade, including the two young women living in the household alongside Sarah, and she may have, at an earlier point in time, also undertaken work in this industry.

In the first half of the nineteenth century, Coventry was becoming overcrowded, and the reasonable-looking façade of Much Park Street hid the congested maze of courtyard buildings located behind it (Prendergast, 2019: 76–7). Complaints from the inhabitants of Coventry included poor sewage drainage within the city due to the construction of mill-dams and poor water supply (Anon., 1845: 33, 43, 87–8). Those residing in the courtyard buildings were often highly impoverished, with crowded, unsanitary housing conditions and diseases such as cholera running rampant (Prendergast, 2019: 81–3). As a domiciliary nurse, Sarah's profession may have been in high demand among the inhabitants of Much Park Street and the wider city.

The high level of staining on Sarah's molars indicates that, at least towards the end of her life, she was possibly a heavy smoker. We could not say if she used a pipe as not enough of her teeth were present to observe pipe-notches. The adoption of tobacco consumption by Sarah may be due to a myriad of factors relating to her perceived social identity, constructed from an intersection between her age, gender, socioeconomic status, cultural and regional backgrounds and her personal preferences. Of importance may be that the area around Much Park Street in Coventry during this period supported a number of Irish immigrants and individuals of Irish descent (Prendergast, 2019). As discussed below, the smoking of pipes held particular significance for those of Irish cultural heritage, particularly of labouring backgrounds. While 1841 census data for Sarah says she was born in the county of Warwickshire, she may have been influenced by the cultural milieu of Much Park Street.

It is difficult to fully understand Sarah's socioeconomic circumstances from the little documentary evidence that exists, but her occupation was probably working class at this time, and her residence on Much Park Street indicates a poor socioeconomic background (Prendergast, 2019). Historical sources, such as court case records and inquisitions, have traditionally linked smoking with women of impoverished backgrounds (Inskip and Muir, 2023). Although the data from the different socioeconomic divisions at St James's Gardens suggest that smoking by women may not have been confined to the working classes, for Sarah, tobacco consumption in particular may have offered a small pleasure, if she could afford little other luxury (Geber and O'Donnabhain, 2020). Contemporary discourse highlights the importance of periodic leisure activities, such as the consumption of tobacco, in providing women with a break from the routine of work in the home or outside of it (Hilton, 2002). Additionally, tobacco smoking is known to reduce appetite (Hughes, 2003), making it a handy substitute for those who could not afford adequate food.

Sarah's age and health may have also been a considerable factor in her choice to use tobacco. The consumption of tobacco, particularly via a pipe, appears to have been commented upon more frequently among older, poorer women, although these women were often described as 'peculiar' or 'eccentric'. Additionally, Sarah's skeleton demonstrated several spinal and degenerative joint diseases and poor dental health, both of which are typical of older age, but which can cause pain. Of greatest note was the unilateral osteoarthritis and complete degeneration of the left temporomandibular joint (the joint that connects the mandible to the cranium – see Figure 5.7), likely as a result of dislocation of the joint and subsequent use. Tobacco consumption may have acted as a rudimentary medical aid, with mild analgesic qualities. Its use as a pain alleviator has been documented throughout its history, including into the eighteenth and nineteenth centuries (Stewart, 1967). During the seventeenth and eighteenth centuries, the boundaries between what constituted medicinal or recreational consumption of drugs – such as tobacco, tea, coffee and opium – broke down. It was also during this time that the concept of addiction to a substance developed (Smail, 2007:183–4). Tobacco, and the way in which it was consumed, may have been seen by Sarah as fulfilling multiple roles: as a pain alleviator, an appetite control, a leisure activity, a signifier of age, class or 'peculiar' or 'other' status and additionally as a 'necessity' born from its addictive qualities.

### Discussion: smoking and identity in industrial England

Analysis of different types of sources has provided a depth of knowledge unobtainable from each type alone, especially on rates of tobacco consumption and how use depended on multiple intersecting aspects of identity, including gender, socioeconomic status, ethnicity and occupation. While tax records and port books reveal key details on the amount of tobacco in England, and historical commentary on tobacco use suggests it was widespread, the osteological evidence indicates that around half of adults from all groups were consuming tobacco frequently enough to leave staining and/or notches on their teeth. Furthermore, due to the limitations of the types of osteological markers used, this represents the minimum amount of use within the groups studied. While we did not undertake a dedicated analysis of the dentition of children, a notable finding is that by 20 years of age some people had

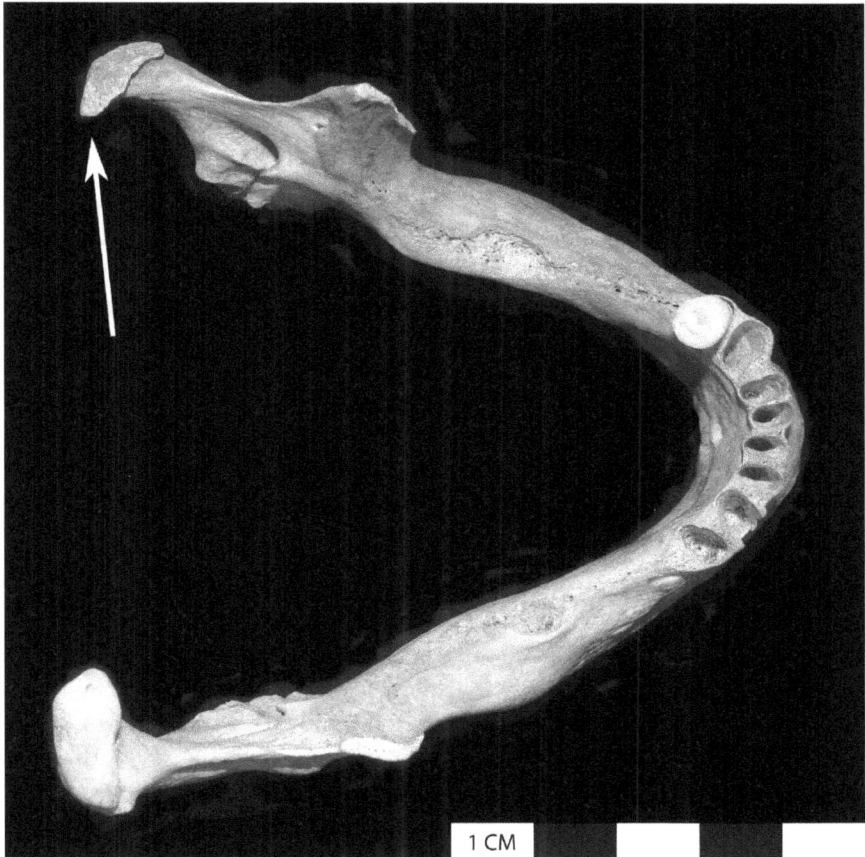

Figure 5.7 Complete degeneration of Sarah Green's left temporomandibular joint (arrow), causing flattening and atrophy of the joint surface.

significant evidence for chronic tobacco use, inferring that use began early in life, perhaps in childhood or adolescence. This adds credence to the concerns of early anti-smoking campaigns in England, who focused strongly on the impact of tobacco on youth (Goodman, 1993: 118), as recorded by social commentators at the time (Billings, 1875). It would be valuable to assess the dentition of children to narrow down the age at which habits were established.

The evidence from clay tobacco pipes and osteological analysis generally supports notions drawn from historical sources about the entanglement of tobacco use with identity. At *prima facie*, gender seems to have played the strongest role in shaping tobacco practice, as it was this aspect of identity for which the biggest differences in tobacco consumption could be found. A key finding here is that while socio-historical commentary presents a picture that women were not big tobacco users, that such an activity would have been 'unseemly' for the majority of well-mannered women during this time period, the osteological evidence from the current study suggests otherwise. In fact, female use rates may be almost as high as men's. Furthermore, this use may have transcended socioeconomic status, as indicated by the data on females from different socioeconomic status burial grounds from St James's Gardens. The lack of agreement between this finding and most historical representations of female smokers has significant implications for understanding female tobacco use in this period.

Historical sources often depict women who smoked during the nineteenth century as being associated with poverty, prostitution and disreputable behaviour, not in keeping with ideas of respectability at the time (McShane, 2021). This may reflect attempts by almost exclusively male commentators to shape and control what they perceived to be a male activity (e.g. Hilton, 2002: 323–4). In certain regions of the country, women who publicly smoked it seems were, thus, vilified and shamed, grouped with others of marginalised status. The negative social perceptions of female smoking likely forced women to consume in a different manner to that of men. While male smoking was inseparable from sociability undertaken in public or shared space or as part of the daily grind, the act of smoking for a woman was likely an intensely private affair, being undertaken for pleasure or solace within her own home or with other women (e.g. McShane, 2021; Rowley, 2003: 184), something hinted at by the inquisition sources or perhaps by Sarah Green who may have used it for medicinal purposes. Unfortunately, female spaces, and what occurred within them, were not subject to the same level of attention as that of public male activities within historical documentation, and we generally lack archaeological evidence from female-dominated spaces. One notable exception is Davies' (2011) study on archaeological pipe assemblages from Hyde Park Barracks, Australia. This prison, which solely housed immigrant and destitute women of British and British/Irish descent from 1862–86, showed that smoking and pipe use were very common among the lower-class women that resided there. The pressure to avoid public smoking may also explain the low level of pipe-notches we find generally in females. Women may have opted for less abrasive mouthpieces or stems, or were careful as to how they used pipes to avoid tell-tale tooth damage that physically embodied smoking (see following paragraphs). They seemingly opted for other modes of delivery; Billings (1875) highlights the practice of rubbing snuff into the gums, which was especially popular with girls and young women.

While social commentary had a strong impact on how and where men and women might use tobacco, it also dictated tobacco practices of the different classes, particularly through bodily control. We can potentially see the effect of this within our analysis of osteological and clay pipe data by socioeconomic status, as well as in court records and inquisitions, which provide insight into the daily lives of people. The clearest difference came from the variation in pipe-notch numbers in men, which can be further augmented by data from other archaeological collections dating to the industrial period, with rates as low as 11.6% in London (Western and Bekvalac, 2020: 94) to up to 97% in a Dutch farming community (Inskip et al., 2023). In our male populations, there were clear variations in the frequency of pipe-notches according to site and status. Men from Barton (46.4%) and the working-class burial ground at St James's Gardens, London (61.3%) having the highest prevalence, and men from Coventry (29.4%) and the high-status London group (22.2%) having the lowest prevalence.

To interpret these differences, it is important to consider what pipe-notches embody, as not all pipes would have caused the formation of notches. The clay 'cutty' pipe has a shorter, thicker stem, which can be clenched between the teeth. Historical sources suggest that these pipes were particularly popular with manual workers, as they freed the hands for work (Brongers, 1964). The habit of holding a pipe between one's teeth may have also extended to periods beyond when the pipe was lit, to avoid the impracticality of repeatedly putting it away and taking it back out. The constant presence of a pipe between the teeth, or even the sight of the notches created by them, would have acted as a visual reminder to others of the individual as a 'cutty smoker'. Learned sources (Anon., 1890; Earle, 1822) describe these notches in relation to sailors, and it is quite likely they could have acted as a physical indicator of lower socioeconomic status/occupational type. It is unsurprising that pipe-notches were most common in men at Barton, where historical records show that the vast majority of the population were engaged in manual labour, and within the working-class group at London, who were also likely to have undertaken manual occupations.

The association between pipes and manual work may then partly explain the low numbers of notches in the high-status men from London. In a strongly stratified society, such as industrial Britain, where physical appearance and bodily control was important, men of higher socioeconomic status might have deliberately avoided using short pipes associated with manual labourers. This effect might be particularly strong in large cities like London, where large groups of middle- and upper-class people resided and socialised. Etiquette books made it clear that having clean and good teeth was a sign of civility (Day, 1840; Hartley, 1860). As such, avoiding short pipes may have also been a choice to prevent the formation of notches, which by association embodied working-class status, a group perceived to undertake immoderate and uncivilised smoking. The high rates of staining in the high-status group suggests that, rather than smoking less than other groups, they were perhaps using more and it remained an important part of elite male identity despite changes in perceptions of public smoking. While at present we cannot tell from osteological methods, this was probably through cigars and other types of pipes with longer and thinner stems, such as the churchwarden or alderman, that were used in leisure smoking (Western and Bekvalac, 2020), as depicted in images of smoking clubs and groups in the eighteenth and nineteenth centuries (Roman, 2022). These pipes were not clenched between the teeth, as they were more fragile and required use of the hand to steady the bowl. In addition, mouth pieces made of whalebone, wood, horn or amber were available for clay pipes and Meerschaum pipes (Penn, 1901), which were far more expensive and less abrasive than clay stems, and became available in England around the nineteenth century. What is interesting is that some high-status men and one high-status woman did have pipe-notches, showing that despite negative social commentary on the use of clay pipes by elites in the later nineteenth century, some made the choice to do so regardless.

The unexpected appearance of notches in high socioeconomic groups, or the low rate identified at Coventry, shows that there are clearly other aspects of life intersecting with gender and socioeconomic status to dictate personal tobacco use. Differences in regional smoking fashions and practicalities may have impacted prevalence rates, and these were also likely to have changed over time. For example, cigar smoking did not become a fashionable alternative to the pipe until the early nineteenth century, and then usually among well-to-do men who had access to the imported and often expensive product (Hilton, 2000: 51–2). It is interesting to consider the population from Coventry who demonstrated the lowest prevalence rate of pipe-notches (20%), but a similar rate of lingual staining to other populations (37.2%). This indicates that while a large proportion of the population was still consuming tobacco, the smoking of abrasive clay pipes was less common. At first, this appears unusual, as much of central Coventry during this period consisted of labourers of poor socioeconomic status, similar to the lower status burial grounds at St James and Barton, and there are plenty of archaeological pipes present. However, the high rate of staining shows they are either smoking pipes less frequently and/or are more likely consuming tobacco in other ways. One possibility is tobacco chewing, which was associated with those in manual classes as, like pipes, it freed up the hands for work (Teare, 1798). One major factor in the low prevalence of pipe-notches may be the involvement of many inhabitants of Coventry within the silk ribbon trade. Silk can be easily damaged by smoke and it is likely workers would not have been permitted to smoke while working with the material, limiting the potential time available to use a pipe. Billings (1875) discusses people that rubbed snuff into the gums in lieu of smoking tobacco. He also described how this approach was used in regions such as Lancashire by those working in spinning and mills, where chewing and smoking tobacco was not permitted. It is highly likely that similar rules might have applied to Coventry. As such, the practicalities of occupation here may have constrained peoples' tobacco choices leading to alternative practices or different modes of use at different points in a person's day.

The choice to use (or avoid the use of) a cutty may also have become linked to perceptions of cultural or group affiliation. In London, for example, multiple pipes with masonic imagery have been identified and may have been used by those of higher status, and decorations associated with Irish identity are common at sites in London. Both the work of Geber and colleagues (Geber and Murphy, 2018; Geber and O'Donnabhain, 2020) and that of Walker and Henderson (2010) link Irish cultural affinity with high frequencies of pipe-notches and, in particular, with poverty. As Geber and O'Donnabhain (2020) explain, the presence of a cutty became frequently incorporated into the often derogatory and racialised caricatures of the Irish poor within English publications. However, such pipes were also co-opted by the Irish to signify cultural belonging and subversive anti-colonial politics through the stamping of the pipe bowl with nationalist insignia and political phrases, such as 'home rule' (Brighton, 2004; Hartnett, 2004). The Irish elite, however, disassociated themselves with the smoking of pipes, perhaps due to its connotations with poverty (Geber and O'Donnabhain, 2020). Thus, the cutty pipe became intimately linked with an Irish labourer's sense of identity, both in terms of socioeconomic status, cultural affinity and political stance. Of note is the greater prevalence of pipe-notches in females from the Kilkenny Workhouse, which, although lower than in males from the workhouse, is still far higher than anything reported for females in England. This indicates that cultural attitudes to the pipe-smoking of women in Ireland may have differed considerably from those in England but may also suggest that the cutty pipe held similar significance in terms of cultural and political identity for Irish women as for men.

Walker and Henderson (2010) suggest that high prevalence rates of smoking noted in the nineteenth-century population from St Mary and St Michael's, London, may be due to a large proportion of Irish immigrants within this burial ground. However, female rates of pipe-notches were greatly reduced (2.9%) in comparison to those from the Kilkenny Workhouse (28.6%), perhaps indicating the pressure from English cultural norms on female behaviour within the Irish immigrant community, a phenomenon also seen in modern migrants (Reiss, *et al.*, 2014). This population also demonstrated very little lingual staining in females (3.9%) and is believed to have come from a poor socioeconomic background (Walker and Henderson, 2010), possibly indicating a lack of access to resources such as tobacco for women of poorer status, at least in this community. Changes in practice could also partly explain the lower rates of pipe-notches in our sample from Coventry and the lack of Irish imagery on the pipes, even though many Irish are recorded as residing and working there.

The prevalence rates of pipe-notches at St Mary and St Michael's are comparable, in both males and females, to our prevalence rates at St James's Gardens. It is evident that smoking among working-class English communities may have been just as common as amongst Irish, although the kind of pipe which causes advanced wear on the teeth may not have been utilised as frequently. Thus, the perception that Irish groups, in particular Irish women, smoked much more frequently than their English counterparts – fitting with derogatory caricatures of the Irish from this period – requires re-evaluation. So, too, does the lack of understanding of tobacco's part to play in the construction of identity among other ethnic minorities in England during this time period. Apart from racist caricatures (see, for example, 'Sea Stores' (Rowlandson, 1812, see Figure 5.1) and 'Sartjee, the Hottentot Venus' (Lewis, 1810)) of ethnic minorities smoking pipes, very little is known of the consumption habits of marginalised groups. As certain types of tobacco consumption were strongly associated with class, gender, regionality and lifestyle, adopting certain methods of consumption may have provided a means for these groups to navigate complex social hierarchies, or to identify with one another via shared practices or iconography, as seen with Irish pipes (Brighton, 2004).

A full exploration of our data is impeded by the absence of research that draws on the embodied actions embedded within the construction, use and discard of clay tobacco pipes, something significantly hindered by the way in which they are used and reported in archaeological scholarship. Osteologically, the accurate identification of smokers also has its limitations, and evidence for other forms of tobacco consumption, such as snuff taking, have yet to be identified in human osteological remains. Additionally, prior to the current study, only Walker and Henderson (2010) have presented prevalence rates of lingual staining. As demonstrated in the current study, a focus on pipe-notches to the exclusion of other forms of evidence for smoking prevents a more nuanced understanding of different types of smoking activities undertaken within different societal groups. In particular, this excludes an understanding of the smoking activities of women in populations where pipe-notches are not frequently found in female dentitions. Therefore, a greater understanding of the composition of lingual staining and more rigorous recording methods for this form of evidence are needed. The development of future scientific analyses (e.g. Badillo-Sanchez et al., 2023; Eerkens et al., 2018) may provide the means to explore the frequency and manner of tobacco consumption among different societal groups further.

## Conclusions

The analysis of multiple types of sources shows that not only was tobacco use extremely widespread in England, but the manner in which it was consumed was tied up with multiple important aspects of their lives. While social commentary on the 'correct' way to use tobacco for men and women, and by upper classes, may have strongly impacted peoples' choices, our work and case study show that group membership, occupation, health and ethnicity intersected with these ideals to produce diverse patterns of individual and group consumption across the country. It appears that derogatory depiction of certain types of tobacco consumption and commentary on the appropriate use of the intoxicant during the industrial period were used as a means to further marginalise certain ethnic, socioeconomic and gender groups. These acts have coloured current perceptions of smoking in the eighteenth and nineteenth centuries, whereby it is assumed that only certain sections of society were undertaking specific tobacco consumption activities. Our work challenges the predominance of historical commentary for smoking as a 'male' activity, and the weight that this narrative has been given in modern analyses of smoking and its relationship to identity, which has resulted in perceptions of smoking as an activity undertaken by, and of greatest importance to, men (Eliot, 2001: 48). This is likely to have contributed to the false perception today that female smoking during the eighteenth and nineteenth centuries was a rare occurrence, isolated to those of poorer socioeconomic or marginalised backgrounds. This work demonstrates, like the work of McShane (2021, 2022), that a shift in perspective yields plenty of evidence for the frequency with which tobacco consumption was woven into the lives of women.

In fact, as our chapter has demonstrated, a wider consideration of the historical, osteological and archaeological evidence suggests that tobacco consumption was utilised broadly across societal groups in different ways and in different public and private spaces. The manner in which people consumed tobacco was likely intimately linked to their social identity, demonstrating the relationship between tobacco consumption and the body as a series of embodied actions dictated by age, class, gender, occupation and regional and cultural backgrounds. Our case study of Sarah Green provides an example of the ways in which these different aspects of identity may have affected the choice to consume tobacco. Furthermore, the choices made by some groups were also important in dictating the use of tobacco by others, with class and occupation evidently structuring factors. The association of the cutty pipe with the poor, labouring classes, people of Irish ethnicity and women of marginalised status may have affected the smoking 'fashions' of the upper classes and particularly of women, who likely often chose pipes or alternative methods that would not have produced notches on the teeth. The combination of historical documentation with osteological and pipe assemblage data has provided a more nuanced understanding, but there is still much to be explored.

## Acknowledgements

We would like to thank Kevin Booth at English Heritage and Dr Simon Mays at Historic England for facilitating access to the Barton-upon-Humber skeletal collection. We would also like to thank Andrea Bradley at HS2 and Michael Henderson and Louise Fowler at MOLA for aiding in access to the St James' Gardens skeletal collection. We would like to gratefully acknowledge the input and help during the course of this research of Maria Serrano Ruber and Dr Diego Badillo Sanchez on the Tobacco, Health and History Project at the University of Leicester. Additional help was provided by Sarah Morriss, Dr Danielle De Carle and Dr Jo Appleby, all also of the School of Archaeology and Ancient History, University of Leicester. Finally, we would like to thank the editors of this book, Dr Lizzy Craig-Atkins and Prof. Karen Harvey, for inviting us to contribute to this volume and for providing feedback on earlier drafts. This research was undertaken as part of the Tobacco, Health and History Project, funded by a UKRI Future Leaders Fellowship grant (grant number: MR/T022302/1), held by Dr Sarah Inskip.

## References

Anon. (1744). 'An extract of the minutes of the Royal Society, of Nov. 8. and 15. 1744. concerning the woman at Ipfwich, who was found burnt to afhes on April 10. Preceding', *Philosophical Transactions*, 43(476): 463–5.

Anon. (1845). *Second Report of the Commissioners for Inquiring into the State of Large Towns and Populous Districts* (London: William Clowes and Sons), vol. 1.

Anon. (1857). 'Singular and awful death. Medical diary of the week', *The Lancet*, 691750: 281.

Anon. (1890). 'The effects of bagpipe playing on the teeth', *The Lancet*, 135(3487): 1438.

Anon. (1898). 'Her last pipe'. *South Wales Echo*, 30 June, p. 2.
Badillo-Sanchez, D., Ruber, M. S., Davies-Barrett, A. M., Sandhu, J. K., Jones, D. J. L., Hansen, M. and Inskip, S. A. (2023). 'Examination of human osteoarchaeological remains as a feasible source of polar and apolar metabolites to study past conditions', *Scientific Reports*, 13: 696.
Barton on Humber Branch Workers' Educational Association (BHBWEA) (1978). *Barton on Humber in the 1850's. Part Two. The Town and the People* (Barton on Humber: Branch Workers' Educational Association).
Besant, W. and Mitton, G. E. (1902). *The Fascination of London* (London: Adam and Charles Black).
Billings, E. R. (1875). *Tobacco; Its History, Varieties, Culture, Manufacture and Commerce* (Hartford: American Publishing Company).
Boulton, J. and Schwarz, L. (2011). '"The comforts of a private fireside"? The workhouse, the elderly and the Poor Law in Georgian Westminster: St Martin-in-the-Fields, 1725–1824', in J. McEwan and P. Sharpe (eds), *Accommodating Poverty* (London: Palgrave Macmillan), pp. 221–45.
Brickley, M. B. (2004). 'Determination of sex from archaeological skeletal material and assessment of parturition', in M. B. Brickley and J. L. McKinley (eds), *Guidelines to the Standards for Recording Human Remains* (Southampton; Reading: British Association for Biological Anthropology and Osteoarchaeology; Institute of Field Archaeologists), pp. 23–5.
Brighton, S. A. (2004). 'Symbols, myth-making, and identity: The red hand of Ulster in late nineteenth-century Paterson, New Jersey', *International Journal of Historical Archaeology*, 8(2): 149–64.
Brongers, G. A. (1964). *Nicotiana Tabacum* (Groningen: Theodorus Niemeyer).
Brooks, S. and Suchey, J. M. (1990). 'Skeletal age determination based on the os pubis: A comparison of the Acsádi-Nemeskéri and Suchey-Brooks methods', *Human Evolution*, 5(3): 227–38.
Bruzek, J. (2002). 'A method for visual determination of sex, using the human hip bone', *American Journal of Physical Anthropology*, 117(2): 157–68.
Buikstra, J. E. and Ubelaker, D. H. (eds) (1994). *Standards for Data Collection from Human Skeletal Remains: Proceedings of a Seminar at the Field Museum of Natural History, Organized by Jonathan Haas* (Fayetteville: Arkansas Archaeological Survey).
Cessford, C. (2001). 'The archaeology of the clay pipe and the study of smoking', *Assemblage*, 6.
Chatterjee, A. K. (2022). 'Oriental dressings, imperial inhalations: The Indian hookah in British colonial culture', *Journal of the Economic and Social History of the Orient*, 65(1–2): 279–324.
Cortes Bárcena, C. (2013). 'Dutch and English clay pipes found in Santander (Cantabria, Spain)', *Journal of the Académie Internationale de la Pipe*, 6: 83–5.
Cruikshank, I. (1807). 'Smoking a Parson!!' [print] (London: The British Museum, accession number: 1872,1012.5081). www.britishmuseum.org/collection/object/P_1872-1012-5081
Cunningham, C. L., Scheuer, L. and Black, S. M. (2016). *Developmental Juvenile Osteology*, 2nd edn (London: Elsevier/Academic Press).

Davies, P. (2011). 'Destitute women and smoking at the Hyde Park Barracks, Sydney, Australia', *International Journal of Historical Archaeology*, 15(1): 82–101.

Davey, P. (1981). *The Archaeology of the Clay Tobacco Pipe. VI: Pipes and Kilns in the London Region*, BAR British Series 97 (Oxford: BAR Publishing).

Day, C. M. W. (1840). *Hints on Etiquette and the Usage of Society; with a Glance at Bad Habits* (London: Longman, Orme, Brown, Green, and Longman).

Denny, E. (1999). 'The emergence of the occupation of district nursing in nineteenth century England' (PhD dissertation, University of Nottingham).

Earle, H. (1822). *On the Influence of Local Irritation in the Production of Diseases Resembling Cancer and other Morbid Alterations of Structure* (London: Woodfall).

Eerkens, J. W., Tushingham, S., Brownstein, K. J., Garibay, R., Perez, L., Murga, E., Kaijankoski, P., Rosenthal, J. S. and Gang, D. R. (2018), 'Dental calculus as a source of ancient alkaloids: Detection of nicotine by LC-MS in calculus samples from the Americas', *Journal of Archaeological Science: Reports*, 18: 509–15.

Eliot, R. E. (2001). '"Destructive But Sweet": Cigarette smoking among women 1890–1990' (PhD dissertation, University of Glasgow).

Falys, C. G. and Prangle, D. (2015). 'Estimating age of mature adults from the degeneration of the sternal end of the clavicle', *American Journal of Physical Anthropology*, 156(2): 203–14.

Gardiner, E. (1610). *The Triall of Tobacco* (London: H.L. for Mathew Lownes).

Gately, I. (2001). *Tobacco: A Cultural History of How an Exotic Plant Seduced Civilisation* (Boston: Grove Press).

Geber, J. and Murphy, E. (2018). 'Dental markers of poverty: Biocultural deliberations on oral health of the poor in mid-nineteenth-century Ireland', *American Journal of Physical Anthropology*, 167(4): 840–55.

Geber, J. and O'Donnabhain, B. (2020). '"Against shameless and systematic calumny": Strategies of domination and resistance and their impact on the bodies of the poor in nineteenth-century Ireland', *Historical Archaeology*, 54(1): 160–83.

Goodman, J. (1993). *Tobacco in History: The Cultures of Dependence* (London: Routledge).

Hartley, C. B. (1860). *The Gentlemen's Book of Etiquette and Manual of Politeness* (Boston: DeWolfe, Fiske and Co.).

Hartnett, A. (2004). 'The politics of the pipe: Clay pipes and tobacco consumption in Galway, Ireland', *International Journal of Historical Archaeology*, 8(2): 133–47.

Higgins, D. (2004). 'Appendix 2: The clay tobacco pipes', in G. Keevil (ed.), *The Tower of London Moat: Archaeological Excavations 1995–9. Historic Royal Palaces Monograph No. 1* (Oxford: Oxford Archaeology), pp. 241–70.

Hilton, M. (2000). *Smoking in British Popular Culture 1800–2000* (Manchester: Manchester University Press).

Hilton, M. (2002). 'Leisure, politics, and the consumption of tobacco in Britain since the nineteenth century', in R. Koshar (ed), *Histories of Leisure* (Oxford: Berg), pp. 319–36.

Hughes, J. (2003). *Learning to Smoke: Tobacco Use in the West* (Chicago: University of Chicago Press).

Hylton, T. (2016). 'The clay tobacco-pipes', in J. Elston (ed.), *Archaeological Excavation on Land at Much Park Street Car Park, Coventry, West Midlands, 2014–2015. Report 16/71* (Northampton: MOLA Northampton), pp. 37–41.

Inskip, S. A. and Muir, A. (2023). 'Material encounters: The alternative use of clay tobacco pipes in England and Wales, c. 1600–1900', *Historical Research*, 96(272): 156–173.

Inskip, S., Zachary, L., Serrano Ruber, M. and Hoogland, M. (2023). 'Pipe smoking and oral health in males from the Netherlands during the 18th–19th century', *Post-Medieval Archaeology*, 57(1): 94–107.

İşcan, M. Y., Loth, S. R. and Wright, R. K. (1984a). 'Metamorphosis at the sternal rib end: A new method to estimate age at death in white males', *American Journal of Physical Anthropology*, 65(2): 147–56.

İşcan, M. Y., Loth, S. R. and Wright, R. K. (1984b). 'Age estimation from the rib by phase analysis: white males', *Journal of Forensic Science*, 29(4): 1094–104.

İşcan, M. Y., Loth, S. R. and Wright, R. K. (1985). 'Age estimation from the rib by phase analysis: white females', *Journal of Forensic Science*, 30(3): 853–63.

Klales, A. R., Ousley, S. D. and Vollner, J. M. (2012). 'A revised method of sexing the human innominate using phenice's nonmetric traits and statistical methods', *American Journal of Physical Anthropology*, 149(1): 104–14.

Le Cheminant, R. (1981). 'Clay pipes bearing the Prince of Wales' feathers', in P. Davey (ed.), *The Archaeology of the Clay Tobacco Pipe. VII: Pipes and Kilns in the London Region*, BAR British Series 97 (Oxford: BAR Publishing), pp. 92–101.

Lemire, B. (2018). 'One British thing: Clay pipes', *Journal of British Studies*, 57: 755–59.

Lewis, F. C. (1810). 'Sartjee, the Hottentot Venus' [print] (The British Museum, London, accession number: 1917,1208.3712). www.britishmuseum.org/collection/object/P_1917-1208-3712.

Lovejoy, C. O., Meindl, R. S., Pryzbeck, T. R. and Mensforth, R. P. (1985). 'Chronological metamorphosis of the auricular surface of the ilium: A new method for the determination of adult skeletal age at death', *American Journal of Physical Anthropology*, 68(1): 15–28.

MacInnes, C. M. (1926). *The Early English Tobacco Trade* (Abingdon: Routledge).

Mann, J. (2011). 'Clay tobacco-pipes', in W. Rodwell (ed.), *St Peter's, Barton-upon-Humber, Lincolnshire: A Parish Church and its Community* (Oxford: Oxbow Books, digital archive), p. 1082.

McCullen, J. T. (1968). 'Tobacco: A recurrent theme in eighteenth-century literature', *The Bulletin of the Rocky Mountains Modern Language Association*, 22(2): 30–9.

McShane, A. (2021). 'Bad habits and female agency: Attending to early modern women in the material history of intoxication', in M. Wiesner-Hanks (ed), *Challenging Women's Agency and Activism in Early Modernity* (Amsterdam: Amsterdam University Press), pp. 25–64.

McShane, A. (2022). 'Tobacco-taking and identity making in early modern Britain and North America', *The Historical Journal*, 65: 108–29.

Oswald, A. (1967). *English Clay Tobacco Pipes* (London: British Archaeological Association).

Pauli, S. (1746). *Treatise on Tobacco, Tea, Coffee and Chocolate* (London: T. Osbourne).

Pearce, J. (2007). 'Living in Victorian London: The Clay Pipe Evidence' (London: Museum of London Archaeology, unpublished report).

Pearce, J. (2022). 'Euston St James: Clay Tobacco Pipe Assessment' (London: Museum of London Archaeology, unpublished report).

Penn, W. A. (1901). *The Soverane Herb. A History of Tobacco* (London: Grant Richards).

Phenice, T. W. (1969). 'A newly developed visual method of sexing the os pubis', *American Journal of Physical Anthropology*, 30(2): 297–301.

Prendergast, T. (2019). 'The Irish in nineteenth century Coventry' (PhD dissertation, Ulster University).

Raffety, S. M., Lednev, I., Virkler, K. and Chovanec, Z. (2012). 'Current research on smoking pipe residues', *Journal of Archaeological Science*, 39: 1951–59.

Reiss, K., Sauzet, O., Breckenkamp, J., Spallek, J. and Razum, O. (2014). 'How immigrants adapt their smoking behaviour: Comparative analysis among Turkish immigrants in Germany and the Netherlands', *BMC Public Health*, 14: 844.

Ritchie, S. and Miles, A. (2011). *52–56 Minories London EC3: Watching Brief Report* (London: Museum of London Archaeology).

Rodwell, W. (2011). *St Peter's, Barton-upon-Humber, Lincolnshire: A Parish Church and its Community. Volume 1: History, Archaeology and Architecture* (Oxford: Oxbow Books), vol. 1.

Roman, C. (2022). 'Smoking clubs in graphic satire and the anglicizing of tobacco in eighteenth-century Britain', *The Historical Journal*, 65(1): 130–48.

Rowlandson, T. (1799). *St Giles's Courtship* [print] (New York: The Met Collection, accession number: 59.533.649). www.metmuseum.org/art/collection/search/745917 (accessed 5 August 2023).

Rowlandson, T. (1812). *Sea Stores* [print] (New York, The Met Collection, accession number: 59.533.1485). www.metmuseum.org/art/collection/search/788067 (accessed 5 August 2023).

Rowley, A. R. (2003). 'How England learned to smoke: The introduction, spread and establishment in England before 1640' (PhD dissertation, University of York).

Schablitsky, J. M., Witt, K. E., Ramos Madrigal, J., Ellegaard, M. R., Malhi, R. S. and Schroeder, H. (2019) 'Ancient DNA analysis of a nineteenth century tobacco pipe from a Maryland slave quarter', *Journal of Archaeological Science*, 105: 11–18.

Schwarz, L. D. (1992). *London in the Age of Industrialisation: Entrepreneurs, Labour Force and Living Conditions, 1700–1850* (Cambridge: Cambridge University Press).

Shammas, C. (1990). *The Pre-Industrial Consumer in England and America* (Oxford: Clarendon Press).

Smail, D. L. (2007). *On Deep History and the Brain* (Berkeley: University of California Press).

Soden, I. (2000). *Excavations at the cathedral church of St Mary, Coventry. Summary report* (Northampton: Northamptonshire Archaeology).

Soden, I. (2003). *Late Post-Medieval Coventry: Resource Assessment c1750–1940* (Birmingham: West Midlands Regional Research Framework).

Stephens, W. B. (1969). *A History of the County of Warwick. Volume 8: The City of Coventry and Borough of Warwick* (London: Victoria County History) vol. 8.

Stewart, G. G. (1967). 'A history of the medicinal use of tobacco 1492–1860', *Medical History*, 11(3): 228–68.

Taylor, A. (2018). 'Venting smoke: The trade and consumption of tobacco in early modern England and Wales, c.1625–1685' (PhD dissertation, University of Sheffield).

Taylor, G. (2008). 'Appendix 3: Other finds assessment. Clay pipe', in C. Clay *Archaeological Evaluation Report: Trial Trenching at Land off Dam Road, Barton-Upon-Humber, North Lincolnshire. Summary* (Lincoln: Allen Archaeology Ltd), p. 10.

Teare, E. (1798). *Treatise on the Use and Abuse of Tobacco* (Doncaster: W Sheardown).

Trickett, M. A. (2006). 'A tale of two cities: diet, health and migration in post-medieval Coventry and Chelsea through biographical reconstruction, osteoarchaeology and isotope biogeochemistry' (PhD dissertation, Durham University).

Trott, K. (2011). 'Appendix 8: Clay pipes report', in C. Clay, M. Allen and K. Trott *Archaeological Scheme of Works: Land off Maltby Lane in Barton Upon Humber, North Lincolnshire* (Lincoln: Allen Archaeology Ltd), p. 56.

Tullett, W. (2019). *Smell in Eighteenth Century England: A Social Sense* (Oxford: Oxford University Press).

Ubelaker, D. H. (1996). 'Pipe wear: Dental impact of colonial American culture', *Anthropologie*, 34(3): 321–7.

Vaughen, W. (1602). *Natvrall and Artificial Directions for Health, Deriued from the Best Philosophers, as Well Modern, As Auncient* (London: Richard Bradocke).

Waldron, T. (2007). *St Peter's Barton-upon-Humber, Lincolnshire: A Parish Church and its Community* (Oxford: Oxbow).

Walker, D. and Henderson, M. (2010) 'Smoking and health in London's East End in the first half of the 19th century', *Post-Medieval Archaeology*, 44(1): 209–22.

Watkins, G. (1979). 'Hull pipes: a typology', in P. Davey (ed.), *The Archaeology of the Clay Tobacco Pipe I: Britain – the Midlands and Eastern England*. BAR British Series 63 (Oxford: BAR), pp. 85–121.

Western, G. and Bekvalac, J. (2020). *Manufactured Bodies: The Impact of Industrialisation on London Health* (London: Oxbow books).

Wilmer, B. (1774). 'An account of a woman accidentally burnt to death at Coventry. By B. Wilmer, Surgeon, at Coventry. In a letter to Mr. William Sharpe.' *Philosophical Transactions*, 64: 340–3.

Withington, P. (2007). 'Company and sociability in early modern England', *Social History*, 32(3): 291–307.

Withington, P. (2011). 'Intoxicants and society in early modern England', *The Historical Journal*, 54(3): 631–57.

Whitely, T. W. (1888). *Humorous Reminiscences of Coventry Life, Coventry Coaching and Coach Roads, and Other Works* (Coventry: T. Burbidge).

Working, L. (2022). 'Tobacco and the social life of conquest in London, 1580–1625', *The Historical Journal*, 65(1): 30–48.

# 6

# Uncovering the lives of late-eighteenth- and nineteenth-century inhabitants of Bristol through osteoarchaeological and documentary analysis

*Heidi Dawson-Hobbis and Jocelyn Davis*

### Introduction

The analysis of human skeletal remains informs us about the lives and deaths of individuals from the past. Burials exhumed from nineteenth-century cemeteries with well-preserved grave markers or coffin plates recording the name of the deceased offer the opportunity to integrate documentary evidence with osteological data to create both historical and osteoarchaeological biographies and to explore how these different sources of data complement each other. The aims of this chapter are to use these data to contribute to our understanding of how the lived experience in terms of disease, accident and occupation may manifest on the skeleton. In the introduction to this volume, Craig-Atkins and Harvey refer to the importance of personal 'ego-documents' as a window into 'the necessarily intimate, personal, individual and interiorized components of lived experience'. In one of the cases presented in this chapter, we were able to utilise such information, transcribed from letters, which allowed access to George Cumberland's own thoughts and feelings. This is the first study that integrates osteological analysis with an exploration of the historical documents available for a nineteenth-century cemetery situated within the city of Bristol, and thus explores urban life away from the capital to assist in addressing the London-centric focus seen in other studies. This chapter aims to contribute to a growing focus on a broad range of people in urban communities, not just the middling or elite, and is a general call for osteoarchaeologists and historians to work together to enable a greater understanding of the lives, deaths and disease processes that affected populations living in the nineteenth century. To explore these aims we will present the osteological and historical evidence for five individuals of differing age, sex and socioeconomic status who were buried in St George's cemetery, Bristol, between 1837 and 1857, with a focus on the evidence for disease (tuberculosis), traumatic injury and the ageing body.

This chapter aims to build on existing work, such as the seminal study which utilised this approach on remains from the crypt clearance undertaken at Christ Church Spitalfields, London. This study provided rich and nuanced information on the lived experience of the individuals exhumed as well as a means to test osteoarchaeological methodologies, which were found to be lacking, particularly in the accuracy of assigning an age-at-death for older adults (Molleson and Cox, 1993). This work was the first to illustrate how osteological and historical data could be explored in tandem to realise 'the potential of skeletal variation as an indicator of lifetime activity' (Molleson and Cox, 1993: 214). As the sample came from a crypt clearance, these individuals were all of 'the middling sort' and therefore lacked diversity of socioeconomic status. Cemetery excavations, such as that at St George's, Bristol, which has a mixture of earthen burials and those interred in burial vaults, are more likely to provide us with individuals more representative of the diversity of urban communities, and in this chapter we aim to represent a range of people from diverse backgrounds.

The invisibility of women, individuals of lower socioeconomic status and children in both history and archaeology began to be discussed in the late twentieth century (Bock, 1989; Lillehammer, 1989) with research now buoyant in these areas in the twenty-first century (Dawson, 2014; Gleadle, 2001; Gowing, 2003; Gowland, *et al.*, 2018; Mant, 2020; Newton, 2012). As archaeology deals in physical remains rather than the written word it enables us to make these groups more visible, particularly in exploring aspects of physical embodiment (Harvey, 2020), such as the effect of disease or trauma to the body, and in the processes of age and degeneration. The increasing rate of clearance of cemetery sites and vaults in advance of development across England creates the opportunity to explore the lives of ordinary people who lived and died in the nineteenth century and contribute to our understanding of how their lived experience in terms of disease, accident and occupation may manifest on the skeleton. Several named skeletal collections from this period have been explored, but the focus has often been in London (Emery and Wooldridge, 2011; Henderson *et al.*, 2013; 2015; Miles *et al.*, 2008; Miles and Connell, 2012; Newman and Hodson, 2021; Scheuer, 1998). Sometimes only a subsample of the population has been available for study, due to a lack of time and funds provided by developers. In other cases, grave markers have not been *in situ* and therefore names cannot always be directly linked to the skeletal remains (Emery and Wooldridge, 2011) or the information from the skeletal remains and the information from coffin plates are presented separately (Connell and Miles, 2010) with no effort made to link the two sets of evidence. The aim of this chapter is to present the first study that integrates the osteoarchaeological analysis with an exploration of the historical documents available for a nineteenth-century cemetery situated within Bristol. This study will aim to add to the growing body of work (Adams and Colls, 2007; Brickley *et al.*, 2006; Gowland *et al.*, 2018) exploring urban life away from the capital to assist in addressing the London-centric focus. This is important as historical comparisons of life expectancy and infant mortality data from urban centres across the UK in the nineteenth century have suggested that these vary, with Bristol appearing to have a higher-than-average life expectancy, and also a low infant mortality rate, when compared to London and other growing cities of the period (Szreter and Mooney, 1998; Williams and Mooney, 1994).

## St George's Cemetery, Bristol

In 2016, the cemetery to the north-east side of the church of St George's, Bristol, was excavated by Avon Archaeology Ltd in advance of building works. The site was purchased in 1819 for use as an overflow burial ground for the church of St Augustine the Less, which was situated approximately 400 m to the south-east. The new graveyard was consecrated in 1820, but subsequently, between 1821 and 1823, a new church was built on the same site, being consecrated in the latter year. This was the present St George's, and although originally a chapel of ease to St Augustine the Less, it was elevated to full parochial status in 1832. The parish boundary was very carefully drawn to run parallel to, and tight against, the eastern wall of the church. This meant that the church itself, and everything to its west, was in the new parish of St George's, but the entire eastern side of the churchyard remained in the parish of St Augustine the Less (Potter, 2017). Under the Public Health Act of 1848, burials at St George's were restricted from 1854 onwards to only one body in each grave and no burials within five yards of a building (Latimer, 1887: 338); the cemetery remained in use until about 1885. The 2016 excavation was carried out in the eastern half of the graveyard, that portion belonging to the parish of St Augustine the Less, and 384 burials were exhumed and recorded from three areas representing three terraces separated by retaining walls (Potter, 2017).

The nineteenth century was a time of rapidly increasing population and urbanisation, with increasing bureaucracy and documentation associated with it. During the nineteenth century, the population of Bristol grew rapidly from 64,095 inhabitants in 1801 – almost tripling in size to 182,552 by 1871 (Latimer, 1887). For the period that St George's graveyard was in use, we have access not only to parish registers, but also street directories, death certificates, census records and newspaper articles, which provide us with a wealth of information relating to age at death, occupation, family status and childbirth, place of birth and causes of death and injury. This gives us the opportunity to compare the osteological analysis to these independent sources of evidence for the named individuals, to aid in our understanding of these individuals' lived experience and how this might manifest on the skeleton.

This chapter will provide the evidence for five named individuals excavated from St George's, Bristol; the first collection excavated from Bristol to have named individuals. The recovery of *in situ* well-preserved grave markers and coffin plates allows the identities of these individuals to be known, facilitating the exploration of the documentary evidence combined with the osteoarchaeological evidence to gain an insight into their lives and deaths. This also creates the opportunity to explore how these different data collection methods, and the information obtained, complement each other. Information obtained on these individuals enables us to reflect on the experience of people who may often be neglected in historical research – including those from the working classes, women and children – as well as explore the lives of a more affluent elderly couple. This chapter also aims to be a call for osteoarchaeologists and historians to work together to enable a greater understanding of the lives, deaths and disease processes that affected populations living in the nineteenth century. While the skeletal and documentary analysis of the St George's skeletal collection, as a whole, is ongoing, the individuals presented here represent a mix of socioeconomic status and range in age from 3 years to 93 years at death. Analysis of osteological and documentary data concerning these individuals is here organised into three case studies: first, the diagnosis of tuberculosis from the death certificates of two individuals and whether these can be confirmed through skeletal analysis; second, the evidence both historical and osteological for accidental injury on one individual illustrating how the two strands of evidence give us a more detailed picture of the repercussions of trauma during the period; and third an exploration of the physical changes associated with the natural processes of bodily events, such as childbirth, and the ageing process in two elderly individuals.

## Methodology

The osteological and documentary evidence for each individual will be explored in order to understand more about the lived experiences of these individuals. Can the information provided by the historical evidence be gleaned from the skeleton and vice versa? It is hoped that in bringing together the skeletal and historical evidence for these individuals that they will complement each other and add to our knowledge of both the individuals themselves and also to the success and limitations of our methodologies.

Individuals were identified either by the presence of an inscribed ledger slab overlying the grave or vault, or that of an engraved coffin plate (depositum) directly overlying the skeleton. These inscriptions provided names, dates of death and sometimes age or date of birth, which were then used to search for additional documentary records related to the individuals and their families. The documentary evidence consulted included, but was not limited to, death certificates (ordered directly from the General Register Office (GRO); parish registers and census records (accessed via Ancestry.co.uk); street directories and poll books (accessed via google books); local newspaper articles (accessed via britishnewspaperarchive.co.uk) and the letters of George Cumberland housed in the British Library and transcribed by Jane Evans (2022). The skeletal remains were initially analysed without any prior knowledge of the documentation that accompanied each individual; this was to ensure there was no bias in the assignment of age and sex determination.

Age estimation for the immature individual was established using standard osteological methods for the dentition (Moorrees, *et al.*, 1963a; 1963b; Smith, 1991) and bony skeleton (Scheuer and Black, 2000). Age and sex determination for the adult remains utilised a variety of methodologies (Brooks and Suchey, 1990; Buckberry and Chamberlain 2002; Buikstra and Ubelaker, 1994; Isçan cited in Bass, 1995; Lovejoy *et al.*, 1985; Meindl and Lovejoy, 1985). Stature estimation was calculated using the prediction equations of Trotter and Glesser, cited in Brothwell and Zakrzewski (2004: 33).

## Tuberculosis

Two of the five individuals examined in detail in this study, Maria McVey Taylor and Thomas Rokeby Price, provide an opportunity to explore the impact of tuberculosis on the skeleton in association with historical evidence for their socioeconomic status. Tuberculosis (TB) is commonly a disease of the respiratory system caused by *Mycobacterium tuberculosis* (and sometimes by other member species of the *M. tuberculosis* (MTB) complex), and is also known as consumption (Magyar, 1999). Tuberculosis was the leading cause of death at the beginning of the nineteenth century (Roberts and Buikstra, 2003: 16), and in 1839 was responsible for 17.6% of all deaths in England (Lane, 2001: 142). The disease can manifest in a variety of different ways in the skeleton and both bone destruction (Martini and Boudjemaa, 1988) and periosteal bone formation (Eyler *et al.*, 1996) have been observed in clinical studies of patients with tuberculosis; however, the former tends to be more readily identified and reported within skeletal remains. The spine is the most commonly affected skeletal region in clinical cases of tuberculosis, for both children and adults (Silva, 1980; Thijn and Steensma, 1990). Termed 'Pott's disease', the cause of bony destruction is from a focal abscess at the anterior surface of the body of one or more vertebrae. The pressure applied can cause localised resorption of the vertebral body creating a scalloped and eroded appearance to the spine (Aufderheide and Rodriguez-Martin, 1998; Ouahes and Martini, 1988). If the destruction of the bone becomes severe, this will eventually lead to the collapse and curvature of the spine known as a pathological kyphosis. Roberts and Buikstra (2003: 225) note that in the past the signs and symptoms of TB could be mistaken for other pulmonary diseases and 'one cannot ever be certain that what is being described in historical data is actually tuberculosis'. The name tuberculosis was assigned in 1839 by Schoenlein, who defined all of the diseases associated with tubercles under this term (McMillen, 2016: 75). Padiak (2009) discusses the retrodiagnoses of TB and the variety of terms used for the disease, in historical documents, due to the manifestation of the disease being variable and the terminology being focused on the part of the body affected. Therefore, socially, these individuals were diagnosed as having TB – whether that fits a modern diagnosis of the presence of the tubercle bacillus or not. Indeed, the tubercle bacillus was not recognised as the specific cause of pulmonary TB until 1882 (Lane, 2001: 142).

## *Maria McVey Taylor (SK293)*

Upon excavation, SK293 was found to have a well-preserved depositum or coffin plate, which enabled the individual to be identified as Maria Taylor, who died on 4 January 1845 (see Figure 6.1a). Maria was the wife of George Edward Taylor, a leather seller. Her cause of death as noted on the death certificate was consumption (see Figure 6.2) and her husband was present at the death, which took place at 8 Host Street. Maria was buried on 12 January.

The remains of Maria Taylor were well preserved and her skeleton was more than 75% complete, with only a few small bones of the hands and feet being absent. Copper alloy staining was present on her left parietal (skull bone), left mandible (lower jaw), left femur (thigh bone) and one vertebral body, indicating the presence of copper funerary dress pins. Her skeleton was generally very gracile and features of the pelvis and skull both indicated a female individual matching the identity from the coffin plate. Her estimated stature was calculated to be 158 ±3.66 cm (5 foot 2 in.).

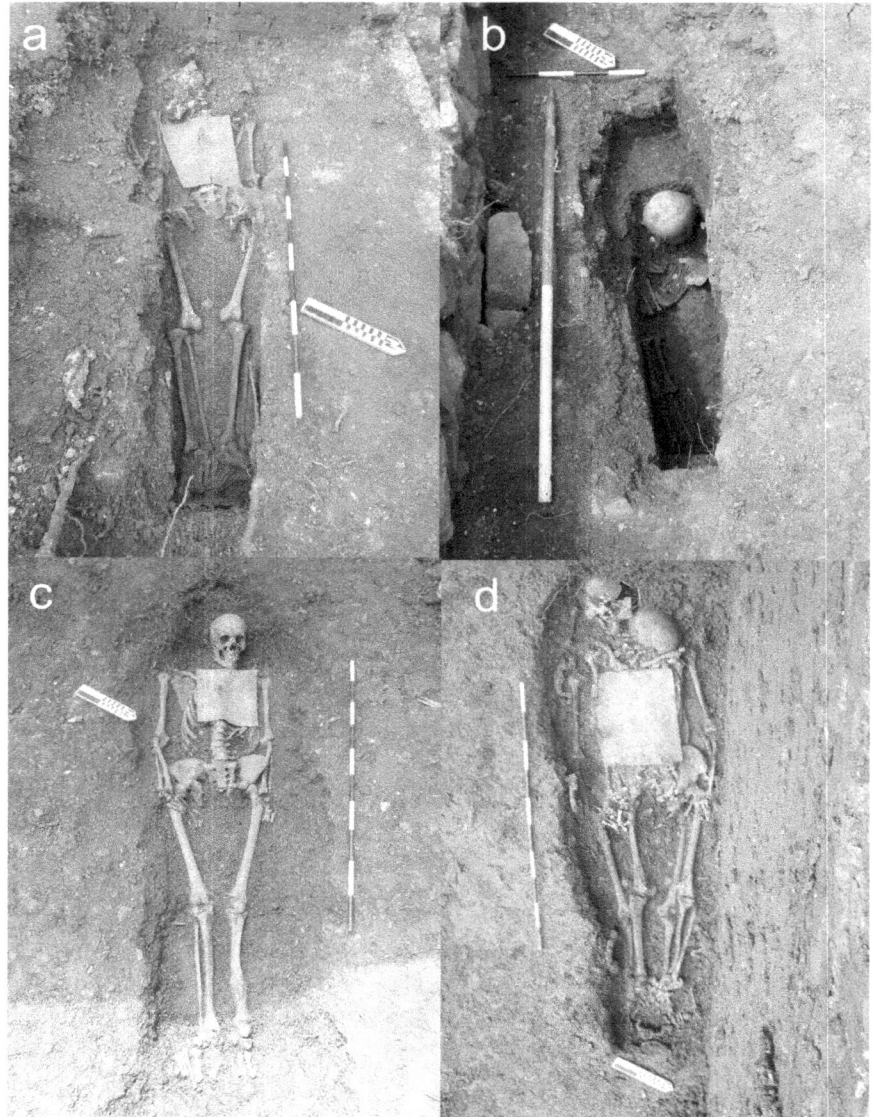

Figure 6.1 Burials on excavation a) SK293, b) SK7, c) SK48 and d) SK273 (upper) and SK272 (lower).

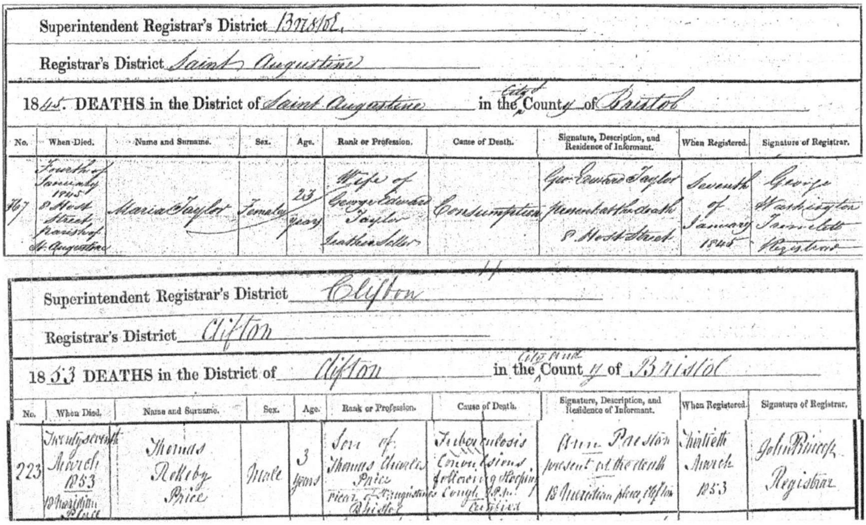

Superintendent Registrar's District Bristol

Registrar's District Saint Augustine

1845 DEATHS in the District of Saint Augustine in the City and County of Bristol

| No. | When Died. | Name and Surname. | Sex. | Age. | Rank or Profession. | Cause of Death. | Signature, Description, and Residence of Informant. | When Registered. | Signature of Registrar. |
|---|---|---|---|---|---|---|---|---|---|
| 167 | Fourth of January 1845 8 Host Street parish of St Augustine | Maria Taylor | Female | 23 years | Wife of George Edward Taylor Leather Seller | Consumption | Geo Edward Taylor present at the death 8 Host Street | Seventh of January 1845 | George Washington Tennelett Registrar |

Superintendent Registrar's District Clifton

Registrar's District Clifton

1853 DEATHS in the District of Clifton in the City and County of Bristol

| No. | When Died. | Name and Surname. | Sex. | Age. | Rank or Profession. | Cause of Death. | Signature, Description, and Residence of Informant. | When Registered. | Signature of Registrar. |
|---|---|---|---|---|---|---|---|---|---|
| 223 | Twenty seventh March 1853 18 Meridian Place | Thomas Rokeby Price | Male | 3 years | Son of Thomas Charles Price [illegible] Bristol | Tuberculosis Convulsions following Hooping Cough [illegible] | Ann Preston present at the death 18 Meridian place Clifton | Thirtieth March 1853 | John Prince Registrar |

**Figure 6.2** Death certificates of Maria Taylor and Thomas Rokeby Price.

The osteological methods suggested an age between 18 and 25 years at death with the sternal end of the clavicle (collar bone) still in the process of fusing, and the death certificate confirmed that Maria Taylor died on the 4 January 1845, aged 23. Although still a young adult, this individual had evidence for poor oral health with antemortem (before death) tooth loss of three upper premolars. She also had carious lesions in six teeth; four small interproximal caries on the upper dentition and two large cavities on the lower second molars. The presence of grade 2 healed cribra orbitalia (as defined by Stuart-Macadam, 1991) may indicate a stress or malnutrition episode earlier in this individual's life. Cribra orbitalia is thought to be associated with iron deficiency anaemia (Mensforth *et al.*, 1978), vitamin B12 deficiency (Walker *et al.*, 2009), parasitic infections (Lewis, 2007: 113), or possibly a combination of all three.

Pathological lesions that are of interest here, related to the cause of death as consumption, are the destruction of bone on the inferior surface of the fifth lumbar vertebrae and on the superior surface of the body of the sacrum (see Figure 6.3). The destruction of the bone is most marked on the left side and there is the presence of small cloacae (pus-containing abscess cavities) at the centre of both elements. There is no evidence for bone formation on either element and none of the other vertebrae are involved.

The skull for this individual was very fragmented, but endocranial lesions (lesions on the internal surface of the skull bones) could still be recorded.

178  The material body

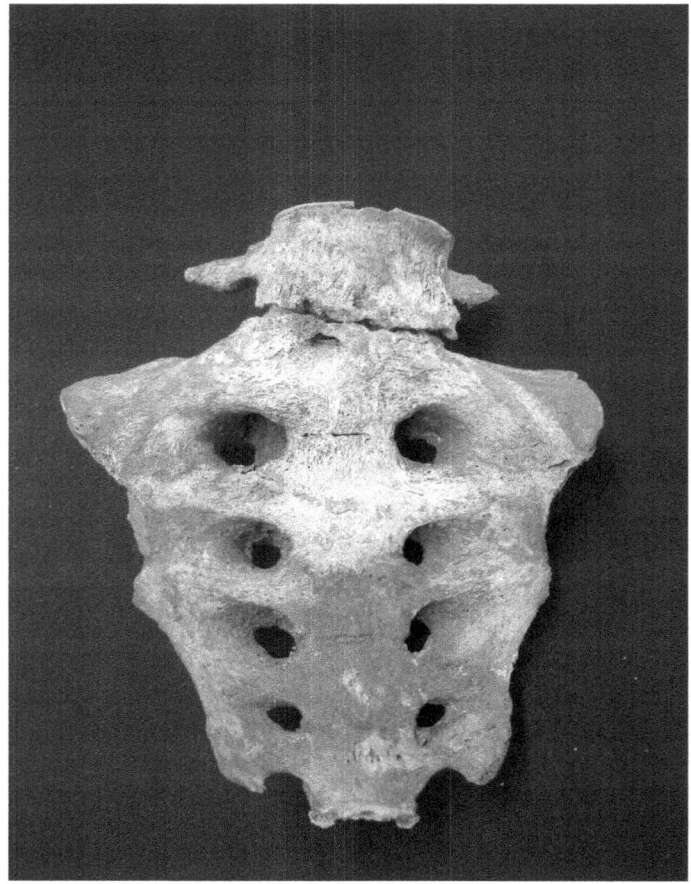

Figure 6.3 Destructive lesions on the sacrum and fifth lumbar vertebrae of SK293, Maria Taylor.

These were most marked on the frontal bone (see Figure 6.4), and also occurred on fragments of the parietal and occipital bones.

In assessing the skeletal lesions present on the remains of Maria we can suggest a diagnosis consistent with TB. While the lesions on the spine are only present at the very base, this localised resorption does permit a diagnosis of TB. Areas of bone formation and resorption termed endocranial lesions (Lewis, 2004) or *serpens endocrania symmetrica* (SES) (Hershkovitz et al., 2002) are also thought to be an indicator of tuberculosis and especially linked to tuberculous meningitis in children (Roberts and Buikstra, 2003: 101). Hershkovitz et al.'s (2002) research focused on adults from the Hamann-Todd

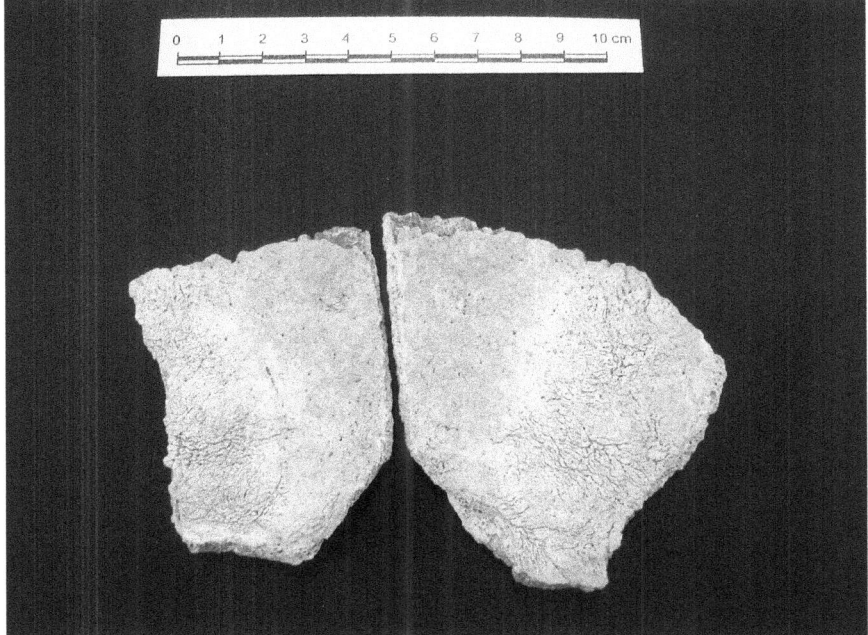

Figure 6.4 Endocranial lesions on the frontal bone of SK293, Maria Taylor.

collection, where they found the frequency of lesions observed was eight times greater in individuals known to have died from tuberculosis. These lesions fit the description of those seen on the skull of Maria and give further skeletal evidence for a diagnosis of TB which matches the cause of death noted on the death certificate. However, while in conjunction the lesions do suggest a diagnosis of TB, neither represent lesions that are pathognomonic (uniquely diagnostic) of the disease and without the diagnosis from the death certificate other types of non-specific infectious disease, such as osteomyelitis of the lower spine, could not be ruled out (Waldron, 2009: 93).

So while Maria had a relatively short life, in which time she contracted and died from tuberculosis, access to the documentary sources in association with her skeletal remains can provide us with greater insight into her life than the skeletal remains alone allow. Maria McVey was born on 3 February 1822, and was baptised on 3 March of the same year, in Canterbury, Kent, and recorded as the daughter of William and Mary McVey. The baptism took place in an Independent chapel, which suggests that the McVey family were Nonconformists. Her parents had had previous children, with the baptism of a daughter in 1813 giving William's occupation as that of a

Bombardier in the Royal Artillery (the equivalent of a Corporal); indeed, four McVey children, including Maria, are listed in Royal Artillery baptism records, two baptised in Canterbury, two in Weedon, Northamptonshire (National Archives, AB91 Army Births and Baptisms, Findmypast.co.uk, accessed 2021).

A William McVey who served in the 3rd battalion of the Royal Artillery has been discovered who may be the same person as Maria's father. He enlisted in 1804, was promoted to Bombardier in $c.$1812, promoted again to Sergeant around 1823, and was finally pensioned off in 1825. He was discharged from the army at Manchester and returned to Glasgow, the place of his birth. The military record notes that he died in October 1826 aged 40 (Findmypast.co.uk, British Army Service Records, accessed 2021). If this is Maria's father, the McVey family would have moved frequently in Maria's early childhood, and the loss of her father may have reduced their circumstances substantially. The family had probably returned to the south of England prior to 1838 as one of Maria's sisters was married in Canterbury in that year. It is possible that Maria's mother moved back to her own parish for poor relief. The loss of her father at a young age, and the reduction in circumstances as a consequence, is in line with the evidence for nutritional deficiency likely during her childhood reflected by the presence of cribra orbitalia.

In 1841, the census records Maria living with her mother and two sisters in Canterbury (Ancestry.co.uk, accessed 2021; all born in Kent). Her mother, Mary, is recorded as a dressmaker, and while no occupation is recorded for the three daughters, it seems unlikely that young women aged between 15 and 26 had no employment of any sort; it is possible that they assisted their mother in her work. Dressmaking was one of the few respectable occupations available to women in the mid-nineteenth century, but was often poorly paid (Thackrah, 1831: 31). Additionally, long hours, often in poor lighting, and sedentary occupation, with 'a bent posture' (Thackrah, 1831: 31), frequently resulted in 'destroy[ing] the health of the young women [...] the digestion especially suffers, and also the lungs' (Evidence taken by Children's Employment Commission February 1841, Appendix to the Second Report 1842, f208).

Maria married George Edward Taylor of Bristol, then a leather cutter, and the son of a bootmaker, on 16 September 1843, at St Marylebone, Westminster. Her father's occupation was recorded on the marriage certificate as 'spirit merchant' (Ancestry.co.uk, accessed 2020). A William McVey has been found in a Glasgow directory of 1825 described as a vintner, which may fit with the soldier described above (McFeat, 1825: 165). There are no McVeys in Canterbury in the Pigots Directory of Kent for 1824 (Pigot, 1824: 378–82). No occupation is given for Maria herself on her marriage certificate, which is not unusual at this period. On the 1851 census, Maria's widowed mother, who is living with her eldest daughter's family, is recorded as a former laundress who was born in Canterbury (Ancestry.co.uk, accessed 2021). There is no evidence to suggest that Maria and her husband had any children in the short time they were married; no baptisms are recorded with their names.

Maria's story presents us with a young child who loses her father and, in consequence, her family were likely to have suffered from a reduction to their socioeconomic status. She appears to have moved around the country during her life, possibly between Glasgow and Canterbury, until her final resting place in Bristol. These are all urban centres and it is likely she worked indoors for long hours to aid her mother in supporting the family until her marriage in 1843. The circumstances of her life led her to contract TB and perhaps her poor health and nutrition during childhood led to her early demise from this disease at the age of 23 years. Our second case illustrates how TB could equally affect individuals from more wealthy backgrounds and the impact that the disease could have on young children.

### Thomas Rokeby Price (SK7)

On initial excavation of Area 1 (the uppermost terrace), three previously unknown ledger slabs were uncovered, including one recording the names and dates of Rhys Uvedale Price, born 18 August 1851, died 20 February 1852, and Thomas Rokeby Price, born November 1849 (date illegible), died (month and date illegible) 1853. Upon excavation of the location of this ledger, two coffin voids were found, a larger one on top of a smaller. A single juvenile skeleton was found collapsed into the lower coffin void (see Figure 6.1b). SK7 was found on osteological analysis to be a child of approximately 2–3 years, and was therefore identified as the older of the two children memorialised, Thomas Rokeby Price. His death certificate stated that he died on 27 March 1853, aged 3 years, of tuberculosis and 'convulsions following hooping [sic] cough' (see Figure 6.2).

The skeletal remains of Thomas Rokeby Price were well preserved and more than 75% complete, with only some of the small bones of the hands and feet, some epiphyseal ends of the long bones and part of the pelvic girdle being absent. Two circular patches of greenish copper alloy staining were seen on his skull (right and left parietal bones) indicating the presence of shroud pins. Pathological lesions were recorded on the skeleton as a marked fine layer of porous woven bone on the shafts of both femora (thigh bones), the right tibia (shin bone) and the left and right ilia (pelvis). Lighter patches of woven bone were also noted on several of the rib ends. No other indicators of disease were noted on the skeleton. Instances of woven bone growth are fairly common findings on infant and child skeletons; in many cases, these are recorded as periosteal new bone growth, periostitis or non-specific infection and the aetiology is unknown.

The range of skeletal lesions on Thomas are quite different to those manifest on the skeleton of Maria. Some of these have been associated with TB in the literature; however, on their own, they would not be confidently diagnosed as TB. Periosteal new bone formation has been seen on the ribs of both adults (Santos and Roberts, 2006) and immature individuals (Santos and Roberts, 2001) of known identity where a cause of death related to tuberculosis was documented, especially where it occurs on the visceral (inner) surface of the ribs. Santos and Roberts (2006) have cautioned that care needs to be taken in diagnosing rib lesions in archaeological remains, as although they appear more common in those with tuberculosis, they are not pathognomonic of this disease. Indeed, other pulmonary infections that have been shown to cause similar rib lesions in clinical settings include pneumonia and actinomycosis (Lambert, 2002). In the case of Thomas, the rib lesions are not on the visceral surface so a diagnosis of TB from these cannot be attempted here. The other lesions across the skeleton are also non-specific, although cases of children with periosteal new bone formation in association with other evidence for TB have been seen. New bone formation has been observed on the long bones (Lewis, 2011; Santos and Roberts, 2001) and in particular the femora (thigh bones) (Dawson and Robson Brown, 2012; Santo and Roberts, 2001), and the ilium and ischium (pelvis bones) (Stirland, 2009).

Thomas Rokeby Price, born November 1849 in Holtby, Yorkshire, was the second child and eldest son of Thomas Charles Price and his wife Ellen (née Taylor). By 1852, Thomas Charles Price was the vicar of St Augustine the Less, Bristol, the parish to which the north-eastern part of the graveyard at St George's belonged. The Rev. Thomas Charles Price was a grandson of Sir Charles Price, 1st Baronet (1747–1818) (Ancestry.co.uk, accessed 2020).

There is surviving documentary evidence that both Maria Taylor and Thomas Rokeby Price suffered from tuberculosis. The evidence from the death certificates recording tuberculosis allows us to recognise that the lesions described on their skeletal remains are likely to be associated with this disease. This is important as often when diagnosing such lesions palaeopathologists would tend to err on the side of caution unless the more classic presentations of destructive lesions to the spine and joint surfaces are in evidence. So here the documentary evidence is key and can provide an insight into the more subtle lesions that occur as a consequence of TB, particularly on young children, but also young adults, such as Maria, where the lesions are clearer but still not pathognomonic.

## Trauma and occupation

The next individual discussed provides us with information on a traumatic injury and leads us to consider how this would have affected their occupation and lifestyle. Usually when presented with healed trauma in the archaeological record, the cause of the injury is unknowable and can only be inferred by the type of fracture. Ives *et al.* (2017) explored hip fractures in skeletal remains from urban cemetery excavations from the eighteenth and nineteenth centuries, determining that accidental falls, both of low and high impact, were often the cause – although underlying conditions such as age-related loss of bone density were also a factor. For the long bones, different types of forces can create different fracture patterns. Oblique fractures tend to occur due to an angulated and rotated force, while spiral fractures occur due to rotational and downward loading stress to the bone; although, when healed, Lovell (1997) notes that they can be difficult to distinguish from each other. Therefore, determining the ultimate cause of the fracture from the skeletal evidence alone can be problematic, with fractures of the leg bones often being attributed to accidental injuries in the past such occupational hazards associated with farm work and manual labour (Burrell *et al.*, 2018; Judd and Roberts, 1999). In this case study we not only have the evidence for the healed trauma on the skeletal remains but a vivid account of the cause of the fracture.

### *Mark Kelson (SK48)*

Upon excavation, SK48 was found to have a well-preserved depositum or coffin plate, with a legible inscription, which identified the individual as Mark Kelson (see Figure 6.1c). Mark Kelson was born in or before 1801, and was baptised on 26 July 1801 in Iron Acton, Gloucestershire, 9 miles north-east of Bristol. He was the son of William Kelson/Kelston and Sophia Pullen, and his father was recorded as a Labourer.[1] As was Maria McVey Taylor, Mark Kelson was recorded as having died at Host Street (no. 24), St Augustine parish, on the 8 July 1857, indicating he was between 55 and 56 years old. Host Street in the mid nineteenth century seems to have been considered a relatively poor area. Latimer (1887: 174) notes that in 1831, large quantities of stolen goods were retrieved from a house on this street, and the street is associated in his account with 'the slums of the city'. This reinforces the relevance of these cases for understanding the lives of the labouring poor.

The remains of Mark Kelson were well preserved with the skeleton being more than 75% complete with only a few small bones of the hands and feet, and the right patella (knee cap) being absent. Copper alloy staining was observed on the frontal bone, lower right ribs and the right femur, showing a similar pattern to Maria Taylor (SK293) in the placement of inferred shroud or funerary dress pins. His age at death based on skeletal degeneration was more than 50 years old; with the Lovejoy *et al.* (1985) auricular surface method suggesting the most precise age of between 50 and 59 years, while that of Buckberry and Chamberlain (2002) gave a range of 39 and 91 years with a mean age of 66 years. Features of the pelvis and skull were consistent with a male individual.

His estimated stature was calculated to be 172 cm ±2.99 cm (5 foot 7 in.). He had lost at least nine teeth antemortem, and the upper wisdom teeth were also missing but appear to have been congenitally absent (i.e. they never erupted). Only one carious lesion was noted in the remaining dentition. There was some evidence for enamel hypoplasia on four teeth, suggesting an episode of stress or malnutrition in childhood, something more common in individuals of low socioeconomic status (Hillson, 2003). At St Martin's, Birmingham, a higher prevalence of enamel hypoplasia was observed on individuals from earth-cut graves (73%) than those from the burial vaults (47%) (Brickley *et al.*, 2006). Some slight degenerative joint disease (osteophytes) was seen on the spine, both shoulder joints, the left knee joint and the right thumb, with more marked degeneration (including porosity) on the left ankle joint. Healed trauma was observed on the left tibia which appears to have broken in more than one place. The line of fracture appears to be oblique, though the fracture may also have been comminuted (comprised multiple fragments); however, the fracture callus obscures this (Lovell, 1997). There is some misalignment of the distal (lower) shaft towards the lateral side of the healed bone (see Figure 6.5). There are still plaques of lamellar (healing) bone observable as well as a cloaca in evidence on the posterior shaft, although the fracture is well healed.

Mark Kelson married Mary Colston on 14 November 1836 in Frome, Somerset. On the 1841 census he and his wife were living on East Street in Bedminster, and he was described as a 'hallier', which is thought to be someone hauling coal or iron ore from the mines.

On Saturday 18 February 1843, a local newspaper, the *Bristol Mercury* (BNA), reported Kelson to have been riding a horse at the top of Union Street, when the animal stumbled and fell upon him. This fall broke his leg, a break which was described as a compound fracture – a fracture in which there is an open wound or break in the skin near the site of the broken bone. He was taken to the Bristol infirmary on the evening of Tuesday 14 February 1843, and treated there. The record of his treatment for a compound fracture survives in the Bristol Archives (BRO 35893, Outpatient admission registers, fiche pages 20–21). The Bristol Royal Infirmary logbooks record the name, age, parish, subscriber, dates of admittance and discharge, distemper

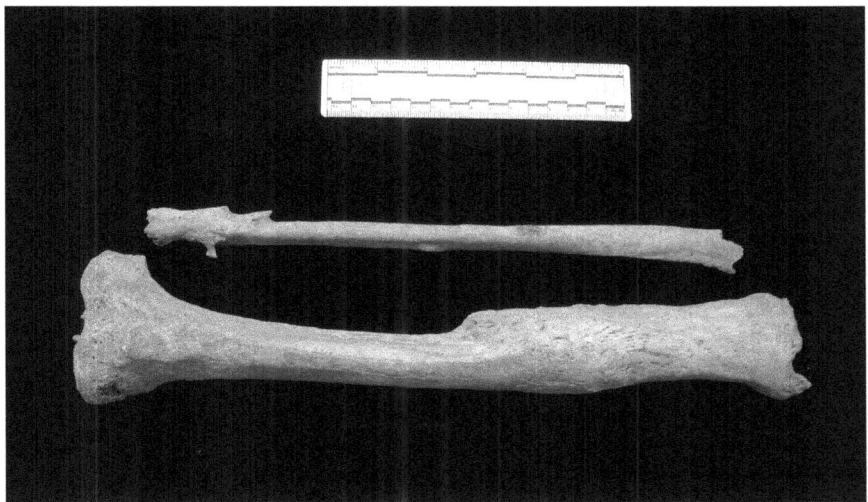

**Figure 6.5** Healed fracture of the left tibia and fibula of SK48, Mark Kelson.

and the result/outcome (Witkin, 2011: 9). In the case of the 'subscriber', Mark Kelson's record states only 'Casualty' rather than a name, meaning that he was admitted as an emergency, which did not require a letter of recommendation from a subscriber (Witkin, 2011: 49); additionally, Witkin (Witkin, 2011: 43) states that most casualty patients were surgical cases, which suggests that amputation may have been considered; Mant (2020: 445) notes that this was often the case for compound fractures in the London general hospitals. His injury is described in the logbook as a 'comp[oun]d fracture', he was admitted on 14 February and discharged in June (possibly the 6th; unfortunately, the date is indistinct in the record), indicating his stay was for approximately 112 days. The result is recorded as MOP, which probably signified 'made outpatient' (Witkin, 2011: 47). It is possible that this information was duplicated from inpatient records. The healing process appears to have taken approximately three months, which appears standard for an adult fracture (Witkin, 2011: 248). Mant (2020: 451) notes the average stay for a compound leg fracture in the London hospitals of the eighteenth century was 121 days, indicating a similar level of care and recuperation. It is unknown whether casualty/emergency patients were required to pay for their treatment.

In this case, we have the cause of the trauma being associated with a horse-riding accident, perhaps indicating a rotational force to the foot and lower leg as it was caught in the stirrup as the horse fell and/or the direct trauma of the weight of the horse to the lower leg. The recording of this incidence in the local papers and subsequent hospital record along with a known date of death also provides us with a very accurate timeframe for how longstanding the fracture is (14 years and 4 months) and it is interesting that, while this is well beyond the time suggested for the remodelling to occur – Lovell (1997) suggests a range of 6–9 years for remodelling of fractured long bones – there were still plaques of lamellar bone present on the shaft. Unfortunately, the right tibia was too damaged to allow a metrical comparison to assess the shortening that had occurred due to the misalignment.

The left fibula also has an oblique fracture in evidence, but at the proximal (upper) end also with some slight misalignment and a small projecting spicule of bone to the anterior. Fractures of the fibula have been associated with accidental injuries involving rotation of the foot (Tucker *et al.*, 2017). It is likely that the degenerative joint disease (DJD) observed on the left ankle has occurred in relation to this incident; this may be due to rotation of the foot during this incident, certainly a possibility if the foot becomes caught in a stirrup. It is also possible that the DJD is secondary to the trauma, with a change to the mobility of Mark Kelson and the misalignment of the lower leg bones causing stress to the ankle joint. Musculoskeletal stress markers, associated with physical activity, are present on some areas of his skeleton, such as the radial tuberosity (lower arm), and costoclavicular area (shoulder), along with marked enthesophytes (ossification at tendon insertion sites) on the proximal ulnae (lower arm), and right calcaneus (heel bone). This evidence is indicative of a physical lifestyle (Hawkey and Merbs, 1995), likely to be associated with his occupation as a 'hallier'.

The injury and its repercussions appear to have created longlasting impacts on Kelson's working life. In the newspaper report from 1843 he is described as being in the employ of a Mr Rowe of Redcliff Street. This may have been Charles and Thomas Roe, who were corn factors at Redcliff Street (*Bristol Poll-Book*, 1841). Between 1848 and 1849, five years after the horse-riding accident, Kelson was listed in city directories as keeping a coffee and eating house, which is described in a newspaper as 'the Tiger's Head Beer-house' (*Canterbury Journal, Kentish Times and Farmer's Gazette*, Saturday 10 June 1848).[2] This seems to have also been known simply as the 'Tiger' (Bristol's Lost Pubs website, accessed 2020), and was situated at 57 Redcliff Street (Hunt & Co., 1848: 78 and 82). It is possible that his injury and associated conditions as discussed above had required him to find alternative employment, at least temporarily, since on the 1851 census he was once more described as a labourer and living as a lodger, in the house of Edward Colston on Lawrence Hill, and recorded as married (although his wife was not present) (Ancestry.co.uk, accessed 2020).

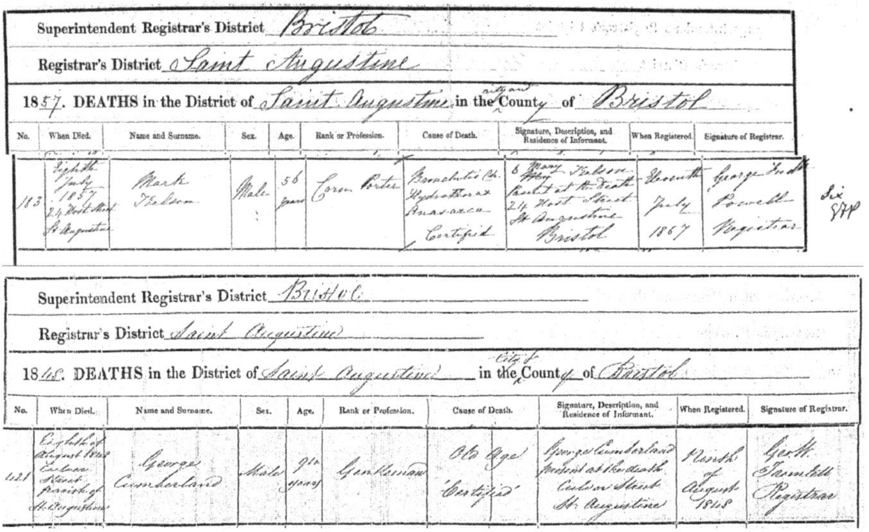

Figure 6.6 Death certificates of Mark Kelson and George Cumberland.

On 8 July 1857, Mark Kelson died at 24 Host Street, St Augustine parish. His death certificate describes him as a Corn Porter, and the cause of his death was recorded as being 'Bronchitis Ch. [chronic]; Hydrothorax [fluid in the pleural cavity]; Anasarca [generalised oedema or fluid retention, caused by organ failure]' (see Figure 6.6). His wife Mary was present at the death. The account of the accident and hospital records alongside the evidence for the injury on Mark Kelson's skeletal remains provide us with a rare example: from the historical record we know the specifics of the cause of trauma and we can also identify this through osteoarchaeological analysis from the healing process to the bone. In this case, the two types of evidence complement each other well and illuminate the repercussions of the accident for Kelson's life.

## Changing bodies due to childbirth and senescence

The final two individuals that will be presented are unusual in terms of the old age that they both managed to attain, and in the fact that there is a wealth of historical documentation for the pair including letters written in their own hands. It is unusual when dealing with archaeological skeletal remains to contemplate that the individuals may have reached much further than the sixth decade of life, as most osteological techniques can only age confidently up to around 50 years of age. The presence of an elderly couple of known age at death can offer us an insight into the degeneration of the skeleton, how this compares to current ageing techniques, and allows us to touch on the personal experience of these individuals and their own ageing bodies. When dealing with females where we have records of the children that they bore, we can also assess the pelvis for areas of degeneration associated with parturition scars (Kelley, 1979; Tague, 1988).

### Elizabeth (SK272) and George Cumberland (SK273)

SK272 and SK273 were excavated together in a location underlying a ledger slab with the following inscription:

SACRED
to the Memory of
ELIZABETH CUMBERLAND,
who died 2nd. Feby 1837
in the 86th. Year of her Age.
Also
GEORGE CUMBERLAND,
Born 27th. Of Novr. 1754,
Died 8th. of Augst. 1848,
In the 94th. Year of his Age.

One skeleton overlay another, and both were found with poorly preserved depositum plates which enabled the uppermost and later burial to be identified as George Cumberland, and the lower, earlier burial to be that of Elizabeth (see Figure 6.1d).

Elizabeth Cumberland was born in about 1752 as Elizabeth Price, the daughter of Rice and Sarah Price. Almost nothing is known about her parents and their status; however, a letter exists which refers to her 'fortune' of £500;[3] this is a significant sum at a time when only one in five families had an annual income of more than £50 (Probert, 2009: 432). An income of £50 per annum has been suggested as the minimum sum 'at which it was possible to aspire to membership of the middling sort' (Langford, 1998: 62); a 'fortune' of ten times this amount suggests that Elizabeth's family should be regarded as such. She died at the Lodge, Culver Street, Bristol, aged 85 or 86 (*Bath Chronicle and Weekly Gazette*, Thursday 9 February 1837). Unfortunately, no death certificate exists as she died just before the commencement of civil registration on 1 July 1837.

The skeletal remains of Elizabeth were well preserved and more than 75% complete, with only the sternum and a few small bones of the hands and feet being absent. Copper alloy staining was observed on the right distal radius and iron coffin studs were adhered to the right femur, humerus (upper arm) and iliac crest (pelvis) and to the left radius (lower arm), indicating a decorated coffin. The skeleton was aged using osteological methods to 60+ years old at death from the auricular surface methods of Lovejoy *et al.* (1985), with those of Buckberry and Chamberlain (2002) suggesting a mean age of 72 years. The skeleton was fairly gracile and features of the pelvis and skull both indicated a female individual. Her estimated stature was calculated to be 168 ±3.51 cm (5 foot 6 in.).

George Cumberland was born on 27 November 1754 (according to his gravestone), the younger son of George Cumberland and Elizabeth (née Balchen), a family described as belonging to the upper middling sort (Greenacre, 2014). From 1769 he was an insurance clerk with the Royal Exchange Assurance Corporation, earning £60 per annum by 1775 (Black, 1912: 86). Cumberland was admitted as a student at the Royal Academy Schools in 1772, where he joined a social circle that included William Blake (the artist and poet 1757–1827), who became a lifelong friend (Greenacre, 2014). In 1784, he received an inheritance which provided him with an annual income of £300, which enabled him to leave his job; between 1785 and 1790 he travelled in Europe, living mainly in Rome. Cumberland was known to his contemporaries as a 'gentleman polymath', and he wrote on a broad variety of subjects including geology, conchology and art theory and history, as well as publishing various works of poetry, fiction and biography. He was in addition an artist, engraver and inventor (Bentley, 1997: 155).

The skeletal remains of George Cumberland were also well preserved and more than 75% complete, with only a few small bones of the hands and feet being absent. Copper alloy staining was observed on the left temporal bone (skull), sternum, parts of the spine, the right-side clavicle, radius, femur and tibia, and the left femur and fifth metatarsal (foot bone). Some iron studs were adhering to the left humerus and fibula, indicating the presence of a decorated coffin, the remains of which including the coffin handles can be seen in Figure 6.1d; iron staining was also observed on the left ulna and right humerus.

The skeleton of George was assigned an age of at least 50 years at death from both the auricular surface methods of Lovejoy *et al.* (1985) and Buckberry and Chamberlain (2002); these could not be scored fully due to *post-mortem* damage on the area. The sternal rib ends confirmed this assessment, suggesting an age range between 54 and 64 years. The ledger slab indicates he died at the age of 93 years. The features of the pelvis and skull confirmed that the individual was a male. Only the humeri (upper arm bones) were complete to enable measurements to be taken to determine estimated stature. Due to some asymmetry of the humeri stature was estimated at 167 cm ±4.05 cm from the left side and 169 cm ±4.05 cm from the right side (around 5 foot 6 in.).

Though Elizabeth and George were buried together, he was not technically her husband. On 23 February 1773, Elizabeth had married Benjamin Cooper, a builder, in the parish of St Dunstan in the West (the groom being of St Clement's East-Cheap), and they had five children who were registered in the 'Protestant Dissenters' Registry of Births from Dr Williams' Library' on 17 October 1799: Ann (born 8 September 1775), Benjamin (born 11 August 1778), Sarah (born 17 June 1780), Elizabeth (born 9 January 1782) and Georgiana (born 17 November 1784).[4] A sixth child, Jane, was born c.1786, but was apparently not registered. Her existence is known from letters and newspaper notices.[5]

While in London, George lodged with the Cooper family (including Elizabeth). Remarkably, in about 1787/88 (certainly before July 1788) he was reported to have taken 'the abused wife and children of his former landlord' back to Italy with him (Stemmler, 1992: fn.20). A letter from George to his mother states that one of the reasons for leaving the country was the 'cold receptions' given to his new family (Stemmler, 1992); this suggests that they may have attempted to live together in England prior to leaving for Italy. The reference to abuse implies that the Cooper's marriage had not been a happy one. However, William George Meredith, the nephew of an associate of Cumberland, recorded an anecdote in his commonplace book of 1829–30 which states that '[t]hey were always very friendly & Cooper used to drink tea with them occasionally' (King, 1972: 155). It is possible that friendly relations were maintained in order to keep in contact with the children left behind with their father, of which there were three according to Meredith. Certainly, these children wrote letters to their mother and visited occasionally (Evans, pers. comm.).

George made a financial settlement with Elizabeth's husband, which involved 'sacrificing above £1500 for [her] emancipation, in addition to the loss of £500 her only fortune'.[6] Elizabeth herself stated in a letter of May 1788, 'I am now your own for you have paid dearly for me' (Stemmler, 1992: fn20); this is the only reference to a letter written by Elizabeth that has been found. Meredith stated that Cumberland had paid £2000 (King, 1972: 155). Such settlements did not amount to a legal divorce, which at this period could only be obtained by a separate Act of Parliament, and as such was an escape route open only to the very rich (Sharpe, 1987: 63). However, much like the wife-sales which were occasionally mentioned in newspapers of the late eighteenth and early nineteenth centuries, the intention of such a transaction would have been 'to deprive the husband of any right of prosecution for damages' (*Kentish Weekly Post*, 18 July 1815). There is no evidence to show that George and Elizabeth ever married legally, which indeed without a divorce could only have happened after the death of her husband (the date of which has not yet been found).

The historical evidence of childbirth is notable in this case. With six children already, Elizabeth bore her first two children with George in Rome: Lavinia (5 November 1788) and George (11 January 1790), who, on the families' return to England in 1790, were both baptised in London on 24 February 1792 (Ancestry.co.uk, accessed 2020). Three further children were born to the couple: Aurora (born 24 April 1792 in London), Sydney (born 1 October 1795 in London) and Eliza Martha (born in 1798 at Bishopsgate, Windsor). The couple moved to Weston-super-Mare in 1803, and then finally to Bristol in 1807 (Greenacre, 2014).

The historical documents therefore contain the names of eleven children borne by Elizabeth. Kelley (1979) and Tague (1988) have both suggested pitting and bone resorption on the pelvic bones can be indicative of childbirth. However, the study by Molleson and Cox (1993) on parity status of the named females from Spitalfields suggests that neither dorsal pitting of the pubis nor the presence of a marked pre-auricular sulcus (both cortical bone defects present on the pelvic bone) appeared to have a relationship to pregnancies. No marked pre-auricular sulcus was noted on Elizabeth's remains and the pubic bones were too damaged to be able to assess the area for dorsal pits. The pubic symphysis (the joint surface where the left and right pelvic bones articulate) was present for the right side and was very porous with marked eburnation (polishing association with complete degeneration of the soft tissues of the joint). This feature has been termed osteitis pubis and has been associated with childbirth in females (Alicioglu, 2008; Lentz, 1995) but also with physical activity associated with collision sports in males (Judd, 2010). The problem here is that the pubic symphysis is also an area that degenerates through age, so whether the extreme destruction of this joint is due to the many children Elizabeth bore or to her advanced age cannot be known.

Evidence of ageing and age-related diseases to the bones and teeth were visible on both Elizabeth and George's remains. Elizabeth Cumberland had lost all the teeth of both the upper and lower jaws antemortem and there was considerable reduction to the bone of the maxilla (upper jaw). As might be expected on an individual of this age, there was evidence for degenerative joint disease across the skeleton including the spine, hips, knee joints, hands, ankles and shoulder girdle. The presence of eburnation suggests a diagnosis of osteoarthritis in the wrists and hands. Most of the dentition of George Cumberland had been lost antemortem with only two teeth (the upper lateral incisor and canine) being still present in the jaw. Marked degenerative joint disease was observed across the skeleton on the spine, the left and right shoulder joint, elbow, wrist and hand. The shoulders, elbows, wrists and hands, as well as the apophyseal joints of the cervical (neck) vertebrae, all showed evidence for osteophyte formation, porosity and eburnation indicating a clear diagnosis of osteoarthritis (Waldron, 2009: 34).

In individuals of this age, degenerative joint disease would be expected. Osteoarthritis is a common finding among the older individuals in skeletal populations. It is a disease of the joints, involving the breakdown of the articular cartilage, and can be caused due to the degenerative changes associated with the wear and tear of old age. It can also be secondary due to trauma causing later problems within the associated joint, which may have been the case with Mark Kelson as described earlier. Initially, the changes to the joint involve new bone formation around the margin of the joint termed marginal osteophytes (MOP), later the joint surface can become pitted and porous and the normal contour of the joint widened or flattened. In severe cases eburnation will be present, this is when the surface of the bone becomes highly polished and smooth, sometimes containing grooves showing the direction of movement of the joint. This polishing occurs due to the constant rubbing of the two articular surfaces or due to the presence of debris within the joint (Waldron, 2009: 28). Osteoarthritis is diagnosed only when either eburnation is present or both MOP and porosity (Waldron, 2009: 34).

A diagnosis of diffuse idiopathic skeletal hyperostosis (DISH) could be made due to specific lesions seen on both Elizabeth and George's spines. Of the twelve vertebrae in the thoracic spine of Elizabeth, the fourth to the eleventh (T4–11) were fused together at the bodies with large flowing osteophytes (bony bridges) down the right side of the eighth to the eleventh thoracic vertebrae. On the spine of George Cumberland, the thoracic vertebrae were also fused from the fourth to the eleventh (T4–11), with the large flowing osteophytes indicative of DISH present on the right side throughout.

Diffuse idiopathic skeletal hyperostosis (DISH) is an extreme condition of bone formation which is diagnosed in skeletal remains by the fusion of the vertebral column with a flowing 'candlewax' type of bone form. This is caused by the ossification of the anterior longitudinal ligament, and tends to be present only on the right side of the thoracic vertebral bodies. The reason that the left side may be spared is postulated to be due to the presence of the aorta descending along the left side of the thoracic vertebrae (Ortner, 2003: 559), although the reasons for this are still unclear. The intervertebral disc spaces remain normal. Although the presence of 'candlewax' ossification of the spine along with enthesophytes present on other elements of the skeleton is indicative of DISH, a diagnosis can only be made when at least four contiguous thoracic vertebral bodies are fused together along the right anterior side and there is the presence of enthesophytes elsewhere on the skeleton (Aufderheide and Rodriguez-Martin, 1998: 97; Waldron 2009,

77). Rogers *et al.* (1987) suggest that while in clinical practice the diagnosis of DISH is only made under these circumstances, it is likely that palaeopathologists will be aware of the early changes associated with DISH, and Waldron (2009: 77) suggests a diagnosis of early DISH when fewer than four vertebrae are fused. In modern populations, DISH is rarely seen in individuals under the age of 50 years and is more common in males than females (Roberts and Manchester, 2005: 159).

The two phalanges of the big toe on the left foot of George Cumberland were fused together as well as a proximal and middle phalanx of another of the toes of the left foot. The bones of the right foot are quite damaged and eroded (post mortem) but there is evidence for a small 'punched out' lesion on the proximal phalanx of the big toe. This could be indicative of gout (the 1$^{st}$ metacarpal is a more common location but is damaged post mortem). Gout is classed as a metabolic disease characterised by an excessive production of uric acid which can become deposited in the soft tissues as crystals (most frequently of the feet) and causes lytic lesions to the bones (Aufderhide and Rodriguez-Martin, 1998: 110).

The letters of George overlap with some of the data in the skeletal record, but provide different information on his bodily experience. According to the letters written by George Cumberland, he suffered from 'anxiety of mind' and 'nervous fever', indicative of mental health issues; as well as asthma, and gout from at least 1824 (when he was laid up in bed, the complaint having started in his toes). He referred in a letter of February 1802, when he was about 47, to reducing his diet 'both eating and drinking', which suggests that he may have struggled with his weight. In later life he was abstemious, drinking only water, possibly a reaction to this and his problems with gout.[7] George was apparently quite accident-prone, noting several incidents in letters to his brother, but tended to write more 'about the illnesses of others than his own' (Evans, pers. comm.). Indeed, when he cut his foot quite seriously while bathing, he made light of it, saying that he could 'hop about very tolerably'.[8]

George Cumberland's letters also refer to Elizabeth (or 'Mrs C.') suffering from 'rheumatic gout' or 'rheumatism' from at least 1803.[9] Unfortunately, her metatarsals (foot bones) had suffered from post mortem erosion and the phalanges (toe bones) were absent; no signs of any pathological lesions associated with gout were therefore observed. A small button osteoma was present on the frontal bone of Elizabeth. This is a small benign form of bone tumour (Waldron, 2009: 173) consisting of a small raised circular area of compact bone. This would be symptomless and is fairly common, occurring on 1% of modern autopsies (Ortner, 2003: 506).

George was blind for the last ten years of his life, but 'retained his faculties to within one day of his death', which occurred on 8 August 1848 at Culver

Street (Obituary in *Manchester Times*, 28 October 1848). His death certificate records his age as 94 (although his dates of birth and death as given on the ledger slab would suggest he was 93) and gives the cause of death simply as 'Old Age' (see Figure 6.6). Interestingly, Bristol was one of the cities to have a specialist eye institution, which was founded in 1810 (Lane, 2001: 91), indicating specialist eye care was available in the city.

The skeletal remains of Elizabeth and George Cumberland are rich in evidence, detailing the physical changes to their bodies as they aged, and can in some instances be aligned with the wealth of historic information that provides insights into their sometimes troubled (by ill health) and unconventional lives.

## Conclusions

The opportunity afforded by the excavation of a named sample of individuals allows us to create meaningful biographies by combining osteoarchaeological and historical methods and enables us to contemplate the lived experience of the inhabitants of late-eighteenth- and nineteenth-century Bristol. The historical evidence enables the discovery of written 'stories' about their lives, while the osteoarchaeological evidence reveals aspects of their lived experience 'written' on their skeletons. These two aspects of evidence allow a fuller recreation of past people's lives. This combined approach also enables researchers to view their studies in a new light by adopting 'a reflective and critical perspective on their own practices' which Craig Atkins and Harvey (this volume: introduction) identify as one of the key strengths throughout this volume. The reporting of human remains can sometimes appear clinical and detached to humanities scholars outside the archaeological disciplines, as in most cases identities are unknown. However, osteoarchaeological research provides an embodied physicality to the study of past lives, which offers its own form of intimacy. Indeed, the same attention can be afforded to all individuals, regardless of whether their lives were documented, and thus the range of embodied experiences that can be obtained is large. In contrast, history focuses on identifiable individuals, providing us with the written detail of people's lives, but the discipline lacks the physical connection with the actual bodies that osteoarchaeological research can bring. An interdisciplinary approach recreates both the written story and the physical person.

Case study one explored two cases where tuberculosis was recorded on the death certificates and whether this disease was observable on the skeletal remains of Maria McVey Taylor and Thomas Rokeby Price. Maria, while still only a young adult, has skeletal lesions that could be identified as TB, although these are not pathognomonic of the disease. The subtle changes manifest on the skeleton of Thomas would not be confidently diagnosed as TB without the death certificate; although such changes are found in association with cases of TB in children, they are also related to other non-specific infections and respiratory diseases. Here the documentary evidence and skeletal analysis combined allows us an insight into the different manifestations and bodily experience of the disease in these two individuals.

Case study two considered that while healed trauma is often easy to identify on skeletal remains, it is much more challenging to discern details about the cause and process of healing. The case of Mark Kelson illustrates how the length of time that bone takes to remodel may, in some cases, be longer than suggested from modern-day clinical observations. It is rarely possible to reconstruct details of the incident responsible for skeletal trauma, but here the association with a well-documented accident allows us to see the cause of the injury. The historical record gave no indication of the outcome, successful or otherwise, of such treatment as he may have been afforded; therefore, the observations on the skeletal remains, which show the misalignment of the healed bone, despite hospital treatment, adds detail to this incident that could not otherwise be gleaned from the historical records. The historical records show that after this accident Mark Kelson changed his occupation from that of a 'hallier' and from 1848 he was working in the Tiger's Head Beer-house; this may be due to him being unable to continue with a highly physical role while recuperating from the injury and possibly due to further complications, such as osteoarthritis of the ankle joint. The presence of musculoskeletal stress markers also indicates the type of physical lifestyle undertaken by Mark, something likely to be the norm for the labouring classes of Bristol.

The third case study focused on the natural life changes that could be observed on the bodies of two elderly individuals in their ninth and tenth decades of life, and how these related to the wealth of documentation available. They provide us with an insight into the degeneration of the skeleton that we might expect to observe in the elderly and allow us the rare opportunity to assess individuals we know to be of advanced years. The appearance of degenerative joint disease allows us an insight into the potential life experience in terms of pain and lack of mobility that may have been present for these two elderly individuals. In clinical patients, the area surrounding the joint will show swelling and be painful; the joint space is also seen to narrow on radiographs (Waldron, 2009). Today, DISH is more common in males than females and rarely occurs below the age of 40 years; it is often seen in patients who suffer from obesity and diabetes (Roberts and Manchester, 2005: 159) and it appears that a rich diet is a major factor in this disease. The condition causes back pain and stiffness of the spine. Gout is also a disease that is seen more often in males and is also associated with similar lifestyle factors, including excessive alcohol consumption (Roberts and Manchester, 2005: 162). This may reflect Cumberland's status as upper middle class and the letter referred to above suggests that diet may have been the cause. From George's letters we can infer that he must have felt unwell and been in pain from this ailment due to him being bedridden. However, while he mentions his ailments, he does not seem to dwell on his own discomfort; and, therefore, trying to elucidate his individual experience of pain is not possible. There was no evidence for the gout that is mentioned in George's letter on the skeleton of Elizabeth, although this may have been due to the lack of well-preserved foot bones available for analysis, the condition may have healed before her death, or that the disease was mistakenly diagnosed.

Molleson and Cox's (1993) seminal work on the named individuals from Spitalfields indicated the problems with methods of age determination in adult skeletons. The accuracy and precision of osteological methods of ageing was poor for the older individuals in this chapter, as would be expected (Mays, 1998: 62). Both of the younger individuals, Thomas and Maria, were still in a stage of dental or skeletal development and therefore the ages assigned using the osteological methods were accurate. In the case of Mark Kelson, the Lovejoy *et al.* (1985) auricular surface method suggested an age between 50 and 59 years while the Buckberry and Chamberlain (2002) method gave a range between 39 and 91 years with a suggested mean age of 66 years. For Elizabeth Cumberland the Lovejoy *et al.* (1985) method suggested an age at death of 60+ years. A range of 53–92 years, with a mean age of 72 years, was obtained using Buckberry and Chamberlain (2002). Due to lack of preservation of the articular surfaces of the pelvis, the sternal rib ends were used to assign an age of 54–64 years to George Cumberland – far younger than his true age of 93 years. Research into the features of skeletal degeneration in advanced age has become more common in the last decade (Appleby, 2017; Falys, 2012; Gowland, 2016). The discovery of more known-age elder individuals, such as Elizabeth and George Cumberland, contributes to a wider exploration, recognition and understanding of the effects of old age on the skeleton.

Our aim has been to explore how osteological analysis of known individuals can offer a more detailed insight into how their lived experience can manifest on their skeletal remains. This has provided us with information about the health and lifestyle of a range of individuals representing the diversity of the inhabitants of late-eighteenth- and nineteenth-century Bristol, including those underrepresented in the historical record: women, children and people of lower socioeconomic status. Osteological data can also add new insights to complement the historical records for those of wealth for whom we have more documentary information, such as George and Elizabeth Cumberland. Drawing on the idea of experience as combined from material and cultural/psychological factors as discussed by Craig-Atkins and Harvey in the introductory chapter to this volume, the historical biographies presented here can also provide more nuanced information of how individuals dealt with and experienced traumatic injury or joint disease. This also provides us with a way of determining how well we can recognise the effects of infectious disease, degenerative joint disease, trauma and the ageing process on the skeleton. Both historians and archaeologists are interested in learning about the lives of people in the past. Working together allows the physicality of the human remains and the written aspects of their lives to be more completely connected, allowing us to learn more about them as individuals but also about human experience. The insights gained from the study of these known individuals can be taken forward in studying those unknown individuals, who make up the majority of human remains recovered from archaeological excavation, by using these combined approaches to 'read' aspects of their lives 'written' on their skeletons and, drawing especially on social history, to gain a better understanding of how those lives would have been lived. The skeletal remains from St Augustine's parish, excavated from St George's cemetery, continue to be analysed and, in collaboration with the historical documentation, will shed new light on the relationship between health, occupation, socioeconomic status and aspects of physical changes to the skeleton relating to disease, injury, childbirth and senescence, on the inhabitants of late-eighteenth- and nineteenth-century Bristol, and how they impacted on their lives.

## Acknowledgements

The authors would like to thank Avon Archaeology Ltd for permission to publish on these five individuals prior to the future monograph publication. We are also grateful to Professor Kate Robson Brown and the University of Bristol for allowing access to the laboratory space for analysis of these remains. Thanks also to Jane Evans for providing information on the letters of George Cumberland prior to publication.

## Notes

1. The Iron Acton parish register of baptisms records the father's profession, uncommon before 1812, and the mother's maiden name, unusual at any time. Accessed at Ancestry.co.uk, 2020.

2 Mark Kelson was a witness in a trial regarding hops stolen from a farmer in Kent; the defendant in the case had rented a room at the Tiger's Head in which the hops were stored for some time. There was, however, no suggestion that Kelson was implicated in the crime.
3 Letter of 11 September 1822, Cumberland Papers: British Library (BL) Add Mss 36509, f120. [PH.0129] (transcribed by Jane Evans, 2022).
4 The Dissenters' register recorded the children's dates of birth, parent's names and maternal grandparents' names. Information from Ancestry.co.uk, accessed 2020.
5 Such as a notice inserted in the *Public Ledger and Daily Advertiser* on Monday 30 September 1822, stating that the partnership between Elizabeth, Georgiana and Jane Cooper and Aurora Cumberland, milliners, had been dissolved (BNA).
6 Letter of 11 September 1822, Cumberland Papers: BL Add Mss 36509, f120. [PH.0129] (transcribed by Jane Evans, 2022).
7 Including a letter written at Axbridge February 1802, Cumberland Papers: BL Add Mss 36500, f76; 21 December 1804, Cumberland Papers: BL Add Mss 36509, f273; 23 Aug. 1823, Cumberland Papers: BL Add Mss 36510, f91.c 1824 (transcribed by Jane Evans, 2022).
8 Cumberland Papers: BL Add Mss 36514, f163v. 1802–3 (transcribed by Jane Evans, 2022).
9 Such as a letter of July 1803, Cumberland Papers: BL Add Mss 36514, f177 (transcribed by Jane Evans, 2022).

# References

## Archives and websites

Ancestry.co.uk (accessed 2020).
BNA (British Newspaper Archive): https://www.britishnewspaperarchive.co.uk/ (accessed 2020).
Bristol's Lost Pubs: https://bristolslostpubs.eu/ (accessed 2020).
BRO 35893 Outpatient admission registers (1739–1844), Bristol Archives.
Cumberland Papers (1748–1836): British Library Add MS 36491–36522. Letters transcribed by Jane Evans (2022).

## Secondary sources

Alicioglu, B., Kartal, O., Gurbuz, H. and Sut, N. (2008). 'Symphysis pubis distance in adults: a retrospective computed tomography study', *Surgical and Radiologic Anatomy*, 30: 153–7.
Adams, J. and Colls, K. (2007). *Life and Death in Nineteenth Century Wolverhampton: Excavation of the Overflow Burial Ground of St Peter's Collegiate Church, Wolverhampton 2001–2002*, BAR British Series 442 (Oxford: BAR Publishing).
Appleby, J. (2017). 'Ageing and the body in archaeology', *Cambridge Archaeological Journal*, 28(1): 145–63.

Aufderheide, A. C. and Rodriguez-Martin, C. (1998). *The Cambridge Encyclopedia of Human Paleopathology* (Cambridge: Cambridge University Press).

Bass, W. M. (1995). *Human Osteology: A Laboratory and Field Manual*, 4th edn (Columbia: Missouri Archaeology Society).

Bentley, G. E (1997). 'The Suppression of George Cumberland's "Captive of the Castle of Sennaar" (1798): Liberty vs Commerce' in *The Yale University Library Gazette* Vol. 71, No. 3/4 (April 1997) (Yale University), pp. 155–8.

Black, C. (1912). *The Cumberland Letters, Being the Correspondence of Rich. Dennison Cumberland & George Cumberland, Between the Years 1771 & 1784* (London: Secker).

Bock, G. (1989). 'Women's history and gender history: aspects of an international debate', *Gender and History*, 1: 7–30.

Brickley, M., Buteux, S., Adams, J. and Cherrington, R. (2006). *St Martin's Uncovered: Investigations in the Churchyard of St Martin's-in-the-Bull-Ring, Birmingham, 2001* (Oxford: Oxbow).

Brooks, S. T. and Suchey, J. M. (1990). 'Skeletal age estimation based on the os pubis: a comparison of the Acsadi and Nemeskeri and Suchey-Brooks methods', *Human Evolution*, 5: 227–38.

Brothwell, D. and Zakrzewski, S. (2004). 'Metric and non-metric studies of archaeological human bone', in M. B. Brickley and J. L. McKinley (eds), *Guidelines to the Standards for Recording Human Remains* (Southampton; Reading: British Association for Biological Anthropology and Osteoarchaeology; Institute of Field Archaeologists), pp. 27–33.

Buckberry, J. and Chamberlain, A. (2002). 'Age estimation from the auricular surface of the ilium: a revised method', *American Journal of Physical Anthropology*, 68: 15–28.

Buikstra, J. E. and Ubelaker, D. H. (eds) (1994). *Standards for Data Collection from Human Skeletal Remains: Proceedings of a Seminar at the Field Museum of Natural History, Organized by Jonathan Haas* (Fayetteville: Arkansas Archaeological Survey).

Burrell, C. L., Emery, M. M., Canavan, S. M. and Ohman, J. (2018). 'Broken bones: Trauma analysis in a medieval population from Poulton, Cheshire', in W. J. Turner and C. Lee (eds), *Trauma in Medieval Society* (Leiden: Brill), pp. 71–91.

Children's Employment Commission (1842). *Appendix to the Second Report of the Commissioners: Trades and Manufactures, Reports and Evidence from Sub-Commissioners, Part 1* (London: William Clowes and Sons).

Connell, B. and Miles, A. (2010). *The City Bunhill Burial Ground, Golden Lane, London: Excavations at South Islington Schools, 2006* (London: Museum of London Archaeology).

Dawson, H. (2014). *Unearthing Late Medieval Children: Health, Status and Burial Practice in Southern England*, BAR British Series 593 (Oxford: Archaeopress).

Dawson, H. and Robson Brown, K. (2012). 'Childhood tuberculosis: a probable case from late medieval Somerset, England', *International Journal of Paleopathology*, 2: 31–35.

Emery, P. A. and Wooldridge, K. (2011). *St Pancras Burial Ground: Excavations for St Pancras International the London Terminus of High Speed 1, 2002–3* (London: Museum of London/Gifford).

Evans, K. J. (2022). *George Cumberland: Farming – Family – Fossils: Aspects of a Somerset Life in Letters 1800–35* (Taunton, Somerset: Somerset Archaeological and Natural History Society).

Eyler, W. R., Monsein, L. H., Beute, G. H., Tilley, B., Schultz, L. R. and Schmitt, W. G. H. (1996). 'Rib enlargement in patients with chronic pleural disease', *American Journal of Radiology*, 167: 921–926.

Falys, C. G. (2012). 'Extending the life course: developing new methods for identifying the 'elderly' in the archaeological record' (PhD dissertation: University of Reading)

Gleadle, K. (2001). *British Women in the Nineteenth Century* (Basingstoke: Palgrave).

Gowing, L. (2003). *Common Bodies: Women, Touch and Power in Seventeenth Century England* (New Haven: Yale University Press).

Gowland, R. L. (2016). 'That "tattered coat upon a stick" the ageing body: Evidence for elder marginalisation and abuse in Roman Britain', in L. Powell, W. Southwell-Wright and R. Gowland (eds), *Care in the Past: Archaeological and Interdisciplinary Perspectives* (Oxford: Oxbow), pp. 71–90.

Gowland, R. L., Caffell, A. C., Newman, S., Levene, A. and Holst, M. (2018). 'Broken childhoods: Rural and urban non-adult health during the Industrial Revolution in northern England (eighteenth-nineteenth centuries)', *Bioarchaeology International*, 2(1): 44–62.

Greenacre, F. (2014, September 25). 'Cumberland, George (1754–1848), writer on art and watercolour painter'. *ODNB*, www.oxforddnb.com/view/10.1093/ref:odnb/9780198614128.001.0001/odnb-9780198614128-e-59709 (accessed 18 December 2020).

Harvey, K. (2020). 'One British thing: A history of embodiment: Ann Purvis, ca.1793–1849', *Journal of British Studies*, 59: 136–39.

Hawkey, D. E. and Merbs, C. F. (1995). 'Activity-induced musculoskeletal stress markers (MSM) and subsistence strategy changes among ancient Hudson Bay Eskimos', *International Journal of Osteoarchaeology*, 5: 324–338.

Henderson, M., Miles, A. and Walker, D. (2013). *'He being dead yet speaketh' Excavations at Three Post-medieval Burial Grounds in Tower Hamlets, East London, 2004–10* (London: Museum of London Archaeology).

Henderson, M., Miles, A. and Walker, D. (2015). *St Marylebone's Paddington Street North Burial Ground: Excavations at Paddington Street, London W1, 2012–13* (London: Museum of London Archaeology).

Hershkovitz, I., Greenwald, C. M., Latimer, B., Jellema, L. M., Wish-Baratz, S., Eshed, V., Dutour, O. and Rothschild, B. M. (2002). 'Serpens endocrania symmetrica (SES): A new term and a possible clue for identifying intrathoracic disease in skeletal populations', *American Journal of Physical Anthropology*, 118: 201–16.

Hillson, S. (2003). 'Wealth, health, diet and dental pathology', in W. H. Metz (ed.), *Wealth, Health and Human Remains in Archaeology, Symposium in het Kader van de Vijfentwintigste Kroon-Voordracht* (Amsterdam: Stichting Nederlands Museum voor Anthropologie en Praehistorie), pp. 7–38.

Hunt, E. & Co. (1848). *Directory and Court Guide for the Cities of Bath, Bristol and Wells* (London: BW Gardiner). https://play.google.com/books/reader?id=SyIO AAAAQAAJ&printsec=frontcover&source=gbs_atb_hover&pg=GBS.RA1-PA82.

Ives, R., Mant, M., de la Cova, C. and Brickley, M. (2017). 'A large-scale palaeopathological study of hip fractures from post-medieval urban England', *International Journal of Osteoarchaeology*, 27: 261–75.

Judd, M. A. (2010). 'Pubic symphyseal face eburnation: An Egyptian sport story?', *International Journal of Osteoarchaeology*, 20: 280–90.

Judd, M. A. and Roberts, C. A. (1999). 'Fracture trauma in a medieval British farming village', *American Journal of Physical Anthropology*, 109: 229–43.

Kelley, M. A. (1979). 'Parturition and pelvic changes', *American Journal of Physical Anthropology*, 51: 541–6.

King, J. (1972). 'The Meredith family, Thomas Taylor and William Blake', *Studies in Romanticism*, 11(2): 153–7.

Lambert, P. M. (2002). 'Rib lesions in a prehistoric Puebloan sample from southwestern Colorado', *American Journal of Physical Anthropology*, 117: 281–92.

Lane, J. (2001). *A Social History of Medicine: Health, Healing and Disease in England 1750–1950* (London: Routledge).

Langford, P. (1998). *A Polite and Commercial People England 1727–1783* (Oxford: Clarendon Press).

Latimer, J. (1887). *The Annals of Bristol in the Nineteenth Century* (Bristol: W & F Morgan).

Lentz, S. S. (1995) 'Osteitis pubis: a review', *Obstetrical & Gynecological Survey*, 50(4): 310–315.

Lewis, M. E. (2011). 'Tuberculosis in the non-adults from Romano-British Poundbury Camp, Dorset, England', *International Journal of Paleopathology*, 1: 12–23.

Lewis, M. E. (2007). *The Bioarchaeology of Children: Perspectives from Biological and Forensic Anthropology* (Cambridge: Cambridge University Press).

Lewis, M. E. (2004). 'Endocranial lesions in non-adult skeletons: understanding their aetiology', *International Journal of Osteoarchaeology*, 14: 82–97.

Lillehammer, G. (1989). 'A child is born: the child's world in an archaeological perspective', *Norwegian Archaeological Review*, 22: 89–105.

Lovejoy C. O, Meindl R. S., Pryzbeck T. R. and Mensforth R. P. (1985). 'Chronological metamorphosis of the auricular surface of the ilium: a new method for the determination of adult skeletal age at death', *American Journal of Physical Anthropology*, 68: 15–28.

Lovell, N. C. (1997). 'Trauma analysis in paleopathology', *Yearbook of Physical Anthropology*, 40: 139–70.

Magyar, L. A. (1999). 'The history of the term tuberculosis', in G. Pálfi, O. Dutour, J. Deák and I. Hutás (eds), *Tuberculosis: Past and Present* (Hungary: Golden Book Publisher Ltd), pp. 25–7.

Mant, M. (2020). '"A little time would compleat the cure": broken bones and fracture experiences of the working poor in London's general hospitals during the long eighteenth century', *Social History of Medicine*, 33: 438–62.

Martini, M. and Boudjemaa, A. (1988). 'Tuberculous osteomyelitis', in M. Martini (ed.), *Tuberculosis of the Bones and Joints* (New York: Springer–Verlag) pp. 52–79.

Mays, S. (1998). *The Archaeology of Human Bones* (London: Routledge).

McFeat, W. (1825). 'The Glasgow Director', National Library of Scotland Directories, https://digital.nls.uk/directories/browse/archive/83434965 (accessed 2020).

McMillen, C. W. (2016). *Pandemics: A Very Short Introduction* (Oxford: Oxford University Press).

Meindl R. S. and Lovejoy C. O. (1985). 'Ectocranial suture closure: a revised method for the determination of skeletal age at death based on the lateral-anterior sutures', *American Journal of Physical Anthropology*, 68: 57–66.

Mensforth, R. P., Lovejoy, C. O., Lallo, J. W. and Armelagos, G. J. (1978). 'The role of constitutional factors, diet and infectious disease in the etiology of porotic hyperostosis and periosteal reactions in prehistoric infants and children', *Medical Anthropology*, 2: 1–59.

Miles, A. and Connell, B. (2012). *New Bunhill Fields Burial Ground, Southwark: Excavations at Globe Academy, 2008* (London: Museum of London Archaeology).

Miles, A., Powers, N., Wroe-Brown, R. and Walker, D. (2008). *St Marylebone Church and Burial Grounds in the 18$^{th}$ to 19$^{th}$ Centuries: Excavations at St Marylebone School, 1992 and 2004–6* (London: Museum of London Archaeology).

Molleson, T. and Cox, M. (1993). *The Spitalfields Project Volume 2: The Anthropology: The Middling Sort* (York: CBA Research Report 86).

Moorrees, C. F. A, Fanning, E. A. and Hunt, E.E. (1963a). 'Formation and resorption of three deciduous teeth in children', *American Journal of Physical Anthropology*, 21: 205–13.

Moorrees, C. F. A, Fanning, E. A. and Hunt, E.E. (1963b). 'Age variation of formation stages for ten permanent teeth', *Journal of Dental Research*, 42: 1490–502.

Newman, S. L. and Hodson, C. M. (2021). 'Contagion in the capital: Exploring the impact of urbanisation and infectious disease risk on child health in nineteenth century London, England', *Childhood in the Past*, 14(2): 177–92.

Newton, H. (2012). *The Sick Child in Early Modern England, 1580–1720* (Oxford: Oxford University Press).

Ouahes, M. and Martini, M. (1988). 'Tuberculosis of the spine', in M. Martini (ed.), *Tuberculosis of the Bones and Joints* (New York: Springer-Verlag), pp. 157–200.

Ortner, D. J. (2003). *Identification of Pathological Conditions in Human Skeletal Remains*, 2nd edn (London: Academic Press).

Padiak, J. (2009). 'Diachronic analysis of cause-of-death terminology: The case of tuberculosis', *Social Science History*, 33(3): 341–56.

Pigot & Co (1824). 'Pigot's Directory of Kent 1824', University of Leicester Special Collections Online: http://specialcollections.le.ac.uk/digital/collection/p16445coll4/id/167102/rec/1 (accessed 2020).

Potter, K. (2017). *Archaeological Excavation at St George's Hall, Great George Street, Bristol Assessment Report and Updated Project Design* (Bristol: Avon Archaeology, unpublished report).

Probert, R. (2009). 'Control over marriage in England and Wales, 1753–1823: The clandestine marriages act of 1753 in context', *Law and History Review*, 27(2): 413–50.

Roberts, C. and Manchester, K. (2005). *The Archaeology of Disease*, 3rd edn (Stroud: Sutton Publishing).

Roberts C. A. and Buikstra, J. E. (2003). *The Bioarchaeology of Tuberculosis: A Global View on a Reemerging Disease* (Florida: University Press of Florida).

Rogers, J., Waldron, T., Dieppe, P. and Watt I. (1987). 'Arthopathies in palaeopathology: The basis of classification according to most probable cause', *Journal of Archaeological Science*, 14: 179–93.

Santos, A. L. and Roberts, C. A. (2001). 'A picture of tuberculosis in young Portuguese people in the early 20th century: a multidisciplinary study of the skeletal and historical evidence', *American Journal of Physical Anthropology*, 115: 38–49.

Santos, A. L. and Roberts, C. A. (2006). 'Anatomy of a serial killer: differential diagnosis of tuberculosis based on rib lesions of adult individuals from the Coimbra identified skeletal collection Portugal', *American Journal of Physical Anthropology*, 130: 38–49.

Scheuer, L. (1998). 'Age at death and cause of death of the people buried in St Bride's Church, Fleet Street, London', in M. Cox (ed.), *Grave Concerns: Death and Burial in England 1700 to 1850*, CBA Research Report 113 (York: Council for British Archaeology), pp. 100–11.

Scheuer, L. and Black, S. (2000). *Developmental Juvenile Osteology* (London: Academic Press).

Sharpe, J. A. (1987). *Early Modern England: A Social History 1550–1760* (London: Edward Arnold).

Silva, J. F. (1980). 'A review of patients with skeletal tuberculosis treated at the University Hospital, Kuala Lumpur', *International Orthopaedics*, 4: 79–81.

Smith, B. H. (1991). 'Standards of human tooth formation and dental age assessment', in M. A. Kelley and C. S. Larsen (eds), *Advances in Dental Anthropology* (New York: Wiley-Liss Inc), pp. 143–68.

Stemmler, J. K. (1992). '"Undisturbed Above Once in a Lustre": Francis Douce, George Cumberland and William Blake at the Bodleian Library and Ashmolean Museum' in *Blake: An Illustrated Quarterly Vol 26 Issue 1* at http://bq.blakearchive.org/26.1.stemmler#n47 (accessed August 2023).

Stirland, A. (2009). *Criminals and Paupers: The Graveyard of St Margaret Fyebriggate in Combusto, Norwich*, East Anglian Archaeology 129 (Norwich, Norfolk: NAU Archaeology/ Historic Environment; Norfolk Museums and Archaeology Service).

Stuart-Macadam, P. (1991). 'Anaemia in Roman Britain: Poundbury Camp', in H. Bush and M. Zvelebil (eds), *Health in Past Societies: Biocultural Interpretations of Human Skeletal Remains in Archaeological Contexts*, BAR Int. Series 567 (Oxford, British Archaeological Reports), pp. 101–13.

Szreter, S. and Mooney, G. (1998). 'Urbanization, mortality, and the standard of living debate: New estimates of the expectation of life at birth in nineteenth-century British cities', *The Economic History Review*, 51(1): 84–112.

Tague, R. G. (1988). 'Bone resorption of the pubis and preauricular area in humans and nonhuman mammals', *American Journal of Physical Anthropology*, 76: 251–67.

Thackrah, C. T. (1831). *The Effects of the Principal Arts, Trades, and Professions, and of Civic States and Habits of Living, on Health and Longevity* (Philadelphia: Porter).

Thijn, C. J. P. and Steensma, J. T. (1990). *Tuberculosis of the Skeleton: Focus on Radiology* (New York: Springer-Verlag).

Tucker, K., Berezina, N., Reinhold, S., Kalmykov, A., Belinskiy, A. and Gresky, J. (2017). 'An accident at work? Traumatic lesions in the skeleton of a 4$^{th}$ millennium BCE "wagon driver" from Sharakhalusan, Russia', *HOMO*, 68: 256–73.

Waldron, T. (2009). *Palaeopathology* (Cambridge: Cambridge University Press).

Walker, P. L., Bathurst, R. R., Richman, R., Gjerdrum, T. and Andrushko, V. A. (2009). 'The causes of porotic hyperostosis and cribra orbitalia: A reappraisal of the iron-deficiency-anemia hypothesis', *American Journal of Physical Anthropology*, 139: 109–25.

Williams, N. and Mooney, G. (1994). 'Infant mortality in an "age of great cities": London and the English provincial cities compared, c. 1840–1910', *Continuity and Change*, 9(2): 185–212.

Witkin, A. V. (2011). 'The health of the labouring poor, surgical and post-mortem procedures at the Bristol Royal Infirmary, 1757–1854: A biohistorical approach' (PhD Dissertation, University of Bristol).

# 7

# Disability, gender and old age in the Industrial Revolution: cultural historical and osteoarchaeological perspectives

*Sophie L. Newman and David M. Turner*

Bringing together theoretical perspectives from disability studies, the history of ageing and osteoarchaeology, this chapter blends textual, cultural and skeletal evidence to examine the ways in which working bodies aged during Britain's industrial expansion of the late eighteenth and early nineteenth centuries. What can a combination of skeletal and documentary evidence tell us about experiences of ageing and living with bodily impairment in the early Industrial Revolution? What insights does the material body provide that are missing from written historical sources? And how can we enhance our understanding of archaeological material by examining cultural narratives of disability and ageing, to provide more nuanced analyses of how these bodies were perceived at the time?

The form, pattern and cause of osseous changes in skeletal remains provides, in Joanna R. Sofaer's words, a 'way of knowing' about the body that reveals the embodied experiences of people in the past (2006: 45; Craig-Atkins and Harvey, this volume: introduction). This is particularly important for understanding the lives of industrial workers or people living on the margins of society, who might otherwise leave few written records of their own, or whose life experiences might be mediated through visual representations or social commentary produced for polemical purposes (Byrnes and Muller, 2017; Southwell-Wright, 2013). Although it is important not to reduce individuals to medical case studies (Sofaer, 2006: 46), or to make assumptions about quality of life from pathological indicators alone (Metzler, 1999; Shuttleworth and Meekosha, 2017), skeletal evidence can inform of the progress of diseases or impairment, of the breaking and remaking of fractured bones, and of the changes in bodily capacity over time associated with ageing. According to Rebecca Gowland, the skeleton of an older person 'represents a life lived, containing skeletal and biographical echoes of a person's childhood as well as later phases of their life' (2017: 239). Using the cross-disciplinary, collaborative approach exemplified by several contributions collected in this volume, this chapter aims to demonstrate the ways in which the study of skeletal remains alongside – and in dialogue with – textual historical evidence can enrich our understanding of populations that have, until recently, been marginalised in studies of industrialisation.

After a brief discussion of the conceptual and methodological issues raised by exploring histories of ageing and disability, we present a detailed analysis of three skeletons recovered during archaeological excavations at Hazel Grove, Stockport and St Hilda's, South Shields to identify skeletal changes that might have signified physical limitations that were disabling or required care. However, embodied experiences during this time period were not simply determined by the presence or absence of pathological features – they occurred within a wider social context of meanings (Harvey, 2020). The chapter proceeds to explore the skeletal evidence in relation to social, cultural and political debates about the body and industrialisation, and what this meant for individualised experiences of debility. Our purpose is not just to *compare* skeletal and documentary evidence, but to explore how archaeological and social historical methodologies can be more fully integrated to understand ageing and disability in this period.

## Approaching disability and old age in the Industrial Revolution

Older people are a relatively neglected demographic within the broader discipline of archaeology. Current skeletal age estimation techniques make it difficult to accurately identify older adults beyond what we now consider middle age (45–50 years) (Appleby, 2018). While there is a growing body of historical scholarship on old age, there have been few studies that explore ageing as an embodied experience, or which explore the relationship between old age and physical impairment (Ottaway, 2007; Pelling and Smith, 1991; Thane, 2000). Old age is not synonymous with disability, but ageing is associated with a multitude of degenerative biological changes leading to potentially debilitating conditions, such as osteoporosis, osteoarthritis and loss of hearing and/or sight. Biological ageing brings on physical changes such as greying and loss of hair, development of wrinkles, stooping of the posture, loss of teeth, weakening of immune response and susceptibility to falls. Injuries can take longer to heal, and periods of illness become difficult to overcome. Chronic pain and impairment can lead to increased frailty, a loss of independence, social isolation and disempowerment in later life (Appleby, 2018). Since impairments in older people are often seen as normal, and somewhat expected, they are much less likely to be framed as 'disability' in the cultural sense compared to impairments in children or working-age adults (Woodward, 2015). What constitutes 'disability' is closely connected to understandings of temporality, ageing and how a particular culture or society conceives of a normative life course (Ljuslinder et al., 2020: 36). In modern Western societies, the construction of 'normal' bodies as able and predominantly youthful or middle-aged means that in younger people disabled bodies are considered 'anomalous and extraordinary', whereas 'visibly marked aged bodies are typically considered so ordinary that they recede from view becoming invisible' (Woodward, 2015: 33).

Ageing and disability are social and biological phenomena and understandings of both the 'process' of ageing and the 'condition' of disability are contextual and change over time (Appleby, 2018: 145; Woodward, 2015: 34). As Gowland points out, the meaning of disablement is not only culturally specific, but also dependent on a range of factors including the construction of particular disease states, the class, gender, age, religious and racial identity of the person concerned, expectations of that person's performance of capabilities pertinent to their identity or stage of their life course, and social, cultural and familial factors influencing the provision of care (2017: 248). Indeed, as work in disability history has shown, the category of 'disability' as a status that entitles a person to particular services and statutory benefits, or pertaining to a person's identity, is itself a relatively modern phenomenon and cannot easily be transposed onto people in the past (Cooter, 2003).

Older and 'disabled' people in the late eighteenth and early nineteenth centuries faced a multitude of adverse social factors, such as a lack of systematic welfare provision, and the reliance on spouses, family or the workhouse for care and support (Ottaway, 2007). The social and economic changes associated with industrialisation have been seen as contributing to increasing marginalisation both of working-age disabled people and of older people. It is argued that the shift from household to factory production, increasing standardisation of the hours of work in relation to an abstract able-bodied ideal, and mechanisation, eventually displaced slower and weaker workers from the labour force, leading to increasing neglect and institutionalisation (Gleeson, 1999; Kuskey, 2016; Oliver and Barnes, 2012: 52–73; Quadagno, 1982: 20). Yet, until recently these assumptions had not been tested by detailed historical or archaeological research. What is emerging from new scholarship on disability and the Industrial Revolution is a more complex picture, which shows that disability was a ubiquitous working-class experience in this period, that 'disabled' people were visible in industrial communities and that the notion of older or disabled people as economically unproductive citizens does not do justice to the diversity of experience (Rose, 2017; Turner and Blackie, 2018).

Aged and disabled bodies were culturally and politically significant during the eighteenth and nineteenth centuries. Fears of widespread worker injury or deformity, especially among younger sections of the workforce, were a major driver of campaigns for regulation of labour in factories and coalmines in the early nineteenth century. Furthermore, as we shall see, during the Industrial Revolution images of bodies becoming 'worn out' or prematurely aged became an important means of conceptualising and critiquing social and economic change. Rather than being marginal to the story of economic progress, older and disabled bodies were important means of understanding its broader implications. The onset of old age was not simply determined by reaching a particular chronological milestone, but by class, occupation and gender. In this context, the history of old age and the history of disability are inextricably linked, not simply because older people were more susceptible to reduced functionality or chronic conditions, but because disablement was itself conceptualised as a form of ageing in working-class communities.

## Case studies

The chapter uses three skeletal case studies from Hazel Grove, Stockport and St Hilda's, South Shields, to examine how the bodily stresses imparted by industrialised society, and the processes of ageing, manifested themselves in individual skeletal biographies.

Skeleton 15 from Hazel Grove, Stockport was one of thirty-nine skeletons recovered during an archaeological excavation of a former Wesleyan Chapel in 2016 (Newman and Holst, 2016). The cemetery associated with the chapel was in use from 1794 to 1910 (Jessop and Beauchamp, 2015), and name plates recovered during the excavation are suggestive of the skeletons dating to the early to mid-nineteenth century (Newman and Holst, 2016). Prior to 1836, Hazel Grove was known as Bullock Smithy, and this rebranding may have been an attempt to overturn the poor reputation of the area (Jessop and Beauchamp, 2015: 16). Throughout the nineteenth century, Hazel Grove continued to grow, and inhabitants were also employed in a number of varying occupations, such as the expanding cotton and silk industries, brickworks, timber yards, a glue works, the hatting trade and nearby coal mines (Jessop and Beauchamp, 2015: 16). Based on the grave goods, coffin fittings and decorative name plates seen in the burials excavated at the former Wesleyan Chapel, it is likely that they are representative of a mix of individuals from working class and wealthier backgrounds (Newman and Holst, 2016).

Skeleton 235 and Skeleton 502 were two of 204 burials recovered during the excavation of the burial ground of St Hilda's Parish Church South Shields between 2006 and 2007 (Raynor *et al.*, 2011). While the cemetery had been in use since *c.*1402, the excavation area relates to the southern section of the burial ground and is split into three burial horizons that date to the eighteenth and nineteenth centuries (Raynor *et al.*, 2011). South Shields was a manufacturing and shipbuilding town that developed in parallel to North Shields across the River Tyne (Hodgson, 1903). The individuals of this population are said to have been representative of a working-class population, employed in local industries, such as the shipyards and port, gas works, salt-works, a glass factory, chemical works and in nearby collieries (Green, 2010; Raynor *et al.*, 2011).

While it has not been possible to identify the individuals concerned via preserved coffin plates and record linkage, the skeletal evidence alone poses questions about embodied experiences of disability, ageing and work in the context of the social and economic development of regions which, although occupationally diverse, were synonymous with key elements of industrial expansion: the cotton textile manufacturing area around Manchester, and the coalfield of North East England (Griffin, 2006; King and Timmins, 2001). A Bioarchaeology of Care approach will be taken for each case study, as proposed by Tilley and Schrenk (2017), in which the skeletal evidence is assessed for the presence of disability requiring care. Ultimately this will enable broader discourse relating to provision of care (or lack thereof) for all three individuals, and connect them to discussions surrounding the cultural intersections between ageing, disability and occupational identity in the eighteenth and nineteenth centuries.

## *Skeleton 15, Hazel Grove, Stockport*

Skeleton 15 from Hazel Grove, Stockport was likely male, and aged between 36–45 years at death (Newman and Holst, 2016). As can be seen in Figure 7.1, the majority of their skeleton was preserved, allowing for the analysis of a suite of skeletal changes potentially indicative of debility experienced during life.

Their spine exhibited severe curvature in the thoracic (torso) region, likely a form of scoliosis termed kyphoscoliosis (see Figure 7.1b). Significant distortions to the shape of the rib cage were evident (see Figure 7.1c), and extensive joint changes and osteoarthritis were seen throughout the vertebral column, in some cases leading to the fusion of ribs to the vertebrae, and between vertebrae. The eleventh right rib (towards the bottom of the ribcage) had fractured at some point in their life, but had failed to heal, instead leaving

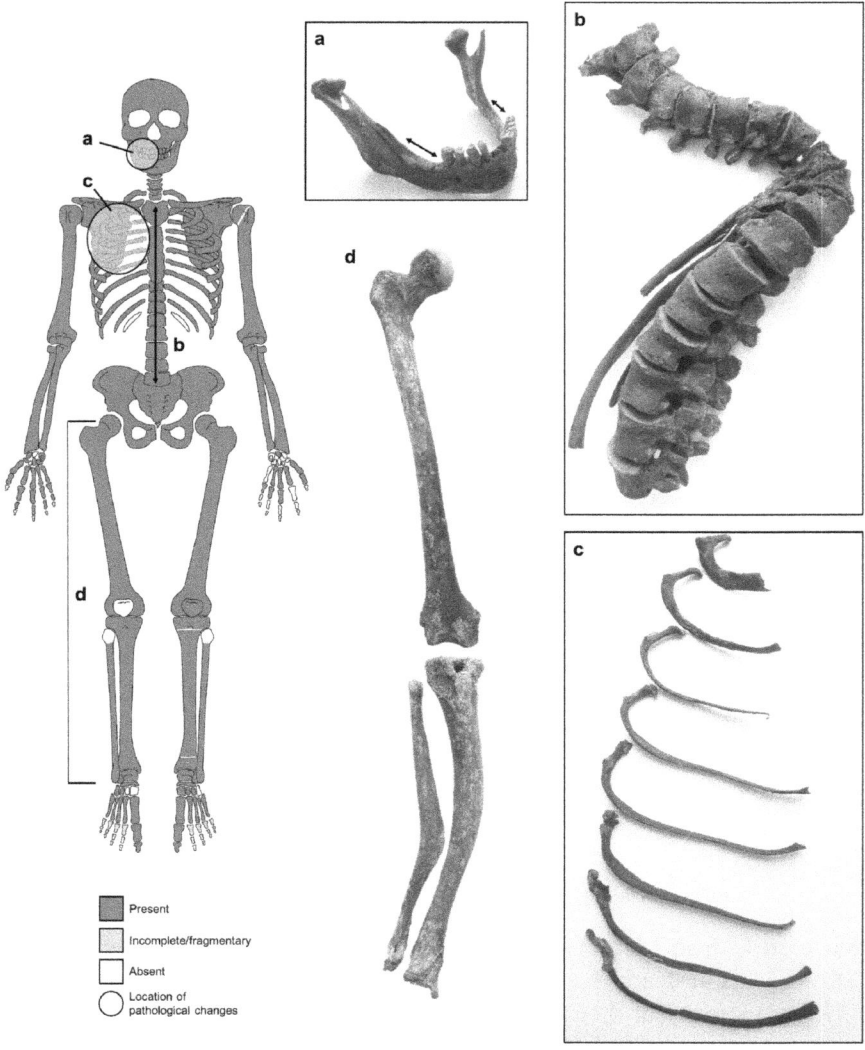

**Figure 7.1** Skeletal elements present and pathological changes seen in Skeleton 15, Hazel Grove, Stockport. a) Antemortem tooth loss of the left and right lower molars of the mandible (arrows); b) thoracic and lumbar vertebrae of the spine, demonstrating kyphoscoliosis and fusion of the 9th–11th ribs on the right side; c) remaining right ribs (1st–8th) showing straightening of the shafts and degenerative changes to the heads (point of articulation with the vertebrae); d) bowing of the right femur, tibia and fibula.

a pseudoarthrosis (false joint) between the two sections. Skeleton 15 also demonstrated severe bowing of the right and left lower limbs (see Figure 7.1d). The femora had notable anterior (forward) curvatures, and the tibiae and fibulae were bowed laterally (outward).

The majority of cases of kyphoscoliosis in the modern day are classed as idiopathic, with no clear causative factors (Issac and Das, 2020). It may also result from congenital conditions and vertebral anomalies occurring during development, continuing to increase in severity throughout the growth period and even after skeletal maturity (McMaster and Singh, 1999; Zeng et al., 2013: 372). Kyphoscoliosis can also develop secondary to other disease factors, such as degeneration of the spine due to age (for example, resulting from osteoporosis and/or osteoarthritis), or following trauma (Issac and Das, 2020). Tuberculosis was also prevalent during the eighteenth and nineteenth centuries, and in a small percentage of individuals destructive lesions on the vertebral bodies can lead to collapse and resultant deformity of the vertebral column (Roberts, 2012: 435). However, no other potential indicators of infectious processes like tuberculosis, such as evidence of inflammatory response on the visceral surfaces of the ribs or destructive lesions on the vertebrae, were present in Skeleton 15. In addition, while gross alterations to vertebral body morphology were evident in the regions of tightest curvature in the spinal column, these had more of a wedged and 'folded' appearance (see Figure 7.1b). When observed alongside the severely bowed lower limbs of this individual, this may be more consistent with an underlying vitamin D deficiency leading to deficient mineralisation and subsequent buckling of the vertebrae under the weight of the body (Brickley et al., 2005).

Deficiencies in vitamin D result from insufficient skin exposure to ultraviolet radiation from sunlight and/or from dietary deficiency (Ives and Brickley, 2014). In the nineteenth century, vitamin D deficiency rickets was found to be particularly abundant in the industrial regions of London, Newcastle and Gateshead, Lancashire, Yorkshire, Cheshire, Derbyshire and Nottingham (Owen, 1889). Its high incidence among urban children is attributed to the thick coal smoke and fogs that diminished sunlight in the cities, rapid urbanisation leading to an abundance of dark and narrow alleyways, nutritionally deficient diets and working indoors (Hardy, 2003; Ives and Brickley, 2014; Roberts and Cox, 2003). Kyphosis and scoliosis of the spine can result from vitamin D deficiencies experienced during the growth period (rickets) and may be retained into adulthood along with bowing of the long bones as indicators of healed vitamin D deficiency rickets (Brickley and Ives, 2008; Holick, 2006; Pettifor, 2003). Such changes have also been associated with vitamin D deficiencies experienced following the cessation of growth (osteomalacia), with significant bending and buckling of weight bearing bones linked to insufficient mineralisation during remodelling. However, a large-scale study of vitamin D deficiency experienced in adulthood has revealed the rarity of such severe skeletal deformities as seen in Skeleton 15 in post-medieval archaeological assemblages (Ives and Brickley, 2014). They are instead seen more frequently in later nineteenth- and twentieth-century pathology museum collections, having been selected for retention as exceptional examples of pathological changes (Ives and Brickley, 2014). The extent of the skeletal changes seen in this individual are perhaps suggestive of severe and chronic episodes of vitamin D deficiency, potentially experienced both in childhood (rickets) and adulthood (Brickley *et al.*, 2005; Ives and Brickley, 2014).

A contemporaneous example of an adult male with severe kyphoscoliosis and lower limb bowing deformities was identified in the skeletal assemblage from St Bride's Church vaults, London (Conlogue *et al.*, 2017: 153). While it was suggested by Conlogue *et al.* (2017) that the changes seen in the bones of the lower limbs of this individual may be related to residual rickets, and exacerbated by the biomechanical implications of the changes seen in their spine, a suggested diagnosis of neurofibromatosis was given (2017: 159). This congenital condition can in some severe cases lead to skeletal abnormalities, including scoliosis and tibial dysplasia.

Whether the severe skeletal changes seen in Skeleton 15 arose due to a congenital condition, such as neurofibromatosis, or due to susceptibility to chronic and recurring vitamin D deficiencies imparted by their physical/social environments, or a combination of the two, this individual lived with them to a relatively advanced age (being approximately 36–45 years of age at the time of death). Spinal curvatures can lead to a hunched appearance and can result in back pain and neurological consequences from compression of the spinal cord, including paralysis (McMaster *et al.*, 1999; Zeng *et al.*, 2013: 372). An increased risk of respiratory failure (often as a result of susceptibility to pulmonary infection) has also been reported in patients with kyphoscoliosis, along with functional impairment, leading to limitations in day-to-day activity (Fuschillo *et al.*, 2015: 96; Zeng *et al.*, 2013: 372). Ability to perform activities such as the lifting and carrying of loads and mobility akin to climbing stairs may have been difficult, and they would have been susceptible to falls and injuries due to changes in gait and bodily imbalance (Conlogue *et al.*, 2017: 169; Issac and Das, 2020). However, as also seen in the individual from St Bride's, the long bones of Skeleton 15 were reasonably robust, and thus presented no evidence of atrophy from lack of use (Conlogue *et al.*, 2017: 158–9). While the presence of extensive degenerative changes in the spine of Skeleton 15, and the ununited rib fracture, are indicative of the additional bodily strains and risks of injury that can accompany cases of severe scoliosis, they too are suggestive of a degree of continued mobility.

It was suggested by Conlogue *et al.* (2017) that the skeletal changes and resultant restrictions on respiratory and cardiac function seen in the individual from St Bride's, and likely too in Skeleton 15, probably had some long-term implications for functionality (Conlogue *et al.*, 2017). However, the authors rightly state that commenting on specific activities associated with daily life that these individuals may have been able, or unable, to undertake is not feasible in the absence of further lines of evidence, and functionality too is dependent on support mechanisms available to them, personal motivation and the specific circumstances in which they lived (Conlogue *et al.*, 2017: 170).

### Skeleton 235, St Hilda's Churchyard, South Shields

Skeleton 235 from St Hilda's Churchyard, South Shields, shows evidence of multiple injuries sustained during life, whether during one event, or recurrent episodes. As can be seen in Figure 7.2, only half of their skeleton was preserved for analysis, but they were likely a male individual aged 36+ years (using methods by: Brooks and Suchey, 1990; Bruzek, 2002; Buckberry and Chamberlain, 2002; Lovejoy *et al.*, 1985; Mays and Cox, 2000; Phenice, 1969). This individual was likely physically active during life, with mild degenerative changes starting to develop in the spine and in both hips and knees.

The glenoid fossa of their right scapula had undergone extensive remodelling leading to loss of the original joint surface, and formation of a pseudoarthrosis on its anterior (front facing) surface (see Figure 7.2a). The proximal end of the right humerus was also grossly altered, with the formation of a new articular surface on its posterior (back) surface (see Figure 7.2b). A large projection of bone had formed on the posterolateral surface (back and outer edge) of the right humerus, perhaps indicative of bone tissue formation following soft tissue damage (termed *myositis ossificans*). This may have been incurred during the original traumatic event, or in response to the unreduced dislocation.

The location of the new articular surfaces evident on the right scapula and humerus suggest that the head of the right humerus had slipped in front of the right scapula, consistent with an unreduced subcoracoid anterior shoulder dislocation. Due to the relatively shallow joint surface of the glenoid fossa, and the reliance on ligaments and musculature to maintain integrity, the highly mobile shoulder is one of the most commonly dislocated joints (Miles, 2000; White *et al.*, 2016: 146). Today, this most frequently occurs in young adult men engaging in riskier activities, such as contact sports, skiing and cycling, leading to high-energy falls onto an outstretched arm (White *et al.*, 2016: 146). The importance of swift treatment of dislocations was recognised in the nineteenth century, and techniques for reduction included pulling on the arm while holding a knee in the armpit of the patient

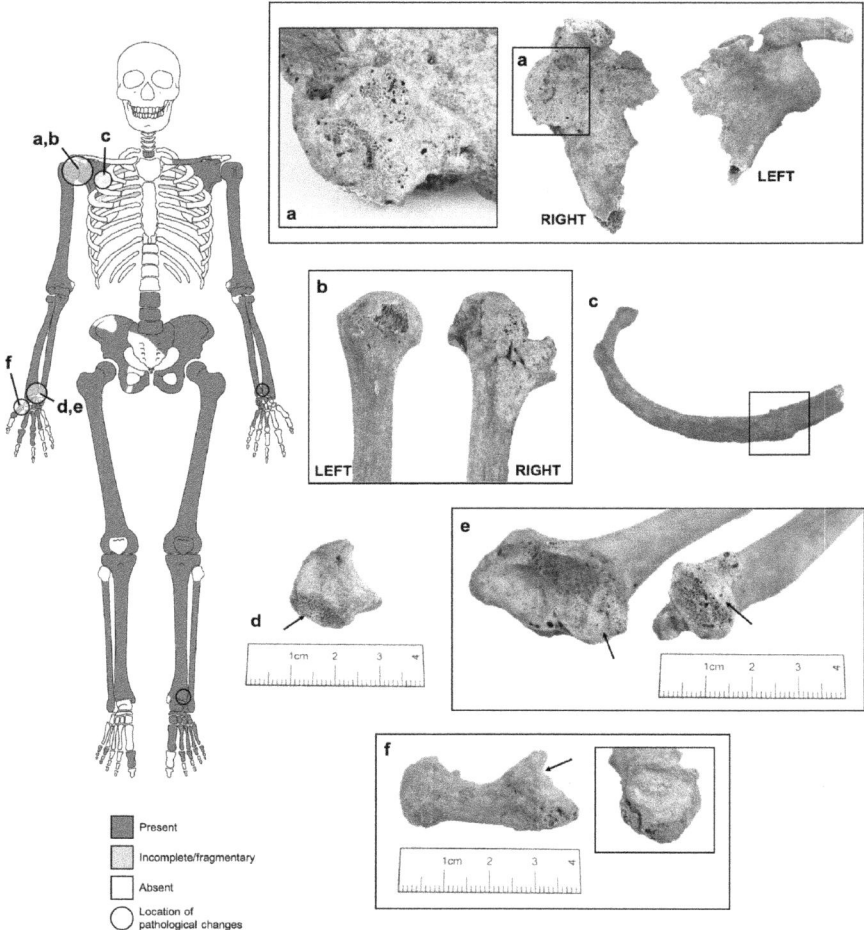

Figure 7.2 Skeletal elements present and pathological changes seen in Skeleton 235, St Hilda's Churchyard, South Shields. a) Anterior view of the left and right scapulae, highlighting evidence of dislocation of the right glenohumeral (shoulder) joint; b) posterior view of the left and right humeri, demonstrating extensive changes seen on the joint surface of the right proximal humerus; c) well-healed fracture seen on the midshaft of the right 3rd rib; d) evidence of possible trauma (arrow) on the right lunate; e) possibly associated osteoarthritic changes seen on the distal joint surfaces of the right radius and ulna, leading to eburnation (arrows); f) medial view (left image) of the right 1st metacarpal (associated with the thumb) showing a well-healed fracture of the proximal joint surface (arrow), and proximal view (right image) of the fractured joint surface of the right 1st metacarpal.

and then finer manipulation of the joint with the arm bent at the elbow, followed by placing the arm in a sling for a few weeks (Cooper, 1822; Miles, 2000). The more time that elapsed following the original injury, the more difficult it became to resolve it satisfactorily due to the fixation of the humerus in its new position and the infilling of the original articular surface (Bowlby, 1887: 189; Cooper, 1822: 1). In addition, modern clinical cases report that the mechanism of the anterior dislocation, whereby the humeral head externally rotates in the joint and slips forward under the force of the fall, can lead to fragmentation of the anterior rim of the glenoid fossa, resulting in a Bankart lesion (White et al., 2016: 147). Continued movement of the humeral head against this Bankart lesion following an unreduced anterior shoulder dislocation could have led to formation of the pseudoarthrosis seen on the right scapula in Skeleton 235 (Walker, 2012: 120).

Skeleton 235 showed evidence of additional healed injuries. A healed fracture was seen on the midshaft of an upper right rib (see Figure 7.2c). Rib fractures may be associated with falls or blows to the torso (Roberts and Manchester, 2010), and the location of this isolated rib fracture in close proximity to the anterior dislocation of the right shoulder could suggest that this injury occurred during the same traumatic event. Also affecting the right upper limb, possible evidence of Kienböck's disease was seen in the right lunate (wrist bone that articulates with the radius), whereby a reduction of blood supply to the lunate following a compression fracture leads to osteonecrosis (see Figure 7.2d; Walker, 2012: 232). This condition is frequently associated with repetitive trauma to the wrist, and typically affects the dominant hand of those aged 20–40 years undertaking manual labour (Walker, 2012: 232). It can lead to pain and swelling, and the development of osteoarthritis (Walker, 2012: 232), such as the extensive secondary osteoarthritis seen at the right distal radioulnar joint in Skeleton 235 (see Figure 7.2e). Evidence of osteoarthritis was also seen in the distal radioulnar joint on the left side, but to a lesser extent. Dysfunction of the distal radioulnar joints can result from trauma, degenerative arthritis, inflammatory conditions such as rheumatoid arthritis, and developmental conditions such as Madelung's deformity (Weiss and Rodner, 2007). No other evidence for the two latter aetiologies were seen in Skeleton 235, so it is likely that the degenerative changes seen in the wrists related to the development of osteoarthritis due to lifestyle or occupational activities, or secondary osteoarthritis resulting from abnormal joint loading following trauma.

A healed fracture was also recorded on the right first metacarpal (bone in the palm associated with the thumb), affecting the proximal joint surface (see Figure 7.2f). Fractures in this location are referred to as Bennett's fractures or Rolando fractures, depending on severity (Carlsen and Moran, 2009). They have been reported following sporting injuries, falls from a standing height, road traffic accidents and assaults (Middleton *et al.*, 2015). They are most commonly seen in males, and predominantly in the dominant hand (Leclère *et al.*, 2012).

Finally, a possible healed avulsion fracture was seen on the distal left tibia, evident as a slight ridge across the posterolateral joint surface. Termed pilon fractures, this type of injury can occur when the talus is pushed up into the articular surface of the tibia, such as following a fall from a height (White *et al.*, 2016: 506). Intra-articular fractures affecting the posterior area of the distal tibial joint surface typically occur when the foot is in plantarflexion (pointed downward) (Sitnik *et al.*, 2017).

It is clear that Skeleton 235 had experienced at least one significant traumatic event during life that may have led to impairment of their right arm. As it is challenging to differentiate between timing of healed fractures in skeletal remains (Mant, 2019), it is not possible to determine whether the additional healed injuries and potential secondary osteoarthritis all resulted from a single traumatic event, or reflect multiple episodes of injury. Whether the injuries and secondary osteoarthritis seen in this individual impacted on their functionality is difficult to determine in the absence of further evidence. The fractures appear to be well healed without added complications, and cases of chronic unreduced or recurrent shoulder dislocations, such as that seen in Skeleton 235, do not necessarily signal permanent functional impairment. Bowlby found that following initial significant impairment of use of the affected limb '… it becomes less painful and stiff, and, after many months, the part i[s] frequently restored to much of its former power', attributing this recovery to the ability of the soft tissue structures of the shoulder to adapt to the newly formed joint (1887: 189). However, Cooper noted a loss of mobility and function of the affected limb in some patients and reported that 'numbness of the fingers is frequently occurring from the pressure of the head of the bone upon a nerve, or the nerves of the axiliary plexus' (1822: 418). Thus, while Skeleton 235 may have experienced difficulty in performing occupational tasks and certain activities associated with daily life during the healing process, permanent significant functional impairment was unlikely.

### *Skeleton 502, St Hilda's Churchyard, South Shields*

Skeleton 502 shows evidence of a significant injury experienced during life alongside more commonplace degenerative changes associated with ageing. Approximately 75% of their skeleton was preserved for analysis (see Figure 7.3), and they were likely a female aged 46+ years (using methods by: Buckberry and Chamberlain, 2002; Bruzek, 2002; Lovejoy *et al.*, 1985; Mays and Cox, 2000).

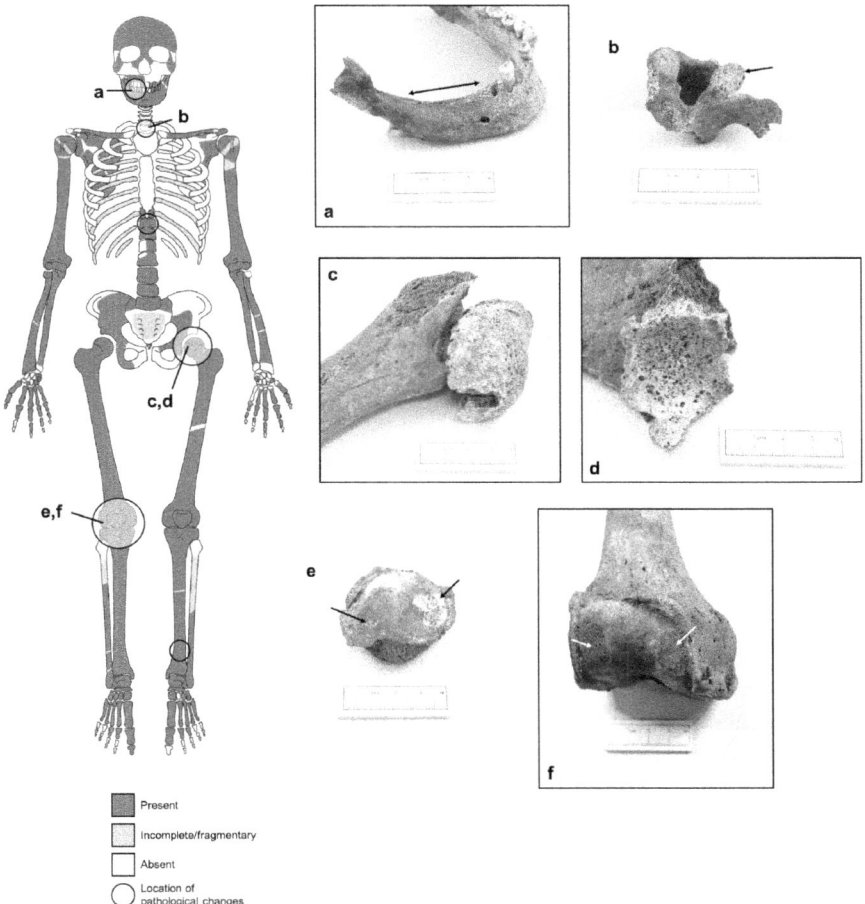

Figure 7.3 Skeletal elements present and pathological changes seen in Skeleton 502, St Hilda's Churchyard, South Shields. a) Antemortem tooth loss of the right 2nd premolar and molars; b) evidence of osteoarthritis in the right superior articular facet of the second thoracic vertebra, showing porosity and eburnation of the joint surface (arrow); c) posterior view of the left proximal femur, with mushroom-like deformity of the femoral head, and osteoarthritic changes to the joint surface; d) posterior view of the left acetabulum (hip joint) showing extensive secondary osteoarthritic changes; e) posterior view of the right patella, showing patches of eburnation (arrows) indicative of osteoarthritis; f) anterior view of the right distal femur with patches of eburnation (arrows) matching that seen on the posterior surface of the patella.

Their bones were light in weight compared to the norm for an adult individual, a feature tentatively suggestive of a decrease in bone mass and density associated with osteopenia or osteoporosis. Progressive loss of bone tissue leading to a heightened risk of fracture in response to minimal force is characteristic of osteoporosis, and fragility fractures tend to occur in load-bearing regions, such as compression fractures in the vertebrae, and in areas vulnerable to injury from trips and falls, such as the ribs, distal radius and the femoral neck (Brickley and Ives, 2008: 151). While it can result from trauma, disease or poor diet, it is most frequently associated with advancing age for males and females, and post-menopausal changes in women (Brickley and Ives, 2008: 151; Morgan et al., 2020). There was only one fracture evident in Skeleton 502 that may be associated with osteoporosis (see below), but due to the multifactorial nature of this type of injury, this cannot be confirmed.

Skeleton 502 had a healed fracture of the left femoral neck (associated with the left hip joint) that had led to extensive secondary osteoarthritic changes to both the femoral head and acetabulum (articular socket on the pelvis for head of the femur; see Figure 7.3c, d). Femoral neck fractures occurring within the capsule of the hip joint (intracapsular fractures) can disrupt blood supply to the femoral head, resulting in avascular necrosis and subsequent collapse, as also seen in Skeleton 502 (Raynor et al., 2011: 74–5; White et al., 2016: 353). Hip fractures are a common injury, with older women being at particular risk, typically as a result of advancing age, osteoporosis or other chronic disease factors (Morgan et al., 2020; White et al., 2016: 352). Hip fractures in older people frequently occur in response to low impact falls from standing height and are associated with a high risk of further morbidity and mortality (Ives et al., 2017; Morgan et al., 2020). Hip fractures in non-elderly patients are rarer, and as such gain less attention in modern clinical literature, but considering the relatively broad age-at-death estimation for Skeleton 502 their aetiology must also be considered. These are more frequently associated with high energy trauma, but can also include those with risk factors for severe injury following falls due to preexisting diseases, or being of 'biologically advanced age' due to osteopenia or osteoporosis (Rogmark et al., 2018). Osteopenia and osteoporosis in younger patients can stem from factors such as malnutrition, medications and excessive alcohol intake or tobacco usage (Rogmark et al., 2018). The fracture to the left femoral neck in Skeleton 502 was well healed, indicating their survival beyond the injury. This is likely due to the fracture location conferring more stability, as has been noted in a large-scale study of hip fractures in post-medieval England (Ives et al., 2017). Despite potential mobility issues that may have occurred during the healing process of the hip fracture seen in Skeleton 502, the evidence of secondary osteoarthritic changes suggests the joint continued to be used.

Degenerative joint changes and osteoarthritis are some of the most common pathologies seen in archaeological skeletal assemblages (Waldron, 2012). While degenerative joint changes and osteoarthritis can arise in response to trauma or disease processes, as seen in the left hip of Skeleton 502 and the previous case studies, they can also be indicative of the cumulative effects of everyday wear and tear on the body during life. While there was no evidence for joint changes or degeneration in the right hip joint of Skeleton 502, their right knee joint did demonstrate extensive osteoarthritic changes (see Figure 7.3e, f). Evidence of osteoarthritis and degenerative joint changes was also seen in the spine (see Figure 7.3b). Degenerative disc disease, whereby the intervertebral discs of the spine begin to deteriorate, was also present in the spine, and may have led to anterior disc herniation in a lower thoracic vertebra (T11). Osteoarthritis was also seen in the left and right pisiform bones (small bones in the wrists), and in the right and left first metatarsals (where the big toe articulates with the foot).

Skeleton 502 had also lost three posterior teeth on the right side of the mandible during life (see Figure 7.3a). Antemortem tooth loss, also seen in Skeleton 15 (see Figure 7.1a), can result from generally poor dental health associated with periodontal disease and dental caries, but also severe tooth wear and trauma (Lukacs, 2012: 560). Antemortem tooth loss is typically seen in increasing frequency in older individuals, perhaps related to the accumulation of dental health risks over time due to poor dental hygiene practices and the finite nature of dental enamel (Roberts and Manchester, 2010).

In summary, degenerative processes affecting spine, wrists and lower limbs were seen in Skeleton 502, alongside a healed hip fracture, ante-mortem tooth loss and tentative evidence for osteoporosis. Some of these skeletal pathologies may be attributable to the ageing process, or may have simply arisen from the advancement of general wear and tear of the body due to differing lifestyles of working-class eighteenth- to nineteenth-century populations. Attributing evidence of degenerative joint changes and osteoarthritis to lived experiences of pain and reduced mobility in past populations can be problematic (Waldron, 2012: 518). A weak correlation exists between joint changes seen in radiological examinations and actual lived symptoms, although some locations may be more liable to cause pain than others, such as the base of the thumb, the medial compartment of the knee and the hip (Waldron, 2012: 518). However, the traumatic event resulting in a hip fracture likely left them requiring assistance with activities associated with daily life during the healing and rehabilitation process, and potential implications for functional changes in gait and mobility beyond this. While the extensive eburnation seen on both the femoral and acetabular joint surfaces of the left hip of Skeleton 502 does suggest continued mobility, large bony outgrowths on the joint margins and the altered morphology of the femoral and acetabular joint surfaces may indicate restrictions to the normal range of movement, and may have resulted in altered gait. In older patients today, ability to live independently and undertake activities of daily living following a femoral neck fracture is reliant on their ease of mobility within the home and support from their wider community (Reuling *et al.*, 2012; Schiller *et al.*, 2015). Such outcomes too are largely dependent on factors such as age, pre-fracture health status of the individual (Reuling *et al.*, 2012) and self-determination (Schiller *et al.*, 2015). Hip fractures in older people are often seen as life-changing events, and modern studies of patients' perspectives of recovery following hip fracture reveal experiences of loss of independence and mobility and a sense of transformation from the normality of their pre-fracture lives, with one older female stating 'Suddenly I feel old' (Bruun-Olsen *et al.*, 2018: 5). Like that seen for older people, younger patients too can face longer-term implications of hip fractures, such as pain, barriers to return to work and reduction in mobility (Rogmark *et al.*, 2018). While more research is needed to determine whether these injuries produced the same feelings of vulnerability in older patients in the past, in the eighteenth and nineteenth centuries medical professionals viewed hip fractures (especially those in the intra-capsular region) as particularly problematic, due to difficulties in promoting union and healing (Degeling, 2009). This was further complicated by the difficulty in identifying such injuries prior to the development of radiography, and approaches to treating older individuals could take the form of 'treat the patient and let the fracture go' (Degeling, 2009: 128). As such, individuals recovering from hip fractures during this time likely faced additional barriers to recovery without the level of treatment seen within modern interventions.

### Reading older and disabled bodies in the Industrial Revolution

In summary, the three case studies are connected by evidence of bodily decline and potential debility experienced during life. This ranged from relatively minor and to some degree invisible indicators of daily wear and tear in the form of degenerative joint changes and antemortem tooth loss, to severe impairments and injuries that likely demarcated their bodies and influenced ability to varying degrees. Within a Bioarchaeology of Care perspective, only one case study (Skeleton 15) exhibited skeletal changes suggestive of long-term care requirements in terms of activities of daily living. However, while Skeleton 235 and Skeleton 502 had likely recovered to some extent prior to their death, evidence of healed injuries gives insight into the impact of periods of rehabilitation experienced during their life course in which they may have been more reliant on their wider communities. How the spinal and limb deformities seen in Skeleton 15, the permanent shoulder dislocation in Skeleton 235 and the healed hip fracture in Skeleton 502 were sustained can only be speculated on in the absence of documentary evidence. However, their susceptibility to the development of these skeletal conditions and their subsequent perception in eighteenth and nineteenth century society was likely influenced by the intertwining of social and biological influences aligned to status, occupation and gender. All three individuals were estimated to be over approximately 35 years of age at the time of death and had persisted alongside their impairments, albeit for an unknown period of time. As will be discussed, in the late eighteenth and early nineteenth centuries, health and appearance were probably more important than chronological factors in determining age; thus, to consider the impact of such bodily changes on their lives requires discussion regarding our interpretation of debility and ageing in this context.

As Pat Thane has argued, there was a long tradition in European history of viewing the onset of old age as beginning in a person's 60s, with more advanced old age beginning at 70 (2020: 389). But ageing was not simply measured in terms of chronological milestones, it was (and is) also a biologically, psychologically and socially influenced process (Appleby, 2018: 146). In eras where people may not have known their exact chronological age, such factors may have been even more significant in determining perceptions of ageing (Western and Bekvalac, 2020: 175). Despite the consistency in defining when old age began, there has been a 'notable disjuncture between the standardisation implied by chronological age and the varied experience of old age' (Thane, 2020: 395). Adult age estimation in human skeletal remains relies on observations of the extent of joint degeneration of key stable joints in the skeleton (notably those of the pelvis). Such methods have been found to systematically underage older adults, in part due to mimicry of reference samples, leading to their relative 'invisibility' in studies of past populations (Buckberry, 2015; Gowland, 2007). No one person ages the same way as the next, and someone's chronological age may differ considerably from their biological or 'functional' age due to the influence (or conversely absence) of chronic illness or bodily degeneration, the nature of which may in turn be influenced by a person's social background, gender, occupation or living conditions (Appleby, 2018). In this way, we may not only lose valuable nuanced information regarding ageing, health and social identity over time, but also risk misattributing individuals to specific age categories and by proxy 'social groups'. In addition, the efficacy of how we apply age estimations on the individual and population level in archaeological skeletal samples becomes further confounded when we consider that ageing is not simply a chronological nor biological phenomenon. On a cultural level, age boundaries become further obfuscated by the temporally and geographically changeable perception of social 'expectation' of a person's role in society and how this aligns to their biological and chronological age (Gowland, 2007). Although official concern with precise age increased during the nineteenth century, thanks to the growth of state bureaucracies and increasing government intervention in aspects of life, perceptions of age continued to depend on physical characteristics (Armstrong, 2003; Thane, 2020: 390).

Physical debility had traditionally been seen as ushering in old age, but as industrialisation developed concerns were increasingly raised that new modes of production were hastening physical decline making people 'old' before the customary 60 or 70 years (Ottaway, 2007: 17). Mechanistic views of the body became prevalent in discussions of the impact of factory work in particular, with workers described as faceless parts of an industrial 'machine'. Debilitated workers, argued factory reformer William Dodd, were liable to be 'cast off as useless lumber; just as a cylinder, or any other piece of machinery would be laid aside when worn out, and with as little remorse' (1968: 106). Similarly, Dr James Kay observed of factory operatives in 1830s Manchester that their labour must 'rival the mathematical precision, the incessant motion, and the exhaustless power of the machine' (1832: 10). Long hours of repetitive or arduous labour in heated environments appeared to speed up the life cycle of workers, with claims made (albeit on shaky empirical foundations) that it brought forward stages such as puberty in factory girls, and the physical signs of old age in adult workers (Gaskell, 1833: 69; Gray, 1991: 38).

This becomes particularly pertinent when considering the skeletal changes seen in Skeleton 15. It was recognised in the early nineteenth century that those working in confined spaces, requiring poor postures, or placing heavy loads on the spine, were at greater risk of developing spinal deformities (Weiner and Silver, 2008). For individuals undertaking manual labour from a young age and into adulthood, such pressures combined with deficiencies in bone quality from vitamin D deficiency could result in the severe pathological changes. In 1831, the Leeds surgeon Charles Turner Thackrah commented that '[t]he limbs consequently, and especially in the growing youth, take the form which is induced by the weight of the body and the posture required in the employ. The spine evidently suffers' (1831: 112). Witnesses before official enquiries into factory work reported that the lower limb deformities presented by Skeleton 15 were prevalent in factory districts. In 1832, Abraham Wildman, a supporter of limiting the hours of labour in factories, reported that there were large numbers of 'ricketty crooked legged children' in Keighley (Yorkshire), and he estimated that about one in ten children were left permanently deformed due to the nature of their work (Report from the Committee, 1832: 156). Accounts of worker 'debility' became central to critiques of the factory 'system' during this period. After a visit to Stockport in November 1841, Dodd observed that factory people were generally 'superannuated before they are forty', compared to 60 in the general population (Dodd, 1968: 173). Dodd's own body appeared to offer living proof of this accelerated decline. Deformed in his arms and legs after spending his early years employed in a factory, fellow reformer Richard Oastler described him at age 37 in 1841 as a 'weak, infirm cripple, even in Nature's prime' (1841: 73). Rather than presenting as an anomalous body, in appearance Skeleton 15 represented a common type of deformity observable in textile factory districts such as Stockport during this period.

As a corollary, the idea that workers in certain industries constituted distinctive 'races' whose size, physical features and life cycles deviated from an idealised pre-industrial agrarian norm, took hold in early nineteenth century England (Turner and Blackie, 2018: 56–9). In *The Manufacturing Population of England* (1833), Manchester social reformer Peter Gaskell argued that industrial manufacture brought about a 'vast deterioration in personal form'. The average height of male factory workers was, he claimed, only five feet six inches. Both sexes had a 'very general bowing of the legs', with 'great numbers of girls and women walking lamely or awkwardly'. Men's hair was often 'thin and straight', and they trudged around with a 'spiritless and dejected air' (1833: 162). Workers in particular trades were instantly recognisable by their bodily peculiarities, and accounts of premature ageing, disease and debility were ubiquitous in descriptions of certain occupations. For example, gaunt features, sallow skin, pale complexion and sunken eyes were all seen as trademark features of ironworkers (Ginswick, 1983: 38). Of coalminers, Thackrah remarked that most 'do not generally exceed age of fifty' due to occupational diseases such as asthma, weakness of vision caused by long hours of working in darkness and 'by the injury which their health has sustained' through arduous labour in cramped, dirty conditions (1831: 28). Many observers of coalmining noted signs of ageing in apparently young men. In 1842, Dr Elliot, who had experience in treating the 'limbs and health' of coalminers and their families in Thornley and South Hetton, County Durham, observed that in 'middle and advanced life' miners usually succumbed to 'articular, muscular, and neuralgic pains'. He remarked that 'premature old age in appearance' was common in coalminers and 'men of 35 or 40 years may often be taken for 10 years older than they really are' (Children's Employment Commission, 1842a: 668).

In addition to the high risks to health that accompanied detrimental domestic and workplace environmental conditions, accidental injury due to occupational hazards and urban overcrowding was a common occurrence, and could lead to significant impairment (Mant, 2019). The multiple healed injuries seen in Skeleton 235 likely occurred due to one or more accidental falls of unknown aetiology. Studies of individuals with multiple injuries within skeletal assemblages are complicated by our inability to differentiate between timings of healed fractures, and loss of visibility of soft tissue injuries in skeletonised individuals, leading to their underestimation in skeletal assemblages (Mant, 2019). As such, an important differentiation must be made between evidence of injury recidivism in the past, whereby an individual exhibits evidence of a combination of healed/healing/unhealed injuries, and an individual with multiple healed injuries (Mant, 2019), such as Skeleton 235. In a study of low-status individuals with multiple fractures and injury recidivism in London (*c.*1666–1837) males were at greater risk of fractures and soft tissue trauma (seen skeletally as ossified soft tissue termed *myositis ossificans*) than females, but frequency of dislocations was not significantly different between the sexes (Mant, 2019). However, those with dislocations were more likely to be over the age of 36 years (Mant, 2019). While instances of multiple injury in the aforementioned study had some association with intentional violence (particularly for male individuals), based on fracture location and type, and comparisons with contemporaneous archival and modern clinical data, the majority were likely accidental in nature and related to hazards presented by living and working in an urban environment (Mant, 2019).

The multiple injuries experienced in life by Skeleton 235 suggest a history of the male body common in industrial societies in this period. In her study of skeletons excavated at the Eerie County Poorhouse in Buffalo, New York, Byrnes (2017) similarly found a high degree of trauma in males from this period, suggesting that poor men were often liable to become injured through work. While we cannot ascertain Skeleton 235's occupation, the potential evidence for Kienböck's disease in their right wrist was suggestive of them undertaking some form of repetitive manual labour. Their multiple injuries too are typical of those experienced by coalminers in the north-east of England and elsewhere in this period. At Haswell Colliery in County Durham, there were twenty-eight reported cases of lower limb injuries in 1849, resulting from rock falls or boys and men being run over by coal trucks (Second Report, 1854: 24–6). Shoulder injuries were a regular, but more infrequently reported, feature of coalmining too, occasioned by 'misadventures in the [mine] shafts, falling of the roof of the mines, and the minor effects of explosions' (Black 1844: 555). The severity of shoulder injuries varied: at Haswell, John Smith a hewer of coal had nine days off work in 1849 with a shoulder injury by a fall of coal, but others needed several weeks to recover, or longer (Second Report, 1854: 24–6). The incomplete healing of the shoulder fracture may indicate the difficulties faced by surgeons in treating these injuries, but it might also reveal a need to get back to work as soon as some degree of functionality began to return. Numerous accounts of workers 'lamed' in industrial accidents but returning to work attest to the importance of 'working through' injuries (Riley, 1997: 135). In Skeleton 235 there are signs that the joints and muscles were still being used after the injury, albeit with reduced functionality. This suggests that individuals may have considered themselves healed enough if they were able to resume earning a living (Turner and Blackie, 2018).

Accounts of workers 'worn out' prematurely by their exposure to industrial capitalism served a political purpose in this period, contributing to gathering calls for workplace regulation. Experiences of older workers varied greatly, but there is evidence to suggest that in occupations involving repetitive or physically demanding work, employment declined significantly above the age of 40. As one Welsh coalmining official reported in 1842, miners were not necessarily 'shorter lived' than other men, but they were 'sooner disabled, and frequently leave underground work at 40 to 45' (Children's Employment Commission, 1842b: 576). Similarly, in Scotland, Dr S. Scott Alison noted that above the age of 30 'it is rare to find a perfectly healthy collier'; by 40 the fast decline of muscular strength meant that many men were capable of no more than two or three days work a week. If a miner survived beyond his 50th year 'by dint of greater strength of constitution, of temperate habits, and attention to the preservation of health', he was still often left 'broken down and decrepit' (Children's Employment Commission, 1842a: 412). Though less dramatic, a similar decline is visible in male factory workers. Table 7.1, which shows men's employment in nineteen Manchester textile factories in 1832, indicates a comparatively large number of sick days taken by youths and young men entering the spinning trade, perhaps in part due to accidents caused by inexperience. During mature adulthood, workers appeared to be at their healthiest, but after age 40 the number of men employed declined and those who remained spent more time off sick, suggesting physical decline. By 40, Engels wrote, male spinners suffered from 'general enfeeblement of frame' and failing eyesight making it difficult to continue their work (1969: 187).

Discussion of worker debility and premature ageing in the early nineteenth century took place in the context of campaigns that were framed in terms of the protection of the persons of 'vulnerable' children and women, while also seeking to extend these protections to adult men by safeguarding their 'property' – their physical ability to work and provide for their families (Gray, 1996: 31). The rhetoric of premature ageing was applied overwhelmingly

Table 7.1 Spinners employed in Nineteen Fine Spinning Mills in Manchester, 1832 (Shuttleworth, 1842: 270–1).

| Age group | Total employed | Number of sick days | Average number of sick days per worker |
|---|---|---|---|
| Under 21 | 8 | 195 | 24.38 |
| 21 to 25 | 184 | 1833 | 9.96 |
| 26 to 30 | 198 | 1031 | 5.2 |
| 31 to 35 | 153 | 860.5 | 5.62 |
| 36 to 40 | 154 | 592 | 3.84 |
| 41 to 45 | 89 | 787 | 8.84 |
| 46 to 50 | 33 | 488 | 14.79 |
| 51 to 55 | 12 | 235 | 19.58 |
| 55 to 60 | 5 | 270 | 54 |
| Above 60 | 1 | 14 | 14 |

to the male body, although some female workers, such as women employed in Scottish coalmines, also described the impact of labour in these terms. Forty-year-old Jane Peacock Watson, a carrier of baskets of coal at West Linton in Peebleshire, testified that the employment of women in coalmines was 'horse-work, and ruins the women; it crushes their haunches, bends their ankles and makes them old women at 40' (Children's Employment Commission, 1842a: 458). Women and young children were banned from working underground by legislation of 1842, and following restrictions on child labour introduced in the 1833 Factory Act, legislation of 1844, 1847 and 1850 further limited the hours of work for women and young persons in factories (Gray, 1996; John, 1984).

Regulation of the hours worked by women and the young served to construct the 'male breadwinner' ideology (Gray, 1996: 8). However, the inclusion of Skeleton 502 reminds us that women were essential agents in industrial society, and due to biological predisposition to conditions such as osteoporosis, may have been burdened with invisible susceptibilities to injuries within domestic and occupational spheres. Physical impairment, combined with visual indicators of age such as tooth loss, could influence employment opportunities. Documentary sources reveal accounts of working-class single women expressing concern for themselves and others associated with the loss of teeth, and by proxy an aged appearance, on employment prospects and perception of redundancy (Vickery, 2013: 884). Historical clinical observations of causes of hip fractures reveal that they occurred due to accidental falls that varied in severity, including trips and falls within the home or on the street, and falls from horses and carts (Ives et al., 2017:

271). Cooper noted in 1822 that in cases of intra-capsular hip fractures 'Women are much more liable to this species of fracture than men; we rarely in our hospitals observe it in the latter, but our Wards are seldom without an example of it in the aged female' (1822: 122). He states that this type of fracture rarely occurred in those under 50 years of age, and that in London they frequently occurred due to accidental falls from elevated footpaths (Cooper, 1822: 124–5).

Contemporary social commentators imagined a bleak future for older people such as Skeleton 502. Industrial urban settlements were, argued Gaskell, no place to grow old. Elderly relatives brought with migrants from rural areas to industrial towns 'who have hitherto lived in open and healthy situations, favourable to the prolongation of life' were apt to 'sink at once beneath the depressing influence of their new abodes', succumbing to chronic diseases brought on by insanitary living conditions (1833: 235). Mid-Victorian census data indicate that industrial towns had lower proportions of older age individuals compared to rural communities, due to the influx of younger migrants and lower life expectancy (Western and Bekvalac, 2020: 187). Nevertheless, older people were still present in these industrial communities, albeit only forming a small minority of the population. For example, in the census of 1861, 3.8% of the population of Hazel Grove, 3% of the population in Manchester, and 4.6% of the population of England and Wales were aged over 65 years (GB Historical GIS, 2018a; 2018b; 2018c). Despite gloomy accounts of older or disabled people being 'cast off as useless lumber', such people remained economically productive if possible. Older women played an important role in providing childcare, allowing their adult daughters to return to work in textile mills or by supplying the domestic labour that serviced heavily 'masculine' industries like coalmining (Jones, 1991; Thane, 2000: 273, 294–5). While we cannot determine the quality of life that Skeleton 502 led from their bones alone, we should not automatically assume that they were devalued, even if their economic role was circumscribed.

Ultimately, debility was a marker of social class. Again, in 1831, Thackrah noted that a 'really fine figure' was rare among urban 'artisans', in contrast to the elite. Although wealthy 'young ladies' were often 'deformed from the want of proper exercise, their brothers are generally well-proportioned' due to their freedom to engage in manly sports and exercises, which gave them a 'decided advantage' 'not only over the sedate sex, but also over the factory boys and apprentices of sedentary artisans' (113). Engels put it more bluntly: 'In Manchester ... premature old age among the operatives is so universal that almost every man of forty would be taken for ten to fifteen years older, while the prosperous classes, men as well as women, preserve their appearance exceedingly well if they do not drink too heavily' (1969: 188). Middle-class descriptions of working-class bodies as a separate 'race', notable for their 'unhealthy' features, premature ageing and deformity, othered physical characteristics that would have been viewed as normal within industrial communities. The anonymous skeletons examined in this chapter all indicate hardships faced by working-class people in industrialising England. The heightened risk of morbidity and mortality alongside general bodily wear and tear were experiences from which others were buffered through their wealth and status.

## Conclusions

In industrialising England, function, health status and appearance were more important than chronological age in shaping perceptions of working-class bodies. Large proportions of the working population were at risk of impairment by occupational injury, disease and poor living conditions and this was frequently conceptualised as premature ageing. These impairments can be seen skeletally, alongside otherwise relatively hidden indicators of wear and tear of the body over time in the form of joint degeneration and tooth loss, as exemplified by the three case studies presented in this chapter. Social status and gender were key factors determining experiences – and perceptions – of debility. The skeletal evidence has revealed the bodily consequences of living with impairment, whether arising from potentially congenital or environmentally mediated conditions such as that seen in Skeleton 15, bodily injury in Skeleton 235, or injury and decline associated with the ageing process in Skeleton 502. While impaired bodies have often been viewed as marginal or 'othered', evidence from a range of official reports, medical sources and social and political commentary suggests that physical difference was an expected and 'normal' feature of nineteenth-century working-class experience. As we have shown in this chapter, by exploring the material body in relation to wider discourses around ageing, disability and debility, we can go beyond viewing the three skeletons as exceptional pathological case studies and see them instead as the remains of people whose experiences were shaped both by their physical characteristics and by the wider culture that gave them meaning (Craig-Atkins and Harvey, this volume: introduction; Harvey, 2020).

Although skeletal evidence cannot inform us of the quality of life experienced by these people or nuances in (in)ability, it instead reveals hidden histories of bodily damage and repair that indicate a need to adapt and 'work through' injury and impairment – a process dependent not simply on the availability of medical care, but also on an individual's wider network of economic support (Turner and Blackie, 2018). If campaigners for industrial regulation used the deformed body to highlight the vulnerability of workers, the skeletal evidence conversely may be more indicative of the resilience of people living with impairment and bodily difference. In turn, documentary evidence can also advocate caution in how we apply and interpret age estimation data within our archaeological analyses of past populations. Much like the wearing down of machinery, industrial society of the early nineteenth century wore down the bodies of its working-class inhabitants, skewing our – and their – perception of who was 'old' in such societies on a social, chronological and, ultimately, biological level.

## Acknowledgements

The authors would like to thank Martin Lightfoot at CFA Archaeology and Malin Holst at York Osteoarchaeology Ltd for permission to publish the case study from Hazel Grove, Stockport in this chapter. We are also grateful to the Department of Archaeology, University of Sheffield for access to the St Hilda's Churchyard, South Shields skeletal collection and associated archive.

## References

Appleby, J. (2018). 'Ageing and the body in archaeology', *Cambridge Archaeological Journal*, 28(1): 145–63.
Armstrong, D. (2003). 'The temporal body' in R. Cooter and J. V. Pickstone (eds), *Companion to Medicine in the Twentieth Century* (London: Routledge), pp. 247–59.
Black, J. (1844). 'Lectures on public hygiene and medical police', *Provincial Medical and Surgical Journal*, 8(36): 551–7.
Bowlby, A. A. (1887). *Surgical Pathology and Morbid Anatomy* (London: J&A Churchill).
Brickley, M., Mays, S. and Ives, R. (2005). 'Skeletal manifestations of vitamin D deficiency osteomalacia in documented historical collections', *International Journal of Osteoarchaeology*, 15: 389–403.
Brickley, M. and Ives, R. (2008). *The Bioarchaeology of Metabolic Bone Disease* (London: Academic Press).
Brooks, S. T. and Suchey, J. M. (1990). 'Skeletal age determination based on the os pubis: a comparison of the Acsádi-Nemeskéri and Suchey-Brooks methods', *Human Evolution*, 5: 227–38.
Bruun-Olsen, V., Bergland, A. and Heiberg, K. E. (2018). '"I struggle to count my blessings": recovery after hip fracture from the patients' perspective', *BMC Geriatrics*, 18: 18.
Bruzek, J. (2002). 'A method for visual determination of sex, using the human hip bone', *American Journal of Physical Anthropology*, 117: 157–168.

Buckberry, J. (2015). 'The (mis)use of adult age estimates in osteology', *Annals of Human Biology*, 42(4): 323–31.

Buckberry, J. L. and Chamberlain, A. T. (2002). 'Age estimation from the auricular surface of the ilium: a revised method', *American Journal of Physical Anthropology*, 119: 231–9.

Byrnes, J. F. and Muller, J. L. (eds). (2017). *Bioarchaeology of Impairment and Disability: Theoretical, Ethnohistorical, and Methodological Perspectives* (New York: Springer).

Byrnes, J. F. (2017). 'Injuries, impairment, and intersecting identities: The poor in Buffalo, NY 1851–1913' in J. F. Byrnes and J. L. Muller (eds), *Bioarchaeology of Impairment and Disability: Theoretical, Ethnohistorical, and Methodological Perspectives* (New York: Springer), pp. 201–22.

Carlsen, B. T. and Moran, S. L. (2009). 'Thumb trauma: Bennett fractures, Rolando fractures, and ulnar collateral ligament injuries', *Journal of Hand Surgery*, 34A: 945–52.

Children's Employment Commission (1842a). *Appendix to the First Report of the Commissioners. Mines. Part 1. Reports and Evidence from the Sub-Commissioners* (London: W. Clowes for HMSO).

Children's Employment Commission (1842b). *Appendix to the First Report of the Commissioners. Mines. Part 2.* (London: W. Clowes for HMSO).

Conlogue, G., Viner, M., Beckett, R., Bekvalac, J., Gonzalez, R., Sharkey, M., Kramer, K. and Koverman, B. (2017). 'A post-mortem evaluation of the degree of mobility in an individual with severe kyphoscoliosis using direct digital radiography (DR) and multi-detector computed tomography (MDCT)', in L. Tilley and A. A. Schrenk (eds), *New Developments in the Bioarchaeology of Care. Further Case Studies and Expanded Theory* (New York: Springer), pp. 153–73.

Cooper, A. (1822). *A Treatise on Dislocations, and on Fractures of the Joints* (London: Longmans).

Cooter, R. (2003). 'The disabled body' in R. Cooter and J. Pickstone (eds), *Companion to Medicine in the Twentieth Century* (London: Routledge), pp. 367–84.

Degeling, C. (2009). 'Fractured hips: surgical authority, futility and innovation in nineteenth century medicine', *Endeavour*, 33(4): 129–34.

Dodd, W. (1842, 1968). *The Factory System Illustrated in a Series of Letters to the Right Hon. Lord Ashley* (London: Frank Cass).

Engels, F. (1892, 1969). *The Condition of the Working Class in England* (London: Panther).

Fuschillo, S., De Felice, A., Martucci, M., Gaudiosi, C., Pisano, V., Vitale, D. and Balzano, G. (2015). 'Pulmonary rehabilitation improves exercise capacity in subjects with kyphoscoliosis and severe respiratory impairment', *Respiratory Care*, 60(1): 96–101.

Gaskell, P. (1833). *The Manufacturing Population of England, Its Moral, Social, and Physical Conditions and the Changes which have arisen from the use of Steam Machinery* (London: Baldwin and Craddock).

GB Historical GIS (2018a). 'University of Portsmouth, Hazel Grove SubD through time. Age and sex structure to age 85 and up' [Online]. Available at:

www.visionofbritain.org.uk/unit/10542212/cube/AGESEX_85UP (accessed 20 May 2018).
GB Historical GIS (2018b). 'University of Portsmouth, Greater Manchester Met.C through time. Age and sex structure to age 85 and up' [Online]. Available at: www.visionofbritain.org.uk/unit/10056925/cube/AGESEX_85UP (accessed 20 May 2018).
GB Historical GIS (2018c). 'University of Portsmouth, England Dep through time. Age and sex structure to age 85 and up' [Online]. Available at: www.visionofbritain.org.uk/unit/10061325/cube/AGESEX_85UP (accessed 20 May 2018).
Ginswick, J. (ed.). (1983). *Labour and the Poor in England and Wales 1849–1851: the Letters to the Morning Chronicle from the Correspondents in the Manufacturing and Mining Districts, the towns of Liverpool and Birmingham, and the Rural Districts: Vol. 3 South Wales-North Wales* (London: Frank Cass).
Gleeson, B. (1999). *Geographies of Disability* (London: Routledge).
Gowland, R. (2007). 'Age, ageism and osteological bias: the evidence from late Roman Britain', *Journal of Roman Archaeology, Supplementary Series*, 65: 153–69.
Gowland, R. (2017). 'Growing old: Biographies of disability and care in later life', in L. Tilley and A. A. Schrenk (eds), *New Developments in the Bioarchaeology of Care: Further Case Studies and Expanded Theory* (New York: Springer), pp. 237–51.
Gray, R. (1991). 'Medical men, industrial labour and the state, 1830–50', *Social History*, 16(1): 19–43.
Gray, R. (1996). *The Factory Question and Industrial England, 1830–1860* (Cambridge: Cambridge University Press).
Green, A. (2010). 'Heartless and unhomely? Dwellings of the poor in East Anglia and north-east England' in J. McEwan and P. Sharpe (eds), *Accommodating Poverty: The Housing and Living Arrangements of the English Poor, c.1600–1850* (Basingstoke: Palgrave MacMillan), pp. 69–101.
Griffin, E. (2006). *A Short History of the British Industrial Revolution* (Basingstoke: Palgrave-Macmillan).
Hardy, A. (2003). 'Commentary: Bread and alum, syphilis and sunlight: rickets in the nineteenth century', *International Journal of Epidemiology*, 32: 337–40.
Harvey, K. (2020). 'One British thing: A history of embodiment: Ann Purvis, ca. 1793–1849', *Journal of British Studies*, 59(1): 136–9.
Hodgson, G. B. (1903). *The Borough of South Shields from the Earliest Period to the Close of the Nineteenth Century.* (Newcastle-upon-tyne: Andrew Reid & Company, Ltd).
Holick, M. F. (2006). 'Resurrection of vitamin D deficiency and rickets', *The Journal of Clinical Investigation*, 116(8): 2062–72.
Issac, S and Das, J. M. (2020). *Kyphoscoliosis*. StatPearls Publishing LLC [Online]. Available at: www.ncbi.nlm.nih.gov/books/NBK562183/ (accessed 17 November 2020).
Ives, R. and Brickley, M. (2014). 'New findings in the identification of adult vitamin D deficiency osteomalacia: Results from a large-scale study', *International Journal of Paleopathology*, 7: 45–56.

Ives, R., Mant, M., De La Cova, C. and Brickley, M. (2017). 'A large-scale palaeopathological study of hip fractures from post-medieval urban England', *International Journal of Osteoarchaeology*, 27: 261–75.

Jessop, O. and Beauchamp, V. (2015). '11–16 Chapel Street, Hazel Grove, Stockport, Gt. Manchester. An archaeological desk-based assessment', Document No: TJC2015.17 (Sheffield: The Jessop Consultancy, unpublished report).

John, A. V. (1984). *By the Sweat of their Brow: Women Workers at Victorian Coal Mine*. (London: Routledge and Kegan Paul).

Jones, D. (1991). 'Counting the cost of coal: Women's lives in the Rhondda, 1881–1911', in A. V. John (ed.), *Our Mother's Land: Chapters in Welsh Women's History 1830–1939* (Cardiff: University of Wales Press), pp. 109–34.

Kay, J. P. (1832). *The Moral and Physical Condition of the Working Classes Employed in the Cotton Manufacture in Manchester* (London: James Ridgway).

King, S. and Timmins, G. (2001). *Making Sense of the Industrial Revolution: English Economy and Society, 1700–1850* (Manchester: Manchester University Press).

Kuskey, J. (2016). 'The working body: Re-Forming the factory body', *Victorian Review*, 42(1): 4–9.

Leclère, F. M. P., Jenzer, A., Hüsler, R., Kiermeir, D., Bignion, D., Unglaub, F. and Vögelin, E. (2012). '7-year follow-up after open reduction and internal screw fixation in Bennett fractures', *Archives of Orthopaedic and Trauma Surgery*, 132: 1045–51.

Ljuslinder, K., Ellis, K. and Vikström, L. (2020). 'Cripping time – Understanding the life course through the lens of ableism', *Scandinavian Journal of Disability Research*, 22(1): 35–8.

Lovejoy, C. O., Meindl, R. S., Pryzbeck, T. R. and Mensforth, R. (1985). 'Chronological metamorphosis of the auricular surface of the ilium: a new method for the determination of skeletal age at death', *American Journal of Physical Anthropology*, 68: 15–28.

Lukacs, J. R. (2012). 'Oral health in past populations: Context, concepts and controversies' in A. L. Grauer (ed.), *A Companion to Paleopathology* (Chichester: Blackwell Publishing Ltd), pp. 513–30.

Mant, M. (2019). 'Time after time: individuals with multiple fractures and injury recidivists in long eighteenth-century (c.1666–1837) London', *International Journal of Osteoarchaeology*, 24: 7–18.

Mays, S. and Cox, M. (2000). 'Sex determination in skeletal remains', in M. Cox and S. Mays (eds), *Human Osteology in Archaeology and Forensic Science* (London: Greenwich Medical Media), pp. 117–30.

McMaster, M. J. and Singh, H. (1999). 'Natural history of congenital kyphosis and kyphoscoliosis', *The Journal of Bone and Joint Surgery*, 81-A(10): 1367–83.

Metzler, I. (1999). 'The palaeopathology of disability in the Middle Ages', *Archaeological Review from Cambridge*, 15(2): 55–67.

Middleton, S. D., McNiven, N., Griffin, E. J., Anakwe, R. E. and Oliver, C. W. (2015). 'Long-term patient-reported outcomes following Bennett's fractures', *The Bone & Joint Journal*, 97-B(7): 1004–6.

Miles, A. E. W. (2000). 'Two shoulder-joint dislocations in early 19th century Londoners', *International Journal of Osteoarchaeology*, 10: 125–34.
Morgan, B., Mant, M., de la Cova, C. and Brickley, M. B. (2020). 'Osteoporosis, osteomalacia, and hip fracture: A case study from the Terry collection', *International Journal of Paleopathology*, 30: 17–21.
Newman, S. and Holst, M. (2016). *'Osteological Analysis, Chapel Street, Hazel Grove, Greater Manchester'*, No.2116 (York: York Osteoarchaeology, unpublished report).
Oastler, R. (1841). *The Fleet Papers; Being Letters to Thomas Thornhill, Esq. of Riddlesworth in the County of Norfolk; from Richard Oastler, His Prisoner in the Fleet*. vol.1 no. 10, 6 March.
Oliver, M. and Barnes, C. (2012). *The New Politics of Disablement*. (Basingstoke: Palgrave-Macmillan).
Ottaway, S. (2007). *The Decline of Life: Old Age in Eighteenth Century England*. (Cambridge: Cambridge University Press).
Owen, I. (1889). 'Geographical distribution of rickets, acute and subacute rheumatism, chorea, cancer, and urinary calculus in the British islands', *The British Medical Journal*, 1464(1): 113–16.
Pelling, M. and Smith R. M. (eds) (1991). *Life, Death and the Elderly: Historical Perspectives* (London: Routledge).
Pettifor, J. M. (2003). 'Nutritional rickets', in F. H. Glorieux, J. M. Pettifor and H. Jüppner (eds), *Pediatric Bone. Biology and Diseases* (San Diego: Academic Press), pp. 541– 65.
Phenice, T. W. (1969). 'A newly developed visual method of sexing the os pubis', *American Journal of Physical Anthropology*, 30: 297–301.
Quadagno, J. (1982). *Aging in Early Industrial Society: Work, Family, and Social Policy in Nineteenth-Century England* (New York: Academic Press).
Raynor, C., McCarthy, R. and Clough, S. (2011). *'Coronation Street, South Shields, Tyne and Wear. Archaeological Excavation and Osteological Analysis Report'* (Oxford: Oxford Archaeology North, unpublished report).
Report from the Committee (1832). *Report from the Committee on the 'Bill to regulate the Labour of Children in the Mills and Factories of the United Kingdom'* (London: House of Commons).
Reuling, E. M., Sierevelt, I. N., van den Bekerom, M. P., Hilverdink, E. F., Schnater, J. M., van Dijk, C. N., Goslings, J. C. and Raaymakers, E. L. (2012). 'Predictors of functional outcome following femoral neck fractures treated with an arthroplasty: limitations of the Harris hip score', *Archives of Orthopaedic and Trauma Surgery*, 132(2): 249–56.
Riley, J. C. (1997). *Sick, Not Dead: The Health of British Working Men during the Mortality Decline* (Baltimore and London: Johns Hopkins University Press).
Roberts, C. (2012). 'Re-emerging infections: Developments in bioarchaeological contributions to understanding tuberculosis today', in A. L. Grauer (ed.), *A Companion to Paleopathology* (Chichester: Wiley-Blackwell Ltd), pp. 434–57.
Roberts, C. A. and Cox, M. (2003). *Health and Disease in Britain* (Gloucester: Sutton Publishing).

Roberts, C. and Manchester, K. (2010). *The Archaeology of Disease*, 3rd edn (Stroud: The History Press).

Rogmark, C., Kristensen, M. T., Viberg, B., Rönnquist, S. S., Overgaard, S. and Palm, H. (2018). 'Hip fractures in the non-elderly – Who, why and whither?', *Injury, International Journal of Care of the Injured*, 49(8): 1445–50.

Rose, S. F. (2017). *No Right to be Idle: the Invention of Disability, 1840s–1930s* (Chapel Hill: University of North Carolina Press).

Schiller, C., Franke, T., Belle, J., Sims-Gould, J., Sale, J. and Ashe, M. C. (2015). 'Words of wisdom – patient perspectives to guide recovery for older adults after hip fracture: a qualitative study', *Patient Preference and Adherence*, 9: 57–64.

Second Report (1854). *Second Report from the Select Committee in Accidents in Coal Mines* (London: House of Commons).

Shuttleworth, J. (1842). 'Vital statistics of the spinners and piecers employed in the fine spinning mills of Manchester', *Journal of the Statistical Society of London*, 5(3): 268–73.

Shuttleworth, R. and Meekosha, H. (2017). 'Accommodating critical disability studies in bioarchaeology', in J. F. Byrnes and J. L. Muller (eds), *Bioarchaeology of Impairment and Disability Theoretical, Ethnohistorical, and Methodological Perspectives* (New York: Springer), pp. 19–38.

Sitnik, A., Beletsky, A. and Schelkun, S. (2017). 'Intra-articular fractures of the distal tibia. Current concepts of management', *EFORT Open Rev*, 2(8): 352–61.

Sofaer, J. R. (2006). *The Body as Material Culture: A Theoretical Osteoarchaeology*. (Cambridge: Cambridge University Press).

Southwell-Wright, W. (2013). 'Past perspectives: What can archaeology offer disability studies?', in M. Wappett and K. Arndt (eds), *Emerging Perspectives on Disability Studies* (Basingstoke: Palgrave-Macmillan), pp. 67–96.

Thackrah, C. T. (1831). *The Effects of the Principal Arts, Trades, and Professions, and of Civic States and Habits of Living, on Health and Longevity* (London: Longman, Rees, Orme, Brown & Green).

Thane, P. (2000). *Old Age in English History: Past Experiences, Present Issues* (Oxford: Oxford University Press).

Thane, P. (2020). 'Old age in European cultures: A significant presence from antiquity to the present', *The American Historical Review*, 125(2): 385–95.

Tilley, L. and Schrenk, A. A. (2017). *New Developments in the Bioarchaeology of Care. Further Case Studies and Expanded Theory* (New York: Springer).

Turner, D. M. and Blackie, D. (2018). *Disability in the Industrial Revolution: Physical Impairment in British Coalmining 1780–1880* (Manchester: Manchester University Press).

Vickery, A. (2013). 'Mutton dressed as lamb? Fashioning age in Georgian England', *Journal of British Studies*, 52: 858–86.

Waldron, T. (2012). 'Joint disease', in A.L. Grauer (ed.). *A Companion to Paleopathology*. (Chichester: Blackwell Publishing Ltd), pp. 513–30.

Walker, D. (2012). *Disease in London, 1$^{st}$–19$^{th}$ centuries. An Illustrated Guide to Diagnosis*. MOLA Monograph 56 (London: Museum of London Archaeology).

Weiner, M.-F. and Silver, J. R. (2008). 'Edward Harrison and the treatment of spinal deformities in the nineteenth century', *The Journal of the Royal College of Physicians of Edinburgh*, 38: 265–71.

Weiss, K. E. and Rodner, C. M. (2007). 'Osteoarthritis of the wrist', *Journal of Hand Surgery*, 32: 725–46.

Western, G. and Bekvalac, J. (2020). *Manufactured Bodies: The Impact of Industrialisation on London Health* (Oxford: Oxbow Books).

White, T. O., Mackenzie, S. P. and Gray, A. J. (2016). *McRae's Orthopaedic Trauma and Emergency Fracture Management*, 3rd edn (Edinburgh: Elsevier).

Woodward, K. (2015). 'Aging', in R. Adams, B. Reiss and D. Serlin (eds), *Keywords for Disability Studies* (New York: New York University Press), pp. 33–4.

Zeng, Y., Chen, Z., Qi, Q., Guo, Z., Li, W., Sun, C. and Liu, N. (2013). 'The posterior surgical correction of congenital kyphosis and kyphoscoliosis: 23 cases with minimum 2 years follow up', *European Spine Journal*, 22: 372–8.

# Index

Note: page numbers in *italic* refer to illustrations and tables.
Note: 'n.' after a page reference indicates the number of a note on that page.

abortions *see under* women
Abraham, Thomas 114
ageing *see under* human bodies
Alison, S. Scott 225
anatomical studies and dissection
    104–7, 108, 109–10, *110*, 114
Anatomy Act (1832) 100
Anderson, Ann 69
archaeology
    approach to human bodies 24
    contrasted with history 23
    documentary evidence 2, 8–9, 12,
        13, 15
    human remains *see* bioarchaeology
archives 27–9
Ariès, Philippe 92
arsenic, as abortifacient 69
Attala, Luci 3, 7
Austin, Richard 126n.43
Austin, W. *121*
Avon Archaeology Ltd. 172

baby-farming *see under* children
Barber-Surgeons' Company 104,
    106–7, *110*, 110–11
Barker, Samuel 30
Barton-upon-Humber 135
    pipes 141, 143
    St Peter's Church burials 135, *146*,
        147, *150*, 152, 159

Beacham, Elizabeth 108
Beemster 147
Bell, Sir Charles 86
Bellers, John 107
Billings, E. R. 158, 161
bioarchaeology (osteoarchaeology)
    4–5, 6, 9, 22, 23, 25, 54, 194
biography 9, 12, 15, 26, 28
Birmingham
    St Martin's-in-the-Bull-Ring burials
        66, 72n.1, 184
Blacktin, Rebecca 29
Blake, William 189
Blow, D. 92
bodies *see* human bodies
bodysnatching 13, 100–27, *121*
    causing disease and death 127n.44
    pervasive by mid-1720s 119
    preventive measures 102–4, *103*
    punishment for 114–15, 116
    women and children preferred
        126n.39
Borić, Dušan 7
Boswell, James 91
Bowen, Joseph 101, 113, 114
Brathwaite (Braithwaite), Thomas
    113–14, 115, 117–18, 122
Bristol 172
    Bristol Royal Infirmary 184–5
    pipes 141, 143

St Augustine the Less 172
St George's Cemetery 171, 172–3, *176*
sex ratios 36
Tiger's Head Beer-house 186
Buffalo (NY), Eerie County Poorhouse 224
bunions (hallux valgus) 95
burials
    burial clubs 56
    burial insurance 64
    cost of 61–3, 64, 66
    infant 47–8, 50, 55, 61–6, 71
    pauper 108
    reuse of plots 63
    unsanctified burial grounds 47–8, 63
    unwanted infants 70
    *see also* bodysnatching; cemeteries; coffins
Byrnes, Jennifer F. 224

Cambridge, bodysnatching 119–20
Canning, Kathleen 9
care 56, 60, 61, 71, 207, 209, 220, 227
cemeteries 65, 136
Chatham, pipes 143
Cheselden, William 109–10, *110*, 111, 113, 119, 120, 122
Chester, pipes 141
childbirth *see under* women
Childers, William 113, 127n.44
children
    and baby-farming 56, 67
    and bodysnatching 126n.39
    childhood 92
    child labour 223, 226
    infant burials 47–8, 50, 55, 61–6, 71
    infanticide 56, 66, 67, 68
    infant mortality 48, 52, 56–61, *58*
    perinatal mortality 55
    and shoes 92–3, *93*
    and smoking 157
    stillborn 64–6, 73n.7
    unwanted 68
    and vitamin D deficiency 211
cigars 138, 160
Clever, Iris 7

Clues, Mary 139
coalmining 223, 224–5, 226
coffins 39–40, 62–3
    anti-bodysnatching measures 104
    box coffins 62
    coffin plates 28, 30, 39, 73n.3
Cole, Hubert 101
Colston, Edward 186
Coltheart, Peter 119
Connor, Bernard 104, 106
consumption *see* tuberculosis
Cooke, Richard 126n.33
Cooper, Benjamin 190
Cooper, Elizabeth *see* Cumberland, Elizabeth
Cooper, Sir Astley 216, 227
Cooper, Samuel 95
Cope, Sir Zachary 111
Corporation of Corpse-stealers 100, 102, 108, 122
cotton, socks 88
Coventry 136, 155
    Holy Trinity Church burials 136, *147, 150,* 154, *154,* 159
    pipes 143–4, 147, 160
    silk ribbon trade 136, 161
Cox, Margaret 191, 196
cribra orbitalia 177, 180
Crossland, Zoe 5
Cruikshank, George 139
cultural turn 2
Cumberland, Elizabeth 14, 15, 188–9, 190–2, 193, 196
Cumberland, George 14, 15, 174, *187,* 188, 189–90, 191–4, 196

Darnall's Chance House 27–8
Darwen 66
Davey, Peter 141
Davies, Peter 158
Demello, Margo 93
Dickinson, William 114
diffuse idiopathic skeletal hyperostosis (DISH) 192–3, 195
disability *see under* human bodies
dissection *see* anatomical studies and dissection
Dod, William 115, 116
Dodd, William 222–3
Douglas, James 106, 118, 126n.40

Douglas, John 118, 127n.44
Dublin, bodysnatching 123n.4
Duden, Barbara 83
Durlacher, Lewis 83, 90, 91

Edinburgh, bodysnatching 119
Ellenborough, Lord 69
Ellis, Richard 123n.2
embodiment 9, 23, 25
Engels, Friedrich 29, 225, 227
Evans, Jane 174
experience 24–5

Factory Act (1833) 226
Fairhurst, Alison 88
Faust, Bernhard 90, 92
Ferne, James 111, 115
fetuses *see* children, infant burials
Fiquel, Hosea 125n.23
Fleming, Robin 26
foundling hospitals 68
Fredengren, Christina 8
Furneaux, Christopher 118, 120

Gambol, George 115
Gaskell, Peter 223
Gay, John 81, 91
Geber, Jonny 147, 161
Gloucester, St Oswald's burials 63–4
Goodman, Jordan 138
gout 193, 196
Gowing, Laura 69
Gowland, Rebecca 27, 205, 207
gravediggers 101, 111, 112
Grecian, Catherine 69
Green, Sarah 15, 134, 154–6, *154*, *157*, 158
Greene, Robert 123n.2
Greenhill, Thomas 109
Gregory, James 90
Griffiths 112
Guttmacher, Alan 101

Hall, J. Sparkes 94
hallux valgus *see* bunions
Hamann-Todd collection 178
handmaiden problem 52
Hartnett, Alexandra 141
Harvey, Karen 6, 92
Haswell Colliery 224

Hauksbee, Francis 119
Hawkins, Sir Caesar 120
Hearne, Thomas 107–8, 111, 113, 115, 119
Hemsley, Catherine 68
Henderson, Michael 146, 161, 162
Hicks, Dan 3, 24
Higgins, David 143
Hilton, Matthew 138
history
    contrasted with archaeology 23
    and experience 24–5
Holbeach 107
Holmes, John 112
Holmes, Michael 112
Hosek, Lauren 9
HS2 136
Hughes, Jason 137
Hull
    pipes 141, 143
    sex ratios 36
human bodies 4–6, 7–8
    and age determination 196
    and ageing 14, 188, 191–3, *195*, 206, 208, 218–19, 221–3, 227, 228
    and archaeology 24
    and childbirth 191
    and disability 206–8, 209–13, *210*, 222–8
    and dissection 106–7, 108, 109–10, *110*, 114, 122n.2
    and DNA 9, 73n.3
    and embodied experiences 1, 4–10, 54
    feet 86, 88, 89, 95
    fractures 183, 184–6, *185*, 195, 213, 215–16, 218, 220, 224, 227
    and gender *see* men; women
    and humours 82–3, 88, 89
    and identity 26–7
    and industrialisation 12, 57, 207, 211, 222–5, 226, 228–9
    and malnutrition 177, 180, 218
    and manual labour 215, 222, 224–6
    as material culture 24
    and materiality 8
    musculoskeletal stress markers 186, 195

and osteobiography 9, 25–6
and shoe wearing 84–96
shoulder dislocation 213–15, *214*
and social status and social identity 39
sweat marks on clothing 88
and tobacco use 144–52, *145*, *146*, *147*, *148*, *150–1*, *153*, *154*, 162
tuberculosis, impact of 174–5, *177–9*, *178*, *179*, 181–2, 194–5
and urbanisation 211
*see also* bodysnatching; osteoarthritis; osteoporosis; teeth
Hunter, John 120
Hunter, William 120, 121
Hyde Park Barracks prison (Australia) 158

infanticide *see under* children
infant mortality *see under* children
Ingold, Tim 3
Ion, Alexandra 8
ironworking 223
Irving, Jane Ann 69

Jedburgh Abbey 64
Joyce, Patrick 3, 4

Keighley 223
Kelley, Marc A. 191
Kelson, Mark 183–7, *185*, *187*, 192, *195*, 196
Kersey, John 102, 108–9, 111, 113–14, 115, 122
Kienböck's disease 215, 224
Kilkenny Union Workhouse 147, 161
kyphoscoliosis 209, *210*, 211, 212

Laidlaw, Mrs 70
Lancercost Priory 63
Laqueur, Thomas 82
Latimer, John 183
Lavater, D. 111
leather, shoes *85*, 86–8, *87*, *91*, 93, *93*
Lee, Lettice 27
Lee, Richard 117
Lee, William 30
Lewis 34
Lincoln, pipes 143

London *105*, 135–6
anatomical studies and dissection 104–6, 119, 120
body size among population 57, 73n.8
bodysnatching 100–1, 108, 112, 114, 115–19, 120, 121–2
Chelsea Old Church burials 72n.1
Christ Church Spitalfields crypt burials 171, 191, 196
foundling hospital 68
New Churchyard 101, 102–4, *103*, 112, 113, 121–2
pipes 141, 142–3, 147, 161
Quaker ground, Whitechapel 112
St Bartholomew's hospital 101, 102, 104, 113, 114
St Bride's Church vaults 212
St Dunstan churchyard, Stepney 123n.4
St James's Chapel coffins, Hampstead 122n.1
St James's Gardens, Euston 136, 142, *151*, 152, *153*, 159, 162
St Mary and St Michael cemetery 146–7, 161, 162
St Saviour's burials, Southwark 115–16, 117
St Thomas's hospital 104, 108–9, 111, 112, 115, 116–17, 122
and smoking 159
Louis-Courvoisier, Micheline 10
Lovell, Nancy C. 183

McNeil, Peter 83, 91
McShane, Angela 138, 139, 163
McVey, William 179–80
Madelung's deformity 215
Manchester 227
 spinning mills 226
Mant, Madeleine 27, 35
Marsh, John 126n.33
materiality 3–4, 7
material turn 2–3, 6, 24
Mead, Richard 115
men
 and accidents 35, 224
 bodily ideal 92

as breadwinners 226
corrupted by luxury 96
and crime 34
and posture 90
sex ratios in port towns 36
and shoes 84, *85*, 86, *87*, 89, 91, *91*, 92, 96
and smoking 134, 137, 138, 149, *150–1*, 152, 159, 163
and urban walking 91–2
and violence 34, 35, 224
Meredith, George William 190
Merleau-Ponty, Maurice 8
Methodism 30–1
midwives 60, 65, 66, 67, 69
Milburn, Ann 69
Miles, Adrian 142
Molleson, Theya 191, 196
Monro, Alexander 117, 119, 127n.44
Moreland, John 23
Morgan, Hester 127n.44
Murder Act (1752) 100
Murphy, Eileen 147, 161
Museum of London Archaeology (MOLA) 101

Newcastle
  abortions 69–70
  midwifery 60
  Trinity House 39
new materialism 3–4
New Poor Law *see* Poor Law
newspapers 55–6
New York City, burials 70
Nicholls, Frank 120
Nisbet, William 87, 89
Norton Priory 141
Nottingham, pipes 143
Nourse, Edward 120
Novak, Shannon 9

Oastler, Richard 223
O'Donnabhain, Barra 147, 161
osteoarchaeology *see* bioarchaeology
osteoarthritis 192, 209, 215, *217*, 218, 219
osteobiography *see under* human bodies
osteoporosis 218

Oxford
  anatomical studies and dissection 107, 120
  bodysnatching 107–8, 111

Pearce, Jacqui 142
Pearson, Mr 68
Perry, Megan 27
Perth, bodysnatching 119
Pett, Grace 139
phenomenology 8
Pilloud, Séverine 10
pilots (ships') 37
pipes (tobacco) 133, 137, 138–9, *140*, 141–4, 156, 158, 159–62, 164
  pipe-notches in teeth 144, *145*, 147–8, *148*, 149, *150–1*, 152, *153*, 159–62
Poor Law 39, 61
  Bastardy Clause 61, 67, 72
Portsmouth 36
Pott's disease 175
praxiography 7, 10
Price, Rhys Uvedale 181
Price, Thomas Charles 182
Price, Thomas Rokeby 174, *177*, 181–2, 194, 196
Prince, Jane 29
Purvis, Andrew 36
Purvis, Ann 14, 15, 22, 35–40, *38*
Purvis, John 36
Purvis, John Skipsey 36
Purvis, Mary 36
Purvis, Thomasine 36
Purvis, William 36, 37, 38

Randal, Phoebe 139
Randell, John 94
Registrar-General's office 56
Resurrectionists 100
Richardson, Ruth 100
rickets 57, 211
Rideout, Simon 109
Ridley, Latimer 125n.29
Riello, Giorgio 83, 91
Ritchie, S. 142
Robb, John 7, 9, 25
Roberts, Charlotte A. 182
Robinson, Robert 30
Roe, Charles and Thomas 186

Rolfe, George 104, 106, 119
Roper, Lyndal 8, 9
Rowlandson, Thomas 139, *140*
Rowley, Anthony R. 138
Royal College of Physicians 106
Ruberg, Willemijn 7
Rublack, Ulinka 7, 8, 82
Rutherford, Julienne 52
Rutty, William 126n.40

St Andre, Nathaniel 118, 119
Santos, Ana Luisa 182
scoliosis *see* kyphoscoliosis
scurvy 57
Secker, Thomas 125n.22
Serle (Searl), Edward 124n.15
sextons 65–6, 101
Sheffield 29–30
    Carver Street Chapel burials 30–1, 66
    life expectancy 34
Shepherd, Sarah 112, 127n.44
shoes 16, 81–3, *85*, *87*, *91*
    illfitting 93–5
    impact of the body 84–9
    impact on the body 90–6
    shoes as protection against evil 85
    socks 88–9
    straight lasted 94–5
    as unnatural 95–6
    used shoes as dangerous 85
    and walking 91
    *see also* leather, shoes
Siena, Kevin 88
Simpson, Emma 33
Simpson, George Henry 33
Simpson, James 14, 15, 22, 29–35
    gravestone *31*
Simpson, John 33
Simpson, Mary 33
Simpson, Rebecca 33
Simpson, Robert (father) 29, 30, 33
Simpson, Robert (son) 33
Simpson, William 32, 33
Skip, Mary 124n.17
Skipsey, Isabella 36
Smail, Daniel Lord 6
Smith, Charles 122n.2
Smith, John 224

smoking 133, 137–8, 157
    and childhood/adolescence 157
    and high socioeconomic status 160
    and Irish 147, 155, 161–2
    and low socioeconomic status 159
    and men 134, 137, 138, 149, 150–1, 152, 159, 163
    and poverty 139, 152, 155
    as source of fatal fires 139
    and women 13, 134, 138–9, *140*, 149, *150–1*, 155–6, 158, 163
    *see also* cigars; pipes (tobacco); tobacco
snuff-taking 133, 137–8, 139, 158, 161
socks *see under* shoes
Sofaer, Joanna 7, 24, 205
Southampton, St Michael burials 124n.15
South Hetton 223
South Shields 35–6, 39
    infant mortality 60
    St Hilda's burials 38, 39–40, 47, *49*, 49–52, *51*, 56, *58*, 62, 209, 213–20, *217*
Spike Island 147
Steele, Louise 3, 7
Stockport 223
    Hazel Grove burials 208, 209–13, *210*, 227
Struve, Christian 85
Stukeley, William 107, 109
surgeons
    and bodysnatching 100, 111, 113–14, 116–17, 119–20, 122
    and dissection 106, 108, 109–11, *110*, 113
    early deaths of 127n.44
    education 104, 114, 120
Swann, June 85, 94
Swaysland, Edward 96
Symonds, Joshua 115

Tague, Robert G. 191
Tarlow, Sarah 5, 22
Taylor, George Edward 180
Taylor, John 'Chevalier' 127n.44
Taylor, Maria McVey 16, 174, 175–81, *177*, *178*, *179*, 194, 196

Teare, Edward 138
teeth
  and ageing 37, 191, 219
  enamel hypoplasia 184
  pipe-notches 144, *145*, 147–8, *148*, 149, *150–1*, 152, *153*, 159–62
  tobacco staining 145–7, *146*, *147*, 148, 149, *150–1*, *153*, *154*, 156, 160
Thackrah, Charles Turner 222, 227
Thane, Pat 221
Thoms, W. J. 66
Thornley 223
tobacco 133–4, 137, 163
  as appetite suppressant 156
  chewing 160
  as pain killer 156
  and social status 137, 138
  staining teeth 145–7, *146*, *147*, 148, 149, *150–1*, *153*, *154*, 156, 160
  *see also* smoking; snuff-taking
Toft, Mary 118
tuberculosis (consumption) 52, 57, 113, 127n.44, 174–81, *178*, *179*, 194–5, 211
Tullett, William 137, 138

Vesalius, Andreas 111
vitamin D deficiency 211–12, 222

Wahrman, Dror 6–7
Wakley, Thomas 64, 65–6
Walker, Don 146, 161, 162
walking, urban 91
Wallis, Katherine 108
Wardrop, James 27
Warner-Smith, Alanna 9
Watson, Jane Peacock 226
Weekes, Hampton 94

Weekes, Richard 86
West Linton 226
Wheatley, Margaret 60
Wildman, Abraham 222
Wilkes, John 91
Withington, Philip 137
Witkin, Annsofie Victoria 185
women
  and abortions 14, 55, 67, 69–70
  and ageing 35, 38, 226
  and bodysnatching 126n.39
  and childbirth 60–1, 191
  and childcare 227
  and coalmining 226
  and crime 34
  and divorce 190
  as domestic servants 68–9
  and dressmaking 180
  and hip fractures 227
  and maternity 52
  and poverty 38–9
  and pregnancy 59–60, 71
  and pregnancy, unwanted 67, 68
  sex ratios in port towns 36
  and shoes 92, 95
  as shopkeepers and dealers 37
  and smoking 13, 134, 138–9, *140*, 149, *150–1*, 155–6, 158, 163
  and snuff-taking 139, 158
  *see also* midwives
Woodward, John 113
wool, socks 88–9
work *see* children, child labour; human bodies, and manual labour
workhouses 61
Working, Lauren 137
Worrell, Catherine 116

York, pipes 141

Milton Keynes UK
Ingram Content Group UK Ltd.
UKHW011351080224
437503UK00007B/119